DRIVE RIGHT

authors

- Owen Crabb
- Randall R. Thiel
- Frederik R. Mottola
- Elizabeth A. Weaver

SAVVAS
LEARNING COMPANY

ELEVENTH EDITION

about the authors

Owen Crabb is a former Driver Education Specialist with the Maryland Department of Education. He has assisted several states in developing driver-education programs. As a member of the American Driver and Traffic Safety Education Association for over 35 years, he has served as President and contributed articles, and is a recent recipient of their Richard Kaywood Memorial Award.

Frederik R. Mottola is Professor Emeritus of Public Health at Southern Connecticut State University and Executive Director of Driver Behavior Institute. He is the creator of the Zone Control System of Space Management and Reference Point Visualizations. He is a consultant and educator for traffic safety education programs for teachers, students, and drivers on local, national, and international levels.

Elizabeth A. Weaver is a former Director of Education and Licensing for the Motorcycle Safety Foundation and Driver Education Specialist for the Idaho Department of Education. She has developed education and training curricula and standards for motorcycle safety and driver education and taught teacher preparation programs for both fields. She served as President of the American Driver Traffic Safety Education Association and the Association for State Supervisors for Safety and Driver Education. Elizabeth is a consultant for traffic safety education and training.

Randall R. Thiel is Education Consultant for the Alcohol-Traffic Safety Program for the Wisconsin Department of Public Instruction. He has taught driver education at the high school level and has been involved in teacher preparation programs at universities in Texas, Pennsylvania, and Indiana.

SAVVAS
LEARNING COMPANY

ISBN-13: 978-0-13-361260-8 (hardcover)
ISBN-10:   0-13-361260-0 (hardcover)
4 5 6 7 8 9 10   V311   14 13 12 11 10

ISBN-13: 978-0-13-367266-4 (softcover)
ISBN-10:   0-13-367266-2 (softcover)

17 20

reviewers

Richard Asbell
Driver Education Instructor
Lennard High School
Ruskin, Florida

Rich Hanson
Trainer of Trainers
Western Oregon University
Portland, Oregon

William E. Howe
Driver Education Instructor
Polk County FL School Board
Bartow, Florida

William H. Massey
Instructor
Boca Raton High School
Boca Raton, Florida

Michael J. McGinley
Retired Coordinator of Driver Education
Retired Traffic Safety Consultant
Oshkosh Public Schools
Oshkosh, Wisconsin

Frederick Nagao
Department of Transportation Driver
 Education Compliance Officer
Honolulu, Hawaii

Gerald L. Ockert, Ph.D
Traffic Safety Education Services
Grand Ledge, Michigan

Judy Ode
Instructional Specialist
Driver Education Coordinator
Umpqua Community College
Roseburg, Oregon

John Papa
Driver Education Coordinator
Lake Park High School
Roselle, IL 60172

Derek Stewart
Driver Education Teacher
Leto High School
Temple Terrace, Florida

Elizabeth Taylor
Driver Behavior Specialist Trainer
Western Oregon University
Department of Transportation
 Safety Division
Everett, Washington

unit 1
THE DRIVING TASK

chapter 1
YOU ARE THE DRIVER

1.1 You Are Part of the System
1.2 Your Driving Task
1.3 Your Driving Responsibilities
1.4 Your Driver's License

chapter 2
SIGNS, SIGNALS, AND ROADWAY MARKINGS

2.1 Traffic Signs
2.2 Traffic Signals
2.3 Roadway Markings

chapter 3
BASIC VEHICLE OPERATION

3.1 Controls, Devices, and Instruments
3.2 Getting Ready to Drive
3.3 Starting, Stopping, Steering, and Targeting
3.4 Driving with a Manual Transmission

chapter 4
PERFORMING BASIC MANEUVERS

4.1 Mirror Usage and Backing Procedures
4.2 Basic Driving Maneuvers
4.3 Parking Maneuvers

chapter 5
MANAGING RISK WITH THE IPDE PROCESS

5.1 The IPDE Process
5.2 Identify and Predict
5.3 Decide and Execute
5.4 Using the IPDE Process

chapter 6
EFFECTS OF DRIVER CONDITION

6.1 Emotions and Driving
6.2 Physical Senses and Driving
6.3 Physical Limitations

chapter 7
ALCOHOL, OTHER DRUGS, AND DRIVING

7.1 Effects of Alcohol on Driving Safely
7.2 Other Kinds of Drugs and Driving
7.3 Traffic Laws Governing the Use of Alcohol
7.4 Coping with Peer Pressure

chapter 8
MANAGING DISTRACTIONS

8.1 Driver Inattention and Distractions
8.2 Distractions Inside the Vehicle
8.3 Distractions Outside the Vehicle

unit 2
BEING A RESPONSIBLE DRIVER

unit 3
CONTROLLING YOUR VEHICLE

chapter 9
NATURAL LAWS AND CAR CONTROL

9.1 Gravity and Energy of Motion
9.2 Traction and Tires
9.3 Vehicle Balance and Control in Curves
9.4 Stopping Distance
9.5 Controlling Force of Impact

chapter 10
NEGOTIATING INTERSECTIONS

10.1 Searching Intersections
10.2 Determining Right of Way and Judging Gaps
10.3 Controlled Intersections
10.4 Uncontrolled Intersections
10.5 Railroad Crossings
10.6 Roundabouts

chapter 11
SHARING THE ROADWAY

11.1 Pedestrians
11.2 Bicycles and Mopeds
11.3 Motorcycles and Scooters
11.4 Trucks, Buses, and Emergency and Specialized Vehicles

chapter 12
DRIVING IN ADVERSE CONDITIONS

12.1 Reduced Visibility
12.2 Reduced Traction
12.3 Other Adverse Weather Conditions

chapter 13
HANDLING EMERGENCIES

13.1 Vehicle Malfunctions
13.2 Driver Errors
13.3 Roadway Hazards
13.4 Collisions
13.5 Insurance

chapter 14

DRIVING IN CITY TRAFFIC

14.1 Adjusting to City Traffic
14.2 Following and Meeting Traffic
14.3 Managing Space in City Traffic
14.4 Special City Situations

chapter 15

DRIVING IN RURAL AREAS

15.1 Characteristics of Rural Driving
15.2 Using Basic Skills in Rural Areas
15.3 Passing and Being Passed on Rural Roads
15.4 Rural Situations You Might Encounter
15.5 Special Driving Environments

chapter 16

DRIVING ON HIGHWAYS

16.1 Classification of Highways
16.2 Entering Controlled-Access Highways
16.3 Strategies for Driving on Highways
16.4 Exiting Controlled-Access Highways
16.5 Highway Problems and Features

chapter 17

BUYING AND MAINTAINING A VEHICLE

17.1 Buying a Vehicle
17.2 Preventive Maintenance
17.3 Fuel Efficiency, Recycling, and Security Systems

chapter 18

PLANNING YOUR TRAVEL

18.1 Environmental Concerns
18.3 Local Travel
18.4 Long-Distance Travel
18.5 Special Vehicles and Trailers

unit 4

DRIVING IN DIFFERENT ENVIRONMENTS

chapter 1

YOU ARE THE DRIVER

1.1 You Are Part of the System

1.2 Your Driving Task

1.3 Your Driving Responsibilities

1.4 Your Driver's License

KEY IDEA

What skills, responsibilities, and license requirements will you have to meet before you drive in the highway transportation system?

 **Before** you can get in a car and start learning the skills that will stay with you for a lifetime, you first need to learn all the fundamentals of the driving task. This chapter will help you learn the first steps in becoming a responsible, low-risk driver.

lesson 1.1
YOU ARE PART OF THE SYSTEM

OBJECTIVES

- Describe the three parts of the highway transportation system.
- Explain how the National Highway Safety Act affects drivers.
- Explain how the National Traffic and Motor Vehicle Safety Act helps keep drivers and passengers safe.

VOCABULARY

- risk
- highway transportation system
- roadway user

You are about to take a driver education course, apply for your driver's license, and join the millions of others who share our country's roads. The key to becoming a safe and responsible driver is to learn about the **risks** of driving and how to manage them. No matter how good a driver you become, the possibility of injury to people and damage to property or vehicles is always present.

The Highway Transportation System

The **highway transportation system**, or HTS, has three parts: roadway users, vehicles, and roadways. The purpose of the HTS is to move people and cargo from one place to another in a safe and efficient manner.

Of all transportation systems, the HTS is the most complex. It has the greatest variety of users, including drivers, passengers, and pedestrians, and it has a wide variety of roadways, from simple rural lanes to complex multi-lane roads and expressways.

Roadway Users   People who use the HTS by walking, driving, or riding are called **roadway users**.

While most individuals consistently drive in a safe and responsible manner, others do not. Even experienced drivers sometimes operate their cars when they are distracted, overly tired, sick, or impaired by medication. To protect yourself and others when these high-risk drivers are on the road, you have to be alert to the risks involved and know how to reduce or control them.

Vehicles   There are more than 240 million registered passenger vehicles in the United States. The vehicles range from lightweight mopeds to tractor trailers weighing many tons. Each of these vehicles varies in how it handles, in its safety features, and in its ability to protect drivers and passengers in the event of a crash. To be a safe driver, you must learn how to share the roads with vehicles whose size and weight add risk to the driving task.

Roadways   The HTS involves more than 4 million miles of paved roads. Driving at night on unlit roads, on unpaved road surfaces, and in hazardous environmental conditions such as rain, snow, and wind have a direct effect on risk for drivers. All skillful drivers are alert to these driving situations and know how to react to each one.

Regulating the HTS

Federal, state, and local government agencies work together to regulate the HTS. The federal government passed two laws to set standards for vehicle and highway safety: The National Highway Safety Act and The National Traffic and Motor Vehicle Safety Act.

By passing the National Highway Safety Act, the federal government created guidelines for motor vehicle safety programs. Included in the guidelines that states must follow are vehicle registration, driver licensing, traffic courts, and highway construction and maintenance.

FIGURE 1   As you learn to drive, you will learn how to navigate the complex mix of people, vehicles, and roadways safely and responsibly.

To keep cars safe, the federal government passed the National Traffic and Motor Vehicle Safety Act, which requires auto makers to install certain safety features into each car. For example, the act requires that safety belts be installed at the factory.

review it 1.1

1. List the parts and purpose of the HTS.
2. Explain how the HTS is regulated.
3. Describe the purpose of the National Highway Safety Act and how it affects states and local governments.
4. Explain the purpose of the National Traffic and Motor Vehicle Safety Act and how it helps keep drivers and passengers safe.

Critical Thinking

5. **Predict**   What do you think might happen if one or more parts of the HTS failed?

IN YOUR COMMUNITY   **Research**   Enforcement agencies play an important role in the HTS. Visit a local police station and find out what percent of officers' time is spent in traffic enforcement. Also ask officers to describe some of the high-risk drivers they encounter. Report your findings to the class.

lesson 1.2
YOUR DRIVING TASK

 OBJECTIVES

- Explain how understanding the social, physical, and mental skills related to driving helps you be a low-risk driver.
- Identify mental, social, and physical factors that might affect your ability to be a safe driver.
- Identify and explain the four steps in the IPDE process.

 VOCABULARY

- IPDE Process
- Zone Control System
- low-risk driving

The driving task includes all the mental, social, and physical skills required to drive. To perform the driving task with low risk, you must develop habits for

- using knowledge and visual skills
- judging speed, time, and space
- anticipating how your car will respond under ordinary and emergency conditions

Mental Skills

Safe, low-risk driving involves critical judgment and continuous monitoring. Monitoring the roadway to stay alert for any unpredictable actions of drivers or pedestrians is a habit you want to develop in order to protect yourself and your passengers.

Social Skills

All drivers bring their own problems and skill levels to our driving world. Like all social tasks, driving requires you to interact with other people. A big part of your driving task will be applying social skills to stressful situations to avoid conflicts. For example, if you can't control an angry driver, you will have to remain calm and patient in order to defuse a potentially dangerous situation. As a courteous driver, you need to make an effort to work with other drivers so that you don't lose focus and make driving mistakes.

Physical Skills

Skills such as smooth use of acceleration and braking and steering controls are examples of physical skills that you need to practice so they become habits. Scanning your rearview mirror every few seconds is another physical skill that you will want to become a habit. You'll need to develop eye-hand coordination so that you'll acquire the habit of using the controls effectively and in a timely manner.

IPDE Process

The **IPDE Process** is an organized system for seeing, thinking, and responding during the driving task. IPDE is an acronym for identify, predict, decide, and execute.

- **I**dentify important information in the current driving situation.
- **P**redict when and where possible points of conflict may develop.
- **D**ecide when, where, and how to communicate, adjust speed, and/or change position to avoid conflict.
- **E**xecute the correct action(s) to prevent conflict.

To help you use the IPDE Process more effectively, you will also learn about the **Zone Control System**, which is a method for managing space around your car. Understanding Zone Control will help you apply the IPDE Process. In that way, you can manage all the information you need to make responsible decisions that reduce the risks of driving.

Once you have mastered the IPDE Process, you will be able to practice **low-risk driving**, which means that you will constantly monitor other vehicles and roadway users around you, and you will not assume others will do what you think they should do. Low-risk driving enables you to actively avoid hazardous situations.

FIGURE 2 Two hikers are in your path of travel. **Execute** What actions should you take?

FIGURE 3 Predict is the second step in the IPDE Process. **Predict** Could you predict a possible conflict in this picture?

---

review it 1.2

1. How do mental, social, and physical habits help you in the driving task?
2. Describe a driving situation where you might need to apply mental skills.
3. Describe a driving situation where you might need to apply social skills.
4. Explain how to use the IPDE Process in the driving task.

Critical Thinking

5. **Analyze** Why should you practice low-risk driving?
6. **Evaluate** How do you think Zone Control supports the IPDE Process to make you a safe, low-risk driver?

IN YOUR COMMUNITY Evaluate the driving habits of drivers in your family. Gather a list of good driving habits that you and your family should keep up, and a list of habits that need to be improved. Set goals for improving unsafe behaviors.

lesson 1.3
YOUR DRIVING RESPONSIBILITIES

 OBJECTIVES

- List three kinds of financial responsibilities drivers have and give an example of each.
- List ways drivers can protect the environment.
- Identify and explain your responsibilities to yourself and to others.

 VOCABULARY

- collision
- operating cost
- fixed cost

Driving is a privilege given to an individual who meets certain requirements determined by state law. As with any privilege, driving has responsibilities. As a licensed driver, you will have legal, financial, and environmental responsibilities. Furthermore, you will be expected to assume responsibility for yourself as well as for others while you are behind the wheel.

Legal Responsibilities

Laws   Your primary responsibility as a driver is to obey all traffic laws. As a law-abiding driver, it is imperative that you avoid drinking and driving.

Collisions   Sometimes, no matter how good a driver you are, you might not be able to avoid a collision. A **collision**, or crash, happens when a vehicle hits another object, whether the object is moving or not. By law, any driver involved in a collision must stop.

FIGURE 4

In 2004, more people between the ages of 15 and 24 died as a result of vehicle crashes than from any other single cause.

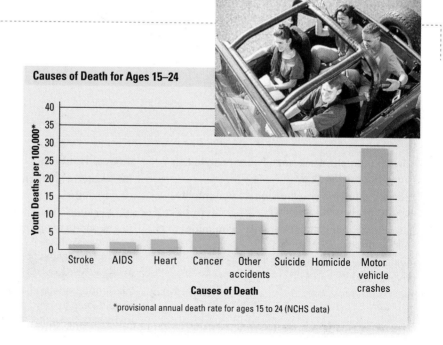

Causes of Death for Ages 15–24

*provisional annual death rate for ages 15 to 24 (NCHS data)

Financial Responsibilities

Operating Costs   As a driver, you are responsible for your **operating costs**, which include costs for fuel, oil, and tires.

Fixed Costs   Your fixed costs include the purchase price of your car, any licensing fees, and your insurance. These are called **fixed costs** because they are not determined by how many miles you drive.

Crash Costs   Of all the possible causes for a collision, driver error is the most common. Being responsible for a car crash that kills another passenger or driver leaves a person with a terrible feeling for life. In addition, traffic crashes cost our nation billions of dollars each year in property damage, time away from work, and medical fees. If a crash is determined to be your fault, you will be responsible for paying for any injuries sustained by the people involved in the collision or damages to any property. Auto insurance is designed to cover the majority of these costs.

Environmental Responsibilities

All drivers have a responsibility to help manage the environmental threats created by motor-vehicle use, including air pollution, water pollution, chemical spills, and pollution caused by the disposal of vehicle-related products. To reduce pollution and preserve our environment, responsible drivers can

- buy and maintain fuel-efficient vehicles
- use fuel-efficient driving habits
- use car pools and public transportation
- recycle used materials
- work for strong policies that encourage energy-efficient driving

Responsibilities to Yourself and Others

Responsible driving involves making rational decisions. As a driver, it is your responsibility to make driving decisions that show respect for yourself as well as for others. Driving recklessly and aggressively, for example, are high-risk behaviors that endanger and show disrespect for other drivers and passengers. By choosing to practice common courtesy and to control

drive
green

Saving Fuel   You can save fuel by doing little things like turning your engine off. United Parcel Service (UPS) drivers are trained never to let their engines idle when at a curb or in a driveway. Even if the driver is out of the truck for a few seconds, the engine is always turned off.

FIGURE 5 It's your responsibility to stay safe; however, saying no to a friend isn't easy.

your anger or frustration, you are demonstrating good judgment and self-control.

Driving can be a social event if your friends are in the car with you. Friends might try to pressure you to engage in risky activities that can affect your ability to drive safely. Showing responsibility for yourself means telling your friends that you have too much respect for yourself and others to give in to negative pressure.

review it 1.3

1. Name three financial responsibilities that drivers have in maintaining and operating a vehicle.

2. Explain how collisions cost the nation billions of dollars.

3. How can you as a new driver protect the environment from vehicle-related pollution?

4. As a driver, how can you show respect for yourself and your passengers?

Critical Thinking

5. **Compare and Contrast** How are crash costs different from fixed and operating costs?

6. **Evaluate** A young driver decides not to use his cell phone while driving. To whom is he being responsible? Explain your answer.

IN THE PASSENGER SEAT **Unsafe Driver** Suppose you have a friend who you think is an unsafe driver. He drives at high speeds, disobeys traffic laws, and frequently takes his eyes off the road. What would you say to your friend to encourage him to drive more safely? List some of the things you'd say and share your strategies with the class.

The purpose of a comprehensive driver licensing program is to make sure only safe drivers are allowed on public roadways. Most licensing programs require applicants to take written, physical, and driving exams.

Graduated Driver Licensing Program (GDL)

To help young drivers adjust to the driving task, many states have a **graduated driver licensing program**. The GDL program requires young drivers to progress through a series of licensing stages. Typically these programs have three stages: learner's permit stage, intermediate license stage, and the full-privilege stage.

Learner's Permit Stage   Supervised conditions require that

- the learner receives a permit to drive when supervised by an adult, licensed driver
- the permit must be held for a minimum period—usually six months—of violation-free and collision-free driving
- other licensed drivers, such as family members, may be asked to provide a minimum number of hours of practice driving

Intermediate License Stage   The learner drives under the following restrictions at this stage:

- The learner must have successfully completed the learner's permit stage and an approved driver-education course.
- Supervised driving may be continued to meet the required hours.
- Night driving is restricted.
- Passengers can be limited in age and/or number.
- The intermediate license must be held for at least six months of collision-free and violation-free driving. If the learner is involved in a collision or receives a violation, the intermediate license stage begins again from the time of the violation or collision.
- Penalties for violations are increased. Many times, violators are required to go to traffic school.

OBJECTIVES

- Describe the stages of a graduated driver license program.
- Explain how a graduated driver license program can help you become a safer driver.
- Explain the implied consent law.
- List the key concepts in a quality driver-education program.

VOCABULARY

- graduated driver licensing program

FIGURE 6
Graduated licensing programs have three stages.

Learner's Permit Stage 6–12 months	Intermediate License Stage 6–18 months	Full-privilege License Stage
Age 15–16	Age 16–17	Age 16.5–18 and on

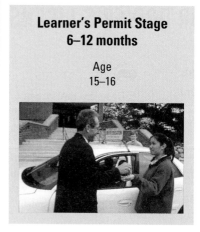  

Full-Privilege License Stage   To graduate to a full, unrestricted license stage, the learner must

- successfully complete the intermediate license stage with no violations and no collisions
- in some states, complete an advanced driver-education course

There was opposition by states to a graduated driver license program when it was first suggested in the 1970s. However, according to research done recently by the Insurance Institute for Highway Safety, "graduated licensing programs have had positive effects on the crash experience of young drivers in the United States and other countries, including Canada and New Zealand. In U.S. states that have adopted elements of graduated licensing, the safety benefits are evident. Almost all studies have found crash reductions from about 10 to 30 percent."

Driver Education and Your License

Quality driver-education programs give you the opportunity to learn and practice the skills you need to be a safe, skilled, and responsible driver. Driver education can also alert you to some of the problems you might face while driving.

The *Drive Right* driver-education program is your start toward becoming a responsible low-risk driver. The program is based in part on the following key concepts:

- Driving is primarily a decision-making process. In this program, you will learn how to use the IPDE Process and Zone Control to become a knowledgeable and skillful driver.

- Your driving will be greatly influenced by your maturity, emotions, and attitude toward responsibility.

- An awareness of the limiting factors for yourself and your vehicle will make you a low-risk driver.

- Drugs and alcohol will impair your ability to be a low-risk driver.

Once you pass your driving-education program, you should take at least one year to ease into full-time driving responsibilities. After you have driven under a wide variety of traffic situations and road conditions, such as night driving and hazardous weather, you can begin to think of yourself as an accomplished new driver.

No driving program can teach you everything you will need to know to be a safe driver. As long as you drive, you will need to improve your skills. Remember, the best drivers never stop learning.

Organ Donor Program   You may indicate your desire to be an organ donor by filling out an organ donation declaration on your driver's license or by signing an organ donor card. The most important step in considering organ donation is discussing your decision with your family.

Implied Consent Laws   All states have enacted the implied consent law. When you get your driver's license, you agree that if you are stopped for cause and charged with drinking and driving, you consent to having a police officer give you a test for the presence of alcohol. If you refuse to take the test, you will lose your license.

safe driving tip

Be Prepared   Never assume what another driver, pedestrian, or cyclist might do. While you are driving, always anticipate that others might enter your path of travel. Be prepared to stop or steer away to avoid a collision.

analyzing data

Driving Performance   One way to analyze driving performance is to measure fatal crashes per million miles driven. The graph shows the fatality rate for different age groups. Study the graph before you answer these questions.

1. **Reading Graphs**   Which does the height of the bars measure?

2. **Analyzing Data**   Which two age groups have the highest number of fatal crashes per one million miles driven?

3. **Inferring**   Suggest some reasons why 40–59-year-old drivers have fewer fatal crashes.

4. **Relating Cause and Effect**   The young drivers on this graph have a high fatality rate per million miles driven. What are some of the biggest risk factors young drivers have that contributed to these fatal crashes?

5. **Execute**   If you were to coach new drivers, what skills would you encourage them to master to avoid having a fatal crash?

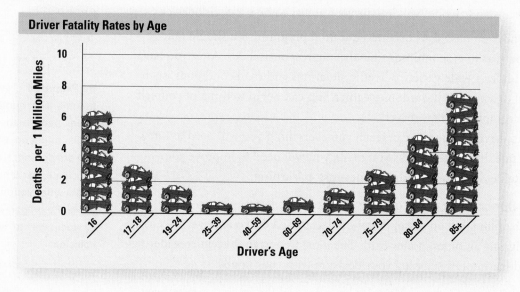

review it 1.4

1. Name and describe the three stages of a graduated driver license program.

2. How can a graduated driver license program help you become a responsible driver?

3. Describe three key concepts of a quality driver-education program.

Critical Thinking

4. **Evaluate**   What do you think is the purpose of the implied consent law?

IN YOUR COMMUNITY   **Research**   Every state has some kind of graduated license program. What are the specific GDL requirements in your state? Compare them to the GDL requirements listed in this book. How are they different from your state's requirements? How are they the same?

CHAPTER 1 REVIEW

Lesson Summaries

1.1 YOU ARE PART OF THE SYSTEM

- The HTS system has three parts: roadway users, vehicles, and roadways.
- The federal government passed the National Highway Safety Act and the National Traffic and Motor Vehicle Safety Act to keep drivers and cars safe.

1.2 YOUR DRIVING TASK

- A driver needs to interact successfully with people, learn the physical skills of driving, and use mental skills to make decisions using the IPDE Process.
- The four steps of the IPDE Process are Identify, Predict, Decide, and Execute.

1.3 YOUR DRIVING RESPONSIBILITIES

- To keep roads as safe as possible, it is your responsibility to obey all laws passed by the state.
- As a new driver, you will assume legal, financial, and environmental responsibilities.
- Your most important new responsibility will be to protect yourself and others.

1.4 YOUR DRIVER'S LICENSE

- The licensing process, driver education, and driving practice work together to produce safe drivers.
- A graduated driver licensing program requires young drivers to go through a series of stages that provide practice driving time.

Chapter Vocabulary

- collision
- fixed cost
- graduated driver licensing program
- highway transportation system
- IPDE Process
- low-risk driving
- operating cost
- risk
- roadway user
- Zone Control System

Write the word or phrase from the list above that correctly completes the sentence.

1. _____ means that you will be actively monitoring other vehicles and roadway users around you.

2. Many states use a(n) _____ to allow new drivers to start driving in stages.

3. The _____ includes roadway users, vehicles, and roadways.

4. The process that includes *identify*, *predict*, *decide*, and *execute* is called the _____.

5. The chance of injuring people or causing property damage is called _____.

6. When a vehicle hits another object, the vehicle is involved in a(n) _____.

7. The system used to manage the space around your car is called the _____.

 **STUDY TIP**

On separate sheets of paper, write each vocabulary word and its definition, leaving space between the words. Cut the words and definitions apart so that each is on a separate strip of paper. Shuffle the pile of vocabulary words and the pile of definitions together. Then with a partner, try to match the vocabulary word with the correct definition.

Checking Concepts

LESSON 1

8. List the three parts of the highway transportation system and explain how they work together.

9. The federal government has established the National Highway Safety Act. How do the requirements of this act protect drivers?

LESSON 2

10. There are social, physical, and mental factors that affect drivers. How do these factors interact to make drivers safe?

11. Name the four steps in the IPDE Process and explain how you would use each step in the driving task.

LESSON 3

12. You will have several financial responsibilities as a driver. Explain how you would assume these responsibilities.

13. Automobiles can endanger our environment in many ways. How can you as a driver help to reduce these dangers?

LESSON 4

14. New drivers have special restrictions while they are in a GDL program. How do these restrictions help to teach new drivers to be safer drivers?

Critical Thinking

15. **Analyze** How does the Zone Control System complement and strengthen the IPDE Process?

16. **Analyze** Why do you think GDL licensed drivers have fewer crashes during the GDL process?

You're the Driver

17. **Identify** What should you try to identify with the IPDE Process while driving?

18. **Predict** Being able to predict with the IPDE Process is a very important step. What is the main thing you should try to predict while driving?

19. **Decide** With the wet and raining road conditions and close following distance pictured, what decision should you make?

20. **Execute** The IPDE Process is an ongoing process used to avoid conflicts. If you sense the oncoming car may turn toward you, what actions should you be ready to execute to avoid a collision with that car?

Preparing for the Test

Choose the letter of the answer that completes the sentence correctly.

1. Which of the following is part of the highway transportation system (HTS)?
   a. passengers
   b. roadways
   c. vehicles
   d. all of the above

2. It's important to learn low-risk driving habits so that you can
   a. complete a qualified driver-education course.
   b. get the attention you want.
   c. actively avoid dangerous driving situations.
   d. use the HTS.

3. If you hold a learner's permit, you can drive
   a. after you attend traffic school.
   b. alone after you complete a driver-education course.
   c. during daylight hours only.
   d. only with a licensed, adult driver.

4. The operating costs of driving include
   a. car insurance.
   b. licensing fees.
   c. the cost of a vehicle.
   d. fuel and tires.

---

drive write

Driving Green Research locations of recycling centers in your area that accept used oil, car batteries, and tires. Visit one or two of the centers and find out how much oil has been recycled and how many tires and batteries have been recycled per month for the past 12 months. Then make a bar graph using the data. In which months were the most oil, batteries, and tires brought in? In which month was the least oil, batteries, and tires brought in? Discuss your findings with the class.

Use the art below to answer Question 5.

5. This sign is important for drivers because
   a. the laws regulating the HTS require that used oil be recycled.
   b. drivers have a responsibility to preserve our environment.
   c. drivers have a responsibility to control driving costs.
   d. GDL programs requires that you know how to recycle oil.

6. If you're involved in a collision, by law you must
   a. get out.
   b. get medical attention.
   c. call your insurance company.
   d. stop.

Use the figure below to answer Question 7.

REQUEST FOR ORGAN DONOR DESIGNATION
ON DRIVER'S LICENSE OR PHOTO ID CARD

DRIVER LICENSE/PHOTO ID NUMBER	LAST NAME(S)	JR., ETC.	FIRST NAME	MIDDLE NAME

DATE OF BIRTH MONTH DAY YEAR	AGE	TELEPHONE NUMBER (8 a.m. to 4:30 p.m.)	E-MAIL ADDRESS (if applicable)

CONSENT OF PARENT, GUARDIAN, PERSON IN LOCO PARENTIS OR SPOUSE AT LEAST 18 YEARS OF AGE
Complete if Applicant is Less Than 18 Years of Age

I hereby certify that I am ☐ Parent, ☐ Guardian, ☐ Person in Loco Parentis or ☐ Spouse at least 18 years of age, of the applicant named herein, that the statements made herein are true and correct to the best of my knowledge and that this request for Organ Donor designation is made with my full consent.

SIGNATURE OF PARENT, GUARDIAN, PERSON IN LOCO PARENTIS OR SPOUSE AT LEAST 18 YEARS OF AGE - IN INK   DATE
CERTIFICATION
I hereby request Organ Donor designation on my Driver's License/Identification Card.

7. The most important action you should take before you sign this card is
   a. getting a photograph of yourself.
   b. arranging for a witness.
   c. checking the laws in your state.
   d. discussing it with your family.

8. The National Traffic and Motor Vehicle Safety Act requires
   a. states to monitor highway construction and maintenance.
   b. the federal government to set guidelines for licensing.
   c. government agencies to regulate traffic courts.
   d. auto makers to install safety features in all cars.

NEXT
MILE

SIGNS, SIGNALS, AND ROADWAY MARKINGS

2.1 Traffic Signs

2.2 Traffic Signals

2.3 Roadway Markings

KEY IDEA

How do signs, signals, and roadway markings communicate information that helps you drive responsibly?

YOU'RE THE DRIVER **You** probably know that you have to stop your car when you come to a stop sign. But do you know and understand the meaning of other traffic signs? What information do signs provide? What risks do they help you identify?

lesson 2.1
TRAFFIC SIGNS

OBJECTIVES

- Describe the shapes and colors of regulatory and warning signs and how to respond to each one.
- Explain how regulatory signs control traffic.
- Explain how guide signs and international signs help you when driving.

VOCABULARY

- regulatory sign
- warning sign
- guide sign
- international sign

Shapes and Colors

You will see many different traffic signs as you drive. Some signs have words only, some have symbols only, and some signs have a combination of words and symbols. While traffic signs may give commands, set limits, or provide alerts, each sign has a specific shape and color. As you can see in **FIGURE 1**, each sign's shape and color has a special meaning. By knowing the meanings of these shapes and colors, you will be able to drive defensively and responsibly.

Regulatory Signs

Signs that set limits or give commands are **regulatory signs**. Regulatory signs control traffic. These signs tell you about a law that is important at that place and, of course, that you must obey. The most important regulatory signs—the STOP sign and the YIELD sign—have unique shapes. All other regulatory signs are either white squares or rectangles with red or black lettering.

Stop Sign A STOP sign tells you where to stop. It may be used where any two—and sometimes more—streets intersect. You may see a STOP sign on two corners or four corners of the intersection. Sometimes when there is a crosswalk, you may see a STOP sign in the middle of the street.

Always come to a complete stop at a STOP sign. The location of a STOP sign or stop line indicates where to make a legal stop. If there is no stop line, make a full stop at the STOP sign before entering the intersection.

FIGURE 1 TRAFFIC SIGN SHAPES AND COLORS

Shapes →

STOP
Octagon
Stop
YIELD
Triangle
Yield
SPEED LIMIT 40
Vertical Rectangle
Regulatory
ST LOUIS 5
MEMPHIS 40
NEW ORLEANS 65
Horizontal Rectangle
Guide
R R
Round
Railroad Crossing
NO PASSING ZONE
Pennant
No Passing
Diamond
Warning
Pentagon
School Zone

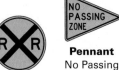

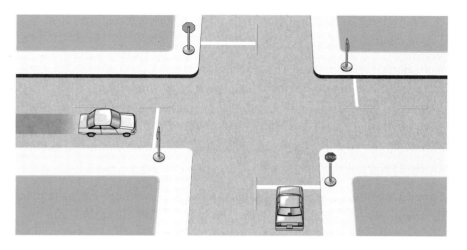

Key

Action car

Other cars in motion

FIGURE 2
The yellow car shows where to stop at a stop line. **Decide** if both cars stopped at the same time, which driver has the right of way at this 4-way stop?

Stop where you can see approaching traffic, but stop before you reach any crosswalk.

If your view is blocked as you approach an intersection and you cannot see cross traffic clearly after stopping, move ahead slowly and prepare to stop again. Make sure the way is clear before driving into the intersection.

At some intersections, STOP signs are posted at all four corners. Each STOP sign might include a small sign that says 4-WAY or ALL WAYS. Follow these rules at a 4-way or all ways STOP sign:

- The driver who stopped first should be allowed to go first.

- When vehicles stop to the right or left of each other at the same time, the driver on the right should be allowed to proceed first.

- When stopped across the intersection facing oncoming traffic, the driver going straight should be allowed to proceed. A driver turning left should wait.

- Show your intention to proceed by moving forward slowly before entering the intersection.

Colors ➡

Red
Stop, yield, or prohibited

Orange
Construction or detour

Yellow
Warning

Black
Regulatory

Blue
Motorist service

Green
Guide

- Check for traffic ahead and to the sides before entering the intersection.

Yield Sign   Yield signs are found where roadways cross or merge. Always slow down and check traffic in front of you and behind you when approaching a Yield sign. By slowing enough ahead of time, you can often proceed without completely stopping. However, always be prepared to stop. Proceed only when it is safe to do so, without affecting the flow of traffic in the lane you are entering.

Speed Limit Signs   Speed limit signs show the maximum—and sometimes the minimum—speed allowed on that roadway. Speed limits are used to manage traffic flow at safe speeds. States are permitted to establish their own speed limits.

Speed limits are set for ideal driving conditions. When traffic, roadway, or weather conditions are not ideal, you must obey the basic speed law. This law states that you may not drive faster than is safe and prudent for existing conditions, regardless of posted speed limits.

A minimum speed limit is set on some roadways, such as expressways, to keep traffic moving safely. This speed limit tells you not to drive slower than the posted minimum speed unless conditions are less than ideal.

An advisory speed limit is set for special conditions such as sharp curves and is often posted below a warning sign. If the road conditions pose possible dangers to drivers, speeds should be even slower. Resume normal speed once road conditions return to ideal, such as after the road straightens out again.

WHAT WOULD YOU SAY?

Safe Speed   It is a rainy night and it is difficult to see the road. Your friend is driving at the posted speed limit, but you think it would be safer to go slower. Suggest two things you could say to persuade your friend to slow down.

FIGURE 3
Visibility, space, and time determine how fast you can drive safely.
Critical Thinking
What are some specific situations when it would not be safe to drive as fast as the posted speed limit?

A speed limit sign tells you the maximum speed allowed in ideal conditions.

In some areas, special speed limits are set for different times of the day. For example, school zones have special speed limits when children are present or during school hours. Night driving speed limits may be lower than daylight limits.

Other Regulatory Signs In addition to STOP signs, YIELD signs, and speed-limit signs, other regulatory signs are used to direct traffic and to control parking and passing. Some regulatory signs have a black symbol inside a red circle that is crossed by a red, diagonal slash. The slash means the action shown by the black symbol is prohibited.

FIGURE 4
REGULATORY SIGNS

Most regulatory signs are rectangles.
Predict What action do you think is prohibited by the sign that is a red circle with a red slash?

| **Turns and Lanes** | **One Way** | **Parking and Passing** |

Warning Signs

A **warning sign** alerts you to hazards or changes in the condition of the road ahead. Most warning signs are diamond-shaped, such as those shown in **FIGURE 5**. Be prepared to slow or stop when you see a warning sign.

FIGURE 5 WARNING SIGNS

Road Narrows (from right)   **Divided Highway Begins**   **Merging Traffic** (from right)   **Alligator Crossing**   **Signal Ahead**

Cross Road   **Sharp Right Curve**   **Left Curve**   **Two-way Traffic**   **Low Clearance**

Pedestrian or School-Zone Signs   A school zone is a portion of a street or highway near a school that is subject to special speed limits. When you see a pedestrian crossing or school-zone sign, be prepared to slow down and proceed carefully. Children might dart out into the street without looking or take other unexpected actions. A school-zone sign, showing only two figures, is posted within a block of a school. A school-crossing sign has lines that represent a sidewalk. This sign is posted near intersections or crossings used by children. Notice the difference between these two signs in **FIGURE 6.**

Railroad Advance Warning Sign   The railroad-crossing advance-warning sign—as seen in **FIGURE 6**—warns motorists of a railroad crossing ahead. Slow down as you approach the train tracks and be prepared to stop. The crossing sign may have the number of tracks posted on it. If there is more than one set of tracks, be sure that a second train is not coming from the opposite direction. Flashing red lights or crossing gates might be added to alert you when a train is coming.

Construction and Slow-Moving-Vehicle Signs   An orange construction sign alerts you that you are about to enter a work zone. Be ready to slow, stop, or drive around workers and equipment. In addition to the signs posted, you must also follow directions from any worker directing traffic. Many states now increase fines for violations in construction zones.

A slow-moving-vehicle sign is an orange triangle bordered with red that warns other drivers that the vehicle is traveling slower than other traffic.

FIGURE 6
REGULATORY SIGNS

Pedestrian Crossing

School Zone

School Crossing

**Railroad
Advance Warning**

Construction

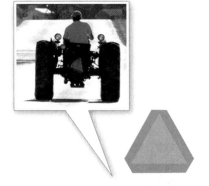

Slow-Moving Vehicle

FIGURE 7 ROUTE SIGNS

U.S. Route Marker

State Route Marker

County Route Marker

Interstate Route Marker

An east-west route is even numbered. A north-south route is odd numbered.

Guide Signs

Guide signs provide a variety of information. **Guide signs** mark routes, intersections, service areas, and other points of interest or information.

Route Signs   Local, state, U.S., and interstate routes are posted with route signs. As you can see in **FIGURE 7**, route signs vary according to the type of roadway. State and county route markers will vary from state to state.

Interstate route signs are red, white, and blue shields. Notice that a special numbering system is used for interstate routes.

Other Guide Signs   You will see a wide variety of guide signs in addition to route signs. As you can see in **FIGURE 8**, green signs provide information on destinations ahead and distances to be traveled. Blue signs highlight highway services such as fuel, food, lodging, and nearby hospitals. Brown signs direct you to recreation areas or cultural points of interest.

A three-figured route that starts with an odd number leads into a city.

A three-figured route that starts with an even number goes around a city.

FIGURE 8 GUIDE SIGNS

ST LOUIS   5
MEMPHIS   40
NEW ORLEANS 65

Mileage and Destinations

Highway Services

ROCKY MOUNTAIN NAT'L PARK ➜

Point of Interest or Recreational Areas

International Signs

International signs, such as those in **FIGURE 9**, convey information by symbols rather than words. Drivers who travel from country to country can understand the meaning of these signs without learning several languages. The United States has adopted several international symbols for use on highway signs. More and more of these symbols will be used as international travel increases.

FIGURE 9 INTERNATIONAL SIGNS

Roundabout

Tunnel

Two-way Traffic Ahead

Road Narrows

Slippery Road

Bicycle Crossing

Falling Rocks

Prohibited for All Vehicles

Construction Site

Danger

review it 2.1

1. How can you recognize a warning sign? How should you proceed when you see one?

2. Compare the action you should take at a STOP sign with the action you should take at a YIELD sign.

3. Describe the kind of information you would find on each of the following guide signs: red, white, and blue shield; green rectangle; blue rectangle; brown rectangle.

Critical Thinking

4. **Apply Concepts** You are approaching an intersection with STOP signs on all four corners. Describe the actions you should take in the following situations. (a) A car on your left is already stopped at the stop line. (b) A car on your right is approaching the intersection at the same time.

5. **Evaluate** How do international signs differ from other regulatory signs? If you were traveling through a European country with an unfamiliar language, how could these signs help you drive safely?

 **Research** Find out about speed-limit laws in your state. Then find the same information about neighboring states. What are the basic speed laws? Are there minimum speed limits? What are the fines for exceeding the speed limit? Note any similarities or differences in the laws. Write a report comparing the laws.

Traffic lights, arrows, flashing signals, lane signals, and pedestrian signals are used to help traffic flow smoothly. Each of these devices is a **traffic signal**.

The lights of traffic signals are easier to see than signs. The color of each light has a specific meaning. Green means go: proceed if the way is safe and clear. Yellow means caution: be ready to stop. Red means stop.

Traffic Lights

Traffic lights are found at intersections and other places where heavy traffic comes together. Traffic lights indicate who has the right of way. The lights may be round or have arrows to indicate direction.

The three colors of a traffic light are shown in **FIGURE 10**. Notice that each color light has a specific position on the signal. When a signal is upright, the sequence of colors is red-yellow-green. Horizontal signals also have the red-yellow-green sequence, with red on the left. This sequence allows drivers who are color blind or whose view is partially blocked to be able to understand the signal.

Red Light You must come to a full stop at a red light. Stop behind the stop line or crosswalk. If there are no stop lines, stop before entering the intersection.

Yellow Light Yellow means caution. Make every effort to stop safely for a yellow light. If you are too close to stop safely when a yellow light appears, proceed carefully through the intersection.

Green Light On a green light, you can proceed, but only once you are sure the intersection is clear.

 OBJECTIVES

- Explain what to do at a green light, a yellow light, and a red light.
- Identify the meaning of arrows, flashing lights, and lane signals.
- Describe the actions to take with pedestrian and traffic-control officers' signals.

VOCABULARY

- traffic signal
- right-turn-on-red
- flashing signal
- lane signal
- pedestrian signal

------ **FIGURE 10** -------------------------------

At a red light, come to a complete stop before the entrance to the intersection.

A yellow light means caution and prepare to stop.

Proceed on a green light only if the intersection is clear.

Check traffic to the left, front, and right before entering the intersection. When approaching a light that has been green for some time, be prepared for the light to turn yellow.

- **Right-Turn-on-Red** At most intersections, drivers are allowed to make a **right-turn-on-red**. This means turning right after stopping when the signal is red. However, some cities restrict such turns.

- **Left-Turn-on-Red** Some states permit drivers to make a left turn after stopping at a red light when turning from a one-way street into another one-way street. A few states permit left turns after stopping at a red light from a left-turn lane into a one-way street. Be sure state laws and local ordinances permit such turns. The intersection and crosswalk must be clear of traffic and pedestrians before you turn either left or right on a red light.

Computerized Traffic Lights On heavily traveled roads, the flow of traffic may be controlled by computer. A computer system coordinates traffic lights at several intersections. With this system, traffic can flow for many blocks at or near the speed limit without stopping.

drive green

Eco-Friendly Traffic Lights Because they reduce stopping and starting and the amount of time that engines spend idling, computerized traffic lights help conserve fuel. They also reduce pollution and CO_2 emissions.

A stop sign and a stop line may be used with a flashing red signal.

FIGURE 11
A flashing red signal means to make a full stop. After you stop, yield to traffic. Proceed only when the intersection is clear.

Other Traffic Signals

Some traffic signals have arrows or flashing lights that regulate the movement of vehicles.

Flashing Signals   A **flashing signal** alerts you to dangerous conditions or tells you to stop. As you can see in **FIGURE 11**, a flashing light may be the only light on the traffic signal. When you see a flashing yellow signal, slow down. Be prepared to stop at the traffic light.

Arrows   Arrows regulate the movement of traffic on a particular path through the intersection. Refer to **FIGURE 12** for the meaning of several colors of arrows. A red arrow means you cannot travel in that direction until the light changes to green. A yellow arrow means to stop or proceed with caution.

A green arrow means you may go in the direction of the arrow. All traffic must flow in the direction that a green arrow is pointing. If you are driving in a lane with a green arrow pointing to the left or right, you must turn in that direction. Remember first to yield to other traffic and pedestrians.

Some cities use left-turn arrows to permit drivers to turn left before oncoming traffic proceeds. Other cities use green left-turn arrows only after oncoming traffic has cleared or has been stopped by a red light. Be cautious if you are unfamiliar with the left-turn signals you encounter. Always be prepared to yield.

Lane Signals   Some streets and expressways have lanes in which traffic is permitted to travel in one direction for one period of time, then in the opposite direction at another time. Switching the direction of travel in these lanes helps control morning and evening rush-hour traffic.

Lights hung overhead with arrows pointing downward indicate whether or not the lane can be used at that time. Each light is a **lane signal**. These signals are different from the arrows that regulate turns. You will learn more about lane signals on expressways in Chapter 16.

FIGURE 12
DIRECTIONAL ARROWS

STOP.
You may not go in this direction.

WARNING.
The red arrow is about to appear.

GO left only.
Be sure that oncoming traffic does not go through the red light.

GO right only.
Yield to pedestrians and vehicles already in the intersection.

GO straight ahead only after yielding to vehicles and pedestrians within the intersection.

FIGURE 13

The walk symbol tells pedestrians they may cross the street. **Decide** When is it safe to make a right turn across this pedestrian crosswalk?

Pedestrian and Officers' Signals

As a driver, you must act responsibly toward pedestrians and traffic-control officers.

Pedestrian Signals   Pedestrian signals are used to ensure the safety of people who are walking. At busy intersections, there may be **pedestrian signals** mounted near traffic lights. Pedestrians should cross only when they face a WALK signal or the symbol of a person walking, as shown in **FIGURE 13**. Pedestrians must wait on a curb when the DON'T WALK signal flashes or remains lit.

Normally, the WALK signal and the green traffic light are lit at the same time for pedestrians and drivers going in the same direction. The DON'T WALK signal usually begins to flash just before the yellow light appears for drivers. If you approach an intersection and see the DON'T WALK signal flashing, predict that your green light will soon change. Some pedestrian signals give times in seconds. You can use these times to help predict when your green light will change. But be careful to watch the pedestrians in the crosswalk; some people move more slowly than the time permitted by the lights.

The DON'T WALK signal will remain on when a green right- or left-turn signal is permitting vehicles to drive through the crosswalk.

FIGURE 14

This police officer is using hand signals to direct traffic.

Pedestrians should wait until their WALK signal is lit. When turning at an intersection, be alert to pedestrians, even if you have a green turn signal.

Traffic-Control Officer's Signals

Sometimes an officer uses hand signals to direct traffic. At night or when there is limited visibility, an officer may use a lighted wand.

- A hand held up with the palm toward you means stop.
- A hand waving you forward means go.

You must obey the signals given by a traffic-control officer, even if those signals contradict the traffic signs or signals.

analyzing data
Pedestrian Injuries

Motor vehicles injure nearly 80,000 pedestrians each year. The chart shows how the number of pedestrian injuries varies according to the time of day. Study the chart before you answer these questions.

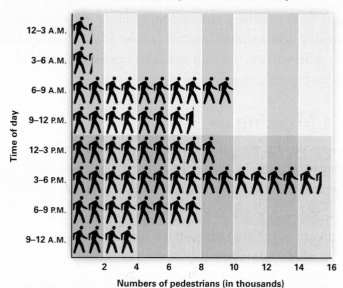

Pedestrian Injuries on Wednesdays

Time of day / Numbers of pedestrians (in thousands)

1. **Reading Graphs** What length of time does each bar on the graph represent?

2. **Analyzing Data** What time period has the greatest number of pedestrian injuries? What time periods have the fewest injuries?

3. **Inferring** Suggest a reason for the increase in the number of injuries from 6 A.M. to 9 A.M.

4. **Relating Cause and Effect** On weekends, there are an average of 3,000 pedestrian injuries between midnight and 3 A.M. How does this rate of injury compare with the data given here? What risk factors do you think contribute to this difference?

5. **Execute** As a driver, what actions can you take to help protect pedestrians?

review it 2.2

1. What should you do when you approach a red light? A yellow light? A green light?

2. Compare the meaning of a flashing yellow light with that of a flashing red light.

3. At an intersection, you see an officer holding his hand up with his palm toward you. What should you do?

Critical Thinking

4. **Relate Cause and Effect** Describe two ways that computerized traffic lights can help traffic flow smoothly.

5. **Decide** At a busy intersection, you would like to turn left. The left-turn signal is green, but three pedestrians are crossing in the crosswalk. What action should you take?

IN YOUR COMMUNITY **Dangerous Intersections** Research local newspapers to find articles about recent accidents in your community. Are some intersections mentioned more often than others? What signs or signals are found at those intersections? Compare your results with those of your classmates.

lesson 2.3
ROADWAY MARKINGS

OBJECTIVES

- Describe the proper actions to take with broken and solid yellow and white lane markings.
- Identify the meaning of special roadway markings, including highway exit ramps, railroad and school crossings, and parking restrictions.
- Explain the function of rumble strips and raised roadway markers.

VOCABULARY

- roadway marking
- shared left-turn lane
- HOV lane
- rumble strip
- speed bump

Markings on the roadway provide many clues to help you drive safely. A **roadway marking** gives a warning or direction. Roadway markings are usually lines, words, or symbols painted on the roadway. Some markings are painted on curbs or other surfaces. As with signs and signals, the colors of roadway markings have specific meanings.

Yellow Lane Markings

Yellow lines separate traffic traveling in opposite directions on two-way roads. Yellow lines may be single or double. Study FIGURE 15 as you read about the meanings of these lines.

Single Lines   A single, broken, yellow line separates two-way traffic. It indicates that you may pass, but only when no traffic is coming from the opposite direction. A solid yellow line indicates that passing is not allowed.

Double Lines   Two solid yellow lines that divide traffic prohibit passing. Some cities permit you to turn left across solid yellow lines into a drive-way or alley after yielding to other traffic.

You may also see a solid and broken line together. This indicates that passing is permitted if you are traveling on the side with the broken line. A solid yellow line on your side indicates that no passing is permitted.

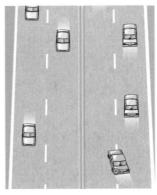

**FIGURE 15
YELLOW
LANE MARKINGS**

Passing is allowed across a broken yellow line.

No passing is allowed across a double yellow line.

No passing is allowed on the side of the road that has the solid yellow line.

FIGURE 16
WHITE
LANE MARKINGS

Broken white lines separate lanes that are moving in the same direction.

Solid white lines identify where changing lanes is hazardous and to mark the edge of the roadway.

White arrows in lanes tell you when and where to turn.

White Lane Markings

Highways that have traffic moving in the same direction use white lines to separate lanes. Broken white lines separate lanes that are moving in the same direction. You may cross these lines when changing lanes. Study **FIGURE 16** as you read the meanings of these lines.

Solid white lines identify locations where changing lanes is hazardous. They keep drivers in their lanes and restrict lane changing. Crossing solid lines is discouraged. Although it may be legal, you should not cross solid white line markings.

Solid white lines are also used to mark the edge of the roadway. These lines help you see the edge of the roadway at night and at times of poor visibility, such as fog or heavy rain. Solid white lines along the edge of a highway may be used to indicate a breakdown lane or bicycle lane.

White arrows in lanes tell you when and where to turn. If you are in a lane with an arrow and the word *only*, you must continue in the direction of the arrow. You may turn or go straight if there is a curved and straight arrow in your lane.

Other Road Markings

A number of painted markings are used to warn of possible dangers and restrictions. Several of these markings are shown in **FIGURE 17**, Roadway Markings, on the next page.

FIGURE 17 ROADWAY MARKINGS

STOP LINES AND CROSSWALKS

Stop Lines
Solid white lines across your lane show where to stop at a stop sign or traffic light.

Stop Lines

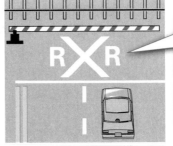

Railroad Crossings
An *X* and two *R*s on each side of the roadway warn you that there is a railroad crossing ahead.

Railroad Crossings

School Crossings
The word *school* indicates a school crossing. Watch for children in the area.

School Crossings

Pedestrian Crosswalks
May be indicated by solid white lines. They often have diagonal or perpendicular lines between them.

Pedestrian Crossings

LANE MARKINGS

High-Occupancy Vehicle (HOV) Lanes A large white diamond symbol and black and white rectangular signs identify HOV lanes. HOV lanes may be reserved for high-occupancy motor vehicles.

Highway Exit Ramps
A special white marking on the roadway indicates the start of an exit ramp. It is dangerous and illegal to cross this area.

Shared Left-Turn Lanes
A center lane with these special pavement markings is designed to be shared by traffic going in both directions for making left turns.

Turning Lanes   On busy streets, a **shared left-turn lane** can help drivers turn left into businesses in the middle of a block. Drivers traveling in either direction may use these lanes. Solid and broken yellow lines with white left-turn arrows pointing in either direction identify a shared left-turn lane.

Reversible Lanes   Many cities use reversible lanes to improve traffic flow during rush hours. Two broken yellow lines mark these lanes. If it is not rush hour, it is legal to cross these lines to pass another vehicle.

Some roadways have high-occupancy vehicle lanes, or HOV lanes. **HOV lanes** are reserved for use by buses and carpools with at least two or three passengers. These lanes are identified with solid yellow or white lines and a diamond. If you travel in these lanes without the minimum number of passengers, you may receive a large fine.

Parking Restrictions   Curbs along a road may be painted red, yellow, or white to indicate that parking is restricted. The meanings of the colors vary from city to city. Red curbs usually mean that you cannot stop or park in the area. No-parking zones are often located near fire hydrants, curves, and intersections.

White curbs usually indicate areas of live-parking only. You may stop for brief periods of time, but may not leave your vehicle. Yellow curbs identify loading zones that are reserved for commercial vehicles.

Handicapped parking markings indicate areas that are reserved for vehicles with drivers or passengers who are disabled. Check for HANDICAPPED PARKING ONLY signs and for pavement markings with the handicapped parking symbol. The curb in these areas may be painted blue. As you can see in **FIGURE 18**, handicapped spaces are usually larger than regular spaces to allow room for loading a wheelchair into a van.

FIGURE 18 DISABLED DRIVER PARKING

It is illegal to park in these spaces without a proper permit.

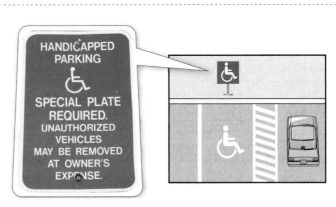

HANDICAPPED PARKING

SPECIAL PLATE REQUIRED. UNAUTHORIZED VEHICLES MAY BE REMOVED AT OWNER'S EXPENSE.

FIGURE 19

White reflective markers are used at the edge of a roadway or between lanes.

Rumble Strips and Reflective Markers

In addition to painted markings, some highways have three-dimensional markers that help ensure safe driving.

Rumble Strips   Rumble strips are short sections of grooved or corrugated roadway. When you drive over these strips, they cause your car to vibrate and make a loud noise. Rumble strips may be used to warn you of an unexpected need to reduce speed or stop, or to warn you that you are driving too close to the edge of the road.

Speed Bumps   Areas such as parking lots and very narrow streets sometimes have raised portions called **speed bumps**. You should drive no faster than about 5 mph over speed bumps. Driving faster may damage your car.

Reflective Markers   Some highways are marked with small reflectors that reflect headlight beams. At night and in bad weather, reflective markers are much easier to see than painted markings. In regions where it rarely snows, these markers are raised.

Reflective markers are color-coded. White markers are used at the edge of a roadway or between lanes. Yellow markers may locate the left edge of an expressway. Red markers warn you that you are driving in the wrong direction. Pull off the roadway immediately if you see red roadway markers.

review it 2.3

1. What is the basic difference between broken white lines and broken yellow lines?

2. How are railroad crossings indicated? How are school crossings indicated? Describe the correct action to take when you see each of these roadway markings.

3. What is a rumble strip? How can a rumble strip help you drive safely?

Critical Thinking

4. **Compare and Contrast**   Compare the correct way to use a shared left-turn lane with the use of a regular left-turn lane.

5. **Decide**   Recently, a friend broke his leg and is now on crutches. You have offered to help your friend go shopping. Should you park your car in the handicapped zone while you help with his errands? Give reasons for your decision.

IN THE PASSENGER SEAT   **Observing Local Markings**   As you drive with a parent or other experienced driver, make a list of the roadway markings you see. Does your community have any shared left-turn lanes? How are passenger crosswalks labeled? Note the location of railroad crossings and school zones.

CHAPTER 2 REVIEW

Lesson Summaries

2.1 TRAFFIC SIGNS

- Regulatory signs, such as STOP signs, YIELD signs, and speed limits, control traffic. Other regulatory signs are used to direct traffic and to control passing and parking.

- Be prepared to slow or stop when you see a warning sign. Most warning signs are diamond-shaped and have black symbols or letters on a yellow background. The warning signs for schools, no-passing areas, construction, and railroads have different shapes and colors.

- International signs convey information with symbols rather than words.

2.2 TRAFFIC SIGNALS

- Green lights mean that you can proceed, but only if the intersection is clear. Yellow lights mean that red lights are about to appear; make every effort to stop safely. Red lights mean that you must come to a full stop.

- Flashing signals alert drivers at intersections and other dangerous locations. Drivers should be alert to pedestrians and signals by traffic-control officers.

2.3 ROADWAY MARKINGS

- Yellow lane markings separate traffic on two-way roads. A broken line means you may pass. Unbroken lines means passing is not allowed.

- White line markings separate lanes of traffic that are moving in the same direction. They may also be used to mark the edge of the roadway, stop lines, and crosswalks.

Chapter Vocabulary

- flashing signal
- guide sign
- HOV lane
- international sign
- lane signal
- pedestrian signal
- regulatory sign
- right-turn-on-red
- roadway marking
- rumble strip
- shared left-turn lane
- speed bump
- traffic signal
- warning sign

Write the word or phrase from the list above that completes the sentence correctly.

1. A sign that alerts you to possible hazards and road conditions is a(n) _____.

2. A(n) _____ is a signal that alerts drivers to dangerous conditions or tells them to stop.

3. A sign set on roadways to keep traffic moving safely is called a(n) _____.

4. A(n) _____ is a center lane used by traffic going in both directions for making left turns.

5. A(n) _____ is used at heavy traffic intersections to tell pedestrians whether they should proceed or wait.

6. A short section of corrugated roadway that warns of hazards is called a(n) _____.

7. A sign that uses symbols instead of words is called a(n) _____.

✓✓✓  **STUDY TIP**

Flashcards Make color flashcards for all the signs shown in this chapter. Work with a partner to test each other on the meanings of the signs.

Checking Concepts

LESSON 1

8. What action should you take at a STOP sign?

9. How should you proceed when you see a YIELD sign?

10. What is the purpose of a speed limit sign?

11. List five situations where warning signs might be used.

12. How do guide signs help you when driving?

LESSON 2

13. What should you do at each of the following traffic lights: green light, yellow light, red light?

14. What action should you take when approaching a flashing red signal?

15. What actions should you take with pedestrian signals?

LESSON 3

16. What is the difference between a shared left-turn lane and a left-turn lane?

17. What is the purpose of a rumble strip?

18. What are six types of special roadway markings?

Critical Thinking

19. **Analyze** What is the difference between a basic speed law, a minimum speed limit, and an advisory speed limit?

20. **Compare** Compare the meaning of a broken yellow line with the meaning of a broken white line.

You're the Driver

21. **Execute** You approach an intersection with a flashing yellow signal. What action should you take?

22. **Execute** You approach an intersection with a red light, but a police officer is signaling you to move forward. What should you do?

23. **Identify** What is the speed limit in this situation? What speed law might make driving at the posted speed limit illegal?

24. **Decide** You want to pass the slower moving vehicle ahead of you. Is it safe to pass here? Is it legal? Why or why not?

Preparing for the Test

Choose the letter of the answer that best completes the statement or answers the question.

1. What does a round traffic sign mean?
   a. yield to other traffic
   b. railroad crossing
   c. stop
   d. pedestrian crossing

2. Yielding in traffic means
   a. allowing others to go before you.
   b. coming to a complete stop every time.
   c. expecting others to stop for you.
   d. speeding up to avoid a collision.

Use the art below to answer Question 3.

3. When you see this sign, you should drive
   a. 45 mph during the day.
   b. at least 45 mph.
   c. 45 mph at night.
   d. no faster than 45 mph.

4. What color is a construction zone sign?
   a. blue
   b. green
   c. orange
   d. yellow

5. Your traffic light changes to yellow as you approach an intersection. In most cases, what action should you take?
   a. Signal for a right turn and slow down.
   b. Go through if no other vehicles are coming.
   c. Accelerate to clear the intersection.
   d. Make every reasonable effort to stop.

6. A solid line and a broken line painted on the center of a two-lane highway means passing is
   a. allowed when the solid line is on your side.
   b. not allowed when the solid line is on your side.
   c. allowed in either direction.
   d. not allowed in either direction.

Use the art below to answer Question 7.

7. To park in a space that is marked with this symbol, you must
   a. reserve the space in advance.
   b. not be able to walk.
   c. have the proper permit.
   d. not be able to find any other parking space.

8. Curbs painted red, yellow, or white are generally designated as
   a. minimum-speed zones.
   b. user-parking zones.
   c. no-parking zones.
   d. limited-time parking zones.

drive write

Speed Limits Do you think the federal government should set national speed limits? Write one or two paragraphs explaining the advantages and the disadvantages.

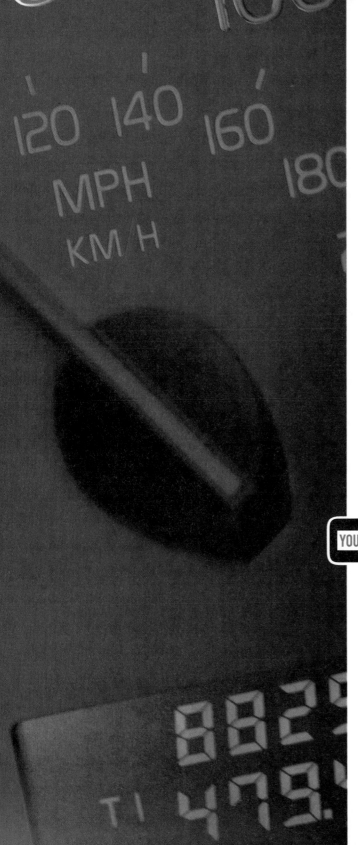

chapter 3

BASIC VEHICLE OPERATION

3.1 Controls, Devices, and Instruments

3.2 Getting Ready to Drive

3.3 Starting, Stopping, Steering, and Targeting

3.4 Driving with a Manual Transmission

KEY IDEA

What is the safest way to get in and out of a vehicle, and how do you check for problems before putting the vehicle into motion? What do you need to learn before you pull into traffic for the first time?

YOU'RE THE DRIVER

To become a proficient driver, you need to know the basic operational controls of your vehicle. Do you know how target usage affects steering control? Do you know how to start and stop the motion of the vehicle in a smooth manner? Can you correctly read the instruments to prevent costly damage to your vehicle?

lesson 3.1
CONTROLS, DEVICES, AND INSTRUMENTS

 OBJECTIVES

- Describe the operational controls of a vehicle and how to use them effectively.
- Identify communication and comfort devices found in most vehicles.
- Identify gauges and warning lights on an instrument panel and explain their purpose.

 VOCABULARY

- shift lever
- cruise control
- shift indicator
- mirror's blind spot
- tachometer
- odometer
- antilock braking system (ABS)

Vehicle Controls

The characteristics and locations of vehicle controls vary from one model to another. However, each control performs the same function in each vehicle.

Steering Wheel (1) The steering wheel turns the front wheels. To steer the vehicle you need to have speed control. With too much speed, the car will go straight even though the tires are turned.

Adjustable Steering Position (2) Some vehicles have options available to help a driver fit behind the steering wheel. Refer to your owner's manual for more information,

Shift Lever (3) The **shift lever** is used to select a gear. The shift lever is most commonly located on the steering column or on the console. The console is the compartment mounted between the front seats.

Cruise Control (4) The **cruise control** device lets you maintain your desired speed without keeping your foot on the accelerator.

Accelerator Pedal (5) The accelerator pedal, located to the right of the brake pedal, is pushed down to increase speed.

Brake Pedal (6) Pushing down on the brake pedal slows or stops the vehicle. Depressing this pedal also turns on the brake lights.

Parking Brake (7) The parking brake keeps the vehicle in place when it is parked. In many cars, the parking brake is a foot-operated pedal located on the far left. Push this pedal down with your foot to set the brake.

FIGURE 1
Devices for starting and controlling the movement of a vehicle.

FIGURE 2
All vehicles have a foot-brake pedal and an accelerator pedal. Some vehicles also have a clutch pedal (**8**) and/or parking-brake pedal.

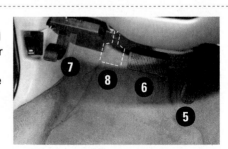

Shift Indicator Positions

The **shift indicator** shows the gear positions of an automatic transmission. This indicator may be located on the steering column, on the instrument panel, or on the console to the right of the driver. Common positions on the shift indicator are P, R, N, D, 2, and 1.

P (PARK) This gear position locks the transmission. Your vehicle should be in PARK before you start driving. You should also shift to PARK every time you stop driving since the vehicle cannot roll in this gear. Never shift to PARK when the vehicle is moving. You can remove the key from the ignition only when the lever is in PARK.

R (REVERSE) This gear is used for backing up. Always come to a complete stop before shifting into REVERSE. When you shift to REVERSE, the backup lights come on. These white lights at the rear of the vehicle illuminate your path at night and tell others that you are backing up.

N (NEUTRAL) This position allows the wheels to roll without engine power. If the engine stalls while you are driving, you must shift into NEUTRAL to restart the engine while the vehicle is moving.

D (DRIVE) This position is for moving forward. To keep your vehicle from jumping forward, keep firm pressure on the brake pedal every time you shift to DRIVE. Some vehicles are equipped with overdrive. In most cars,

FIGURE 3

overdrive is shown as a D with a circle or square around it. Driving in this gear saves fuel and can be used for all normal forward driving.

LOWER GEARS   The numbers 2 and 1 located to the right of D represent lower gear ratios (some indicators have L2, L1, or D2, D1). These positions allow the engine to send more power to the wheels at lower speeds. You should use the lower gears when you are towing heavy objects or going up and down steep hills.

Devices for Safety, Communication, and Comfort

Locate and understand the operation of the following devices on any vehicle you drive before you put the car in motion.

Safety Belts (9)   Always wear your safety belt when the vehicle is in motion; it is your best protection against injury in a collision. Fasten the belt to a snug fit. Most states require drivers and front-seat passengers to wear safety belts. Some states require all passengers to use safety belts.

Head Restraints (10)   Most vehicles have head restraints, padded devices on the backs of the seats. Head restraints help reduce whiplash injuries in a collision, especially if the vehicle is struck from the rear.

Inside and Outside Rearview Mirrors (11,12)   The inside mirror (11) shows the view through the rear window of the vehicle. The left and right outside mirrors (12) show views to the side and rear of your vehicle.

FIGURE 4
Safety devices help protect you and your passengers.

Even when these mirrors are adjusted properly, there are areas around the vehicle that the driver cannot see. These areas, called the **mirror's blind spots**, are shown in **FIGURE 12** on page 54.

Horn (13) The horn is usually located on the steering wheel. In some areas, two quick taps on the horn convey a friendly message, but a prolonged blast of the horn sends out a warning signal to other users of the roadway.

Hazard-Flasher Control (14) This switch may be located on the steering column or on the instrument panel. When the hazard flasher is on, both front and rear turn-signal lights flash at the same time.

Turn-Signal Lever (15) This lever is located on the left side of the steering column. Move the lever up to signal a right turn and down to signal a left turn. The turn signal stops flashing when the steering wheel is straightened. You may need to manually cancel the signal light by moving the lever back to the neutral position.

Windshield Wipers and Washers (16) One switch usually operates both the wipers and the washers to clean the windshield. This control is often mounted on the turn-signal lever. Use a windshield anti-freeze solution in the windshield washer container under the hood in winter if you live in a cold climate.

Light Switch (17) The light switch is usually a knob or switch located on the left of the instrument panel or on the turn-signal lever. In some vehicles, it may be a separate lever attached to the steering column. This device controls headlights, taillights, and side-marker lights, as well as the instrument panel, license plate, and dome lights. You can change the headlights from low to high beam by using the dimmer switch, usually located on the turn-signal lever.

Hood Release Lever (18) This lever is usually located on the left side under the instrument panel. Pull the lever to release the hood. You will also need to operate a second release under the front of the hood before the hood can be raised.

FIGURE 5

The controls on your car may look different, but all vehicles have similar controls.

Heater, Air Conditioner, and Defroster Heating and air-conditioning systems warm or cool the inside of the vehicle.

The defroster keeps the windshield and windows free of moisture. Most vehicles have a separate switch for a rear-window defroster.

Sun Visor Sun visors are located above the windshield on the driver and passenger sides. Pull the visor down or to the side to help cut glare from bright sun. Always make certain the edge of the visor is not pointing towards you, which could cause injuries during a crash.

Seat Adjustment Lever This lever is usually located at the lower front or left side of the driver's seat. In vehicles with electric seats, the controls are usually on the lower left side of the driver's seat or mounted on the door.

Instrument Panel

The instrument panel contains gauges, warning lights, and sometimes a message center. It is the panel directly in front of the driver's seat. No matter where these gauges and lights are located, their purposes are the same. You can make sure the warning lights are working if they light when the ignition switch is turned on before starting the engine.

Important Vehicle Gauges

These gauges measure the operational condition of the vehicle. It is extremely important that you detect any abnormal reading as soon as possible.

- **Fuel Gauge (1)** The fuel gauge shows how much gasoline is in the tank. It's a good idea to keep the tank at least half full during cold weather.
- **Temperature Light or Gauge (2)** This light or gauge warns you when the coolant in the engine is too hot.
- **Oil Pressure Warning Light or Gauge (3)** This warning light or gauge signals you when the oil is not circulating through the engine at the proper pressure. However, it does not tell you the amount of oil in the engine.
- **Alternator Warning Light or Voltage Meter (4)** If this light comes on, or the gauge shows "discharge" while the engine is running, the alternator is not generating enough electricity to run the vehicle. The alternator warning light indicates that the electricity is being used from the battery. The more electricity used, the sooner the battery will go dead.

safe
driving tip

Cruise Control Cruise control should never be used when road surfaces are wet or slippery or in heavy traffic. You have much less control if a conflict occurs. Using cruise control in areas of steep grades wastes fuel and puts added stress on the engine.

- **Brake System Warning Light (5)** This warning light serves two purposes. First, the light reminds you to release the parking brake before moving the vehicle. Second, if the light comes on while you are pressing the foot brake or while you are driving, part or all of the braking system is not working properly. If this occurs, brake gradually to a stop, have the vehicle towed, and have the problem corrected.

- **Speedometer (6)** This instrument tells you the speed at which you are traveling in both miles per hour and kilometers per hour. Some vehicles have a digital speedometer.

- **Tachometer (7)** Some vehicles have a **tachometer** that indicates the engine revolutions per minute (RPM). Engine damage may occur if the RPMs rise too high while the vehicle is being driven. This is indicated by a red zone on the gauge.

- **Odometer (8)** The **odometer** indicates the total number of miles the vehicle has been driven. Some vehicles have an additional trip odometer that can be set back to zero to measure the number of miles driven during a certain period of time.

- **Antilock Braking System Light (9)** This light tells you if the **antilock braking system (ABS)** is functioning properly. ABS keeps the wheels from locking if the driver brakes hard. If the ABS light comes on while driving, it indicates a problem with the system.

- **Safety Belt Light (10)** This light reminds you to fasten your safety belt before moving your vehicle. This light comes on when you turn

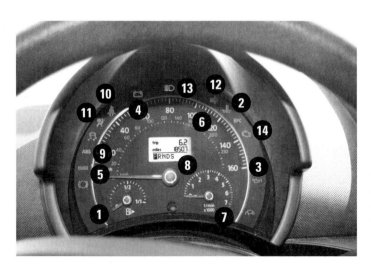

FIGURE 6
The location of the gauges and warning lights varies from one vehicle to another.

the key. In some vehicles, the light stays on for a few seconds after the engine is started and there may also be a beeping sound.

- **Air Bag Warning Light (11)** When the ignition is turned on, the air-bag light comes on for a few seconds and then goes off. This tells you that the air bags are in proper working condition. If the air bags are not in proper operating condition, the warning light will stay on.

- **Turn-Signal Indicators (12)** These indicators tell you the direction you have signaled to turn.

- **High-Beam Indicator (13)** This light glows when the high-beam headlights are on. This indicator usually appears as a small blue light in some area of the instrument panel.

- **Check Engine Light (14)** The check engine light can either blink or remain constant, depending on the problem. A blinking light indicates a problem that needs immediate attention. However, whenever the check engine light comes on, you should have the vehicle checked by a service technician.

- **Message Center** Many vehicles have a message center that provides drivers with important information. Typical reminders include check engine oil, low-washer fluid, and door ajar. Refer to your owner's manual for the meanings of the messages whenever they appear in the message center.

review it 3.1

1. Identify three operational controls and explain how to use them.

2. Why is it important to check your indicator lights every time you start the car?

3. Explain how safety devices inside your car help keep you safe.

Critical Thinking

4. **Evaluate** Do you think it would be a good habit to place the shift selector into PARK when passengers exit the vehicle with the engine running? Explain your thinking.

IN YOUR COMMUNITY **Investigate** Use the Internet to research new innovations in vehicle controls, devices, and instruments. Make a summary of your findings and their sources, and share it with the class.

Before you take your place behind the wheel to drive, you should follow certain checks and procedures. People who get into a vehicle and drive away with little thought or concern for themselves or others are demonstrating high-risk driving behaviors.

Before Opening the Door

1. Have your keys in your hand. Hold your keys while approaching the vehicle. If you have a **key fob**, a hand-held remote control, you can lock or unlock the vehicle's doors from a distance.

2. Look under the vehicle. It is easier to see under your vehicle from a distance. Inspect beneath your vehicle as you approach it and before getting in. You may be able to detect a potential problem by looking for water or oil marks under the vehicle

3. Look at and around the vehicle. Checking all around your vehicle is especially important to avoid injuring someone or damaging your vehicle. Be alert for small children playing near your vehicle. Many deaths each year are attributed to driveway backups.

4. Glance at the tires. Look at the tires to check for cuts, tread wear, and sidewall bulges.

5. Check the windshield, windows, headlights, and taillights. Make sure the windows, windshield, headlights, and taillights are clear. If windows are covered with snow or ice, clear them completely.

6. Look inside the vehicle. Looking into the vehicle before opening the door will allow you to detect any possible problems. If your vehicle is parked on the street, walk from the front of the vehicle toward the back. This way you can see oncoming traffic and reduce the risk of being hit.

Get Into the Vehicle

Watch the traffic. Do not open the door if an oncoming vehicle is near. Get in quickly and close the door. Then take the following steps:

OBJECTIVES

- Describe how to reduce risk while walking to your vehicle.
- Explain outside checks you can make before getting into the vehicle.

VOCABULARY

- key fob

FIGURE 7

As you approach the car, hold the key fob with your finger ready to activate the panic button if needed.

1. Lock all doors. Put the key in the ignition so you have two hands free to make proper adjustments. Lock the doors to be secure from carjackers and to have better protection during a crash.

2. Adjust your head restraint. Adjust the middle of the head restraint to ear level.

3. Adjust your seat. Adjust the seat for comfort and best control of foot pedals and steering wheel. Sit with your back firmly against the seat. The seat should be high enough so that your chin is no lower than the top of the steering wheel. Your body should be at least 10 inches away from the hub of the wheel to avoid injury from the airbag during a crash.

    Place your hands at the 9:00 and 3:00 positions on the steering wheel, or slightly lower. Your hands should be in a balanced, comfortable position with your elbows slightly bent. Reach for the accelerator and brake pedal with your right foot to judge a comfortable distance. Your knees should be slightly bent.

4. Check and adjust all mirrors. The inside mirror should be adjusted to a level position to show the maximum outside view through the rear window. Adjust the left and right outside rearview mirrors so they show the slightest amount of the side of the vehicle.

5. Make sure passengers buckle up. Before starting the vehicle, make sure you and all passengers put the safety belts on.

review it 3.2

1. How should you enter the vehicle when it is parked on a street?
2. What checks should you make before opening the door to the car?
3. How can you tell when you are positioned properly behind the steering wheel?

Critical Thinking

4. **Analyze** While approaching the vehicle, why is it a good habit to hold the key in your hand?

IN YOUR COMMUNITY **Stolen Vehicles** Use the Internet to find data about vehicles that were stolen in your state because 1) the doors were left unlocked, 2) the keys were left in the car, and 3) both the keys were left in the car and the doors unlocked. Then find the same data for the United States. Make a bar graph to compare the data and share your findings with the class.

STARTING, STOPPING, STEERING, AND TARGETING

It doesn't take much skill to start, stop, and steer the vehicle. However, it takes considerable skill and practice to develop habits that will allow you to move the vehicle smoothly as you accelerate, steer, and brake.

Starting the Engine

Use this procedure to start the engine of a vehicle with an automatic transmission.

1. Set the parking brake. The parking brake should already be on from the last time it was parked. The parking brake is the primary means of preventing the vehicle from moving until you are ready to put it in motion.

2. The shift lever should be in PARK. The engine can only be started from the PARK or NEUTRAL positions. If you are starting the vehicle after the engine has stalled, shift into NEUTRAL to restart the engine.

3. Place your right foot on the brake pedal. This will keep your foot off the accelerator pedal and in position when the parking brake is released.

4. Insert the key and turn the ignition switch to ON. Continue turning the key to start the engine. Release the key as soon as the engine starts to avoid damage to the starter.

5. Check the gauges, warning lights, and fuel supply.

6. Turn on the headlights if they don't come on automatically after starting the car. Get in the habit of driving with your headlights on during the day to help other drivers see your vehicle.

OBJECTIVES

- Explain why you should make smooth acceleration and braking actions.
- Explain how the use of targets will help develop good visual searching and steering habits.

VOCABULARY

- target
- braking point
- wheel lock-up

FIGURE 8

IGNITION AND STARTER SWITCH

With the shift selector in PARK or NEUTRAL, insert and turn the key to the start position.

Lock: position of key when engine is off. Steering wheel and shift lever are locked in position.

On: position of key when engine is running.

Start: position of key to start engine; release when engine starts.

Accessory: can be used to run accessories (lights radio, etc.) without running engine.

FIGURE 9

Critical Thinking
Explain the advantages of holding the steering wheel at a 9:00-3:00 or 8:00-4:00 position.

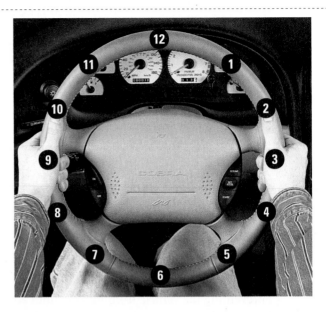

Hand Positions for Controlled Steering

Steering is not just a matter of pointing the vehicle in the direction you want it to go. Controlled steering involves effective use of vision and a comfortable and balanced hand position on the steering wheel.

Refer to **FIGURE 9** and imagine that the steering wheel is the face of a clock. Place your hands at either the 9:00 and 3:00 positions or the 8:00 and 4:00 positions. A 9-3 or an 8-4 position will give you a balanced grip and help you avoid injury if the airbag in your vehicle's steering wheel deploys during a collision.

Always keep your knuckles and thumbs on the outside of the rim of the steering wheel to reduce injury in a collision.

FIGURE 10

Don't use the road lines as a guide for where to look when you practice steering.

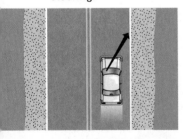

Use of Targets and the Steering Wheel

Using a target helps you steer the vehicle with pinpoint accuracy. A **target** is a fixed object far out in the distance that appears to be in the center of the path you intend to drive. A target serves as an aiming point for where you want your vehicle to go. Using targets will give you the ability to steer your vehicle accurately. To steer the vehicle, turn the steering wheel so that the center of it is aligned with the target.

Two popular methods for turning the steering wheel are hand-over-hand and hand-to-hand, as shown in **FIGURE 11**.

Hand-over-Hand Steering   This method is best to use when you need to make tight right turns, or to make quick steering actions to correct a skid. This will give you maximum movement of the steering wheel in a short period of time.

1. Begin with the hands in a balanced 9-3 position.

2. To make a right turn, begin with the right hand at the 3 position, and pull down to the 5 position.

3. Move the left hand up to the 12 position, grip the wheel, and pull down to the 5 position.

4. Cross the right hand over the left hand to the 12 position and continue turning to the 5 position.

5. To straighten the steering wheel, turn the steering wheel back using the left side of the steering wheel.

6. To make a left turn, use the left side of the steering wheel starting at the 9 position.

Hand-to-Hand Steering   This method is best when there is a need for small steering adjustments, such as making a left turn or going into a slight curve. This method will keep your body balanced behind the steering wheel and prevent your hands from crossing the area of the steering wheel in which the air bag is stored.

1. Begin with your hands in the 8-4 position.

2. To make a left turn, grip the wheel with your right hand at the 4 position.

3. Slide your left hand to the 10 position. Grip the wheel and pull down to the 7 position.

FIGURE 11

4. Push the right hand up to the 2 position. Slide the left hand up to the 10 position.

5. With your left hand, pull the steering wheel down to the 7 position while sliding the right hand down to the 4 position.

6. Continue to pull and push as more steering is needed.

Hand-over-Hand Steering

Putting the Vehicle in Motion

A vacant parking lot is a good place to practice good driving behaviors. You have the opportunity to repeat your actions often during a short period of time.

1. Put your right foot on the brake. Keep the ball of your foot on the brake pedal, and the heel of your foot on the floorboard.

2. Shift into DRIVE by placing your open palm under the shift lever and moving it towards your body and into the DRIVE position.

3. Keep your foot on the brake pedal. Locate the parking brake and release the lever without looking at it to keep you alert to the driving scene around you. Release the parking brake.

4. Check your path of travel. Before taking your foot off the brake, check the path of travel you want the vehicle to take. Look to the left, front and right of your vehicle. Check the rearview and outside mirrors.

5. Make blind-spot area checks. Even with side view mirrors, there are blind spots where you may not be able to see another vehicle alongside you. You should look over your shoulder towards the side you will be moving into, or move your head forward while checking the outside mirror.

FIGURE 12

The dark shading indicates blind spots. Never rely only on your rearview mirrors alone when checking for vehicles to the rear.

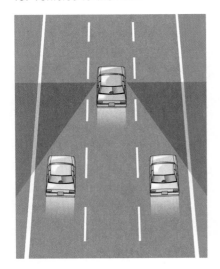

Acceleration Control

When you are ready to move, take your foot off the brake and allow the vehicle's idling engine to begin moving the vehicle before pressing the accelerator pedal.

Press the accelerator smoothly. Once the vehicle is moving at the engine's idle speed, the force added by accelerating will be smooth. This is because idle speed is able to move the vehicle from a rest position more lightly than most drivers are able to accelerate.

Accelerate smoothly, and then work to maintain a steady speed. Decelerate gradually. Practice releasing partial pressure from the accelerator.

Braking Control

There are several techniques you can practice to acquire the best braking control.

- **Braking Point**   As you practice using the brakes, try to feel the vehicle's **braking point**, which is the point at which the brakes begin to work and slow the vehicle.

- **Constant Braking Pressure**   Apply constant pressure to the pedal when braking. A constant "squeezing" pressure on the brake pedal will activate the brakes without causing your wheels to lock up. **Wheel lock-up** occurs in a vehicle without ABS when the brakes are applied with such force that the wheels stop turning and the tires begin to slide on the pavement.

- **Normal Smooth Stop**   To make a smooth stop, release some braking pressure one or two seconds before the vehicle comes to a complete rest. For a smooth stop, keep the ball of your foot on the pedal while lifting your toes. This will release enough braking pressure—without affecting the braking action—so that the vehicle will be level at the moment of total stop.

- **Hard, Smooth Stop**   For hard stops, apply maximum braking pressure at the start of braking without locking the wheels, and hold that position. You can still make a smooth braking action by pulling back your toes during the last one or two seconds before the vehicle comes to a full stop.

- **ABS Braking**   When the ABS system activates, your brake pedal may begin pulsating, which is normal. Do not release your foot pressure.

safe driving tip

Develop the habit of turning your head in the direction you want to go before turning the steering wheel. This will help you stay mentally ahead of the vehicle. Your eyes should always precede the vehicle on the path you want to travel.

Exiting the Vehicle

Check the location. Make sure your vehicle is parked in the best possible location. Is it legally parked?

1. Keep your foot on the brake until the shift selector is in PARK and the parking brake is set.

2. Set the parking brake to secure the vehicle.

3. Shift to PARK.

4. Take your foot off the brake.

FIGURE 13

The driver is facing traffic after he exits the vehicle. **Evaluate** Why is it important to face traffic once you're out of the car?

5. Turn off the headlights and accessories to prevent unnecessary drain on the battery.

6. Take off your safety belt.

7. Close the windows before turning off the ignition.

8. Turn the ignition off and remove the key. Keep the key in your hand.

9. Check for traffic to be certain that it is safe for you to open the door.

10. Open the door as little as necessary and close it as soon as possible.

11. Lock the doors after you are certain you have your keys. Walk to the rear of the vehicle, so that you can face traffic to detect any problems.

review it 3.3

1. What are targets, and how are they used while steering the vehicle?

2. How do you use the brake to make a smooth stop? Why is this a good habit?

Critical Thinking

3. **Analyze** Why should you turn your head before turning the steering wheel?

IN THE PASSENGER SEAT **Locating Targets** Use your time as a passenger to practice your targeting skills. Look as far ahead as possible until you see a fixed target such as a window on a house, a utility pole, a traffic sign, or a tree. Then, see if the path the vehicle will travel is clear.

DRIVING WITH A MANUAL TRANSMISSION

It will be easier to learn good manual transmission skills after you have learned how to use the steering wheel, brake pedal, and accelerator, and have developed skills to manage space.

Manual Transmission

The purpose of a **transmission** is to convert engine speed into power to turn the wheels of a vehicle. When a vehicle is stationary, it takes more power to set it in motion than when it is already moving. Putting a vehicle in motion requires a gear selection that will give the most power at the expense of speed. As speed is increased, there is less need for power. Shifting gears in the transmission changes how the speed of the engine is transferred to the vehicle's wheels. While the lower gears of the transmission provide the greatest power, the higher gears allow for the highest speeds.

The purpose of the **clutch** is to connect the rotating engine shaft to the gears in the transmission. This connection is made with clutch plates held together by friction. When the clutch pedal is pressed down, the engine gets separated from the transmission, which allows the driver to change gear selection in the transmission. After the gear selection is made, the pressure on the clutch pedal is removed and the engine and transmission apply power to the vehicle's wheels.

Advantages and Disadvantages of Manual Transmission

One of the advantages of a manual transmission is better fuel economy. Cars with manual transmissions are less expensive and require less maintenance than cars with automatic transmissions. Plus the driver has more control over how power is applied.

Driving a car with a manual transmission means that the driver has one hand off of the steering wheel on a continual basis, which could result in less control during a critical steering situation.

OBJECTIVES

- Describe what a transmission does.
- Compare the advantages and disadvantages of manual transmissions.

VOCABULARY

- transmission
- clutch
- semi-automatic transmission

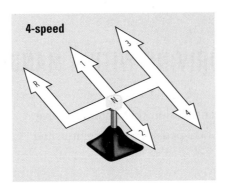

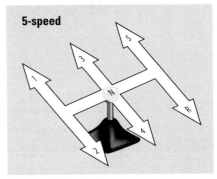

FIGURE 14
Typical patterns of gear positions for manual transmissions. Positions may vary, especially for REVERSE (R).

Inexperienced drivers may place too much of their attention on shifting the gears, thus creating distractions from traffic scenes. A driver may inadvertently shift to the wrong gear, causing damage to the engine and transmission. There is a greater workload on the driver during heavy stop-and-go traffic.

To learn how to drive a car with a manual transmission, you can find detailed lessons on the Internet. You can also ask a licensed driver to help you.

Semi-Automatic Transmission

Many auto manufacturers are producing **semi-automatic transmissions**, also known as a "clutchless manual transmission." The clutch is replaced with electronics that allow the driver to shift gears manually by merely moving the shift lever.

review it 3.4

1. Explain the purpose of a transmission.
2. Explain the function of a clutch.
3. List three advantages and three disadvantages to operating a vehicle with a manual transmission.

Critical Thinking

4. **Analyze** Why do you think some people may prefer driving a car with a manual transmission rather than one with an automatic transmission?

IN YOUR COMMUNITY **Research** Search the Internet for auto manufacturers that make vehicles with semi-automatic transmissions as an option. Read about how they work. Write a brief summary of your findings and share it with the class.

CHAPTER 3 REVIEW

Lesson Summaries

3.1 CONTROLS, DEVICES, AND INSTRUMENTS

- The accelerator, brake pedal, steering wheel, and shift selector allow you to start and stop the motion of the vehicle and to change its direction.
- Safety belts not only protect you and passengers during a crash, they also allow you to remain behind the steering wheel to maintain control of the vehicle.
- Signal lights, brake lights, headlights, and the horn are communication devices.
- Always check the four major engine operational gauges or warning lights.

3.2 GETTING READY TO DRIVE

- Having your key in hand and being alert to the area surrounding your car will increase your safety as you approach your parked vehicle.
- Be alert for small children playing near your vehicle and look for objects that you may back into.
- Proper seating position can, in part, determine how well you will be able to control the vehicle.

3.3 STARTING, STOPPING, STEERING, AND TARGETING

- Learning to use targets for steering the vehicle will help you develop correct use of vision. The vehicle will go where the eyes are looking.

3.4 DRIVING WITH A MANUAL TRANSMISSION

- There are advantages and disadvantages to having a vehicle with a manual transmission.

Chapter Vocabulary

- antilock braking system (ABS)
- braking point
- clutch
- cruise control
- key fob
- mirror's blind spot
- odometer
- semi-automatic transmission
- shift indicator
- shift lever
- tachometer
- target
- transmission
- wheel lock-up

Write the word or phrase from the list above that completes each sentence correctly.

1. When _____ occurs, the tires stop rotating.

2. A(n) _____ serves as an "aiming point" for where you want the vehicle to go.

3. The _____ is used to select a gear.

4. A(n) _____ lets you open or close your vehicle's doors from a distance.

5. In an automatic transmission, the _____ shows the positions of the gears.

6. When drivers brake and feel the brakes slowing down the vehicle, they are feeling the _____ of the vehicle.

7. The _____ indicates engine revolutions per minute.

8. The _____ keeps the wheels from locking if the driver brakes hard.

✓ ✓ ✓ **STUDY TIP**

Controls and Panel Lights Look at all the controls and the instrument panel of a car that is parked. Try to name each control and its function. Then turn the ignition key to the ON position and name each warning light and its function.

Checking Concepts

LESSON 1

9. How does too much speed affect steering?

10. What might you feel when ABS brakes are activated?

11. Why is it good practice to manually cancel the signal light after making a lane change?

LESSON 2

12. Why is it a good habit to look under, around, and inside the vehicle before you open the door?

13. Explain how keeping the key fob in your hand while approaching your parked vehicle keeps you safe.

LESSON 3

14. What techniques do you use to come to a smooth stop?

15. How does the use of targets help you to steer the vehicle?

16. Why is it important to keep your right foot on the brake pedal while starting the engine?

LESSON 4

17. What are three advantages and three disadvantages of operating a vehicle with a manual transmission?

Critical Thinking

18. **Compare and Contrast** List the similarities and differences between hand-over-hand steering and hand-to-hand steering.

19. **Evaluate** How does being too close, too far, and too low from the steering wheel affect your control of the vehicle?

You're the Driver

20. **Execute** How should you approach and enter a vehicle that is parked at a curb?

21. **Decide** Why is it important to look under and around your car before getting in?

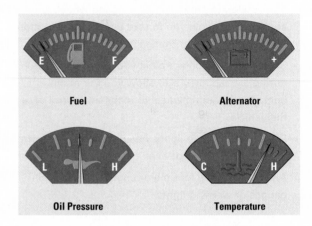

Fuel   Alternator

Oil Pressure   Temperature

22. **Identify** While you are driving, the gauges on the instrument panel could look like the pictures above. What problems might you have? What should you do?

23. **Evaluate** Is the driver in the picture below in a safe steering position? How might he achieve more controlled steering?

Preparing for the Test

Choose the letter of the answer that best completes the statement or answers the question.

1. You can never rely completely on your rearview mirrors when changing lanes because
  a. they may not be properly adjusted.
  b. they are too far apart.
  c. they are too small.
  d. they have blind-spot areas.

2. While approaching your parked car, the first step before getting in, should be
  a. have the key in your hand.
  b. bend down to search under the car.
  c. check tire pressure with a reliable tire gauge.
  d. open the door carefully.

3. To make a smooth braking action, you should
  a. release some braking pressure 1–2 seconds before the car stops.
  b. jam on the brakes to lock the wheels and then release all unnecessary braking pressure.
  c. shift into NEUTRAL 1–2 seconds before the car stops.
  d. slowly apply pressure to the brake pedal until the car is fully stopped.

4. A parking lot is a good place to practice the first in-vehicle lesson because
  a. more time can be spent on advanced techniques without traffic.
  b. you have the opportunity to repeat your actions often.
  c. you need a big space to practice driving maneuvers.
  d. you may not be able to legally drive on the street.

Use the art below to answer Question 5.

5. To avoid injury from an airbag in your vehicle's steering wheel during a collision, keep your hands between the
  a. 9 and 3 or 8 and 4 positions.
  b. 5 and 7 or 8 and 4 positions.
  c. 10 and 2 or 11 and 1 positions.
  d. 9 and 3 or 10 and 2 positions.

Use the art below to answer Question 6.

6. The most important safety feature shown here will prevent all of the following except that it
  a. will slow down your body gradually if you're in a crash.
  b. prevents you from being thrown into the crash.
  c. keeps you from being thrown out of the car in a crash.
  d. will not keep unbelted passengers from crashing into you.

drive write 🚗

Every driver has a responsibility to be sure their car is in peak condition, which saves fuel and money. Write one or two paragraphs explaining how the instrument panel in a vehicle helps drivers stay safe on the road.

chapter 4

PERFORMING BASIC VEHICLE MANEUVERS

4.1 Mirror Usage and Backing Procedures

4.2 Basic Driving Maneuvers

4.3 Parking Maneuvers

KEY IDEA

What methods can you use to accurately and safely maneuver your vehicle when changing lanes, turning, stopping, backing, and parking?

 **YOU'RE THE DRIVER**

As a driver, you'll make right and left turns, park your vehicle, and drive backwards. Do you know the procedures to keep you risk-free while performing these maneuvers? Do you know how to control steering and judge space accurately in order to park safely?

lesson 4.1
MIRROR USAGE AND BACKING PROCEDURES

OBJECTIVES

- Explain when the rearview and outside mirrors should be checked.
- Explain what a convex mirror is and how it can be used to eliminate blind-spot areas.
- Explain why backing is a high-risk maneuver, and how to minimize the risk.
- List the steps for safely backing a vehicle.

VOCABULARY

- convex mirror

FIGURE 1
A convex mirror attached to the outside mirror on the driver's side allows a wider view.

Using mirrors effectively is essential for getting timely and accurate information about conditions behind your vehicle. Driving large vehicles makes good mirror-usage skills even more important. Backing situations present high crash risks, but correctly using mirrors and adhering to backing guidelines will minimize these risks.

Mirror Usage

There are three mirrors that come as standard equipment on most vehicles: the inside rearview mirror and two outside mirrors. In addition, convex mirrors can be added to help compensate for blind spots.

Inside Rearview Mirror   Check the inside rearview mirror when you see something in the path you intend to travel, and before and after making a turn at an intersection, to get an update on traffic behind you. Check before and after passing another vehicle to see whether the car behind you is in position to pass you and the other vehicle. Check the mirror before and after making a lane change. Make two or three quick mirror checks rather than one prolonged check, and be on the lookout for aggressive drivers who may be weaving in and out of lanes.

Outside Mirrors   Before moving the vehicle to either side, check the outside mirror on the side to which you will be moving. To check for a vehicle in the mirror's blind spot, you can look over your shoulder in the direction you wish to move, or move your head forward while checking the outside mirror.

Convex Mirrors   The best way to eliminate blind spots is by attaching a convex mirror to each outside mirror. Outside mirrors on the driver's side have a flat surface, which shows a limited range of view. The surface of a **convex mirror** is curved outward like the exterior of a ball, which allows a wider view of the area to the side and rear of the vehicle. When you see something that is in both the flat and the convex mirror, you should judge its position to your vehicle by use of the flat mirror.

When you can see something in the convex mirror, but not in the flat mirror, then it is in the blind-spot area. It will be unsafe to move into its path.

Backing

Backing is a high-risk maneuver because drivers cannot see behind their vehicles; in most vehicles, they cannot see the pavement within 45 feet of the rear. Therefore, obstructions lying on the pavement can go undetected. Always walk to the rear of the vehicle before getting into it to check for a safe path for the tires to travel.

Procedures for Backing

1. Place your foot firmly on the brake, and shift into reverse.
2. Use a target to aim the car toward. Look over your right shoulder to see your targeting path.
3. Check all three mirrors to supplement looking over your shoulder.
4. Travel no faster than a crawl by slightly releasing brake-pedal pressure.

Backing Straight   When backing straight, put your left hand on the steering wheel at the 12:00 position. Move the top of the steering wheel in the direction you want the back of the vehicle to go.

Backing Left or Right   When backing left or right, start with both hands on the wheel. This will allow easier head movement to check all four corners of the vehicle during the turn. Pull the wheel from the top down in the direction you want the back of the vehicle to go. Be sure to check not only the rear as you back but also the swing of the front of the vehicle before turning takes place.

DID YOU KNOW?

Passenger-side mirrors are slightly convex, resulting in a smaller image than that of the driver's side. The warning "Objects In Mirrors Are Closer Than They Appear" is placed on it to prevent anyone from being fooled by the smaller image. However, the curvature is not great enough to eliminate blind-spot areas.

review it 4.1

1. What effect does the curvature of a mirror have on image size and your perception of its distance from your vehicle?
2. What does it mean when you can see something in the convex mirror attached to an outside mirror but not in the flat mirror?
3. What outside checks should you make before backing any vehicle?

Critical Thinking

4. **Relate Cause and Effect**   Explain how using mirrors correctly helps you to be a low-risk driver.
5. **Apply Concepts**   Name two situations where you need to use the outside mirrors.

 **IN THE PASSENGER SEAT**   **Watch Out!**   Your friend is ready to back out of his driveway and is not looking to the rear. What would you say to him?

lesson 4.2
BASIC DRIVING MANEUVERS

OBJECTIVES

- Explain situations and timing for communication using signal lights.
- Explain how to make left and right turns.
- Explain three methods for making a turnabout, and state which is the safest.
- Explain the factors to consider in deciding which type of turnabout to use.

VOCABULARY

- turnabout

Performing basic driving maneuvers properly depends upon using speed control, steering control, and good visual habits with consistency. Once you learn how to perform one maneuver, you can then use the behaviors frequently to develop them into habit.

Signaling

Being a safe and responsible driver requires communicating your intentions to others on the road. The most common method of communication is through the use of turn-signal lights. Develop the habit of signaling every time you plan to turn, change lanes, pull to the side, or re-enter the traffic flow. Signal at least five seconds in advance of beginning any maneuver to give other drivers adequate time to react to your actions.

Even though all vehicles have turn-signal devices, there will be times when you have to use hand signals for further protection, as shown in **FIGURE 2**. Use your right hand to maintain steering control.

Entering Traffic Flows

You should avoid backing into a traffic flow. Pulling out forward will reduce risk and provide the best visibility for observing approaching traffic. Follow these steps for entering a traffic flow.

1. Check to your left, front and right zones before entering a traffic flow. Find a safe space to enter within the traffic flow.

FIGURE 2

Right turn

Left turn

Slow or stop

2. Select the proper and legal lane to enter and accelerate smoothly until operating at travel speed.

3. After entering a traffic flow, cancel the turn signal manually if necessary.

4. Re-evaluate the rear zone for fast approaching vehicles.

Making Right and Left Turns

Make left and right turns only after checking for traffic and pedestrians. Be sure to search the mirrors when making any braking action.

The numbers in **FIGURE 3** match the following steps for turns:

1. Position your vehicle in the correct lane for the turn. For a right turn, use lane position 3 if there are no parked vehicles. For a left turn, use lane position 2, the lane nearest the center line. (On a one-way street, this could be in the far left lane.) Signal five seconds before the turn.

2. Brake early to reduce speed.

3. Search the left, front, and right zones for vehicles, pedestrians, and bicyclists.

4. Slow to about 10 mph just before the crosswalk.

5. For a right turn, check to the left again before turning. Then look in the direction of the turn. Begin turning the wheel when your vehicle's front bumper is even with the curb line.

6. For a left turn, check traffic to the left, front, and right. Be certain there is no oncoming traffic, and that the path you intend to enter is clear. Turn your head and the steering wheel to the left once the car enters the intersection to look into the lane you will enter.

7. Turn into the nearest lane of traffic going in your direction. Halfway through the turn, accelerate as you return the wheel to the straight-ahead position.

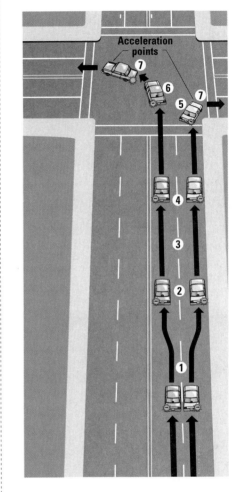

----- FIGURE 3 --------

Steps for making left turns (yellow car) and right turns (white car)

FIGURE 4

Move into lane position 2 and check your blind spot.

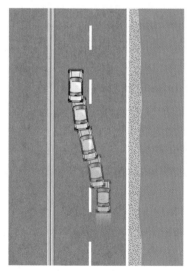

When clear, move into lane position 3 and check the rear zone.

Lane Changes

Before deciding to make a lane change, consider whether it is necessary, beneficial, and legal. Look for an opening in rear traffic that might occur.

Procedures for Changing Lanes

1. Put your signal light on and use lane position 2 or 3 to bring you closer to the lane you will enter.
2. Check your mirror and blind spot. Avoid unintentionally moving the steering wheel.
3. Gradually ease into your new lane.
4. Release the signal lever. Check behind you. Get the best speed and lane positioning to blend in with the traffic flow.

Turning the Vehicle

The safest way to turn your vehicle around is to drive around the block. If this is impractical, there are several ways to accomplish a **turnabout**. A turnabout is when you turn your vehicle around to go in the opposite direction. Take these precautions when you plan to make a turnabout:

- Be sure local laws permit the turnabout.
- Select a location with at least 10 seconds of visibility in each direction.
- Do not make a turnabout near hills or curves or within 200 feet of intersections.
- Never attempt a turnabout in heavy or high-speed traffic.
- Continually check all around you for traffic, bicyclists, and pedestrians.

Midblock U-turn Make sure local and state laws permit this type of turnabout. Solid pavement markings in the center of the road indicate that a U-turn is prohibited. You need at least two wide lanes to make a U-turn.

1. Pull to the far right edge of the road and stop.

2. Check the front and back, and your left-rear blind spot. If the front and rear are clear, signal and turn sharply left while moving slowly.

3. When the vehicle is headed towards your target area, recheck your rear and accelerate to the speed of traffic.

Back Into a Driveway on the Right Side Know your state law for the use of driveways. Avoid backing beyond the sidewalk.

1. Check behind you and check the driveway. Tap your brake lights to signal to drivers behind you.

2. Shift into reverse and if it is clear, begin turning. Back only until the vehicle is straight.

3. Signal left and make the left turn when the path is clear.

FIGURE 5

A midblock U-turn is risky because you must cross oncoming traffic.

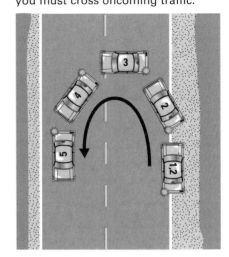

FIGURE 6

Using a driveway on the right side has the advantage of letting you reenter traffic going forward.

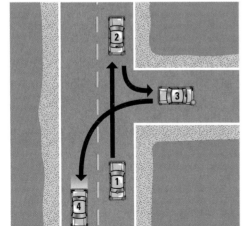

A riskier option is to pull into a driveway on the left side.

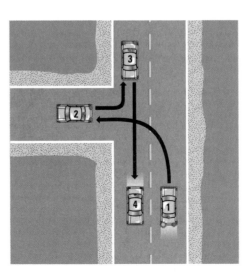

FIGURE 7
The three-point turnabout should only be done in a lightly traveled area.

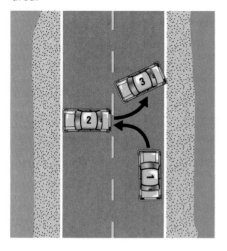

Pull Into a Driveway on the Left Side   If there is no acceptable driveway on the right and you must use a driveway on the left, it increases your risk because you will need to back out of the driveway into traffic.

1. Use the same procedures as making a left turn.

2. When traffic is clear, back out and stay as close to the curb as possible.

Three-Point Turnabout   This is a dangerous maneuver and should only be performed where there will be no traffic that you cause to stop while you complete the turnabout.

1. Pull as far to the right side of the road as you can. Check in front of and behind you. Make a blind-spot check and signal for a left turn.

2. If your path is clear, turn sharply left and stop before reaching the curb.

3. Recheck for traffic, shift to reverse, and turn sharply while backing slowly. Back only as far as necessary to complete the maneuver.

4. Check traffic again and signal left. Move slowly forward while steering toward your new target area.

review it 4.2

1. Explain how and when braking and acceleration actions should take place when making a moving right turn.

2. Explain how lane positioning is used before and after making a lane change.

3. What is the safest way to perform a turnabout?

Critical Thinking

4. **Compare and Contrast**   How is making a midblock U-turn different from a three-point turnabout?

5. **Analyze**   Which stages of the turnabout would cause you to be at fault if your car were hit by an approaching vehicle?

   **Research**   Investigate your state's laws on turnabouts. Which of the turnabouts described in this lesson are legal in your state, and which are illegal? Which has the highest risk and which has the lowest risk?

PARKING MANEUVERS

Parking your car is a skill that you need to practice. To park easily, you need to control the vehicle with steering, braking and an understanding of reference points. There are three basic ways to park: angle parking, perpendicular parking and parallel parking.

Angle parking spaces can be at the curb of a street or in a parking lot. **Perpendicular parking** is only used in parking lots. Finally, **parallel parking** is a method of backing between two vehicles that are parked alongside a curb.

A **reference point** is some part of the outside or inside of the vehicle, as viewed from the driver's seat, that relates to a part of the roadway.

Knowing reference points enables you to put your vehicle exactly where you want it. Once you know and can use reference points, you can apply them to any vehicle that you drive.

The reference points on a vehicle that are typical for most drivers are called **standard reference points**. A **personal reference point** is an adaptation of a standard reference point for your own vehicle. The **forward reference point** is when steering should begin during a maneuver.

OBJECTIVES

- List the advantages and disadvantages of angle, perpendicular, and parallel parking.
- Describe how to perform each parking maneuver.
- Explain the differences among the three parking maneuvers.

VOCABULARY

- angle parking
- perpendicular parking
- parallel parking
- reference point
- standard reference point
- personal reference point
- forward reference point

Angle and Perpendicular Parking

Some cities use angle parking spaces on the street to increase the number of curbside parking spaces. It is the easiest parking procedure to perform, but the most dangerous to exit because you will be backing into traffic.

To park in an angle space, follow these steps:

1. Check behind you. Check the parking space to see if it is legal and clear of obstacles and pedestrians. Tap your brake lights to warn drivers behind you.

2. You should have at least six feet of side space away from the parked vehicles. Your forward reference point is the center of the space at the curb.

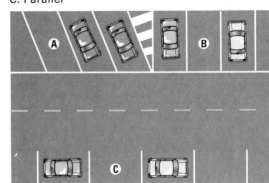

FIGURE 8
A. Angle   B. Perpendicular
C. Parallel

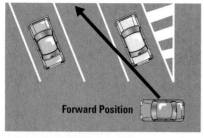

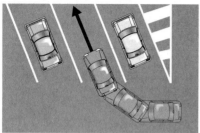

FIGURE 9 Angle parking in a parking lot is intended for head-in parking only. Most angle parking spaces will be on your right side.

3. Quickly turn the steering wheel while the vehicle is moving slowly.

4. Line up with a target at curbside, such as a parking meter. Straighten the car and tires.

5. Place the tip of the bumper even with the curb.

To perpendicular park, you can follow the same steps as for angle parking except you will need at least eight feet of side space from the parked vehicles.

Leaving an Angle or Perpendicular Space Backing out of a parking space is a high-risk maneuver because you will be backing into a potential traffic flow with your view blocked. Back slowly! Look behind you and to the sides for approaching vehicles and pedestrians.

1. Creep straight back by controlling speed with your brake. When your front bumper is even with the rear bumper of the vehicle that is on the opposite side of where the back of your vehicle will go, begin to turn the steering wheel.

2. Stay close to the parked cars when backing to reduce risk from approaching traffic. Straighten the tires, shift to a forward gear. Proceed forward as you check the front. Recheck behind you for fast-approaching vehicles.

Perpendicular Back-In Parking You can reduce the risk of perpendicular parking by backing into the space, eliminating the need to back out of it.

1. Signal a right turn. Check traffic to the rear, and tap your brake lights.

2. Position your vehicle so that its side is 3 feet from the parked cars, and your body appears to be aligned with the center of the parking space.

3. Select a target 45 degrees to your left, using the outer edge of the driver's side mirror.

FIGURE 10
Perpendicular back-in parking

2

3

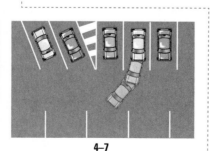

4–7

4. Align your vehicle with the target using the least forward motion possible, while quickly turning the steering wheel.

5. Line up your car with the parking space. Straighten your tires and shift to REVERSE.

6. Back until the corner of the car parked next to your space is in your rear window's blind spot, then quickly turn the steering wheel all the way to the right while backing slowly.

7. When your car is properly aligned in the space, straighten your tires. Back until the back line of the space appears to be in the middle of the rear side window.

Parallel Parking

Use parallel parking to park your vehicle parallel to the curb. Select a space that is five to six feet longer than your vehicle. When parking on the right, the front of your vehicle will swing far to the left.

1. Signal a right turn and flash your brake lights. Evaluate the parking space to be sure it is legal and clear of objects. Stop about three feet away from the parked cars.

2. Then pull forward so that your rear bumper is even with the rear bumper of the vehicle parked in front of the space you want to enter.

3. Back slowly, controlling speed with your brake. When the back of the passenger's seat is even with the rear bumper of the front vehicle, straighten the wheels. Look over your shoulder, through the rear window.

4. When your front bumper is even with the front vehicle's back bumper, turn the wheel sharply left towards the street. Continue to back slowly to clear the front car's rear bumper. Check to the back and front continually.

5. Straighten your tires and center the car when your vehicle is parallel to the curb.

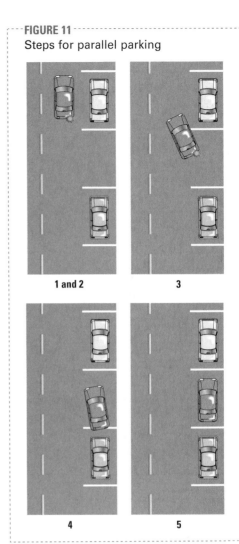

FIGURE 11

Steps for parallel parking

1 and 2   3

4   5

Leaving a Parallel Parking Space   You are responsible for avoiding a collision when leaving a parallel parking space. You must search for a safe gap in the flow of traffic, and yield to all oncoming vehicles. To begin exiting the space:

1. Slowly back straight until your rear bumper almost touches the vehicle behind you. Turn the wheels sharply left as you stop. Signal a left turn. Check your left mirror and the blind-spot area.

2. Move the vehicle forward slowly. Check the right-front corner of your vehicle for clearance.

3. When you are halfway out of the parking space with your passenger door aligned with the street-side corner of the parked car, turn your wheels slowly to the right.

4. Scan the front again, and accelerate as you center your vehicle in the traffic lane.

FIGURE 12 PARKING ON HILLS

When parking uphill against a curb, turn the front wheels to the left.

When parking uphill or downhill where there is no curb, turn your wheels to the right.

When parking downhill against a curb, turn the front wheels to the right.

review it 4.3

1. List the three basic types of parking methods.
2. Explain why street-side angle parking is the most dangerous parking method.
3. Why is reverse-angle parking safer than angle parking?
4. How should the tires be turned when parked uphill with a curb?

Critical Thinking

5. **Analyze** Explain why backing out of a parking space puts other drivers in a high-risk situation.

IN YOUR COMMUNITY   **Observe Traffic** Locate a busy parking lot with perpendicular parking spaces. Spend thirty minutes observing drivers parking. Record the number of drivers who

a. pulled forward into a front space.

b. backed into the space.

c. pulled in forward requiring the need to back out.

d. had near-misses, and what actions the drivers were taking when they had them.

e. did not search properly while backing.

Share your findings with the class.

CHAPTER 4 REVIEW

Lesson Summaries

4.1 MIRROR USAGE AND BACKING PROCEDURES

- You can eliminate a mirror's blind-spot areas by placing a convex mirror on the outside corners of both the driver- and passenger-side mirrors.
- When your foot covers the brake pedal, your eyes should automatically go to the rearview mirror.

4.2 BASIC DRIVING MANEUVERS

- The most common method of communicating is by the use of signal lights. Develop the habit of signaling every time you plan to turn, change lanes, pull to the side, or reenter the traffic flow. Signal at least five seconds before you begin any maneuver.
- Use lane position 2 to get 3-6 inches from the center line of the road for left turns, and lane position 3 to get 3 feet from the curb or road shoulder for right turns.
- A turnabout is a maneuver for turning your vehicle around to go in the opposite direction.

4.3 PARKING MANEUVERS

- Angle parking and forward perpendicular parking maneuvers are performed almost exactly the same way. The only difference is that you will need a wider side position for parking forward into a perpendicular space than when angle parking.
- Backing out of parking spaces is a high-risk maneuver.

Chapter Vocabulary

- angle parking
- convex mirror
- forward reference point
- parallel parking
- perpendicular parking
- personal reference point
- reference point
- standard reference point
- turnabout

Write the word or phrase from the list above that completes the sentence correctly.

1. When you turn your vehicle around to go in the opposite direction, it's called a(n) _____.
2. While executing a parking maneuver, you should begin steering at the _____.
3. In _____, you have to back into a parking space that is between two vehicles.
4. A(n) _____ allows a wider view of the side and rear of the vehicle than a flat-surface mirror.
5. A(n) _____ is a part of the vehicle from the driver's point of view relative to a part of the roadway.
6. An adaptation of a standard reference point for your own vehicle is a(n) _____.

 **STUDY TIP**

With classmates, move two chairs to represent a perpendicular parking space. Have one student pretend that she is in a car and have her demonstrate the correct maneuvers involved in backing into the parking space. Other classmates should use the book to evaluate her maneuvers. Take turns and repeat for all parking positions.

Checking Concepts

LESSON 1

7. Explain why you are able to see more in a convex mirror than in a flat mirror.

8. Why is it a good habit to check the rearview mirror as your foot begins to apply the brake?

9. Why is it a good habit to check to the rear of the vehicle before getting into it when backing is necessary?

LESSON 2

10. Explain how to signal stop or slow, right turn, and left turn using hand signals. Why is it important to know how to use these hand signals?

11. Why is it important to reevaluate your rear zone when making a turn or a lane change?

12. Explain which is the most dangerous type of turnabout and how you can minimize the risk.

LESSON 3

13. Which of the three parking maneuvers should you practice first, and which should you practice last?

14. Why is covering the brake with your foot important when you're backing out of any parking space?

Critical Thinking

15. Analyze What is the difference in the forward position for making a right turn and for making a left turn?

16. Analyze Why should you know how to use both hand signals and turn signals?

You're the Driver

17. Identify Explain to your friend why it's important to make a visual check behind the car and check all three mirrors before backing a car.

18. Predict If you're backing straight, why should you be aware that you may need to move the top of the steering wheel right or left?

19. Decide You're the driver in the situation below and you need to make a turnabout. Which type of turnabout would you choose and why?

20. Decide In which direction should the front wheels be turned for the vehicles parked facing uphill and for the vehicles parked facing downhill? Why is correct wheel placement important when parking on hills?

Preparing for the Test

Choose the letter of the answer that best completes the statement or answers the question.

1. The rearview mirror should be checked
   a. at least once every 10 seconds.
   b. more often than searching the target area.
   c. whenever you apply the brakes.
   d. whenever you see a speed-limit sign.

2. Which statement is true?
   a. Angle parking at the curb is safer than parallel parking.
   b. Backing out of a perpendicular parking space is safer than backing into the space.
   c. Parallel parking is the most dangerous of all parking types.
   d. An angle parking space is the easiest type to get into.

3. When backing, you should
   a. only look over your right shoulder.
   b. use mirrors to supplement looking out the rear window.
   c. keep both hands on the steering wheel while backing straight.
   d. keep your left hand at the bottom of the steering wheel.

Use the photo below to answer Question 4.

4. The driver is using a hand signal to show that she is
   a. making a right turn.
   b. making a left turn.
   c. going to stop.
   d. slowing down.

5. Which statement is false?
   a. Backing is as safe as driving forward.
   b. Reduce risk by backing into perpendicular parking spaces.
   c. Angle parking usually requires backing into traffic flows.
   d. Convex mirrors give a wider view than flat mirrors.

6. During a parking maneuver, you begin steering at
   a. the standard reference point.
   b. the personal reference point.
   c. any reference point.
   d. the forward reference point.

Use the photo below to answer Question 7.

7. The driver of this car has parked
   a. uphill against a curb.
   b. downhill against a curb.
   c. in an angle parking space.
   d. in a parallel parking space.

drive write

You are on a four-lane road when you realize you are going in the wrong direction. What are your choices for turning around? Which choice will have the least amount of risk? Explain in one or two paragraphs why backing out of a driveway is not a good choice.

chapter 5

MANAGING RISK WITH THE IPDE PROCESS

5.1 The IPDE Process

5.2 Identify and Predict

5.3 Decide and Execute

5.4 Using the IPDE Process

KEY IDEA

How does learning and using the IPDE Process help you to be a low-risk driver?

YOU'RE THE DRIVER As a driver, you'll be faced with many situations that present some kind of risk. Are you aware of the driver-contributed risks involved in driving? How can you manage risks posed by other drivers? Learning an organized system for driving helps you to understand how to manage risk in order to be a safe driver.

lesson 5.1
THE IPDE PROCESS

OBJECTIVES

- Describe three factors that contribute to the degree of risk you face when driving.
- Name the four steps in the IPDE Process and explain how IPDE helps you to be a low-risk driver.
- Explain the three steps in the Zone Control System and how they contribute to low-risk driving.

VOCABULARY

- risk factor

Drivers who use an organized system will be better equipped to manage risk and thus reduce the possibility of damage or harm. Good searching habits and the ability to manage space on the roadway are basic tools for low-risk driving. The IPDE Process along with the Zone Control System can help you enjoy low-risk and low-stress driving.

Understanding Risk Factors

All activities throughout a person's life involve some degree of risk. When driving a vehicle, the possibility of a crash is always present. The driver, vehicle, roadway, and environment contribute to the **risk factors**, or anything that can increase the possibility of a collision, involved in driving. As you drive, be aware that all of the risk factors—either separately or together—play a major role in the level of risk you face.

Driver-Contributed Factors   As a driver, you create risk when you don't give your undivided attention to the driving task. Adjusting the radio, combing your hair, using a cellular phone, and eating or drinking while driving affect your ability to be a low-risk driver.

Driver-contributed risk factors also apply to other drivers on the roadway. Drivers who take unnecessary chances can increase your level of risk and chance of conflict.

Vehicle-Contributed Factors   As a driver, it is your responsibility to properly maintain your vehicle. Vehicles with bald tires, a dirty windshield, broken headlights, or worn wiper blades contribute to the possibility of a crash.

Roadway- and Environment-Contributed Factors   Conditions such as bright sun, dark shadows, and glare contribute to driving risk. Road construction, a sharp curve in the road, or ice and snow also create risk for drivers. Because some degree of risk is always present, try to make sure nothing about your own condition or the condition of your vehicle further increases your level of risk.

The IPDE Process

Safe driving depends on your ability to see and analyze traffic situations correctly. However, that alone is no guarantee that you will identify all critical clues and make correct driving responses in every situation. Because driving is primarily a thinking task, drivers who develop a system that deals with all traffic possibilities have fewer close calls and fewer crashes than drivers who don't use an organized system.

The IPDE Process is an organized system of seeing, thinking, and responding. IPDE actually represents the four steps for safe driving: identify, predict, decide, and execute.

You begin the IPDE Process by "reading" traffic situations to gather information in order to make your decision and execute them. To process information properly, you must identify hazards and predict points of conflict. You then decide how to avoid the conflict by executing the correct action.

The Zone Control System is an organized method for managing six zones of space surrounding your vehicle. Zone Control allows you to see and respond to changes in the traffic environment at a time when best control can be achieved.

The Zone Control System includes the following steps: 1. See a zone change. 2. Check other zones. 3. Create time and space by getting the best speed control, lane position, and communication.

Using the IPDE Process in conjunction with the Zone Control System will help you develop behaviors that will make you a safe and responsible driver.

FIGURE 1 THE IPDE PROCESS

1 Identify

Use visual search pattern to identify
- open and closed zones
- specific clues
- other users
- roadway features and conditions
- traffic controls

2 Predict

Use knowledge, judgment, and experience to predict
- actions of other users
- change of direction
- points of conflict
- consequences of your actions

3 Decide

Decide to use one or more actions to
- change or maintain speed
- change direction
- communicate

4 Execute

Execute your decisions to
- control speed
- steer
- communicate
- combine actions

---

review it 5.1

1. Describe three risks posed by drivers, vehicles, and the roadway and environment. What actions could you take to reduce the risks posed by these factors?

Critical Thinking

2. **Relate Cause and Effect** Explain how the IPDE Process helps you reduce the risks involved in driving.

3. **Analyze** What do you think would happen if you tried to use the steps in the IPDE Process in a different order?

IN THE PASSENGER SEAT **Record Risk Factors** For one week, record the number of driver-, vehicle-, roadway-, and environment-contributed risk factors you notice while in the passenger seat. Make a graph to compare the factors. Which one did you notice most often? Explain to the class why you think it occurred most often.

lesson 5.2
IDENTIFY AND PREDICT

 OBJECTIVES

- Explain what it means to identify as it relates to the IPDE Process.
- Identify the positions of each of the six zones of the Zone Control System.
- Identify the eight steps of an orderly visual search pattern.
- Explain how knowledge and experience help you make accurate predictions.

 VOCABULARY

- identify
- zone
- open zone
- line of sight
- target area
- closed zone
- target-area range
- 12–15-second range
- 4–6-second range
- orderly visual search pattern
- field of vision
- depth perception
- scanning
- ground viewing
- predict

The identify and predict steps of the IPDE Process are critical in every driving environment. These two steps begin your thinking process for every situation you encounter. With practice and experience, these steps will seem like a natural part of driving. As you search your path to identify possible problems, you will be making judgments and predictions about what conflicts may occur.

Identify

The first step of the IPDE Process is **identify**. This step involves much more than just seeing. You must know when to look, where to look, how to look, and what to look for.

Any aspect of the Highway Transportation System (HTS) can become a hazardous situation. This includes the roadway, your own vehicle, other vehicles or pedestrians, and traffic controls. Clues you identify may cause you to change direction or speed, signal others, or perform any combination of maneuvers. The sooner you identify a possible hazard, the more time you will have to react safely.

Zones   The Zone Control System helps you make quick and accurate use of the IPDE Process by setting a standard of what to identify and what to do when you find it. A **zone** is one of six areas of space around a vehicle that is the width of a lane and extends as far as the driver can see, as shown in **FIGURE 2**.

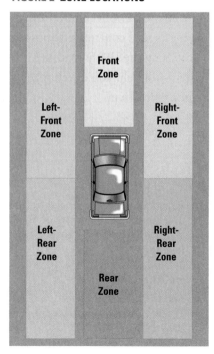

FIGURE 2 **ZONE LOCATIONS**

Front Zone

Left-Front Zone

Right-Front Zone

Left-Rear Zone

Right-Rear Zone

Rear Zone

An **open zone** is space where you can drive without a restriction to your line of sight or to your intended path of travel. Your **line of sight** is the distance you can see ahead in the direction you are looking. Your intended path of travel is the space your vehicle will occupy. Your path of travel is directed toward the target area. The **target area** is the section of the roadway where the target is located in the center of your intended path, and the area to its right and left.

A **closed zone** is a space not open to you because of a restriction in your line of sight or intended path of travel, such as a red traffic light. The sooner you identify a closed zone, the more time you have to respond. With more time, the better chance you have to achieve control of the situation by lowering the degree of risk.

Searching Ranges   In order to keep alert to the conditions of your zones, there are three searching ranges that need to be evaluated as shown in **FIGURE 3**. A searching range is a certain distance ahead of the vehicle where the intended path of travel is systematically evaluated. The first searching range is the **target-area range**, which is the space from your vehicle to the target area. You search this range to detect early any conditions that might affect your intended path of travel.

Next you will search the **12–15-second range**, which is the space you will travel in during the next 12–15 seconds. This range is where you need to identify changes in your line of sight or path of travel to make decisions about controlling your intended path. Try to identify the possibility of closed zones by searching to the left and right.

The **4–6-second range** is the space you will travel in during the next 4–6 seconds. In this range you need to get the final update of how you are controlling your intended path of travel.

Orderly Visual Search Pattern   You can use any of several patterns to help develop your own identifying process. An **orderly visual search pattern** is a process of searching critical areas in a regular sequence. To use an orderly visual search pattern, look for clues in and around your intended path of travel in a systematic manner.

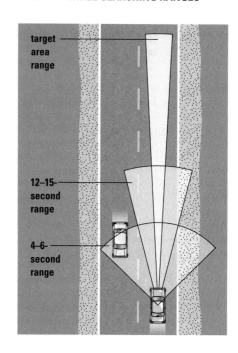

FIGURE 3 THREE SEARCHING RANGES

target area range

12–15-second range

4–6-second range

Below is an example of an orderly visual search pattern for straight-ahead driving.

1. Look ahead to your target-area range.
2. Evaluate your left-front, front, and right-front zones in the 12–15-second range. Search driveways and intersections for possible changes in your line of sight and path of travel.
3. Glance in the rearview mirror to check your rear zones.
4. Evaluate your 4–6-second range before entering that space.
5. Look ahead again to evaluate another 12–15-second range.
6. Check your 4–6-second range.
7. Glance in the rearview mirror.
8. Check your speedometer and gauges.

You will repeat this pattern continually as you move forward. Each look or glance should last only an instant as you evaluate your zones and the areas to the left and right. Be careful not to stare as you search. Practice using your orderly visual search pattern as a passenger—in addition to when you are driving—so it will become a safe driving habit. You will then be able to adjust your search pattern for any maneuver or driving environment.

Aspects of Vision   Different driving environments and traffic situations present a variety of visual search problems. As you gain driving experience, you will learn what kinds of clues and situations are most important to identify in order to keep an open zone in your path of travel. The primary aspects of vision necessary for driving include central vision, peripheral vision, and depth perception.

The area you can see around you while looking straight ahead is called your **field of vision**. Many of us can see an area of about 90 degrees to each side, for a total picture of 180 degrees. The area you can see clearly and sharply is seen with your central vision. This is a narrow cone of only up to 10 degrees. The area you can see to the left and right of central vision is your side vision, or peripheral vision. As the distance from central vision increases toward the outer edge of peripheral vision, the less clearly you can identify clues and events.

Depth perception, or the ability to judge the relative distance of objects correctly, is especially important for driving.

safe driving tip

Avoid Staring
Beginning drivers sometimes fixate for several seconds on the same clue or event. They do not look far enough into target-area ranges, and often drive with swerves and jerky movements. Do not let yourself become a "stare" driver.

You must be able to judge distances correctly in order to pass and follow vehicles, and judge stopping distances.

You should always look ahead 12–15 seconds into your target area as you drive. Looking far ahead with your line of sight will help you identify clues and analyze situations before your zone becomes closed. There are many restrictions to your line of sight such as curves, hills, large vehicles, weather conditions, buildings, trees, or even a dirty windshield.

Scanning   Develop the art of **scanning**, glancing continually and quickly with very brief fixations through your orderly visual search pattern. You are looking and seeing as you scan, but not staring at any one event or clue. Staring blocks out side vision, causes lack of attention, and tends to create high-risk driving habits. Keeping your eyes moving helps you stay more alert with your attention at a higher level. You are then more likely to keep up with all the changes in your field of vision.

Selective Seeing

Knowing where and how to look does little good if you do not know what to look for in your target area. Develop the technique of selective seeing in your identifying process. Selective seeing means that you identify and select only those clues and events that restrict your line of sight or can change your intended path of travel.

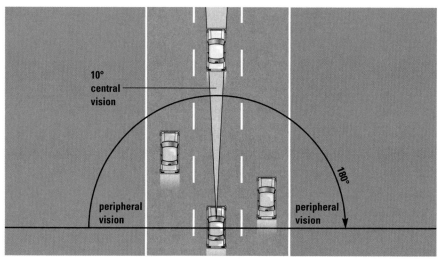

FIGURE 4   You see most clearly in the area of central vision, but peripheral vision is equally important.

FIGURE 5 The red car is parked. **Identify** What clues do you have that the car might pull out and close your zone?

Look for Open Zones Use your visual search pattern to look for specific driving-related clues that might cause an open zone to close. You might identify exhaust coming from a tailpipe or a driver sitting in a car, indicating that a car might be about to enter your path of travel and cause your front zone to close.

The kinds of clues you search for will change as you drive in different environments. When driving in the city, search for intersections, parked cars, pedestrians, and traffic. On open highways, search areas much farther ahead. Look for crossroads, slow-moving vehicles, and animals. Any of these can suddenly cause an open zone to close, resulting in the need to change your intended path of travel or reduce your speed. When you drive on expressways, speeds are higher and scanning all zones becomes even more critical. Regardless of the driving environment, you should always look for other roadway users, roadway features, changing conditions, and traffic controls that may affect your intended path of travel.

Look for Other Users Look for other users who might affect your intended path of travel. Watch for movement of other roadway users, especially in areas that have shadows or shade. Watch for pedestrians and bicyclists. A large truck is easy to identify. However, it creates a restriction in your line of sight and may prevent you from seeing another user. Develop the habit of ground viewing as part of your visual search pattern. **Ground viewing** is making quick glances to the roadway in front of your vehicle. When other vehicles are approaching, use ground viewing to see where they are headed by checking the direction of their front wheels.

Always be on the lookout for problem drivers. Drivers who speed and drivers who pass without enough room or in a no-passing zone are problem drivers. Others frequently change lanes, trying to get ahead of the normal traffic flow, and can cause a sudden change in your open-zone condition.

Look for Roadway Features and Conditions The roadway itself is another important area to watch. Identify intersections, hills, and curves early. Be aware ahead of time that the width of your lane might be reduced for road construction or other obstacles. An intersection is a high-risk area where the management of your path of travel needs constant attention. Stopped traffic or entering traffic can cause line-of-sight restrictions or even a closed zone. A hill is a line-of-sight restriction that could hide a closed zone as you go over the hill.

▶ **Change from multilane to single lane** Multilane roadways often narrow into single-lane roadways. Identify signs warning you of this change early enough to avoid a closed zone in your intended path. When signs indicate roadway repairs ahead, you can expect your front zone to close. Check your left-front, right-front, and rear zones before moving into the through lane. Drivers who wait until the last instant and then try to squeeze into the through lane are demonstrating high-risk behavior with no concern for other drivers.

▶ **Change in width of lane** Standing water, patches of snow, potholes, or objects in the roadway can cause an open zone to close. Identify the conditions early and then check your rear zone to find out if there will be a problem if a stop is needed.

FIGURE 6
Drivers need to look for many different possible conflicts in close traffic. **Identify** What hazards could challenge a driver in this situation?

FIGURE 7   Is it safe to drive around the object?

▶ **Roadway surface**   Identify the roadway surface and condition each time you begin to drive. There will be times when the weather will change while you are driving. Roadway surfaces may be dry when you start out and then become wet and slippery with rain, snow, or ice as you are driving. Be prepared to adjust your driving for changing weather conditions that might affect the roadway surface. A gravel surface can cause sliding or skidding just like a wet or slippery surface.

▶ **Roadside hazards**   Your identification process should keep you scanning for bicyclists, pedestrians, parked vehicles, and animals. Watch for shopping center entrances and exits, roadside stands, and restaurants. Other drivers can appear from almost any location and cause your open zone to close. Continual scanning of your target areas will help you identify these other drivers in time to avoid sudden actions or conflict.

Look for Traffic Controls   Learn to look in different places for traffic controls. At major intersections, controls can be overhead, in the center of the road or on a corner. Identify traffic controls as early as possible so you are ready to respond appropriately.

Predict

Once you have identified a hazard, predict how this hazard might affect your intended path of travel. When you **predict**, you take the information you have identified and imagine what might happen. You predict where possible points of conflict may occur. Your predictions will be based upon those conditions that could reduce your line of sight or change your intended path of travel.

If you had to face just one hazard at a time, you could more easily predict the possible outcome. However, most of the time you will be faced with more than one possible hazard or conflict, so predicting can become more complex.

How to Predict   Predicting involves what is happening in your zones, what could happen, and if it does happen, how the change could affect you. To predict, you must evaluate the situation and make a judgment about the possible consequences. The more complex a situation is, the more difficult it is to identify and predict. As you gain driving experience, you will become more selective about which hazards or possible conflicts are critical.

Scanning your target areas can help you predict hazards that may affect your path of travel. Your ability to predict and make sound judgments will improve as you gain knowledge and experience.

What to Predict   Nearly all predictions you make as a driver will be related to predicting changes in zones and looking for an alternative path of travel. Three major elements in the traffic scene that you must make predictions about are the actions of other roadway users, your control of your vehicle, and the consequences of your actions.

Predicting Actions of Others Do not assume other roadway users will always take the correct action. Instead watch for clues to what they might do to alter zone conditions.

The most important types of predictions to make concerning the actions of others are:

- **Path**   Where might the other driver go? What zone might be closed? Will I have an open zone for escape?

- **Action**   What action will other users take? Is more than one action possible? Where will I be then?

- **Space**   Will I have an open zone?

- **Point of Conflict**   If I have no open zone for escape, where might our paths cross and a conflict occur?

FIGURE 8

What might you predict will happen if you were this driver?

FIGURE 9

FIGURE 9

Vehicles and pedestrians make this a hazardous situation. **Predict** What dangers should you be cautious of?

Imagine that you are driving toward the intersection in **FIGURE 9**. The oncoming driver is signaling for a right turn. Assume the worst and predict that the driver will turn left into your front zone. Also predict that the pedestrians will step off the curb and close your right-front zone. By making these predictions, you will be able to slow, swerve, or stop in order to avoid a conflict.

Predicting Control of Your Vehicle Speed is probably the most important factor in maintaining control of your vehicle. Always be prepared to adjust your speed for different zone conditions and situations. Different traffic, roadway, and weather conditions can change the amount of time and space needed for safe reactions.

The basic requirement for vehicle control is traction. Traction is the actual gripping power between the tires and the roadway surface. The more traction there is, the greater the gripping power.

In **FIGURE 10**, the driver knows the roadway is icy and wet and that visibility is restricted by the weather. The driver should predict that stopping will take longer than if the roadway were dry. Based on this prediction, the driver should check the rear zone, and then slow, and brake earlier.

Knowledge One basic part of your driving knowledge comes from the study of traffic laws and driver-education material. Whenever you drive, you also gain knowledge by gathering more information and learning from others.

Think of storing driving knowledge as adding to your safe-driving memory bank. The more you drive, the more you add to your memory bank of knowledge. This knowledge will help you identify and predict more quickly and accurately to increase your chances of becoming a low-risk driver.

Judgment   Making a judgment about a traffic situation involves measuring, comparing, and evaluating. As you drive, you judge speed, time, space, distance, traction, and visibility. You make judgments about your own driving performance as well as the actions and performance of other roadway users. Make every effort to develop the ability to make sound judgments that lead to accurate predictions.

Experience   In addition to knowledge, experience helps you improve your ability to predict accurately. Exposure to a wide variety of driving experiences provides a solid base for making sound judgments later.

In many situations, you may have a choice of actions to predict. Try to judge and compare the possible consequences before deciding on the best action.

FIGURE 10
Identify the risks in this situation and predict how they will affect your path of travel.

---

review it 5.2

1. Explain selective seeing and why it's important for drivers.

2. Explain how using an orderly search pattern helps you to be a safe driver?

3. Explain how knowing the zones around your car helps support your ability to identify and predict?

4. Why is it important to predict as you drive?

Critical Thinking

5. **Analyze** The first step of the IPDE Process is Identify. As a driver, why is it important for you to identify and not just to see?

6. **Analyze** Why is knowing how and what to predict an important skill for drivers to master?

IN THE PASSENGER SEAT **Changing Paths** As you ride with an adult, licensed driver, record all the roadway features and other driver-created situations that caused you to change your path of travel. Did you find that there were more or fewer of these situations than you expected? Report your findings to the class.

lesson 5.3
DECIDE AND EXECUTE

OBJECTIVES
- Name the three decisions you must make when applying the IPDE Process.
- Describe the three different lane positions available to you within your lane.
- List the three most important actions you can take to avoid conflict.

VOCABULARY
- execute
- space cushion
- minimize a hazard
- compromise space

Once you have identified a situation and predicted a possible conflict, your next step is to decide. Deciding, like predicting, is also a mental task. There is probably no task more important, though, than making wise decisions and then executing actions to avoid conflict. Drivers must continually identify and predict until they have enough information to make correct decisions.

Once you make a decision, the **execute** step of the IPDE Process will follow. To execute a decision means that you carry out the action that you have decided upon. In order to do this, you will use your vehicle's controls and safety devices.

Decide

As you follow your intended path of travel, your decision might be to maintain speed, change speed, change direction, or communicate your plan to others, or you might decide to use a combination of these actions. Be prepared to rethink your decisions as zones close and greater hazards are presented.

Decide to Change Speed
Any decision you make will be influenced by the speed of your own vehicle as well as the speed of other vehicles. Many drivers think that slowing down is the only way to avoid a predicted point of conflict. However, in many situations, you will decide to maintain your speed. Your other choices of actions, rather than

FIGURE 11
The driver of the yellow car decided to accelerate to provide space for the passing driver to return to the right lane. **Explain** What might have happened if the driver of the yellow car had decided not to accelerate?

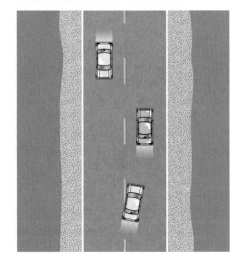

maintaining your speed, are to decelerate, brake, or accelerate. Base your decision about speed control on your evaluation of the situation as well as the possible consequences of your actions.

Decide to Change Direction   In order to change your position in the roadway, you will steer to the right or left. A greater change of direction might even be a lane change.

You can use an escape path into an open zone to avoid conflict. This area of space all around your vehicle is called a **space cushion**.

Three different lane positions are available to you within your lane, as shown in **FIGURE 12**.

Lane position 1   This should be your selected and safest position under normal driving conditions. In this position, you have the most space around your vehicle.

Lane position 2   You might decide to use this position when there is a closed right-front zone with an open left-front zone. Just a slight adjustment to the left is necessary.

Lane position 3   Use this position when there is a closed left-front zone with an open right-front zone.

There may be times when the situation requires a greater change in direction than the three lane positions. You may decide that the best position, in some situations, is to straddle a lane line. In these situations, return to lane position 1 as soon as it is safe to do so.

In order to make consistently low-risk decisions, try to detect a changing zone condition at least 15 seconds ahead in your searching area. This gives you ample time to decide on the best action.

Decide to Communicate   The decision to communicate with other users of the roadway helps reduce the possibility of conflict. You can decide to communicate with others by using lights, horn, vehicle position, eye contact, and body movement.

FIGURE 12 LANE POSITIONS

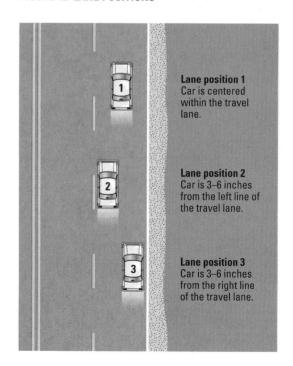

Lane position 1
Car is centered within the travel lane.

Lane position 2
Car is 3–6 inches from the left line of the travel lane.

Lane position 3
Car is 3–6 inches from the right line of the travel lane.

Use hand signals to communicate to other drivers.

A change in direction or speed can be executed with less risk if you have communicated your intentions to other users. Try to avoid changes in speed or direction without communicating first. Sudden actions can result in high-risk situations.

After deciding the best method of communicating, you will execute that action to inform others of your decision. The driver in **FIGURE 13** is using body movement by waving the driver on the left through the intersection first.

Traffic Flow

The IPDE Process and the Zone Control System will help you make decisions that will enable you to avoid hazards and conflicts in your intended path of travel. The safest position in traffic is the place where the fewest vehicles surround you. Your objective is to keep your vehicle surrounded by space. Continually analyze your left, front, and right zones and make decisions to adjust your speed or direction if one of your zones begins to close. By deciding to adjust your speed or direction, you will avoid unnecessary stops and thus reduce your risk of conflict.

Use the following techniques to manage time, space, and distance in order to maintain your safe path of travel.

Minimize a Hazard   You always want to **minimize a hazard**, or reduce the possibility of conflict, by deciding to put more distance between yourself and the hazard. As you can see in **FIGURE 14**, the yellow car is approaching the parked cars on the right. The driver predicts a car door might open. Since there is no oncoming traffic, the driver decides to steer away from the parked cars into lane position 2. After passing the parked cars, the driver will return to lane position 1. The driver has minimized the hazard by using more space.

FIGURE 14
Minimize the hazard of the parked cars by moving to lane position 2.

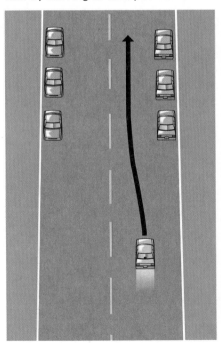

Separate Hazards   There will be times when you face more than one hazard at the same time. When this occurs, do not try to handle both or all hazards at once.

Instead, decide to adjust your speed to let them separate so you can deal with only one hazard at a time. By following this strategy, you will be more effective in dealing with each hazard separately.

The driver in **FIGURE 15** sees an approaching truck. The driver and the truck are both headed for the same one-lane bridge. If nothing changes, the driver's car and the truck will meet on the bridge at the same time. To avoid trouble, the driver slows to allow the truck to clear and separate from the bridge. The driver can then avoid the truck and center the car while crossing the bridge.

Compromise Space   Sometimes hazards cannot be minimized or separated. When this occurs, you must decide to **compromise space** by giving as much space as possible to the greater hazard.

The truck in **FIGURE 16** might enter the front zone of the yellow car to avoid the parked car that's pulling out on the left. The cars on the right present a lower level of risk. The driver of the yellow car should decide to steer close to the parked cars on the right while braking to reduce speed. This is an example of the yellow car driver making a compromise decision since there is no way to let these hazards separate.

Execute

Carrying out your decision in order to avoid conflict is the execute step in the IPDE Process. This step involves the physical skills used in driving. In most cases, you will execute routine actions and maneuvers. More important actions, however, involve timing and placement of your vehicle to avoid conflict. The important actions you will execute are

- control speed
- steer
- communicate

FIGURE 15

In this situation, you decide to slow to allow the hazards of the oncoming truck and bridge to separate.

FIGURE 16

The driver of the yellow car is compromising space to give more space to the greater hazard—the truck.

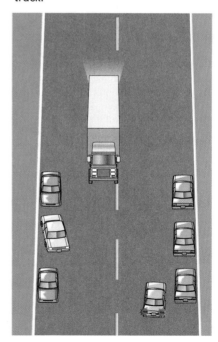

Control Speed   When you decide to control speed, you may have to maintain your speed or you may have to decelerate, such as when you approach a red light. If you merely release the accelerator far enough before the intersection, you often will arrive at the intersection when the light is green. In this situation, you also may use gentle pressure on the brake if more slowing is needed.

When greater deceleration is needed, you will execute the action of firm braking. The amount of braking needed will vary with the situation, the speed of your vehicle, the condition of the roadway, and the condition of your brakes.

Always check your rear zone before decelerating or braking in any manner. Avoid locking the brakes in an emergency stop. Locked brakes make steering impossible because the wheels must be turning to provide traction for steering. Some newer vehicles have an antilock-braking system. Such a system helps prevent loss of steering control. An antilock-braking system, through the use of computers, helps stop your vehicle in an emergency. All you need to do is to apply the brakes firmly and continuously. No pumping action is needed.

As the driver of the car in **FIGURE 17** enters the intersection, the white car from the right makes a right turn and enters the driver's path. The

FIGURE 17 Assume that your vehicle has an antilock-braking system. **Execute** What procedures would you follow to avoid conflict?

driver avoids locking the brakes so as not to lose steering control. Locking the brakes could have caused the car to slide and result in a conflict.

Steer   When you decide to steer away from a possible conflict, execute just the amount of steering needed. If you turn the steering wheel too much, you can lose control of your vehicle, especially at higher speeds.

Not steering enough can also present a problem. Try to steer just enough to avoid a conflict without making jerky or sudden movements. Drivers who keep space cushions around their vehicles usually have an escape path to steer into, thus reducing risk.

Communicate   In many instances, your only action will be to communicate. When you communicate, you must do it early enough so other users know your intentions. Communicate by using the following:

▶ **Headlights, taillights, and brake lights**   Use headlights during periods of reduced visibility. Using headlights during daylight hours, as shown in **FIGURE 18**, is a safety practice that makes your vehicle more visible to other drivers. Some new vehicles are equipped with daytime-running lights—headlights that come on automatically whenever the vehicle is operated. The advantage of these lights is to improve the visibility of the vehicle. Research shows that the use of daytime headlights reduces daytime crashes of all types.

▶ **Turn-signal lights**   Turn them on three to five seconds before making any change in direction.

▶ **Parking lights and hazard flashers**   When you are parked along the roadway but not in an emergency situation, have your parking lights turned on. If your vehicle is disabled, turn on your hazard flashers. Be prepared to change your path of travel when you see the blinking or flashing lights of a stopped delivery truck.

▶ **Back-up lights**   White back-up lights let others know you are backing up. Look for back-up lights on vehicles in parking lots.

safe driving tip

Daytime Lights   Some cars are equipped with daytime-running lights. Research shows that your chance of being in a daytime crash is reduced by daytime-running lights or using low beam headlights all the time.

FIGURE 18

Your vehicle can be seen more easily if your headlights are on, even during the day.

FIGURE 19

Be prepared to change your path to drive around stopped vehicles.

▶ **Horn**   A light tap is usually enough for a warning. In an emergency, a loud blast may be necessary.

▶ **Vehicle position**   The position of your vehicle in the roadway communicates a message. It indicates to others your intended path of travel. Other drivers may or may not see a light signal, but the position of the vehicle in the lane sends a message.

▶ **Eye contact and body movement**   Try to develop eye contact with other roadway users. You can communicate many messages this way. Body movements such as a wave of the hand may tell a driver to proceed.

Combine Actions   You often will need to execute a combination of actions. Sometimes you might need to accelerate and steer at the same time.

If you were driving alongside the parked truck in the picture above, you would need to combine several actions. You would first check your rear zone and your left-front zone to see if they were open. Then you would communicate by signaling as you brake and steer around the open car door. The precision and timing with which you execute these actions will determine whether or not a conflict will occur.

review it 5.3

1. Explain how communication and deciding to change speed or direction help you to be a low-risk driver.

2. Describe three situations where you would use each of the three lane positions.

3. List the three actions you can execute to avoid conflict and explain how these actions help you prevent conflicts.

Critical Thinking

4. **Decision Making**   You approach a parked car that is about to pull away from the curb. What sequence of actions should you execute to avoid any possible points of conflict?

5. **Evaluate**   How does knowing and using the different lane positions help to minimize risk?

IN THE PASSENGER SEAT   **Communication**   Make a list of the communication strategies listed in this chapter. Then, as you drive with an experienced adult driver for one week, record the number of times and under what circumstances you noticed each strategy used by drivers. How might you have communicated in the same circumstances? Discuss your findings with the class.

lesson 5.4
USING THE IPDE PROCESS

Using the IPDE Process and the Zone Control System helps you plan and execute **maneuvers**, or actions, to reduce hazards. It is up to every driver to manage space, time, and speed in order to further increase safety within the HTS.

You must continually practice using the IPDE Process so that it will become habit. Once you have developed the habit, you will identify open and closed lanes, make accurate predictions and correct decisions, and execute maneuvers more successfully.

Putting IPDE Into Action

Use the four steps of the IPDE Process in order. Identify the hazards or events, then predict how they might affect your intended path of travel. You then perform the third step, deciding. Finally, you execute your maneuvers based on your decisions.

Selective Use of IPDE   There will be times when you do not carry out the complete IPDE Process. Conditions may change in one or more zones so the process need not be completed. You can use the IPDE Process selectively by beginning a new cycle before completing the previous one.

As you become a more experienced driver, you will learn the more important clues and trouble spots in different areas of the HTS. You will then be able to adjust your selective application of the IPDE Process for those specific areas.

OBJECTIVES
- Describe what is meant by selective use of the IPDE Process.
- Explain why the IPDE Process takes time to learn and use.

VOCABULARY
- maneuver

-----FIGURE 20 --

Can you identify the possible points of conflict in this photograph? **Decide**   What would you decide to do?

IPDE Takes Time and Practice

Remember that the IPDE Process takes time to put into action. You must have time to identify clues and changing zones. You must have time to predict the actions of others and the possibility of closed zones. The more complex the traffic situation and the more risk factors present, the longer it takes to carry out the IPDE Process.

Practice is necessary for the development and improvement of any skill. As you ride with other drivers, practice the I-P-D steps of the IPDE Process. You can then judge if the actions taken by others were based on correct decisions.

FIGURE 21 Do you know what actions to take to avoid a conflict in this situation?

review it 5.4

1. Explain what is meant by selective use of the IPDE Process.

2. What factors can cause the IPDE Process to take more time?

Critical Thinking

3. **Apply Concepts** Although you learn the steps in the IPDE Process in order, there may be times when you might have to begin the next step before finishing the previous one. Describe a driving situation where you might have to use the IPDE Process selectively.

4. **Compare** Risk factors change depending on the driving environment. Explain why driving on the highway during rush hour presents more risk factors than driving in your neighborhood at any time.

IN YOUR COMMUNITY **Research** Distractions are one of the major causes of traffic crashes for drivers of all ages. Emotions, other drivers, and being in a hurry can cause experienced drivers to temporarily forget their good driving skills. Research the major causes of traffic crashes among teens, 20–39 year olds, 40–59 year olds, and among the 60+ years population. Draw a graph to represent your findings, and share it with the class.

CHAPTER 5 REVIEW

Lesson Summaries

5.1 THE IPDE PROCESS

- The IPDE Process is an organized system that includes the following steps to avoid conflict: identify, predict, decide, and execute as they relate to driving.
- The Zone Control System is designed to help drivers manage the space around their cars.

5.2 IDENTIFY AND PREDICT

- There are eight steps in an orderly visual search pattern: look ahead; evaluate your zones; check the rearview mirror; evaluate and check your 4–6-second and 12–15-second ranges; and check your speedometer and gauges.
- Selective seeing means that you identify and select only those clues and events that restrict your line of sight or can change your intended path of travel.
- In order to predict how hazards might affect your path of travel, you have to evaluate the situation and make a judgment about the consequences.

5.3 DECIDE AND EXECUTE

- When driving, there are three main decisions you can make: minimize the threat of a single hazard by adjusting speed and direction; allow two hazards to separate; or adjust and split what little space there is between the hazards with a compromise decision.
- The three main actions you can execute when driving are speed control, steering, and communicating.

5.4 USING THE IPDE PROCESS

- The IPDE Process takes practice and time.

Chapter Vocabulary

- 4–6-second range
- 12–15-second range
- closed zone
- compromise space
- depth perception
- execute
- field of vision
- ground viewing
- identify
- line of sight
- maneuver
- minimize a hazard
- open zone
- orderly visual search pattern
- predict
- risk factor
- scanning
- space cushion
- target area
- target-area range
- zone

Write the word or phrase from the list above that completes the sentence correctly.

1. The first step in the IPDE Process is _____.

2. When you search critical areas in a regular sequence as you drive, you are using a(n) _____.

3. One of the hardest skills to learn in driving is picking a point or points where you might have a conflict with others. This ability to anticipate is called _____.

4. When there is no line-of-sight or path-of-travel restriction to a zone, that zone can be called a(n) _____.

5. Checking your _____ will let you see hazards in your intended path of travel ahead of time.

6. _____ is the space from your vehicle to the target area.

Checking Concepts

LESSON 1

7. The ultimate risk in driving is having a crash. Name two risk factors for each of the three risk factor groups that could increase risk?

LESSON 2

8. Why are there six zones in the Zone Control System?

9. How does an orderly visual search pattern help make you a low-risk driver?

10. Explain why the predicting step in the IPDE Process is one of the hardest to practice on a regular basis.

LESSON 3

11. Describe two situations where you would want to separate hazards and two situations where you would need to compromise space.

12. You are driving and predict a point where a crash is going to happen between your car and a truck if nothing changes. What decision choices do you have to avoid a crash?

LESSON 4

13. Name three types of situations where you might select only the identify and predict steps in the IPDE Process as you drive.

Critical Thinking

14. **Apply Concepts** How do you use the identifying process known as orderly visual search pattern?

15. **Compare** Describe the difference between separating a hazard and minimizing a hazard.

You're the Driver

16. **Decide** What are the three basic decisions you make in the Decide step of the IPDE System?

17. **Execute** You see the flashing lights of a parked delivery truck in your path of travel. What actions should you take to avoid potential conflict?

18. **Predict** In this situation, the bike riders and driver have not seen each other. The yellow hedge presents a line of sight restriction. If nothing changes, what might happen?

19. **Execute** How would knowledge and experience help the driver approaching the STOP sign execute a safe stop?

Preparing for the Test

Choose the letter of the answer that best completes the statement or answers the question.

1. To avoid last minute moves, you should be looking down the road to where your vehicle will be in about
   a. 4–6 seconds.
   b. 6–8 seconds.
   c. 8–12 seconds.
   d. 12 seconds or more.

2. A school bus ahead of you in your lane is stopped with red lights flashing. You should
   a. stop, then proceed when you think all of the children have exited the bus.
   b. slow to 25 mph and pass cautiously.
   c. stop as long as the red lights are flashing.
   d. slow to pass if no students are visible.

Use the photo below to answer Question 3.

3. When you tailgate other drivers
   a. you can frustrate the other driver and make them angry.
   b. your actions can result in a traffic citation.
   c. you cut your response time and ability to avoid problems.
   d. all of the above

4. The safest precaution you can take regarding the use of a cell phone and driving is
   a. use hands-free devices so you can keep both hands on the steering wheel.
   b. keep your phone within easy reach so you won't need to take your eyes off the road when you need to use it.
   c. wait until your car is stopped and out of traffic to call.
   d. make sure you have a safe following distance before calling.

Use the art below to answer Question 5.

5. You see a traffic officer holding this sign. You should obey his or her instructions
   a. only if you see orange cones on the road ahead.
   b. unless they conflict with existing signs, signals, or laws.
   c. during times of extreme traffic congestion.
   d. all the time

6. You must obey instructions from school crossing guards
   a. at all times.
   b. only during school hours.
   c. unless you do not see any children present.
   d. only if there are no traffic lights.

drive write

IPDE Process Identify, predict, decide, and execute are actions you will need to practice until they become habits. Which do you think will be the most difficult for you? Write one or two paragraphs explaining why it's difficult and what you can do to gain confidence in performing it.

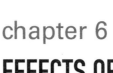

chapter 6

EFFECTS OF DRIVER CONDITION

6.1 Emotions and Driving

6.2 Physical Senses and Driving

6.3 Physical Limitations

KEY IDEA

How do your emotions, physical senses, and physical capabilities affect your ability to drive?

Driving involves some risk, as do many other activities. You can keep your driving-related risks low if you are mentally alert, emotionally fit, and physically healthy. How can your senses help lower risks involved in driving? How can drivers compensate for physical disabilities?

lesson 6.1
EMOTIONS AND DRIVING

 OBJECTIVES

- Describe how emotions can affect your ability to drive.
- Explain how passengers can help a driver.
- Describe the influence emotions have on your willingness to accept risk.
- Explain how you can manage your emotions while driving.

 VOCABULARY

- emotion
- aggressive driving
- road rage

How Emotions Affect Driving

An **emotion** is a strong feeling. Anger, fear, and joy are examples of emotions. Emotions add a special flavor to life.

How you think and act depend a lot on your emotions. When emotions affect your thoughts and actions, they can also affect your decision-making skills and ability to assess risk. Strong emotions block your ability to judge and reason.

In Chapter 5, you were introduced to the concept of risk and how to manage risks using the IPDE Process with the Zone Control System. Emotions can lead you to assume more or less risk than normal. You can reduce the negative effects of emotions and better manage risks by using courteous driving strategies. When you do this, you empower yourself, as courtesy can influence others' emotions.

Mental Effects of Emotions   Strong emotions interfere with your ability to think, reason, make wise decisions, and respond appropriately to situations. They can increase your chances of making a mistake. Emotions can also affect the way you make judgments and decisions in a driving situation.

In some instances, strong emotions may cause you to focus on only one event. You could miss other important events in a driving situation. In **FIGURE 1**, a driver suddenly moves into your lane without warning. If you focus only on that driver's actions, you might overreact and cause a conflict with the driver behind you. Your overreaction could upset or anger that driver. Instead of getting upset, you and the driver behind you could each increase the space between you and the vehicle ahead of each of you. Drivers need to reduce their risks; emotional responses like seeking revenge increase risk.

Physical Effects of Emotions   Strong emotions can cause changes in your bodily functions. Your

-------- **FIGURE 1** --------
A vehicle suddenly cuts into your lane.
Decide   What response will best minimize risk with the vehicles ahead of and behind you?

heartbeat speeds up, your breathing quickens, your digestion slows, and your muscles tighten. If you are angered, your mind and body may prepare to fight. If you are afraid, your focus may become flight. These emotions prevent you from properly applying the IPDE Process.

The more tasks there are in a given driving situation, the more complex and stressful the situation. During rush hour, drivers often display more discourteous driving behaviors as a result of traffic congestion. Heavy traffic can cause stress and fatigue in drivers.

Everyone encounters different stresses in life. Stress is not always bad. Sometimes it helps people perform better and accomplish things. However, continued emotional stress exhausts a person and can lead to adverse effects, including heart disease and digestive disorders.

FIGURE 2
The driver might remain angry long after the people have cleared his path.

Anger While Driving

You usually rely upon a set of assumptions or expectations when driving. You assume that others will drive and act in a safe, responsible manner. You might be tempted to react angrily when you must change your expectations.

In normal driving situations, other drivers might interfere with your intended speed or path of travel. They might slow or change lanes improperly. They might not yield, may fail to signal, or may not move quickly enough when a traffic light changes. Sometimes you might think that other drivers are trying to irritate you. As a result, you might become angry.

Anger seems to occur and be displayed more often than any other emotion. Anger is one of the hardest emotions to control. When you are angry, your body and mind may respond with an urge to fight, which can block your ability to think rationally. Anger may cause aggression or road rage. According to the American Automobile Association (AAA), **aggressive driving** is driving without regard for others' safety, and **road rage** is driving with the intent to harm others.

In **FIGURE 2**, the driver is angry at the people who are talking and blocking his way. If he cannot maintain emotional control, he might remain angry and react aggressively.

Anger can impair all of your driving skills. You might take risks you would not take if you were calm. You also might not see everything

WHAT WOULD YOU SAY?

Staying Calm You are riding with a friend in the center lane of a three-lane highway. A driver behind you starts honking the horn, flashing high-beam lights, and tailgating. What are two things you could say to help your friend manage the situation and drive safely?

you should see, which can cause you to miss important clues. You might force other drivers to stop or swerve abruptly. These last-second actions can cause conflicts and added stress not only for you, but for other drivers as well. Good drivers never surprise other drivers.

What might you do when you become angry while driving or encounter other drivers who are? Here are a few options:

- Think positively.
- Leave punishment to police; your acts may only aggravate the situation.
- Model good behavior.
- Consider that other drivers may have good reasons for their actions.

Other Emotions and Driving

Sorrow, depression, and anxiety are other emotions that can adversely affect driving. These emotions can also slow body processes and reduce mental alertness.

Anxiety differs from anger. You might be anxious when driving in an unfamiliar, difficult situation. You might have trouble identifying hazards when you are confused. You might even feel panic-stricken. As a responsible driver, work to recognize difficult situations and try your best to cope. It may mean delaying driving, but your risks will be reduced.

Excitement and happiness can also prevent you from fully concentrating on your driving task. A happy, excited driver can be just as impaired as an angry driver. After an emotionally intense event, try to deal with your emotions before you get behind the wheel. If not dealt with, your emotions could impair your driving abilities.

FIGURE 3 You find yourself in this situation on the highway. **Apply Concepts** How would you feel?

Emotions and the IPDE Process

The successful use of the IPDE Process requires total concentration on the driving task. In a tight, high-stress situation, you need even more time to use the IPDE Process to keep from making wrong or late decisions, because your emotional condition can drastically affect your driving ability.

Think how emotions could affect your driving if you were beside the truck pictured in **FIGURE 3**. The car

ahead has slowed, forcing you to slow. The truck driver
has just decided to pass the car. You are not sure what
the driver ahead is going to do. Another truck is
behind the passing truck. As a result, the driver ahead
and the truck drivers could cause you to make quick,
irresponsible decisions.

Passengers and Emotions

Peer pressure can be a very strong force, depending
upon the situation. In a baseball game, team spirit can
help win the game. In a vehicle, your passengers can
strongly influence the way you drive.

In most group situations, one or more people
need to assume responsibility and lead the group.
When you are driving, you must be the leader and
take control. You are responsible for the safety of your
passengers.

In **FIGURE 4**, a championship soccer match has
just ended. Everyone is going to celebrate. Emotions will be running high.
The driver will be under special pressure to concentrate on the driving task.
To make sure that nothing goes wrong, the driver must be the leader and
maintain control of the situation.

Passengers can help the driver maintain control while driving. Here
are actions you, as a passenger, can take to assist a driver:

- Avoid saying or doing anything that might distract or upset the driver.
  Refrain from heated discussions. Talk about positive events.

- Discourage the driver from taking reckless actions. Be prepared
  to intervene if the driver endangers others by driving recklessly.
  Encourage the driver to let someone else drive, or refuse to ride in the
  same vehicle. Do what you must to protect yourself and others.

- Compliment the driver for doing a good job of driving in a difficult
  situation. You might need the same support when you are the driver.

FIGURE 4
Spirits might run high after winning
a game. The driver is responsible
for his or her passengers. **Apply
Concepts** How can the driver deal
with his or her emotions before driving?

Effects on Risk Taking

Your emotions have a big influence on the amount of risk you are willing to take. You probably will be more likely to take risks if you are angry than if you are happy. When a driver cuts you off after passing, you might want to get even by taking chances that you would not normally take.

Mature, responsible drivers do not let their emotions cause them to take unnecessary risks. Taking a chance while driving can be deadly. You must be mature enough to adjust your behavior so that you do not drive into or create high-risk situations. You also must be mature enough to refuse to take part when other people suggest activities that could endanger you, your passengers, or other drivers.

Your emotions might also affect how you would drive on the same roadway at different times. For example, if you were driving an injured friend to the hospital, your concern might cause you to drive fast, increasing the risks. An hour later, you probably would not drive home in the same manner. You then would drive more cautiously and courteously.

On the other hand, sometimes you might be so uninterested in your trip that you don't give your complete attention to the driving task. Driving the same route over and over may cause you to pay less attention to the driving task.

Controlling Emotions

During some performances, like a concert or a play, you are asked to hold your applause until a certain point. You must manage your emotions until the proper time. In driving, you must develop this same type of emotional discipline. You must strive to keep emotions from affecting your driving ability.

Coping with Emotions   High-stress driving situations can cause emotions to surface. These techniques can help you manage your emotions while driving:

- Use the IPDE Process to drive in an organized manner. Learn and use correct driving procedures until they become habits. You then will be more likely to execute the proper action, even when under emotional stress.

FIGURE 5   You drive on this street every day. **Identify** If you were upset and angry, do you think you could miss identifying the potential hazard on the right?

FIGURE 6   You're the driver. **Execute** If you stay in control, what affect might you have on the passengers in your car?

- Anticipate emotion-producing situations and adjust your expectations. Say to yourself, "I know there will be delays during rush hour, so I will allow more time to get home. I will not let the actions of others bother me."

- If you encounter an aggressive driver, do not challenge the driver. Avoid eye contact, ignore gestures or verbal comments, and remain calm. Adopt a "yield" attitude.

- Try to adjust your route to avoid irritating traffic situations.

- If you are tired, make a special effort to manage your emotions. A tired person can become upset more easily.

- Analyze your mistakes. Learn from them so that you are less likely to repeat them.

- Keep courtesy as one of your personal rules of the road.

Goal of Emotional Control   Emotions are complicated and powerful forces. Learning about emotions and how to manage them is something most individuals work at all their lives. Maintaining an attitude of "I will always work to manage my emotions when driving" is a big step toward actually mastering your emotions. If you can manage your emotions and maintain your driving ability, those skills will help keep the risks of driving, as well as your stress level, low.

drive green

Haste Makes Waste   Stay calm when driving. Aggressive driving behaviors such as rapid and excessive acceleration, over-braking, and driving at high speeds waste fuel.

review it 6.1

1. How can a strong emotion like anger affect your ability to drive?

2. How can passengers help a driver?

3. What affect can emotions have on your willingness to take more risks?

4. What are some things you can do to help manage your emotions while driving?

Critical Thinking

5. **Compare and Contrast**   How are the effects of anxiety and fear on driving similar? How do they differ?

6. **Decide**   You have a big date tonight, but you have to stay late after school. You need to run errands before the date, and rush-hour traffic has begun. What can you do to avoid strong emotions from affecting your driving before you get behind the wheel?

IN THE PASSENGER SEAT   **Observe Traffic**   When riding as a passenger, look for signs of road rage and aggressive driving and take note of the traffic conditions in that area. Report the types of driver behaviors you noticed and the traffic conditions that were associated with those behaviors to your class.

lesson 6.2
PHYSICAL SENSES AND DRIVING

OBJECTIVES

- Define visual acuity and the parts of your field of vision.
- Describe factors that can affect and limit vision.
- Explain how your senses help you drive.
- Describe the importance of managing sensory distractions.

VOCABULARY

- visual acuity
- field of vision
- central vision
- peripheral vision
- fringe vision
- tunnel vision
- color blindness
- depth perception
- night blindness
- glare resistance
- glare recovery time
- speed smear

Your senses play a vital role in using the IPDE Process. You use your abilities to see, hear, smell, and detect motion to know what is occurring in and around your vehicle.

Driving, like other activities such as sports and mowing the lawn, exposes you to risks. As you drive, your senses help you stay alert and be aware of changing situations. Using your senses to help you drive can give you a better chance of maintaining control over your vehicle and minimizing your driving risks.

Seeing

More than 90 percent of the information you gather while driving is received through your eyes. You must be able to clearly and quickly identify closing zones in your intended path of travel.

Your brain directs your eyes to focus on objects in and around your path of travel. Information is sent to your brain and combined with stored information. As a result, you can identify hazards, predict conflicts, decide to maintain or adjust your speed and position, and execute your decisions.

Visual Acuity   When driving, you need the ability to see things clearly both near and far away. For example, you may need to read the gauges on your instrument panel in one instant, then identify oncoming traffic in the next. The ability to see things clearly is called **visual acuity**.

A person with normal visual acuity—called 20/20 vision—can read 11/32-inch letters on an eye chart from 20 feet away.

You must pass a visual acuity test in order to obtain a learner's permit, and possibly again when you apply for your driver's license. Most states require a minimum corrected visual acuity of 20/40 to drive. A person with 20/40 vision must be twice as close to an object to see it as clearly as a person with 20/20 vision must be. With 20/200, the person would have to be 10 times closer. If you need to wear glasses or contact lenses to pass the vision test, then you must wear them when you drive.

Field of Vision Your field of vision is all the area that you can see around you while you are looking straight ahead. While looking straight ahead, most people can see about 90 degrees to each side, or about half a circle. There are three types of vision that are part of your field of vision.

Central Vision The straight-ahead part of your field of vision is called your **central vision**. As shown in **FIGURE 7**, your central vision is a small, 10-degree cone-shaped area. As you drive, direct your central vision to your target area and 12–15 seconds ahead to identify zone changes.

Peripheral Vision Surrounding your central vision is **peripheral vision**. Your peripheral vision is sensitive to light and motion.

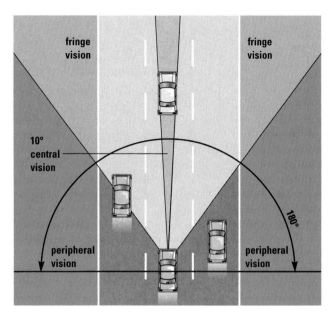

FIGURE 7 You can see most clearly in the area of central vision, but the fringe vision is also very important for driving.

Fringe Vision The part of your peripheral vision closest to your central vision is called **fringe vision**. Your side fringe vision is used to monitor a zone condition after it has been clearly identified in central vision. The upper fringe vision is used to detect changes in the rear mirror. The lower fringe vision is used to monitor reference points for vehicle position.

Some people see less than a total of 180 degrees. A narrow field of vision—140 degrees or less—is called **tunnel vision**. A driver who has tunnel vision must compensate with more frequent head and eye movements.

FIGURE 8 Use your central vision to check your target area and front zones. Use your fringe vision to check reference points and detect changes in your rearview mirror.

Factors That Affect Vision

There are many other aspects of vision besides visual acuity and your field of vision that affect how well you see when you drive. Good vision for driving also means understanding our ability to perceive colors and depth and to our limitations while driving at night, in glare, or at highway speeds.

Color Vision Color vision is the ability to distinguish one color from another. Not being able to distinguish colors is called **color blindness**. Being able to see the colors red, green, and yellow is particularly important since these colors give the messages stop, go, and slow or caution. The most common type of color blindness is difficulty distinguishing red and green. This type of color blindness is hereditary and affects many more men than women.

A color-blind driver can compensate by

- remembering the order of the lights in a traffic signal. If the lights are vertical, the red light is at the top. If horizontal, the red light is on the left.

- knowing the meanings of traffic signs by their shapes.
- reading all signs that appear with traffic signals.
- checking all zones and 90 degrees to the left and right before proceeding at traffic signals.
- taking cues from other drivers.

Depth Perception The ability to judge distance between yourself and other objects is **depth perception**. When driving, you must judge the distance between your vehicle and other vehicles and objects. Accurate judgment is more difficult when other vehicles or objects are moving.

A driver can compensate for poor depth perception by

- using a following distance greater than three seconds.
- allowing for additional clear distance ahead before passing.
- allowing greater distances at night than during the day. Darkness hides many visual cues that you use in the daytime.

FIGURE 9

Here is the same intersection in the day and at night. **Compare and Contrast** What objects that you can see in the daylight are hard to see at night?

Night Vision   The ability to see at night varies from person to person. Some people who see clearly in the daytime have poor night vision. Not being able to see well at night is called **night blindness**.

All people see less at night than in daylight: colors are harder to identify and details of objects do not appear as sharp.

Your night vision is limited to the area lit by headlights, streetlights, and other lights. In rural areas, you might be in total darkness except for moonlight and the area lit by your headlights.

At night, you might not be able to see anything to the sides. You might have difficulty reading signs and roadway markings. Compare the two pictures in **FIGURE 9**, which show the same location during the day and at night. Notice how little you can see at night. Your ability to judge distances accurately also decreases at night.

Glare   Glare occurs in the daytime when bright sunlight is reflected off shiny surfaces. Sunroofs and convertibles with their tops down let in additional sunlight that can produce glare. At night, glare occurs when bright lights reflect off shiny surfaces. The term **glare resistance** describes the ability to continue seeing when looking at bright lights. Glare resistance varies from person to person. Some people are more sensitive to light than others.

Sudden glare can blind a person temporarily, especially at night. Headlights turn toward you at intersections. Bright lights appear from over hills and around curves. A vehicle using high-beam headlights approaches from behind. Your pupils open wide at night to let in all available light. When your eyes are suddenly exposed to bright lights, your pupils contract. You might be temporarily blinded before your pupils can adjust to the bright lights.

The term **glare recovery time** describes the time your eyes need to regain clear vision after being affected by glare. Your pupils can take 5–10 seconds to readjust. At 40 mph, you would travel more than the length of a football field while partially blinded.

Take these steps to avoid or recover from glare:

- Avoid looking directly at bright lights. Use the right edge of the roadway as a guide.

- Anticipate glare situations and glance away or squint.

FIGURE 10
Some vehicles in sunny conditions can reflect a lot of light into your eyes. **Identify**   What can you do to avoid having your vision affected by glare?

FIGURE 11 When you drive at high speeds, your fringe vision is reduced so your side vision is less clear.

- Use side fringe vision rather than central vision to check your lane position and the location of oncoming vehicles.
- If you are impaired by glare, slow until your vision clears.
- Wear sunglasses and use your vehicle's sun visor in bright sunlight.
- Adjust your rearview mirror for night use.

Vehicle Speed and Vision   As your vehicle's speed increases, your need for accurate vision also increases. Yet, at higher speeds, you have less time to see clearly. Your field of vision is narrowed. At 55 mph, your clear, side-vision area is less than half as wide as at 20 mph.

Objects off to your sides become blurred and distorted as your speed increases. This blur, or **speed smear**, as shown in **FIGURE 11**, has an effect much like tunnel vision. Your eyes tend to focus far ahead to where the roadway appears to come to a point. You see less and less of what is happening on the sides. Make sure you move your eyes and increase the frequency of your side glances when driving at highway speeds.

Other Senses and Driving

Sometimes you need to depend on senses other than vision to identify hazards during travel. In complex driving situations, you may have to use more than one sense at a time.

Hearing   Your sense of hearing can alert you to the sounds of vehicle horns, train whistles, emergency-vehicle sirens, and the engines and brakes of trucks and buses. You can also get early warning of mechanical problems by listening for unusual noises from your vehicle.

Drivers who have sounds blocked from them can be dangerous to themselves and others. Driving with closed windows and with the stereo or a headset on may make a driver unaware of critical traffic sounds. Talking on a cellular phone while driving creates a similar hearing problem.

Drivers who are deaf know that they must compensate for what they cannot hear. They use their eyes more than drivers who have normal hearing.

Smell   Your sense of smell can identify an overheated engine or over-heated brakes. Smelling exhaust fumes inside your vehicle can give you an early warning of the presence of deadly gases.

Sense of Motion   Certain sensations can give you clues to the movement of your vehicle. Your sense of balance tells you that you are veering right or left, changing speed, or going around a curve. A sudden vibration of the vehicle or jerk of the steering wheel might warn you of a mechanical prob-lem, a flat tire, or a change in the roadway surface.

Managing Sensory Distractions

You increase or decrease your risk of becoming involved in a collision by changing the level of control you have over your vehicle. Impairment or inadequate use of vision, hearing, smell, and motion will affect your ability to manage risks. Anything that distracts you from using your senses and concentrating on the driving task will increase your risk of a collision.

The driving scene can change quickly, and you need to be alert to changes so that you make decisions and act quickly. As a driver, you are responsible for maintaining control and managing any distractions. Remember that the more distractions you can eliminate, the better you will be able to use your senses to manage risks and avoid collisions while driving.

Audio   An audio system in your vehicle can cause distractions. You need to keep the volume at a level that allows you to hear important traffic sounds such as sirens and horns. Also, do not wear headphones while driving. Headphones will block traffic sounds, and it is illegal in many states to wear them while driving. Avoid changing radio sta-tions and CDs or controlling portable music players while driving. You increase your risk of a collision any time you take your eyes off the road and a hand off the steering wheel.

Cell Phones   Cell phones can be helpful in a vehicle in emergencies, but they are dangerous to use while driving. Research studies have found that drivers talking on cell phones were four times more likely to be involved in a collision. Some states have passed laws prohibiting people from talking or sending text messages on a cell phone while driv-ing. You should turn off your cell phone when you drive. If you need to use the phone, pull off the road and stop the car.

FIGURE 12
Talking on a cell phone while driving creates risk for you and your passengers. **Predict**   What do you think could happen if you aren't paying attention to your driving?

analyzing data

Reported Aggressive Driving Behaviors

Recently, a study about driving on San Diego interstates was conducted in order to find out some common aggressive driving behaviors that drivers observed while on the freeway. People were told to report observed behaviors using their cell phones and almost 1,794 calls were received. The circle graph shows the results of the complaints. Study the graph before you answer these questions.

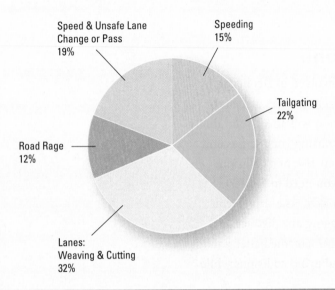

Speed & Unsafe Lane Change or Pass 19%

Speeding 15%

Tailgating 22%

Road Rage 12%

Lanes: Weaving & Cutting 32%

1. **Reading the Chart** What does each segment in the graph represent?

2. **Analyzing the Data** Which behavior was observed most often? Which behavior was observed least often?

3. **Inferring** Suggest some reasons people might have for weaving and cutting in lanes? For tailgating?

4. **Relating Cause and Effect** Road rage and speeding were reported almost the same number of times. Do you think road rage might have been a result of drivers who were speeding? Explain your reasoning.

5. **Execute** As a driver, what can you do to make sure that you never become an aggressive-driver statistic?

review it 6.2

1. What is your field of vision? What part of your field of vision provides you with your clearest vision?

2. Describe three factors that affect your vision.

3. How do your senses of hearing, smell, and motion help you assess driving situations?

4. How can sensory distractions affect the risks you take while driving?

Critical Thinking

5. **Evaluate** Your senses help you drive. Rank the senses described in this lesson from most important to least important and explain your reasoning.

6. **Relate Cause and Effect** It is a bright and sunny day, and you have a doctor's appointment for an eye exam. How might this affect your ability to drive? What could you do to avoid or reduce the risks of driving after the appointment?

IN THE PASSENGER SEAT **What Might You Say** You don't want to scare or alarm your grandfather, who is driving, but you see a deer at the edge of the road ahead. You are not traveling very fast. Has your grandfather spotted the deer or not? What might you say and how could you say it so as not to startle him?

PHYSICAL LIMITATIONS

A **disability** is a diagnosed physical or mental impairment that inter-feres with or prevents normal activity or achievement in a particular area. Many experienced drivers have learned to respond to different disabilities. Generally, driving is possible for many people who have even moderate to severe disabilities. However, a disability needs to be recognized before it can be properly addressed.

Temporary Disabilities

Sometimes you must drive even though you are not at your physical best. You may be dealing with a temporary disability. A **temporary disability** is a disability that can improve and clear up. While you can compensate for some temporary disabilities, with others you should not drive.

Fatigue   Mental or physical work, emotional stress, or loss of sleep can cause fatigue. You may not think of fatigue as being a disability, but fatigue lessens your fitness to perform tasks, including driving. It dulls your senses and slows both mental and physical processes. If you are fatigued, you will need more time to use the IPDE Process.

Fatigue can also cause drowsiness. Drowsy driving is estimated to cause at least 100,000 collisions each year. If you find that you can't stop yawning, your eyes keep closing, or you can't focus or concentrate on the driving task, you're probably drowsy and shouldn't be driving.

Rest is the only safe remedy for fatigue. However, people often need to drive even when they are tired. If you are tired after work or school, take a break for a few minutes before you drive. Stop every two hours. Walk, stretch, get a beverage or snack. Use your orderly visual search pattern to keep your eyes moving. Be active—listen to the radio, sing, or talk with your passengers. Stop in a safe, well-lighted place if you feel you can't drive safely anymore. Lock the vehicle and take a nap.

Temporary Illness or Injury   Any illness, even a cold, can impair driv-ing to some extent. A temporary physical injury, such as a broken bone or a sprained ankle, also can impair your driving.

OBJECTIVES

- Describe what you can do to combat fatigue.
- Explain how medicines, carbon monoxide, and smoking affect a driver.
- Describe what drivers who have permanent disabilities can do to compensate.

VOCABULARY

- disability
- temporary disability
- carbon monoxide
- permanent disability
- chronic illness

----**FIGURE 13**-----------------
Identify What clues suggest to you that the driver is fatigued?

WHAT WOULD YOU SAY?

Hey, Wake Up!

Your friend is driving you home from the movies. You notice the vehicle is starting to drift. You look over and see your friend's eyes are closing. What are some things you could do or say?

When an illness is temporary, many drivers do not recognize its influence on their driving skills. Being under the influence of medicines can increase your chances of being in a collision. Be aware of the side effects of medicines by reading the labels.

Effects of Medicines Many medicines have side effects that can interfere with your driving ability and risks. For example, medicine that reduces headache pain or relieves allergies might also cause drowsiness, dizziness, or reduced alertness.

If you take medicine, read the label to learn the possible side effects. The label shown in **FIGURE 14** warns users not to drive while taking this medicine. Ask your physician or pharmacist about side effects. If you must drive after taking medicine, try to choose a quiet, less-congested route.

If a medicine's label indicates that you should not drive or operate vehicles or machinery, do not attempt to drive. If you begin taking a new medicine and there is no specific warning about driving, be safe and maintain an even greater following distance than normal until you know how it will affect you.

Effects of Carbon Monoxide Your vehicle's exhaust fumes contain **carbon monoxide**, a colorless, odorless, and tasteless gas. Carbon monoxide is present in all engine exhaust gases.

You can sometimes detect carbon monoxide in a vehicle because the gas mixes with other exhaust fumes that do have an odor. However, you cannot tell how concentrated the carbon monoxide is by the odor of the exhaust fumes. Carbon monoxide may be present even without an odor.

Small amounts of carbon monoxide can cause drowsiness, headaches, muscular weakness, mental dullness, and nausea. Too much carbon monoxide can cause death.

Be alert for the danger of carbon monoxide in heavy traffic and in enclosed areas such as tunnels and underground parking facilities. Your heater or air conditioner vents might draw in exhaust fumes from the car ahead.

FIGURE 14

A medicine can affect you differently at different times. If possible, drive to your destination before taking the medicine.

Leaving a rear window open might create a slight vacuum that pulls in exhaust fumes.

If your vehicle is parked in a garage at home, open the garage door before starting the engine.

In stop-and-go traffic, maintain a 3-second following distance. Stop where you can see the tires of the vehicle ahead touching the pavement. In traffic jams, especially in enclosed areas, turn off the engine when possible.

Smoking   Be aware that smoking while driving is dangerous. Smoking raises the carbon monoxide level and reduces the oxygen level in a person's blood. Smoke residue accumulates on windows and affects vision.

Discourage your passengers from smoking. Carbon monoxide from tobacco smoke can affect even nonsmokers in an enclosed area such as a vehicle. If someone does smoke in your vehicle, open a window to provide fresh air.

Permanent Disabilities

Disabilities such as epilepsy, blindness, and loss of a limb are considered **permanent disabilities** because these are conditions that cannot be cured or improved. Many permanent disabilities, however, do not prevent people from driving. Special vehicle equipment and controls, as shown in **FIGURE 15**, can make it possible for many people with permanent disabilities to drive.

Most drivers with permanent disabilities understand that the disability itself may put them at a higher level of risk, and they learn how to compensate for those limitations.

Some drivers with permanent disabilities have special license plates or window cards with the handicapped symbol. The symbol also appears on license plates or window cards of drivers who often transport disabled people. Vehicles with these license plates can park in specially marked areas in parking lots and on streets.

Aging

As a nation, we are healthier and living longer. As a result, more older drivers are using the roadways. One in six drivers is over age 65. Eighty percent of drivers over age 75 take prescription medications.

Adaptive equipment allows for hand operation of gas and brake pedals.

FIGURE 15
There are many types and combinations of adaptive equipment available to help those with mild to severe physical disabilities maintain independence.

Aging slows reflexes, dulls vision and concentration, can make muscles weaker and inflexible, and reduces depth perception and field of vision. Failure to yield the right of way is the main factor in collisions involving older drivers. However, drivers over 65 are still involved in fewer collisions per mile driven than those under 30.

Chronic Illnesses

A **chronic illness** is an ailment that lasts over a period of years. Some chronic illnesses have little effect on driving. Other illnesses, such as heart disease, could seriously impair a person's ability to drive.

Some chronic illnesses require regular medications that can cause side effects that interfere with driving. Some people have diseases that cause sudden loss of consciousness or muscle control. Before these individuals can receive a driver's license, they must provide medical proof that their chronic illness is under control.

Whatever the illness or disability, everyone who can perform driving tasks safely and successfully can be licensed to drive when all other requirements are met. Sometimes people with certain disabilities are required to be tested more frequently to maintain driving privileges.

safe driving tip

It is illegal to park in handicapped-designated parking spaces unless you have special identification.

---

review it 6.3

1. What can you do to avoid the effects of fatigue while driving?

2. What are some possible indicators of exposure to excessive amounts of carbon monoxide? What should you do if you notice these symptoms?

3. How are drivers with permanent physical disabilities able to drive?

Critical Thinking

4. **Compare and Contrast** How might people with temporary and permanent disabilities approach driving differently?

5. **Evaluate** Why does fatigue probably cause so many accidents today?

IN YOUR COMMUNITY **Handicapped Parking** Is there misuse of handicapped parking in your community? Select an often-visited location, such as the post office or a grocery store, that has specially designated handicapped parking spaces. Visually observe the spaces on two different Saturdays to see how many vehicles use them. Also note if the vehicles are authorized to use the space by having a special license plate or card inside the car. Remember that you can't always see a person's disability, so you must observe the vehicle. Report your findings to the class.

CHAPTER 6 REVIEW

Lesson Summaries

6.1 EMOTIONS AND DRIVING

- Emotions affect how you drive. Controlling your emotions helps you reduce and manage risk.

- As a passenger, you can help the driver remain calm and focused on the driving task.

- Control your emotions; don't let emotions control you when driving. Strong emotions result in focusing on a single item or event rather than the big picture.

6.2 PHYSICAL SENSES AND DRIVING

- Visual acuity is how well you see objects. You use your central vision to see things clearly. Your fringe and peripheral vision allow you to see a wider angle than central vision, as much as 180 degrees to the sides.

- Color blindness, depth perception, night vision, glare, and speed can affect your vision while driving.

- Your senses of hearing, smell, and motion help you drive safely.

- Limit sensory distractions while driving. Operating the car stereo, talking on the phone, playing loud music, and wearing headphones all divert your senses away from driving.

6.3 PHYSICAL LIMITATIONS

- Fatigue is a temporary disability that impairs driving. Rest is the best solution.

- Medications and carbon monoxide have physical effects on drivers.

- Many people with permanent disabilities can drive. Special adaptive equipment and learning how to compensate are critical for operating a vehicle safely.

Chapter Vocabulary

- aggressive driving
- carbon monoxide
- central vision
- chronic illness
- color blindness
- depth perception
- disability
- emotion
- field of vision
- fringe vision
- glare recovery time
- glare resistance
- night blindness
- peripheral vision
- permanent disability
- road rage
- speed smear
- temporary disability
- tunnel vision
- visual acuity

Write the word or phrase from the list above that completes the sentence correctly.

1. _____ is driving in a way that causes harm to others.

2. _____ is the time your eyes need to regain clear vision after being affected by glare.

3. A person with a condition that limits their normal daily activities for a limited time is said to have a(n) _____.

4. The narrow, 10-degree area that drivers can focus on is called their _____.

5. A person who has difficulty distinguishing colors has _____.

6. A condition that permanently limits a person's daily activities is called a(n) _____.

 **STUDY TIP**

Vocabulary Cards Write vocabulary terms on one side of a card and definitions on the other side. Try to define each word. Flip the card over to check your response.

Checking Concepts

LESSON 6.1

7. What effects can strong emotions have on your ability to drive?

8. What can you do to control your emotions while driving?

9. How are aggressive driving and road rage similar? How do they differ?

LESSON 6.2

10. What roles do central vision and fringe vision play in your driving?

11. How can drivers compensate for poor depth perception?

12. How can senses other than vision assist you when driving?

LESSON 6.3

13. What can you do to combat fatigue?

14. How can you avoid carbon monoxide?

15. How can permanently disabled drivers compensate for their disabilities?

Critical Thinking

16. Apply Concepts Besides there being less light, why might many older drivers avoid driving at night?

17. Decide You are stopped in heavy traffic and have no alternative other than waiting. A driver pulls up behind you and starts yelling and blowing the horn. What should you do to maintain control of your emotions? Why is this important?

You're the Driver

18. Compare and Contrast How is a driver with a broken leg similar to a driver who is paralyzed from the waist down? How do they differ?

19. Evaluate What are the physical and emotional effects of vehicle speed on a driver?

20. Identify How are the passengers in the picture below affecting the driver? What should they be doing to help?

21. Decide What affect could the argument between the two people in the picture below have on the driver's ability to drive?

Preparing for the Test

Choose the letter of the answer that best completes the statement or answers the question.

1. The vision that is sensitive to movement and light is a person's
   a. peripheral vision.
   b. central vision.
   c. tunnel vision.
   d. field of vision.

Use the photo below to answer Question 2.

2. In order for a person to park in this space, what is required?
   a. A person riding in the vehicle must be in a wheelchair.
   b. An able-bodied person must be present to assist the disabled person.
   c. The vehicle must have a special license plate or card inside.
   d. The vehicle must have special equipment.

3. When is glare resistance worst?
   a. when driving in a blinding snowstorm
   b. when driving in traffic during heavy rain
   c. when driving in thick fog during the day
   d. when driving in very sunny conditions

4. In order to drive with any disability, the most important thing a driver should do is
   a. drive at off-peak times.
   b. have a cell phone at all times.
   c. use alternative routes.
   d. know how to compensate for the disability.

Use the art below to answer Question 5.

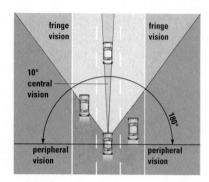

5. The part of your vision that you use to focus and to direct attention toward your target is called
   a. field of vision.   c. fringe vision.
   b. central vision.   d. peripheral vision.

6. What can a driver do to avoid or recover from glare?
   a. Squint and glance to the side.
   b. Speed up and change lanes.
   c. Turn on high-beam headlights.
   d. Close his or her eyes and hit the brakes.

7. Where is carbon monoxide most likely to be found?
   a. in fuel
   b. in an engine
   c. in the passenger compartment
   d. in a vehicle's exhaust

8. Which is the best way for a driver to prevent fatigue?
   a. Talk to yourself.
   b. Sing.
   c. Open a window.
   d. Get ample rest before driving.

drive write

Persuasive Argument Who do you think is at greater risk when driving: a driver who, through an injury, has a temporary disability, or a licensed driver who has a permanent disability? Write one or two paragraphs explaining your response.

chapter 7

ALCOHOL, OTHER DRUGS, AND DRIVING

7.1 Effects of Alcohol on Driving Safely

7.2 Other Kinds of Drugs and Driving

7.3 Traffic Laws Governing the Use of Alcohol

7.4 Coping With Peer Pressure

KEY IDEA

How does understanding the effects of alcohol on a person's driving ability help keep you and others safe?

YOU'RE THE DRIVER ▶ **Alcohol** is the most abused drug in the United States, and it is the deadliest when someone drives after even one drink. Drinking impairs your judgment and decreases your skills.

127

EFFECTS OF ALCOHOL ON DRIVING SAFELY

 OBJECTIVES

- Explain how alcohol affects the mental and physical abilities needed for driving safely.
- Define blood-alcohol concentration (BAC).
- List and explain factors that affect blood-alcohol concentration.
- Compare myths and truths about the use of alcohol.

 VOCABULARY

- euphoria
- inhibitions
- alcoholism
- blood-alcohol concentration (BAC)
- designated driver

Alcohol is the most commonly used drug in our society. It is by far the most frequently used drug that leads to drivers being fatally injured. Even though it is illegal for teenagers to buy or consume alcohol, they represent a significant percentage of alcohol abusers. For teenage drivers in particular, the combination of inexperience and alcohol can be fatal.

All states enforce a minimum drinking age of 21. Laws against underage drinking and driving are vigorously enforced. Alcohol-related educational programs in schools and communities have increased. Unfortunately, despite these efforts to enforce laws and educate young drivers, alcohol-related collisions are still a major safety problem.

Alcohol Facts

Some people may not be aware that alcohol is categorized as a drug because it can be purchased legally by anyone over 21 years old. It is categorized as a drug because of the effects it has on the central nervous system.

There are different types of alcohol, including

- ethyl alcohol, or ethanol, also known as grain alcohol
- isopropyl alcohol, or isopropanol, also known as rubbing alcohol
- methanol, or methyl alcohol, also known as wood alcohol

Ethanol, or what is commonly referred to as alcohol, is found in the alcoholic drinks people consume.

The effects of drinking alcohol vary from person to person; however, everyone who drinks alcoholic beverages is affected to some degree. One of the most serious problems of drinking alcohol is people who drink and drive. Even a small amount of alcohol in your bloodstream can affect your coordination and ability to think clearly.

Alcohol and Your Driving Ability

Regardless of the type of alcoholic drink, as soon as the alcohol from even one drink reaches the brain, it affects the way a person thinks and behaves. The same amount of alcohol doesn't affect all people the same way; in fact, alcohol doesn't even affect the same person in the same way in all situations. The best way to avoid changes in your behavior and thinking is to abstain from drinking.

Effects on the Central Nervous System   It may be surprising to learn that alcohol is classified as a depressant. Alcohol acts on the central nervous system like an anesthetic, slowing the activity of the brain. Alcohol is not digested in the stomach. It is absorbed directly into the blood stream through the walls and linings of the entire digestive tract.

Once alcohol enters the bloodstream, it quickly flows to the brain. Alcohol has the greatest effect on the parts of the brain that control judgment and reasoning—the two most critical mental skills needed by drivers. Physical abilities become impaired soon afterward.

Effects on Judgment and Reasoning   A driver impaired by alcohol has a decreased ability to reason clearly and make sound judgments even though the driver may feel that these abilities are sharper, quicker, and more accurate than usual. But in fact, the opposite is true.

A person in this condition can develop a false feeling of well being, or **euphoria**. People who are in a euphoric state of mind may take chances they normally would not take, chances that may be deadly when behind the wheel of a car.

Alcohol also weakens a person's **inhibitions**, the forces of personality that restrain or hold back impulsive behaviors. As alcohol content in the body increases, a driver's inhibitions relax to the point that the driver might drive too fast, take needless risks, or even drive into high-risk situations without knowing or caring.

A driver whose judgment and reasoning abilities are impaired by alcohol cannot properly use the IPDE Process or Zone Control techniques. The driver is less able to interpret correctly what he or she sees. Scanning scenes may become erratic and the target area may become unclear.

FIGURE 1

EFFECTS OF ALCOHOL ON BEHAVIOR

Number of drinks in one hour	BAC	Effects
1 serving 	0.02–.03%	Inhibitions are lessened. Judgment and reasoning begin to be affected.
3 servings 	0.05–.09%	Unable to think clearly. Judgment and reasoning are not reliable. Muscular coordination is impaired.
4 servings 	0.10–.12%	After four drinks, hearing, speech, vision, and balance are affected. Most behaviors are affected.

Effects on Vision   One of the most dangerous effects of alcohol is impaired vision. Impairment occurs in visual acuity, peripheral vision, night vision, color vision, and depth perception. Impaired vision combined with diminished judgment and slow reaction time can cause a driver to be in a conflict. For example, the driver in **FIGURE 2** might not be able to identify the pedestrian in time to stop safely.

------- FIGURE 2 -------

A driver who's been drinking may have difficulty reacting. **Apply Concepts**   Why might a driver who has been drinking have difficulty seeing the pedestrian and avoiding conflict?

Visual acuity   After only a few alcoholic drinks, a driver's visual acuity and ability to focus become impaired. In addition, because alcohol distorts vision, it reduces the effectiveness of the driver's orderly visual search pattern. A driver who's been drinking is more likely to fixate his or her eyes in a stare, thus hindering the scanning and searching process. The driver is likely to look straight ahead or at any object that attracts his or her attention. A driver who stares is unaware of vehicles that may be to the side or to the rear.

Reflex action   Alcohol also affects the reflex action of the eyes. At night, this impairment can be critical. As headlights of oncoming vehicles come closer, the pupils of the eyes normally become smaller to shut out excess light. This reflex keeps you from being blinded by the glare of the headlights. When the lights have passed, the pupils enlarge again to let in all available light.

After a few drinks, this reflex action is impaired. The pupils do not become smaller quickly as the headlights approach, and they are slow to open after the bright lights pass. As a result, the driver can be temporarily blinded and may continue to have blurred vision for some time afterward.

Blurred vision   After excessive drinking, a person might see multiple images. Each eye normally picks up a separate image of an object. These two images are coordinated by the brain so that the person sees only one image. After several drinks, however, coordination of the images becomes impaired. When driving, the person might see numerous images of a roadway centerline or of traffic signs.

Depth perception   Alcohol impairs depth perception as well. The drinking driver may misjudge the distance of oncoming or cross-traffic vehicles, and actually see a vehicle farther away than it actually is. In addition, drivers who drink cannot accurately determine the speed or distance of approaching vehicles. These drivers even lose the ability to judge their own speed or stopping distance.

Peripheral vision Drinking also affects peripheral vision, narrowing it so the driver must turn and look to the sides for potential problems. Thus not only is the driver unable to avoid hazards, the driver actually becomes a hazard.

Physical Effects of Alcohol As alcohol enters the part of the brain that controls muscular movements, reflexes and balance begins to slow down. A driver who has been drinking alcohol may recognize a dangerous situation but the brain takes longer to process the information and react to the danger. Muscular coordination becomes slow and clumsy. A driver impaired by alcohol might oversteer, brake late, or accelerate suddenly.

As a person continues to drink, the center of the brain that controls breathing and heartbeat can become impaired. If a large amount of alcohol is consumed in a short period of time, the drinker becomes unconscious and death may follow. Long-term use of alcohol can lead to **alcoholism**, an addiction to alcohol.

Abusing alcohol or drinking inappropriately not only causes problems for drivers, but also has the potential to create problems for families and communities.

Alcohol in the Body

The amount of alcohol detected in a person's bloodstream is called **blood-alcohol concentration** (BAC). The level of intoxication is determined by the percentage of alcohol in the bloodstream. Beer, wine, and liquor can be thought of as "drinks." In standard sizes, all drinks have about the same amount of alcohol, as shown in **FIGURE 3**.

The word *proof* describes the strength of liquor. By dividing liquor's proof number by two, you can determine its approximate percentage of alcohol.

Factors Affecting BAC The percentage of alcohol in the bloodstream depends on the amount of alcohol consumed, the period of time (over which) alcohol is consumed, and body weight.

WHAT WOULD YOU SAY?

Peer Pressure You and your friend are at a party. Although you're not drinking, you notice that your friend is drinking. You know she is driving home after the party. What would you say to your friend?

FIGURE 3
The alcohol content of drinks varies. A standard drink can add about 0.02 to 0.03 percent to a person's BAC.

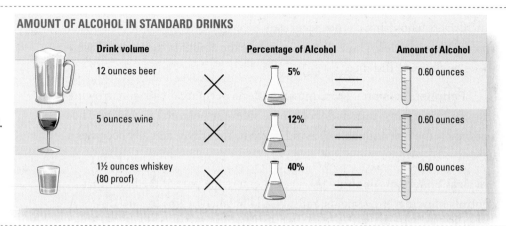

AMOUNT OF ALCOHOL IN STANDARD DRINKS

	Drink volume		Percentage of Alcohol		Amount of Alcohol
	12 ounces beer	×	5%	=	0.60 ounces
	5 ounces wine	×	12%	=	0.60 ounces
	1½ ounces whiskey (80 proof)	×	40%	=	0.60 ounces

The more a person drinks, the higher the BAC. A person's BAC rises more rapidly if less time elapses between drinks. If other factors are equal, a heavier person may be affected less by the same amount of alcohol than a person who weighs less.

To a lesser degree, some types of food in the stomach may make a difference in the rate of absorption of alcohol. However, even with food in the stomach, the absorption rate of alcohol into the bloodstream is rapid. When alcohol is mixed with carbonated beverages, the rate of absorption is even faster.

The safest decision a person can make about drinking alcohol is to abstain entirely.

Controlling Impairment

Alcohol is absorbed in the bloodstream very quickly but is slow to leave it. Alcohol continues to circulate throughout the body until the liver oxidizes it. The body rids itself of alcohol at a rate of about three fourths of a standard drink per hour.

After consuming three drinks in one hour, a person needs more than four hours to oxidize and eliminate most of the alcohol. Remember, only time can reduce the body's BAC and a person's degree of impairment.

Fact or Fiction?

▶ *Drinking black coffee, taking a cold shower, or exercising can make a drunk person sober.* **FICTION** These activities do not reduce BAC. The person may seem more alert but the BAC is not reduced.

FIGURE 4

The Time It Takes for the Body to Rid Itself of Alcohol		
Number of Drinks	**BAC Range**	**Approximate Time to Eliminate Alcohol**
	0.02–.03	1½ hours
	0.04–.06	3 hours
	0.06–.09	4 to 5 hours
	0.08–.12	5 to 7 hours

*The number will vary depending on the alcohol content of the drinks and rate of consumption.

If you drink faster than your body can eliminate the alcohol you've consumed, your BAC rises and eventually you will get drunk.

FIGURE 5
This woman has had several drinks at a party and now she's ready to go home.
Apply Understanding
Is there a way the woman can lower her BAC more quickly so that she can drive home within the hour?

▶ *One drink won't hurt.* FICTION Taking one drink can make it easier to take a second and third drink.

▶ *Beer will not make me drunk.* FICTION One 12-ounce can of beer contains as much alcohol as an average cocktail.

▶ *Driving is easier after a few drinks.* FICTION Consuming alcohol diminishes your driving abilities.

▶ *Young people cannot become problem drinkers.* FICTION Young people can become problem drinkers even as teenagers. There is no age limit to becoming an alcoholic.

Reducing Driving Risk

As a responsible driver, you can help reduce the risk of drinking and driving.

One way to reduce the risks of drinking and driving is to appoint a person to be a **designated driver**. The designated driver decides not to drink in order to stay sober so that he can drive without impairments.

Although you are a responsible driver, your friends may decide to drink and drive. Responsible friends can encourage friends to limit their drinking by getting them involved in other activities, encouraging them to decide on a limit of drinks in advance, asking them to avoid drinks with a high concentration of alcohol, encouraging them to sip a drink slowly so that they don't consume more than one alcoholic drink per hour, and making them aware of their behavior.

analyzing data

Blood Alcohol Concentration

Blood alcohol concentration (BAC) is a measure of the amount of alcohol in the bloodstream per 100 mL of blood. A BAC of 0.1 percent means that one tenth of 1.0 percent of the fluid in the blood is alcohol.

The graph shows the relative risk of being involved in a fatal crash as a result of the BAC of the driver. Study the graph before you answer the following questions.

1. **Reading Graphs** What does each bar on the graph represent?

2. **Analyzing Data** What trends do you see in the number of fatal crashes from age 17 to age 66+ based on the two ranges of BAC?

3. **Drawing Conclusions** Are young drivers less affected by alcohol than older drivers? Why do you think younger drivers in fatal crashes were less likely to have a BAC of 0.10 or more?

4. **Inferring** How does the consumption of alcohol affect driving risk for the average driver?

5. **Making Judgments** To minimize crashes and fatalities due to drunk driving, what do you think should be the legal limit of blood alcohol for drivers?

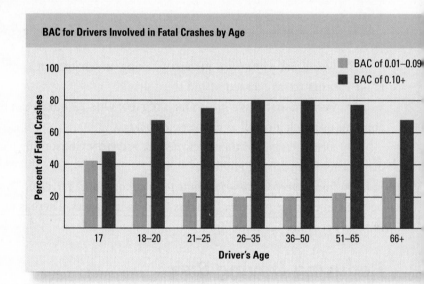

BAC for Drivers Involved in Fatal Crashes by Age

review it 7.1

1. What are some mental effects that alcohol can have on a driver who has been drinking? What are some physical effects?

2. What is BAC and what relationship does this have to one's driving abilities?

3. What factors can affect a person's BAC?

4. What are some common myths and facts about alcohol?

Critical Thinking

5. **Relate Cause and Effect** In order for one's BAC to rise, what has to occur?

 **Alcohol-Related Crashes** Visit your local law enforcement agency to get data for all reported crashes that were alcohol related for the past five years. Then compare your state's data for the same years. Share your findings with the class.

OTHER KINDS OF DRUGS AND DRIVING

Besides alcohol, there are many other types of drugs, legal and illegal. When used properly, most legal drugs have a positive effect. However, even medicines designed to be beneficial can cause hazardous driving situations.

Types of Drugs

Most drugs are classified according to the effects they have on the central nervous system and bodily functions. Some drugs depress, or slow down, the central nervous system. Other drugs stimulate, or speed up, the central nervous system. When legal drugs are taken as directed, they are relatively safe. However, any drug can become dangerous if it is taken in excess, combined with other drugs, or misused or abused.

Over-the-Counter Medicines   Drugs that are available without a doctor's prescription are called **over-the-counter medicines**, or OTCs. Many OTCs have side effects that can cause drowsiness, dizziness, slowed reaction time, and poor judgment.

When buying any medicine, read the label for warnings that could affect driving. Check with a pharmacist if you are not sure of labeling or possible side effects. Be sure to tell the pharmacist about any other medicines you might be taking in order to prevent possible drug interactions that can magnify side effects or pose a health threat.

Prescription Medicine   Drugs that cannot be purchased without a doctor's order, or prescription, are called **prescription medicines**. The law requires that drugs that have serious side effects or are potentially addictive be dispensed only under a physician's direction and guidance.

Depressants   A **depressant** is a class of drugs that depress, or slow down, the central nervous system. Depressants such as alcohol, barbiturates, sleeping pills, and tranquilizers are taken to relieve tension, calm nerves, or even treat high blood pressure.

A driver using depressants can become very relaxed, uninhibited, and less able to identify, predict, decide, and execute activities.

 **OBJECTIVES**

- Explain the difference between over-the-counter medicine and prescription medicine.
- Explain how depressants, stimulants, and hallucinogenic drugs affect a driver.
- Describe the effects of combining alcohol with other drugs.

 **VOCABULARY**

- over-the-counter medicine
- prescription medicine
- depressant
- stimulant
- synergistic effect

Stimulants   A **stimulant** is a drug that speeds up the central nervous system. Amphetamines are a type of stimulant. At first, stimulants create a feeling of high energy and alertness; however, once the feeling of alertness wears off, the driver quickly becomes very tired.

Some people misuse stimulants in order to stay awake while driving for long periods of time. Unfortunately, stimulants can create high-risk situations once the immediate effect wears off.

Hallucinogens   Hallucinogens are unpredictable, mind-altering drugs that can alter personality and cause panic or terror because they distort a person's sense of direction, distance, and time. Driving while under the influence of hallucinogens creates potentially deadly situations.

Marijuana is another powerful, mind-altering drug that affects the brain and other parts of the central nervous system. Marijuana can impair judgment, memory, depth perception, and coordination. A person who uses marijuana may think that the effects of the drug have worn off after a few hours, but in reality, driving abilities may be impaired for a very long time.

Combining Drugs

You should not take more than one prescription or over-the-counter medicine at the same time without consulting your doctor or pharmacist. In particular, alcohol and medicine are a potentially dangerous combination. If a person drinks alcohol while taking an antihistamine for a cold, for example, the central nervous system is slowed down much more than taking each by itself. When other drugs are combined with alcohol, the effects of both drugs can be multiplied. This is known as a **synergistic effect**.

review it 7.2

1. How does the purchase of over-the-counter medicines differ from the purchase of prescription medicines?

2. What effects do depressants, stimulants, and hallucinogens have on a driver?

3. What effect would combining alcohol with one or more other drugs have on a person's driving ability?

Critical Thinking

4. **Analyze**   All medicines are either over-the-counter or prescription. Why are some over-the-counter medicines not out on the shelves and readily available to all customers?

IN YOUR COMMUNITY   **Read Carefully**   Read the labels for the different medicines that you and others you live with commonly use. How many of the labels indicate warnings about driving? Compare your findings with your classmates.

TRAFFIC LAWS GOVERNING THE USE OF ALCOHOL

All 50 states have become uniform in requiring a person to be 21 years of age to purchase or consume alcoholic beverages. In an effort to further reduce alcohol-related collisions and fatalities, all states have set **illegal** *per se* **laws** establishing BAC levels of 0.08 or greater. Illegal *per se* laws are state laws that make it a criminal offense to operate a motor vehicle

- at or above a specified alcohol concentration in either the blood, breath, or urine; or
- with any amount of a drug, usually a controlled (illegal) substance, in the body.

Alcohol-related vehicle crashes dropped among teenagers after states raised the legal drinking age to 21. Young drivers are less likely than adults to drive after drinking. However, the risk of collision is substantially higher when teenagers drive after drinking.

Traffic Laws and Alcohol

Every state has an **implied consent law** for drivers. Implied consent means that anyone who operates a motor vehicle automatically consents to be tested for BAC and other drugs if stopped for suspicion of drug use while driving. If the driver does not cooperate with the police officer and refuses to be tested for BAC, the driver's license can be suspended.

Some states have a **zero tolerance law**, which means that if you are a driver under 21 years of age and you have a BAC greater than 0.02 (depending on the laws in your state), you are guilty of breaking the law. Some states have also adopted a policy of "zero tolerance means zero chances," which means drivers under the age of 21 receive harsh penalties for even their first offense.

A person who serves alcoholic beverages to an intoxicated individual may be liable for the damages caused by that individual. This is an example of a **dram shop law**. In some states, a person who serves the alcohol may also be liable for injuries sustained by the intoxicated individual.

OBJECTIVES

- Explain what is meant by the implied consent law.
- Describe zero tolerance levels of impairment, and tell how impairment can be detected and measured.
- Explain what actions a driver should take when stopped by a police officer.

VOCABULARY

- illegal *per se* laws
- implied consent law
- zero tolerance law
- dram shop law
- driving while intoxicated (DWI)
- driving under the influence (DUI)
- operating while impaired (OWI)
- field sobriety test
- nystagmus

Parents, or any adult, who decide to host parties and knowingly provide alcohol to individuals under the age of 21 can be sanctioned under their state's dram shop laws.

Levels of Impairment

Because research has demonstrated that the vast majority of drivers who have been drinking are significantly impaired at 0.08 percent, the Federal Government encouraged states to adopt a uniform level of 0.08 BAC, and states complied. All states have set a BAC level of 0.08 BAC at which drivers can be charged with **driving while intoxicated (DWI)**, or in some states driving while impaired (DWI).

Some states may use different terminology to describe drivers who are convicted of operating a vehicle above the legal limit. Some might use driving while intoxicated or impaired, others may use **driving under the influence (DUI)** or **operating while impaired or intoxicated (OWI)**.

Tests for Impairment

Law enforcement agencies place a high priority on enforcing DWI and DUI laws. Several tests, which can be administered in a police station or on the roadside, can be used to evaluate a person suspected of DWI or DUI.

Chemical Testing Chemical analysis of blood, urine, or breath can accurately determine BAC. The breath test is a widely used and simple analysis.

The breath-test machine most commonly used for determining BAC is an intoxilyzer. The person breathes into the intoxilyzer tube that determines the BAC. The results of the test are then displayed on both the intoxilyzer screen and a paper printout.

Field Sobriety Testing Law officers in many states can give a field sobriety test when they suspect a driver of DWI or DUI. A **field sobriety test** includes a series of on-the-spot roadside tests such as coordination and eye checks that help a police officer detect driver impairment.

FIGURE 6

The intoxilyzer can determine a person's BAC. The results of the test are admissible evidence in court.

One eye-check test is the horizontal-gaze **nystagmus** test, which refers to the involuntary jerking of the eyes as the person gazes to the side. Most people show some nystagmus as their eyes track from straight ahead to the side. The test determines the point where the jerking begins. As a person's BAC level increases, the jerking begins at an earlier point.

Trained officers can accurately estimate a person's BAC to within 0.02 percent of chemical test readings.

Other field sobriety tests can determine both physical and mental impairment. A person's balance, coordination, the ability to follow simple instructions, and the ability to perform two tasks at once may be tested. The inability to perform two tasks at once is called divided-attention impairment.

A simple divided-attention test might require the driver to walk heel to toe a certain number of steps while at the same time giving an oral count of the number of steps taken.

FIGURE 7

The police officer has stopped this driver on suspicion of intoxication and is conducting a field sobriety test, a finger-to-nose check.

Penalties for Conviction

The penalties for conviction of driving while intoxicated and driving under the influence involve one or more of the following:

- suspension or revocation of driver's license
- payment of a fine
- serving a prison term
- community service

The most common penalty is suspension of the driver's license for a specified amount of time. Penalties are most severe if an intoxicated driver is involved in a collision. If a fatality results from the collision, the driver could be found guilty of manslaughter or even murder.

Drivers who are convicted of a second DWI or DUI offense usually receive much harsher penalties than for the first conviction. Licenses can be revoked for as long as three years; prison sentences can be longer; and fines can be higher.

DID YOU KNOW?

Underage Drinking and Driving If you are under 21 and drive after consuming alcohol, you are breaking two laws. You are breaking the law against underage drinking and the law against driving while under the influence of alcohol.

FIGURE 8

If stopped by a police officer, remain calm, stay in the vehicle, keep hands in plain sight of the officer, and follow the officer's directions.

If You Are Stopped by a Police Officer

When a driver sees the flashing lights of a police vehicle in the rearview mirror, it is usually a signal to pull over and stop. If you see such a signal, slow your vehicle until you are sure the officer is signaling you. Pull over to the right and stop in a safe place. You might need to pull into a parking lot or a side street out of the way of traffic. Keep your hands visible as the officer approaches.

Stay in your vehicle and follow the instructions the officer gives you. You will be required to show your driver's license, and in states with mandatory insurance laws, you will need to show your certificate of insurance.

review it 7.3

1. What is the implied consent law for drivers, and what is likely to happen if a driver refuses to take a BAC test if asked to take one by a police officer?

2. What are zero tolerance levels of impairment and how can they be measured?

3. What are two things you should do if you are ever stopped by a law enforcement officer?

Critical Thinking

4. **Apply Concepts** Why do you think implied consent is not specifically limited to those who have received and hold a driver's license?

5. **Analyze** If drinking under the age of 21 is illegal in all states, why do some state's zero tolerance laws prohibit driving with a BAC level of 0.02 as its level instead of a BAC level of 0.00?

 **BAC Testing** What law enforcement agencies are in your area? What BAC testing equipment do they use? Interview a representative from each agency that is responsible for the agency's BAC testing equipment. Find out the cost for each piece of equipment, and how many of each type the department has to use. Share your findings with the class.

COPING WITH PEER PRESSURE

People's decisions are influenced by many factors, including pressure from individuals or groups. These influences can create conflicts or uncertainty about decisions that affect a person's future. Many decisions are made based on positive peer pressure or negative peer pressure.

Understanding Peer Influence and Pressure

Peers greatly influence each other because people naturally want to belong to, and be accepted by, a group. Some of the strongest influences in a person's life are the attitudes and actions of friends and peers.

Peer pressure and peer influence are factors that affect peoples' decisions and actions. **Peer pressure** is an external force that results from peers trying to influence you to do certain things or act a certain way. **Peer influence** is an internal force created out of a desire to be accepted.

Positive Peer Pressure   When peers exert a pressure on you in a positive way, they want to help and encourage you to do your best and stay safe. Students in **FIGURE 9** are demonstrating positive peer pressure by cheering for their friends.

Talking a friend out of drinking alcoholic beverages at a party or refusing to ride with someone who has been drinking are examples of positive peer pressure. Exerting positive peer pressure on friends can also help strengthen self-esteem in young people because they can see themselves as leaders.

Negative Peer Pressure

Negative peer pressure occurs when others, who don't have your best interests in mind, encourage you to do something that you believe is wrong or dangerous. For example, friends who tell you that you can drive safely after consuming alcohol are exerting negative peer pressure.

Some people might also

 OBJECTIVES

- Describe how peer influence and peer pressure might affect a person's decision about drinking and driving.
- List five steps involved in making a responsible decision.
- Explain the meaning of peer education.
- Explain why everyone should share the responsibility of preventing friends from drinking and driving.
- Identify five different ways to say no to peer pressure.

VOCABULARY

- peer pressure
- peer influence
- peer education

FIGURE 9
These girls are cheering for their friend as she races past them.

submit to negative peer influence, which occurs when a person feels pressure to use alcohol or other drugs just to fit in with a group. Refusing to do things that you believe are wrong and being able to say no to others are signs of responsible, mature behavior and positive peer influence.

Peer Refusal Skills

Refusal skills are all about being able to say no. Knowing ahead of time why, when, and how to say no empowers you and others who hold similar beliefs not to be pressured and to say no.

Sometimes, it's easy to say no, and other times it's not so easy. The desire to be accepted is strong, but when the influence being exerted upon you involves what you believe to be a bad decision with short- or long-term negative consequences, knowing different ways to say no empowers you to be a responsible person.

Different situations call for different ways to say no. Below are some examples of ways you can say no, especially when you are facing negative peer pressure.

Use Humor   A joke can change the tone of things if you feel the conversation is too serious. Humor also helps to change the direction or focus of the peer pressure being exerted upon you.

Walk Away   Say no and walk away, or just walk away from the person or people trying to engage you in behavior that is not in your best interest.

Ask a Question   Say no and then rephrase the suggestion as a question. For example, you might say, "No. Why would I want to risk not being able to get my driver's license?"

Repeat No   Keep saying no. It can buy you time to consider another response. The more you say no, the easier it is to reaffirm your position.

Avoid the Situation   If you know your friends will be trying to influence you to do something you think is wrong or do not want to do, avoid situations where they have the chance to exert their pressure and influence.

Ignore the Pressure   Don't respond when asked to participate in hazardous behavior. Divert your attention or start a conversation with someone else.

Prepare Reasons   Have a reason for saying no and share that reason. You could say, "I signed a contract with my parents agreeing not to drink, and I need to honor that agreement."

Provide Alternatives Suggest an alternative activity to the irresponsible behavior being suggested.

Use Teamwork Team up with others who feel the same way you do and who will support you when you say no. Sometimes having others around you who will say the same thing makes saying no a little easier.

Be Firm If all else fails, firmly say, "No, thanks!" in such a way that the other person understands that you will not be persuaded to do anything dangerous or against your values.

It takes time, effort, and practice to fully develop different and effective refusal skills. The more you plan ahead and practice, the easier it becomes to apply refusal skills effectively. You want to be accepted by your peers, as we all do, but keep in mind that you have the right and a responsibility to yourself, your family and loved ones to say no when faced with negative pressure to put yourself in danger.

Making Responsible Decisions

Learning how to make responsible decisions can help you be more in control of your life. Following the five steps listed in **FIGURE 11** will help you make responsible decisions.

Each person must make his or her own decision whether or not to drink alcohol. The best decision is to choose not to drink. However, as a nondrinker, you must share the concern and care about people who drink and drive.

Although people hesitate to interfere in other people's lives, most people wisely realize that they are being caring friends when they prevent friends from driving after drinking.

Student Programs

Underage drinking is a national problem with many causes and no simple solutions. Many schools have student

----- FIGURE 10 -----
You are walking home from school and you see your friend's car parked nearby. Besides your friend, there are two other people in the car nearby who you don't know. As you walk over to talk to your friend, someone extends a beer to you. **Refusal Skills** What are two ways you could say no?

FIGURE 11 STEPS FOR MAKING RESPONSIBLE DECISIONS

1. Know when a decision is needed.

2. Consider the choices.

3. Consider the consequences and ask yourself these questions:
   - Is it legal?
   - Is it safe?
   - What would my parents and other family members think?
   - Does it show respect for myself and others?

4. Decide which choice is best.

5. Evaluate your decision to know if it was a responsible one.

programs that educate students on how to combat underage drinking. Communities also offer support and education programs to combat drinking.

Peer Education   **Peer education** is a process in which young people help other young people make decisions and determine goals. Peer programs may be known by many other names, including peer counseling, peer mentoring, or peer helpers.

Many young people are more sensitive to the thoughts and opinions of their peers than to the thoughts and opinions of adults. Peer groups have properly trained peer leaders who can be more than a friend or a considerate listener. Peer leaders learn specific skills such as communication and problem solving in order to help others deal effectively with problems through activities that develop cooperation, trust, support and confidence.

Many schools have developed programs through the assistance of other organizations to help influence people about the harmful effects of alcohol as well as the problem of drinking and driving, including Mothers Against Drunk Driving (MADD), Alliance Against Intoxicated Motorists (AAIM), and Students Against Destructive Decisions (SADD).

review it 7.4

1. How do peer pressure and peer influence differ? How might peer pressure influence your decision to drink and drive?

2. What are the five steps for making responsible decisions?

3. Why should everyone share the responsibility of not letting friends drive after drinking?

Critical Thinking

4. **Apply Concepts**   Why is it a good idea for young people to develop more than one way to say no?

IN YOUR COMMUNITY   **Is It Worth the Risk?**   Does your state or city have sanctions against underage individuals being at a party where alcohol is present and being consumed? Interview a local police officer to find out. Then create a chart listing the potential sanctions for underage individuals attending such a function.

CHAPTER 7 REVIEW

Lesson Summaries

7.1 EFFECTS OF ALCOHOL ON DRIVING SAFELY

- A person's BAC is affected by the amount of alcohol consumed, the time over which alcohol is consumed, a person's body weight, and the presence (or lack) of food in the stomach.

7.2 OTHER KINDS OF DRUGS AND DRIVING

- Drugs can cause a driver to lose inhibitions and can impair judgment, memory, depth perception, and coordination.
- Combining alcohol with other drugs often results in synergistic effects, which means the effects are multiplied.

7.3 TRAFFIC LAWS GOVERNING THE USE OF ALCOHOL

- Anyone who operates a motor vehicle is assumed to have given consent to a BAC test.
- If an officer signals you to stop, slow down, pull over, and stop as soon as it is safe to do so.

7.4 COPING WITH PEER PRESSURE

- To make a responsible decision, consider your options and consider the consequences before you decide.

 **STUDY TIP**

Make flash cards for all the vocabulary words. On the back of each card, write the definition. With a partner, quiz each other on the meanings of the words and then offer one example for each definition. Take turns.

Chapter Vocabulary

- alcoholism
- blood-alcohol concentration (BAC)
- depressant
- designated driver
- dram shop law
- driving under the influence (DUI)
- driving while intoxicated (DWI)
- euphoria
- field sobriety test
- illegal *per se* laws
- implied consent law
- inhibitions
- intoxicated
- nystagmus
- operating while impaired (OUI)
- over-the-counter medicine
- peer education
- peer influence
- peer pressure
- prescription medicine
- stimulant
- synergistic effect
- zero tolerance law

Write the word or phrase from the list above that completes the sentence correctly.

1. A(n) _____ is a drug that tends to slow down the central nervous system.

2. _____ requires a doctor's permission to obtain.

3. _____ is the amount of alcohol in a person's blood, expressed as a percentage.

4. The forces of personality that restrain a person's impulsive behavior are called _____.

5. The involuntary jerking of the eyes as a person gazes to the side is called _____.

6. A(n) _____ is an effect that often results when taking two or more medications or drugs.

7. _____ are laws that state if a person has a BAC over a certain amount, they are legally impaired.

Checking Concepts

LESSON 1

8. What effect does alcohol have on a person's driving ability?

9. What measurement is used to determine a person's level of impairment?

10. What are three factors that affect the amount of alcohol in a person?

LESSON 2

11. How can depressants affect a person mentally?

12. How might a person be affected if they combine alcohol with some other medication?

LESSON 3

13. If a state has a zero-tolerance level of 0.02 percent BAC, what does this mean?

14. What effect does an implied consent law have on a driver?

15. What should a driver do if they are stopped by a police officer at night?

LESSON 4

16. What steps should a person take if he or she wishes to make a responsible decision about alcohol?

17. State three ways to say no to your peers?

18. How does peer influence affect a person's decision to be a responsible driver?

Critical Thinking

19. **Analyze** Why is it important to practice refusal skills?

20. **Compare** Compare the different BAC tests that the police can request a person to take if stopped.

You're the Driver

21. **Identify** Using the framework of IPDE, explain how alcohol affects your ability to drive.

22. **Decide** What strategies can you use to overcome negative peer pressure as it relates to drinking as well as drinking and driving?

23. **Predict** The driver in the picture below has been pulled over by police for suspicion of driving while under the influence of alcohol. What types of tests might the driver be asked to take? What can the tests detect and measure?

24. **Decide and Execute** Why is it important that this woman read the labels before she takes over-the-counter medicine and drives?

Preparing for the Test

Choose the letter of the answer that best completes the statement or answers the question.

1. All states have adopted illegal *per se* laws establishing a BAC level of
   a. 0.15 percent.
   b. 0.10 percent.
   c. 0.08 percent.
   d. 0.02 percent.

2. The most common penalty for a first-time conviction of DWI or DUI is
   a. driver's license suspension.
   b. a prison term.
   c. payment of a fine.
   d. vehicle impoundment.

Use the art below to answer Question 3.

YOU DRINK YOU DRIVE YOU LOSE

3. This sign refers to
   a. underage drivers.
   b. commercial drivers.
   c. race-car drivers.
   d. all drivers.

4. To which of the following groups do implied consent laws specifically apply?
   a. underage drinkers
   b. passengers
   c. underage-drinking pedestrians
   d. drivers

Use the art below to answer Question 5.

KNOW WHEN TO SAY WHEN

5. What does the above message most likely refer to?
   a. knowing when it is safe to drink
   b. peer refusal skills
   c. responsible adult drinking tip
   d. tip for controlling passengers' emotions

6. A two-ounce shot of 86-proof liquor contains
   a. 86 percent alcohol.
   b. the same amount of alcohol as 20 oz. of 4.5% beer.
   c. 43% of its volume as alcohol.
   d. the same amount of alcohol as 3–5 oz. of wine.

7. The part of a person's brain first affected by alcohol is the part
   a. controlling reasoning and judgment abilities.
   b. controlling vital functions.
   c. of the brain controlling visual perception.
   d. of the brain controlling eating habits.

8. What advice should you give to a friend who is planning to go to a party and drink?
   a. Don't drink on an empty stomach and drive.
   b. Don't drive; make sure there is a designated driver.
   c. Just be careful if you drive after drinking.
   d. Wait an hour after your last drink before driving.

drive write

Age Limit Do you think the legal drinking age should be lowered to 18 or remain at 21? Write two or three paragraphs supporting your position, citing facts and figures from reliable sources.

chapter 8

MANAGING DISTRACTIONS

8.1 Driver Inattention and Distractions

8.2 Distractions Inside the Vehicle

8.3 Distractions Outside the Vehicle

KEY IDEA

How can you manage distractions that take your focus away from the driving task?

YOU'RE THE DRIVER ▶ **Many** different things can distract you while driving. Some distractions come from inside the vehicle and others from outside the vehicle. When you drive, are you easily distracted, or are you able to cope with distractions better than others?

DRIVER INATTENTION AND DISTRACTIONS

 OBJECTIVES

- Describe what is meant by driver inattention.
- Identify how distracted driving differs from inattentive driving.
- List the four categories of driving distractions.
- Describe what drivers can do to avoid driver inattention and distraction.

 VOCABULARY

- driver inattention
- distracted driving
- cognitive distraction
- visual distraction
- auditory distraction
- biomechanical distraction

Drivers who reach for items on the dash or in the glove compartment, eat or drink while driving, tune the radio, or chat on a cell phone are inattentive drivers. According to the NHTSA, driver inattention is a major factor in most crashes and near-crashes. In one study, it was determined that 80 percent of crashes and at least 65 percent of near-crashes involved some form of driver inattention within three seconds prior to the crash.

Driver Inattention and Distracted Driving

Driving is a complex task. Safe driving requires drivers to stay focused on the driving task. When a driver's awareness and focus drift to anything other than the driving task, it is called **driver inattention**. Drivers who are inattentive may look but not see conflicts ahead or around their vehicles.

Driver inattention may be unintentional. Fatigue, for example, is usually not an intentional physical condition, yet fatigue often causes drivers' attention to drift away from the driving task.

When an event, person, activity, or object draws a driver's attention away from the driving task, it is an example of **distracted driving**. Distraction occurs when a driver chooses to do something that is not necessary to the driving task.

A key difference between driver distraction and driver inattention in general is that driver distraction is caused by an event that directs the focus of a driver away from the driving task. If a drink falls out of its holder and spills onto the floor while a driver is making a turn, the driver is likely to become distracted, as he or she quickly focuses on the falling cup rather than the turn. Having taken his or her eyes off the road, the driver will most likely have to make a dangerous, unplanned steering recovery, which has the potential of conflict with other vehicles. Driver inattention, on the other hand, does not necessarily deal with a specific event.

FIGURE 1 ATTENTION STATUS OF DRIVERS IN CRASHES

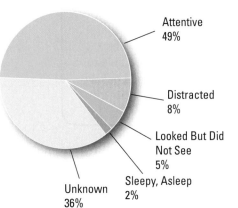

Attentive 49%

Distracted 8%

Looked But Did Not See 5%

Sleepy, Asleep 2%

Unknown 36%

Distraction Classifications

The NHTSA groups driver distractions into either those that occur inside the vehicle or those that occur outside the vehicle. These distractions fall into four different categories: cognitive, visual, auditory, and biomechanical.

Cognitive Distractions   A **cognitive distraction** is when your mind is lost in thought or in a daydream. Talking on a cell phone while driving is a cognitive distraction. You are not focusing mentally on the primary task of driving.

Visual Distractions   A **visual distraction** is anything that causes you to take your eyes off the roadway ahead, as shown in **FIGURE 2**.

Auditory Distractions   Any distractions caused by sounds are **auditory distractions**. A crying child or a siren can easily divert a driver's attention away from the driving task.

Biomechanical Distractions   Any mechanical act not specifically related to driving that is performed by a driver is a **biomechanical distraction**. Biomechanical distractions include pushing a button, turning a dial, or picking up a CD or soft drink.

There are things you can do when driving to avoid being distracted. If you are fatigued, stop and stretch, or switch drivers. Limit conversations with passengers; avoid emotional conversations.

Read the owner's manual to understand how to work the controls and any particular features in the car. Adjust your seat, mirrors, and radio presets before entering traffic.

Take control of the environment inside your vehicle by setting rules for passengers and securing loose objects. After all, not only are your life and vehicle at stake, but so are those of others.

FIGURE 2
Some distractions have intentionally been placed in strategic locations to catch drivers' attention.

review it 8.1

1. When is a driver considered to be inattentive?
2. What criterion determines whether something is a driving distraction?
3. Describe the four categories of driver distractions and give an example of each.
4. What actions can a driver take to avoid being distracted?

Critical Thinking

5. **Compare and Contrast**   How does a situation involving driver inattention differ from a situation involving driver distraction? How are they similar?

IN THE PASSENGER SEAT   **Help with Distractions**   As a passenger, what can you do to help keep a driver from being distracted?

lesson 8.2

DISTRACTIONS INSIDE THE VEHICLE

 OBJECTIVES

- Identify five different categories of inside-the-vehicle distractions.
- Explain why cell phone usage while driving can be distracting.
- Describe how a driver can reduce inside-the-vehicle distractions.

 VOCABULARY

- projectile

Driver distractions or inattentive driving are estimated to play a part in one out of every four motor vehicle crashes. This means drivers who are distracted or inattentive are a factor in 1.5 million collisions each year, and more than 4,300 crashes each day in the U.S.!

The AAA Foundation for Traffic Safety suggests that when a driver's eyes are away from the driving scene ahead for more than two seconds, the odds of being in a crash or near-crash double.

Cell Phones

Cell phones, once considered a luxury item, are now used by a substantial majority of Americans. While some people use cell phones only for making calls, many newer models also act as multimedia systems that can take and share photos, send and receive text messages, act as navigational systems, and access the Internet. As the usage and capabilities of cell phones have increased, so, too, has the potential for driver distractions.

Hazards Distractions such as reaching to pick up a cell phone, making or receiving a call, and sending or receiving a text message are common with

FIGURE 3
CELL PHONE BEHAVIOR COMPARED BY SELECTED DEMOGRAPHICS

Driver Cell Phone Use as Observed from the Roadside		
	Drivers holding phones to their ears	Drivers speaking with headsets
All Drivers	5%	0.6%
Males	4%	0.4%
Females	6%	0.8%
Apparent Age:		
16–24	8%	0.7%
25–69	4%	0.6%
Drivers with:		
no passengers	6%	0.8%
at least one passenger	2%	0.1%

cell phone usage. In particular, carrying on a conversation on a cell phone while driving causes a lack of focus on the driving task since your attention is on the conversation.

Conversations can be a cognitive distraction. Many drivers unknowingly reduce their vehicle speed while talking on a cell phone. This behavior can cause conflict if vehicles behind are driving at the speed limit, especially at night.

As awareness of the hazards of cell phone usage while driving has increased, efforts have been made to reduce driver distraction. Educating the public about the hazards of cell phone usage while driving, the introduction of hands-free technology, as shown in **FIGURE 4**, and even legislation in some states outlawing non-emergency cell phone usage while driving are some of the efforts being made to promote low-risk driving.

Vehicle Equipment or Controls

Advancements in technology have resulted in many different systems and components for vehicle safety, comfort, information, control, and entertainment. Unfortunately, these advancements have also created increased opportunities for driver distraction. Drivers who are unfamiliar with new controls and displays can easily overload themselves with cognitive distractions.

Many of today's vehicles are equipped with video entertainment systems. Some states have laws prohibiting any visible video displays within view of the driver.

Elaborate vehicle sound systems have volume capabilities that can hinder a driver's ability to hear other vehicles and can create an audible distraction to people outside the vehicle.

In some communities, local ordinances prohibit very loud volume levels. Responsible drivers keep their sound systems down to levels at which they are able to hear other vehicles around them and they do not distract others.

FIGURE 4 This driver is using hands-free technology to send and receive calls without having to remove a hand from the steering wheel.

FIGURE 5
Speakers and sound systems, such as the one in this photo, have become quite popular. **Predict** What distractions might be related to such a system?

Although a vehicle navigation system provides drivers with information about a vehicle's position and guides drivers to a destination, it is a source of potential distraction.

Drivers' focus can be diverted because they look at the screen, listen to directions, or try to input data into the system while driving. Passengers can help reduce driver distraction by becoming an extra set of eyes and ears when using a vehicle's navigational system.

Other Distractions

Animals or insects that fly into your car, eating and drinking, and even passengers can create distractions.

Animals and Insects   A driver who is allergic to bee stings may panic and focus all attention to a bee in the car instead of the roadway ahead and surrounding traffic. Before driving, check to see if there are any insects in the vehicle and deal with them before you start driving. If you are already in traffic and notice a bee or insect, stay calm, and look for a spot to safely pull out of traffic and stop; then deal with the bee or insect.

Large animals that move around can distract drivers and even block their view. Holding a pet while driving is not only an unsafe behavior, it also places the pet at a higher risk of being injured or killed should a crash occur.

Food and Drink   Eating or drinking while driving can create both visual and biomechanical distractions. Drivers may look at their food instead of

FIGURE 6   If you have a pet, invest in a pet safety belt and make sure you use it any time you have your pet in the vehicle.

the road, and when they remove a hand from the wheel to hold the food or drink, they leave only one hand to control the steering wheel. In extreme cases, drivers have been seen driving along with both hands holding food and drink items.

Passengers The behavior of passengers can easily distract a driver. Yelling or screaming, engaging in loud or emotional conversations, turning up the sound-system volume, or tossing objects around inside the vehicle can easily divert a driver's attention away from the roadway. If a passenger becomes disruptive, and the behavior continues after asking them to stop, pull over safely, stop the vehicle, and resolve the situation before getting back into traffic.

Research has shown that young, novice drivers are more likely to be distracted by peers in the vehicle while driving than older, more experienced drivers. As the number of passengers increases, so does the likelihood of driver distraction and the risk of being involved in a crash.

Loose Objects Objects hanging from the rearview mirror could move and fall due to a sudden stop or a turn taken too quickly. The same holds true for items placed on top of the dashboard or the rear window ledge. Such objects could even become **projectiles**, flying objects that could be a hazard to a driver or passenger. Before driving, clear all areas of loose objects. Secure or place them so they won't move around and become distractions or projectiles.

FIGURE 7

A cluttered back window ledge can block a driver's view of the traffic scene behind. **Identify** What type of impact force do you suppose an airborne tissue box traveling 55 mph would have on a passenger or driver?

review it 8.2

1. What are five different categories of inside-the-vehicle distractions?

2. Why is dialing a cell phone or text messaging while driving distracting?

3. What are ways a driver can reduce inside-the-vehicle distractions?

Critical Thinking

4. **Apply Concepts** Why is it a good idea to limit passengers for young, novice drivers?

IN THE PASSENGER SEAT **Drivers and Cell Phones** When riding as a passenger in a vehicle, look for other drivers at intersections. Make a note of each driver you observe, and if they are talking or using a cell phone. Also note any other inside-the-vehicle distractions you see. Share your findings with your class.

lesson 8.3
DISTRACTIONS OUTSIDE THE VEHICLE

 OBJECTIVES

- Identify the categories of outside-the-vehicle driver distractions.
- Explain how outside-the-vehicle distractions differ from distractions inside the vehicle.
- Describe how a driver can avoid outside-the-vehicle distractions.
- Explain ways a driver can avoid becoming a distraction to others.

 VOCABULARY

- gawking
- rubbernecking

Driving distraction-free is not easy. It takes commitment and a constant effort to stay focused on the driving task.

Outside-the-vehicle distractions are often more difficult to deal with than inside-the-vehicle distractions. With inside-the-vehicle distractions, you have more control of the environment, situation, and passengers. However, you have little, if any, control over people, objects, or events outside the vehicle.

Animals Outside the Vehicle

Animals, birds, reptiles, and many other creatures have the potential to be distractions, even when they pose no hazard to a driver's path of travel.

When drivers experience a situation involving an animal or bird that they rarely see, they often take their eyes off the road for longer than a quick glance. If there is something you would like to get a better look at, look for a safe place to pull out of traffic and stop your vehicle. Then take the time to appreciate the view or take a picture.

FIGURE 8

The driver has never seen an alligator in the road before. **Evaluate** How might a distraction like this cause a traffic conflict for other drivers approaching from the rear?

Objects Outside the Vehicle

While driving, you will come across some unusual objects on or along the road such as debris that has fallen off vehicles, signs and billboards, parked and disabled vehicles, and emergency vehicles.

In many cities, electronic traffic information signs are installed or temporarily placed close to the road.

These signs and boards are placed in such locations to reduce the distance you need to move your eyes and head to read their messages. The messages displayed are short yet informative, reducing the likelihood they will present a driving distraction while allowing drivers to read them.

Emergency vehicles are common distractions to drivers. Drivers often take their attention away from their immediate path of travel to try to see the emergency vehicle. If there are passengers, ask them to help you find the emergency vehicle. This allows you to maintain focus on the driving scene ahead.

Scenes and Events

Crash and Fire Scenes   Two major forms of distraction associated with crash scenes are **gawking**, which is when a person stares, and **rubbernecking**, which is when a person continually looks all around the scene. If you ever come upon a long line of backed-up traffic at a crash scene, you may have noticed how drivers often proceed past the scene very slowly, gawking at the crash scene before finally accelerating back up to highway speed. Their gawking is often what causes the traffic backlog, not the actual crash.

Gawking that causes a traffic backlog is often a major cause of rear-end collisions. Drivers coming onto the scene suddenly are unable to slow and stop before crashing into the vehicle ahead.

A large fire is quite a dynamic scene, requiring a lot of personnel and equipment. Within the first few minutes after a large fire has been identified, the traffic around the event becomes chaotic. Such a scene might include drivers striving to get out of the way or police vehicles helping to create a traffic perimeter around the area.

FIGURE 9

A variable electronic message sign (VMS) like this provides drivers with traffic information including traffic congestion information, estimated travel times to certain locations, and possible alternative traffic routes. They are also used to display AMBER alert information.

FIGURE 10

Predict   What can you do to avoid becoming distracted and becoming a hazard to others?

Emergency vehicles arriving and getting into position help create confusion and congestion. People may also wander around in an emotionally overwhelmed state making them unaware of the dangers around them.

Public Events   Imagine trying to exit a stadium parking lot after a major sporting event, with pedestrians walking and running all around you. Not only do you have to pay attention to the traffic ahead and to your sides, but you also have to pay attention to the crowds and their actions, which are a source of potential hazards and conflicts to your path of travel.

Events can also create visual distractions to drivers who take their eyes off the roadway and try to look at what's happening on the fields. Looking out at a soccer field, for example, could distract a driver long enough to avoid noticing—and being able to react to—pedestrians or a vehicle pulling out of a parking spot to enter the traffic flow.

As a driver, try to stay focused on the roadway and driving task ahead. Don't allow yourself, your actions, or your vehicle to become a distraction to others.

DID YOU KNOW?

Distractions   In a recent study, interviews were held with drivers who had been involved in crashes where at least one vehicle had to be towed. Of those drivers, 8.3 percent claimed to have been distracted. Of those distracted drivers, 29.4 percent reported outside-the-vehicle distractions.

---

review it 8.3

1. What are the four most common categories of outside-the-vehicle distractions?

2. Why can outside-the-vehicle distractions be more difficult to deal with than inside-the-vehicle distractions?

3. How can drivers empower themselves to avoid becoming distracted by objects and events outside the vehicle?

4. How can drivers avoid being a distraction to others?

5. What can drivers do to minimize inside-the-vehicle distractions?

Critical Thinking

6. **Analyze**   Why do you think some states have restrictions on the types, placement, and size of non-traffic signs and advertisements along their roadways?

IN YOUR COMMUNITY   **Outside Distractions**   Signs, billboards, and electronic advertisements are used by businesses and organizations to inform, create awareness, and advertise. Does your community have certain requirements or restrictions regarding such items? Is any consideration based on traffic safety issues? Research and share your findings with your classmates.

CHAPTER 8 REVIEW

Lesson Summaries

8.1 DRIVER INATTENTION AND DISTRACTIONS

- Driver inattention takes place when a driver's focus and attention are not on the driving task for any reason.

- Although distracted driving is a form of driver inattention, it differs in that it is usually triggered by some event.

- Almost every driving distraction can be labeled as a cognitive, visual, auditory, or biomechanical distraction.

8.2 DISTRACTIONS INSIDE THE VEHICLE

- Using a cell phone can divert a driver's mental and visual attention from the driving task.

- Drivers can minimize distractions within their vehicles by knowing the locations of controls; keeping the radio volume down to a level where they can still hear other vehicles' horns, and sirens of emergency vehicles; securing any objects or pets brought into the car; avoiding the use of electronic devices and cell phones while driving; not eating or drinking while driving; limiting conversations with passengers; limiting the number of passengers; and controlling passengers' behaviors.

8.3 DISTRACTIONS OUTSIDE THE VEHICLE

- Outside-the-vehicle distractions are usually related to people, animals, objects, or events.

- The biggest difference between an outside-the-vehicle distraction and an inside-the-vehicle distraction is that drivers have very little, if any, control over outside-the-vehicle distractions.

Chapter Vocabulary

- auditory distraction
- biomechanical distraction
- cognitive distraction
- distracted driving
- driver inattention
- gawking
- projectile
- rubbernecking
- visual distraction

Write the word or phrase from the list above that completes the sentence correctly.

1. When a driver's mental focus is on something other than the driving task, it is said to be a(n) _____.

2. When a driver stares at something, they are _____.

3. _____ occurs when a triggering event shifts a driver's focus away from the driving task to the event.

4. A(n) _____ causes drivers to take their eyes off the roadway.

5. When a driver's mind wanders or isn't focused on the driving task, it is called _____.

6. When a driver reaches over to pick up an object while driving, it is a(n) _____.

7. A loud sound that distracts a driver's focus away from the roadway is called a(n) _____.

 **STUDY TIP**

Categorize With classmates, interview experienced drivers about driving distractions. Write each one on a separate card. As a group, sort the cards into cognitive, audible, biomechanical, and visual distractions.

Checking Concepts

LESSON 1

8. What differentiates distracted driving from inattentive driving?

9. What steps and actions can drivers take to avoid driving inattentively or being distracted?

LESSON 2

10. What categories are associated with inside-the-vehicle distractions?

11. What steps or actions can a driver do to reduce distractions inside their vehicle?

12. How does hands-free technology help drivers from becoming distracted?

LESSON 3

13. What are the four categories of outside-the-vehicle distractions?

14. What might cause the driver of a vehicle to become a distraction to other drivers?

Critical Thinking

15. **Analyze** Why is it important to know how to operate the car's controls and equipment before starting the car?

16. **Relate Cause and Effect** How do advancements in technology create risk for you as a driver?

17. **Evaluate** Explain which is more difficult for a driver to manage: inside- or outside-the-vehicle distractions?

You're the Driver

18. **Execute** You are driving with an infant sibling safely secured in a child-safety seat in the back. Suddenly the baby begins to cry very loudly. What action should you take?

19. **Decide** You are using your vehicle navigation system as you drive some friends to a concert. Your friends tell you that the concert is in a different city than you had thought. What should you do to avoid being distracted while trying to recode your navigational device?

20. **Identify** How many different potential distractions can you identify in this picture?

21. **Identify and Predict** You are driving in a large urban area on a major highway. What do you see ahead that might help you? Why?

Preparing for the Test

Choose the letter of the answer that best completes the statement or answers the question.

1. Which of the following is more of a traffic hazard than a distraction?
   a. a muffler in your lane ahead
   b. a deer carcass on the shoulder
   c. a disabled vehicle on the side of the road
   d. a police vehicle following behind

2. When is using a cell phone while driving appropriate?
   a. on an open road with no traffic
   b. never
   c. to report an emergency
   d. to call home

3. What is the main purpose for passenger restrictions as part of GDL laws?
   a. to limit liability
   b. to reduce time on the road for novice drivers
   c. to gain driving experience with fewer distractions
   d. to reduce double dating

Use the photo below to answer Question 4.

4. Using this device while driving is an example of
   a. both cognitive and biomechanical distractions.
   b. both auditory and biomechanical distractions.
   c. a cognitive distraction only.
   d. an auditory distraction only.

5. Which of the following statements is not correct?
   a. Watching a DVD while driving is a driving distraction.
   b. Daydreaming is an example of driver inattention.

   c. Talking on a cell phone using hands-free technology is a distraction.
   d. Making a voice-activated cell phone call is not a distraction.

6. Distractions outside a vehicle are more easily managed
   a. during the morning than the afternoon.
   b. if the situation does not pose a threat to any of your zones.
   c. if it involves an animal alongside the roadway.
   d. if it can be identified within your immediate 3-second path of travel.

Use the photo below to answer Question 7.

7. This meal may become a biomechanical distraction because
   a. you will have to look at the wrapping to remove it.
   b. your friends will want you to share it.
   c. you will have to think about getting it home before it gets cold.
   d. you will take one hand off the steering wheel to eat while driving.

---

drive write 🚗

GDL Passenger Restrictions for All States   Should all states adopt uniform passenger and night-time driving restrictions for novice drivers? Write two or three paragraphs to support your position. Then submit it to your local newspaper for potential publication in its editorial section.

chapter 9

NATURAL LAWS AND CAR CONTROL

9.1 Gravity and Energy of Motion

9.2 Tires and Traction

9.3 Vehicle Balance and Control in Curves

9.4 Stopping Distance

9.5 Controlling Force of Impact

KEY IDEA

How do the laws of motion affect your ability to control your vehicle?

> **YOU'RE THE DRIVER** If you had been the driver of this car and were using your safety belt, an air bag would have helped to protect you from serious injury. To be a safe driver, you need to know about the laws of motion. How do these natural laws affect your ability to control your car and help you drive safely?

163

lesson 9.1
GRAVITY AND ENERGY OF MOTION

OBJECTIVES

- Describe how inertia affects your vehicle while going straight and while driving through a curve.
- Define momentum.
- Identify the factors that affect energy of motion.
- Explain how gravity affects your vehicle.

VOCABULARY

- inertia
- momentum
- energy of motion
- gravity

The motion of your vehicle is subject to the natural laws of motion. These laws include inertia, momentum, energy of motion, and gravity. In emergency situations, these natural laws can work for or against you.

Inertia, Momentum, and Energy of Motion

Objects that are at rest tend to stay at rest and objects that are moving tend to keep moving. This is the law of **inertia**. Inertia keeps a parked car at rest. For the car to move, it must be acted upon by forces produced by the engine. Once the car is moving, inertia causes the car and everything in it to continue moving in a straight line at a constant speed until acted upon by another force. FIGURE 1 shows three examples of how inertia affects passengers in cars.

You can feel inertia when a car brakes rapidly. The force of friction on the brakes causes the car to slow down. But as the car slows down, inertia causes your body to continue to move forward. You feel this inertia as you are pressed against your safety belt. If you were not wearing a safety belt, your body would continue to move forward until it was stopped by the dashboard or the windshield.

You also experience inertia when a car accelerates rapidly. As the car accelerates, you seem to be pushed back into your seat. But no force is pushing you back. Instead, your body continues to move at the old speed, while the car speeds up.

FIGURE 1

Vehicle weight and speed determine how much inertia is generated.

As car decelerates

As car accelerates

Around a curve

You also experience inertia when a car drives around a sharp curve. You feel as if you are being pulled toward the outside of the curve because inertia causes your body to continue in a straight line.

Momentum is the tendency of an object to stay in motion, or the inertia of an object in motion. The amount of momentum depends upon the object's weight and speed. Heavy vehicles have more momentum than light vehicles moving at the same speed. A fast car has more momentum than a slow car.

A moving object also has **energy of motion**, or kinetic energy. A vehicle's energy of motion changes in proportion to the weight of the vehicle. The more a vehicle weighs, the greater its energy of motion.

A vehicle's energy of motion is proportional to the *square* of its speed. If you double your speed, your vehicle will have *four times* as much energy of motion and will need *four times* as much distance to stop.

Gravity

Gravity is the force that pulls all things to Earth. Gravity also acts on you and your car.

The pull of gravity affects you as you drive up and down hills. When you drive uphill, the pull of gravity will cause you to lose speed.

When going downhill, gravity's pull will make you go faster. To control your speed, ease up on the accelerator and brake early. On a long downhill stretch, shift to a lower gear so the engine can slow the vehicle.

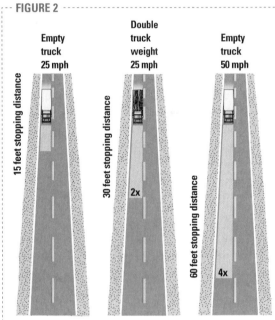

-- **FIGURE 2** --

A vehicle's energy of motion increases with weight and speed.

---

review it 9.1

1. How does inertia affect your vehicle and passengers?

Critical Thinking

2. Relate Cause and Effect Which would cause a greater change in energy of motion: doubling the weight of a vehicle or doubling its speed? Why?

IN THE PASSENGER SEAT **Laws of Motion** As a passenger, pay attention to situations in which the vehicle accelerates, slows down, and enters a curve. Record the effects you feel in the passenger seat under these conditions. Write a paragraph describing your findings.

lesson 9.2

TIRES AND TRACTION

OBJECTIVES

- Explain how traction controls your car.
- Describe the importance of tread and proper inflation in maximizing traction.
- Identify the driver actions that depend on traction and how they relate to vehicle control.
- Identify three factors that can reduce traction.

VOCABULARY

- friction
- traction
- tread
- blowout

How do you control your vehicle? Certainly the steering wheel, accelerator, and brake pedal are important. But you may be surprised to learn that your tires are a key part of your control system. The way your tires interact with the surface of the road is essential to safe driving.

Friction and Traction

The force that keeps a tire from sliding on the road is friction. **Friction** is the force that acts between materials as they move past each other. Friction is caused by tiny irregularities on the surface of the objects that are touching. You can feel the force of friction by rubbing your hands together—friction makes your hands get warmer.

When tires roll over the surface of the road, they create a form of friction called **traction**. Traction makes it possible for your vehicle to grip the road so you can control speed and direction. Press the accelerator and the tires on the drive wheels rotate. The traction of the tires on the roadway pushes your vehicle forward.

Squeeze the brake pedal and the friction of the linings against the brakes slows the four wheels. As the tires on these wheels slow, traction between the tires and road will slow your vehicle. Traction also enables your vehicle to turn left or right when the front wheels turn.

Tire Tread and Traction

The place where a tire touches the road is called its *footprint*. **FIGURE 3** shows each tire's footprint. Footprints are small—each is about the size of an adult's hand. These footprints are all you have for traction on the surface of the road.

The grooved surface of a tire is called **tread**. Tread provides the traction for starting, stopping, and gripping the road. This gripping action is critically important in preventing skids and hydroplaning. When the

FIGURE 3

The four footprints of your tires on the road are the only contact between your car and the road.

road is wet, water flows through the grooves in the tread and away from the tire, allowing the tire to grip the road.

A tire's ability to grip the road increases as the amount of tread touching the road increases. Tire size also affects the amount of tread and traction on the road. Use care when putting larger tires on a vehicle because they alter the performance characteristics of the vehicle. Check the owner's manual for your vehicle for the maximum recommended size of tire.

Inflation and Traction

Properly inflated tires can mean the difference between keeping or losing control. **FIGURE 4** shows how too much or too little pressure can change the amount of tread on the road. A properly inflated tire will grip the road better than an underinflated or overinflated tire.

Underinflation   When you drive on an underinflated tire, only the tire's outer edges provide traction. The outside edges will wear out first, shortening the life of the tire. In an emergency, the underinflated tire will not perform properly—it will accept less stress before losing its grip on the pavement. An underinflated tire is likely to heat up and fail more quickly than a properly inflated tire.

Overinflation   If a tire has too much pressure, only the center of the tread will grip the road. The footprint will be smaller, so the tire will have less traction. Over time, the overinflated tire will wear out its center tread more quickly than a properly inflated tire.

Temperature   Weather can change the pressure in your tires. If the air gets colder, tire pressure will drop. Your tires may become underinflated in cold weather. Hot temperatures will increase pressure, and may cause overinflation.

Check your tires' pressure on a regular basis to make sure they have the right amount of air. To assure an accurate reading, check tire pressure when your tires are cold, before you start driving.

---- **FIGURE 4** ----

Too much or too little pressure can change the amount of tread, or footprint, on the road.

Proper Inflation

Properly inflated tires grip evenly.

Underinflation

Underinflated tires grip only by the outer edges.

Overinflation

Overinflated tires grip only in the center.

Using Traction

When you drive, you use traction to accelerate, brake, and steer. Even under ideal conditions, your tires provide a limited amount of traction.

If you release the accelerator and brake hard, braking may consume most of your traction, while acceleration may consume little. In an emergency situation, all your traction might be consumed by hard braking and steering, leaving no reserve traction. If the steering and braking requirements of traction exceed the amount available, the vehicle will skid and you may lose control. Always try to regain traction by adjusting your braking and steering force.

Here is an example of changing traction forces. You enter a curve at 55 mph. As you reach the middle of the curve, you realize you are going too fast, so you quickly brake and turn the wheel sharply into the curve. Braking and steering require far more traction than is available. In this situation, you would lose control of your vehicle.

How could you have managed your traction to remain in control? By using IPDE and searching at least 12–15 seconds ahead, you could have identified the curve and reduced your speed before entering the curve. At a slower speed, the hard braking and steering would have been unnecessary and the traction capability would have been sufficient to maintain control.

Many vehicles today have four-wheel or all-wheel drive. That means all four wheels have pulling power. Traction control devices are available on most new vehicles, and will be covered in more detail in Chapter 17.

Ensuring Good Traction

Three things are required to achieve ideal levels of traction. First, your vehicle must be in good condition. Second, the road surface must be smooth and clear. Finally, your actions must maximize traction.

Vehicle Condition A new vehicle is easy to control. But as a vehicle ages, you need to work hard to maintain it properly. If you allow tires, shock absorbers, or parts of the steering system to wear, traction and control will be reduced.

Tires are your lifeline to traction, so it is important to keep them in good condition. Check their pressure and inspect their tread regularly. Replace older tires before they are worn out. A worn, bald tire is dangerous and will not grip a wet or icy road. Because it has no tread, the tire can

easily be punctured. If this happens, the tire could suffer a **blowout**, when all of the air escapes at once.

Good shock absorbers, or "shocks," are essential for maintaining traction. Worn shock absorbers will cause your tires to bounce on a rough road, leaving you with less traction. Replace worn shock absorbers to maximize control.

Road Condition   When you drive on a dry, flat road with good tires, your traction is excellent. But your traction will be reduced when that same road is covered with rain or snow. Your traction is also reduced when you drive on gravel roads, or roads covered with sand, leaves, or oil.

Icy weather can be especially dangerous for driving. Ice can reduce traction so much that you may lose steering, braking, or acceleration control. Be alert that water will freeze in shaded areas and on bridges before it does on regular roads.

When you see the road condition is about to change, reduce your speed before you reach the area of reduced traction. To check how much traction you have, brake gently to see how your vehicle responds. If your vehicle does not slow or if your antilock brakes start to work, reduce your speed even more.

Driver Action   Your actions affect your ability to manage traction. Quick turns and excessive speed, especially in a turn, can consume a great deal of traction. So can hard braking in a curve or on a slippery surface. Maximize your traction by steering, accelerating, and braking gently and smoothly. Lesson 3 will give you more information about how to maintain control of your vehicle.

review it 9.2

1. Explain why friction is important in controlling your vehicle.
2. What three actions consume traction? Why is it wise to never exceed traction capability?
3. What steps can you take to ensure that an older car will have good traction?

Critical Thinking

4. **Apply Concepts**   How do overinflated and underinflated tires affect traction?

IN YOUR COMMUNITY   **Use Technology**   With the owners' permission, examine the tires of at least 10 vehicles. Check for signs of worn tread or bald spots. Use a tire-pressure gauge to determine the tire pressure of each of the vehicles. Record your findings. Then write a brief report that includes the percentage of vehicles with overinflated or underinflated tires, and worn or bald tread.

lesson 9.3

VEHICLE BALANCE AND CONTROL IN CURVES

OBJECTIVES

- Define center of gravity.
- Identify the key factors that can affect a vehicle's balance.
- Describe how speed, the sharpness of the curve, vehicle load, and road shape affect control in a curve.

VOCABULARY

- vehicle balance
- center of gravity
- pitch

Vehicles of different sizes and shapes handle differently. Small vehicles are light and can accelerate quickly. Sports cars are low to the ground and handle well in curves. Vans and SUVs can be unstable on steep slopes. What makes some vehicles more difficult to control than others?

Vehicle Balance

Your ability to control your vehicle is affected by its balance. **Vehicle balance** is the distribution of a vehicle's weight on its tires as they contact the ground. The only time a vehicle is in perfect balance is when it is not moving. Whenever a vehicle accelerates, brakes, or turns, the changing weight on each tire affects its balance.

Center of Gravity The point around which an object's weight is evenly distributed is called its **center of gravity**. The center of gravity is the balance point. If you could balance the car on your finger, your finger would be directly under the center of gravity.

For a perfectly symmetrical object, such as a bowling ball, the center of gravity is exactly at the center of the object. But the weight of a car is not evenly distributed throughout the car's body. The chassis weighs more than the roof. The front end with the engine weighs more than the back end. So the center of gravity is not in the center of the vehicle, but closer to the wheels and more toward the front.

Stability A vehicle with a center of gravity that is close to the ground is more stable and less likely to roll over than one with a high center of gravity. Passenger cars typically have a low center of gravity. Taller, narrower

---

FIGURE 5

A vehicle's stability decreases as its center of gravity rises.

Center of gravity

Center of gravity

Center of gravity raised

vehicles such as SUVs, pickups, and vans have a higher center of gravity and tend to be less stable.

Installing large tires or carrying heavy cargo can raise a vehicle's center of gravity. This can have a significant impact on vehicle control if a vehicle's center of gravity is already high.

Balance and Steering

Maneuvers that shift weight to different areas of the vehicle cause changes to the vehicle's balance. Sudden weight shifts can throw a vehicle out of balance, sometimes with deadly consequences.

To understand the motion of your vehicle, it is useful to imagine three axes crossing at the center of gravity. Your vehicle may rotate around these axes in three ways: pitch, roll, and yaw.

Pitch   A tilting motion from front to back is called **pitch**. When you apply the brakes, the motion shifts more weight onto the front tires and less on the rear tires. When you accelerate, more weight is put on the rear tires and less weight on the front tires. This changing weight on your tires can increase or reduce traction.

If you brake too hard, your front tires may slide, or skid. The loss of traction in the front will result in a loss of steering control. To correct this, lift your foot off the accelerator. Do not apply the brakes. Look and steer to the target area to regain steering control.

Roll   A vehicle may also tip to the side, or roll. Strong or sudden acceleration, braking, or turning can cause a vehicle to roll over. The greater your speed and the harder you steer, the greater the risk of rolling. Reduce speed and steer smoothly, using only the amount of steering needed to make your maneuver.

Yaw   Your vehicle may rotate clockwise or counterclockwise, or yaw. When the rear tires lose traction, a vehicle may yaw. In extreme cases, a vehicle may spin completely around.

Forces in Curves

Inertia and traction work on your vehicle as you drive through a curve. Your ability to control your vehicle in a curve is affected by the sharpness of the curve, the speed and weight of your vehicle, and the shape of the roadway.

FIGURE 6

Pitch force is in effect when a vehicle's front or back end rises or falls. A vehicle can pitch due to rapid acceleration or braking.

During rapid acceleration, the vehicle's weight pitches to the rear.

During hard braking, the vehicle's weight pitches to the front.

FIGURE 7
Roads may be level, have a crowned surface, or have a banked curve.

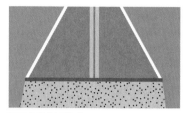

Level road

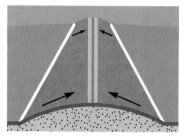

Crowned surface

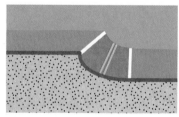

Banked curve

Sharpness of Curve   The sharper the curve, the more traction your tires need to grip the road in order to overcome inertia.

Speed   The momentum of your vehicle increases with speed. The faster you go, the more traction you need to overcome your momentum. If you go too fast, your vehicle may not be able make the turn.

Load   Carrying a heavy load, such as passengers and cargo, changes the center of gravity, which alters the weight distribution on the wheels and affects how the vehicle handles. To maintain control, reduce speed when you are heavily loaded.

Shape of the Road   The shape of the roadway affects your ability to control your car. **FIGURE 7** shows three different types of road surfaces. Many roads are level. Other roads have a crowned surface. The crowned surface helps rainfall drain from the roadway and prevents flooding. However, it is more difficult to maintain traction if a curve has a crowned surface. Gravity will tend to pull your vehicle to the side of the roadway.

Some roadways are banked, or tilted so one side is higher than the other. A curve that is higher on the outside than it is on the inside is called a banked curve. When you drive around a banked curve, the force of gravity pulls you downward and into the curve. This helps you overcome inertia.

review it 9.3

1. What is a vehicle's center of gravity?
2. Describe three ways that a vehicle may move around its center of gravity.
3. List four factors that can affect your control as you drive around a curve.

Critical Thinking

4. **Relate Cause and Effect** You are in a pickup truck with a full load of lumber. How will this load affect your vehicle's center of gravity? Why is it important to know this?

IN YOUR COMMUNITY **Dangerous Curves** With a team of classmates, locate several curves in your community that have reduced-speed warning signs. Record the street's name, the legal speed limit before the curve, and the reduced speed limit indicated for the curve. Present a report to your classmates with your judgment as to why the speed for the curve is reduced.

lesson 9.4
STOPPING DISTANCE

When you have to stop quickly, you must do three things. You must perceive the hazard in your path of travel, react, and brake to a safe stop.

Total Stopping Distance

The distance your car travels from the time you first perceive a hazard until you reach a full stop is your **total stopping distance**. You should always be able to stop within the distance you can see ahead. Refer to **FIGURE 8** as you read how the time required to perform each of the three actions determines total stopping distance. Notice that it will take you almost 300 feet, or the length of a football field, to stop if you are traveling at 65 mph.

Perception Time and Distance   The length of time it takes you to identify a hazard, predict a conflict, and decide to brake is your **perception time**. Perception time for alert drivers is about three fourths of a second. The distance your vehicle travels during your perception time is your **perception distance**.

OBJECTIVES
- Describe the three actions that determine total stopping distance.
- Identify key factors that affect braking distance.

VOCABULARY
- total stopping distance
- perception time
- perception distance
- reaction time
- reaction distance
- braking distance

FIGURE 8
Total stopping distance is based on good brakes and tires on dry, level concrete pavement.

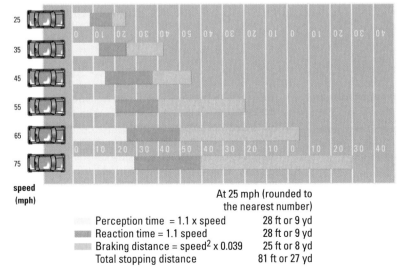

speed (mph)

	At 25 mph (rounded to the nearest number)
Perception time = 1.1 x speed	28 ft or 9 yd
Reaction time = 1.1 speed	28 ft or 9 yd
Braking distance = speed^2 x 0.039	25 ft or 8 yd
Total stopping distance	81 ft or 27 yd

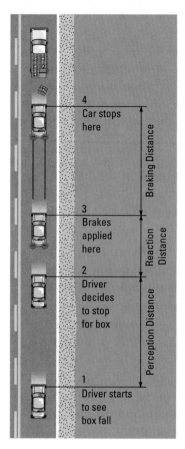

FIGURE 9
TOTAL STOPPING DISTANCE

4
Car stops here

3
Brakes applied here

2
Driver decides to stop for box

1
Driver starts to see box fall

Braking Distance

Reaction Distance

Perception Distance

Perception time varies greatly, depending upon visibility, your alertness, and your line of sight. Sometimes it takes longer to perceive a complex driving situation than to brake to a stop. You can improve your perception time by using IPDE and knowing when and where to search for potential hazards. Always search at least 12–15 seconds ahead.

Reaction Time and Distance   Once you identify a hazard, the length of time you take to apply the brake is your **reaction time**. An alert driver's reaction time is about three fourths of a second. The distance your vehicle travels while you react is called your **reaction distance**.

Braking Distance   The distance your vehicle travels from the time you apply the brake until you stop is your **braking distance**. In order to stop, your brakes must overcome your energy of motion. Braking distance is proportional to the square of your speed. If you were traveling at 40 mph, your braking distance would be four times longer than if you were traveling at 20 mph.

Factors That Affect Braking Distance

The most efficient way to stop is in a straight line. This allows the braking force to be distributed to all four tires. But many factors can increase the distance it takes to stop. Factors that can affect total braking distance include driver ability, speed, vehicle condition, roadway surface, hills, and the weight of the vehicle's load.

review it 9.4

1. In the order they occur, list the three actions that determine total stopping distance.

2. List six factors that can increase your braking distance. Which of these can the driver control?

Critical Thinking

3. **Relate Cause and Effect**   What law of motion controls stopping distance?

4. **Calculate**   Use Figure 8 and the calculation formulas to calculate total stopping distance for speeds of 20, 30, 40, 50, 60, and 70 mph.

IN YOUR COMMUNITY   **Evaluate Reaction Times and Distance**   With an adult, stand on the corner of a busy intersection with a traffic light. Use a stopwatch to determine the amount of time it takes for vehicles to stop for the red light. To identify when a driver has started braking, watch for the forward pitch of the vehicle. Calculate the average reaction time and stopping distance of each car.

If you have seen a traffic collision, you know that it can happen in the blink of an eye. Collisions can be violent, but if you know how to protect yourself and your passengers, you can reduce the risk of injury.

Force of Impact

The force with which a moving object hits another object is called **force of impact**. Three factors determine the force of impact—speed, weight, and the time between initial impact and stopping.

Speed　A vehicle's momentum is proportional to its speed and weight. Any reduction in speed will reduce the damage inflicted. Always try to reduce speed in an emergency.

Weight　The heavier a vehicle, the more damage it will cause in a collision. A vehicle weighing twice as much as another vehicle will hit a solid object twice as hard.

Time Between Impact and Stopping　How quickly a vehicle stops affects the force of the impact. If a truck hits a stone wall, the force of impact is great because the collision occurs in a brief moment. But if the same truck hits a patch of bushes, the truck will come to a stop more gradually, and there will be less damage. That is why traffic engineers put cushioning materials, such as barrels half full of sand, in front of solid roadside objects.

Safety Belts

When a vehicle hits an object, inertia causes the driver and passengers to continue forward until they hit either the inside of the vehicle or their restraint devices. A restraint device is any part of a vehicle that holds an occupant in place during a crash. A device you must engage, such as a safety belt, is an **active restraint device**. A device that works automatically, such as an air bag, is a **passive restraint device**.

Wearing a safety belt is your first defense in an emergency. Safety belts hold you in place and prevent you from being thrown from the vehicle.

 OBJECTIVES

- List three factors that affect the force of impact in a collision.
- Identify the proper use of safety belts.
- Describe how air bags have been improved and how to get the maximum benefit from air bags.
- Explain how child passengers can be protected.

 **VOCABULARY**

- force of impact
- active restraint device
- passive restraint device

FIGURE 10
You and each of your passengers should always wear safety belts whenever the car is moving.

During a crash, safety belts distribute the forces of rapid deceleration over larger and stronger parts of the body: the pelvis, chest, and shoulders.

A typical safety belt consists of a lap belt and a shoulder belt securely fastened to the vehicle's frame. Safety belt webbing is flexible, so it can stretch slightly during a collision. In a collision, the reels of the belt will suddenly tighten up and hold you in place.

Any time you are in a vehicle, you need to wear a safety belt. Make it a habit to check that all your passengers are buckled up, too. Follow these steps to maximize protection from your safety belt:

1. Adjust your seat back to an upright position and sit all the way back. Make sure your safety belt is not twisted.

2. Click the safety belt's latch into the buckle.

3. Adjust the lap portion of the safety belt so it is low and snug across your hips. The bottom portion of the belt should just touch your thighs. This adjustment will ensure that the crash forces are applied to your pelvic bones instead of your internal organs.

4. Adjust the shoulder belt snugly across your chest and collarbone.

You risk serious injury if you wear your shoulder belt under your arm or behind your back.

Air Bags

An air bag is a balloon-type device that automatically inflates to protect you. In a collision, air bags inflate, cushioning the force of impact as you are thrown forward. If a collision happens in the blink of an eye, air bags work even more quickly.

Frontal air bags   Air bags that deploy only when there is a crash at the front of the vehicle are called frontal air bags. The first generation of air bags deployed so rapidly and powerfully that they were dangerous to some passengers.

Advanced frontal air bags have been required on all cars and light trucks since September 2006. Advanced frontal air bag systems have sensors that can detect the size and seat position of an occupant, whether the occupant is wearing a seat belt, and the severity of the crash. The airbag then deploys with the appropriate speed and intensity for the situation.

Side air bags   Other air bags, called side air bags, are designed to protect your head and chest in a collision. Side impact air bags can protect occupants from injury and from ejection during a rollover.

Using Air Bags Effectively   Air bags are designed to work with safety belts. If you are not securely fastened into your safety belt when the bag deploys, you risk greater injury.

Keep your hands on the steering wheel between the 9:00 and 3:00 or 8:00 and 4:00 positions, as shown in **FIGURE 11**. This steering position also gives you the best control.

Adjust your seat so that your chest is at least 10 inches away from the hub of the steering wheel.

As a front seat passenger, move your seat as far back as possible. The passenger-side air bag is two to three times larger than the driver-side air bag and will deploy much farther out from the dashboard.

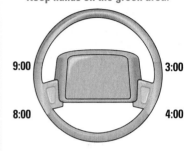

FIGURE 11
A balanced hand position will provide good steering control and avoid injury if the air bag deploys.

Keep hands on the green area.

Child Passenger Safety

All states have laws that require proper restraints for infants and children traveling in vehicles. These laws are usually specific to the age and weight of the child.

Safety belts usually do not fit children until they are between 8 and 12 years old. Until then, children who have outgrown a car seat with a harness are safer in a booster seat.

FIGURE 12

It's important to know the proper ways to install and use child safety-restraint seats.

Infants one year old or younger and weighing up to 20 pounds should be carried in a rear-facing car seat.

Children older than age one and more than 20 pounds should be carried in a forward-facing car seat.

All children younger than 13 years should sit or be carried in the back seat.

FIGURE 13
Adjust your head restraint to reach the middle of the back of your head.

Other Protective Devices

Along with safety belts and air bags, automobile manufacturers are making vehicles safer for all of us. Here are a few recent improvements:

- **Crush zones**　The front and rear ends of vehicles are designed so that they will be crushed during a collision. As the front or rear end crumples, it absorbs much of the force, greatly reducing the impact on the driver and passengers.

- **Energy-absorbing bumpers**　Bumpers are designed to absorb low levels of impact (under 5 mph) without damage.

- **Side-impact panels**　Reinforced panels on the sides of a vehicle help absorb crash energy. Side panels also reduce the risk of objects penetrating the passenger compartment.

- **Penetration-resistant windshields**　To protect against flying glass, vehicles now have windshields made with a thin layer of plastic between two layers of glass.

- **Head restraints**　Padded headrests on the top of seats are designed to protect you against whiplash injuries. However, to get this protection, you must adjust your headrest to the proper head height, as shown in **FIGURE 13**.

review it 9.5

1. Name the three factors that affect the force of impact. Which of these can a driver control?

2. What four steps should you take to put on a safety belt properly?

3. You are driving a car with air bags. What are three key steps you should take to protect yourself?

4. Why is it important that children ride in the rear seat of a car with proper safety equipment for their age and size?

Critical Thinking

5. **Apply Concepts**　Why must automotive engineers understand physical laws when designing safer vehicles?

 **Seat Belt Laws**　Compare your state's seat belt laws to six other states across the nation. How do the laws differ? Analyze what factors may cause states to have different seat belt laws. Write a report and share it with your class.

CHAPTER 9 REVIEW

Lesson Summaries

9.1 GRAVITY AND ENERGY OF MOTION

- Inertia is the tendency of an object to remain at rest, or to continue at the same speed and in the same direction, unless acted upon by another force.

- Momentum is a measure of inertia in motion; a vehicle's momentum depends upon its speed and weight.

- A vehicle's energy of motion, or kinetic energy, is proportional to its weight and to the square of its speed.

- Gravity affects driving up and down hills.

9.2 TIRES AND TRACTION

- Friction between tires and the surface of the road is called traction.

- To provide the most traction, tires must have good tread and be inflated properly.

9.3 VEHICLE BALANCE

- Every vehicle has a center of gravity that is affected by the vehicle's height and load.

- Control in curves is affected by speed, the sharpness of the curve, the shape of the roadway, and vehicle load.

9.4 STOPPING DISTANCE

- Total stopping distance includes perception distance, reaction distance, and braking distance.

- Braking distance is affected by the driver's ability to see and react; vehicle speed; condition of the vehicle and road surface; momentum; and vehicle load.

9.5 CONTROLLING FORCE OF IMPACT

- The force of impact is determined by a vehicle's speed and weight, and the time between impact and stopping.

- Proper use of restraint devices can protect against injury in collisions.

Chapter Vocabulary

- active restraint device
- blowout
- braking distance
- center of gravity
- energy of motion
- force of impact
- friction
- gravity
- inertia
- momentum

- passive restraint device
- perception distance
- perception time
- pitch
- reaction distance
- reaction time
- total stopping distance
- traction
- tread
- vehicle balance

Write the word or phrase from the list above that completes the sentence correctly.

1. The amount of time it takes to perceive something in your path of travel is known as _____.

2. The amount of time it takes to execute an action, such as applying the brakes, is _____.

3. The _____ is the point around which an object's weight is evenly distributed.

4. A motion in which a vehicle tilts from back to front is known as _____.

5. The friction between a tire and the surface of the road is called _____.

6. _____ is the force that pulls all things to Earth.

Checking Concepts

LESSON 1

7. Describe how inertia acts on the motion of a vehicle entering a curve.

8. What factors affect energy of motion?

LESSON 2

9. Why is tread essential to controlling a vehicle?

10. When is it important to check your traction?

LESSON 3

11. How does a vehicle's center of gravity affect its stability?

LESSON 4

12. If your perception and reaction time increase, what happens to your braking distance?

13. How does driving up or down a hill affect braking distance?

LESSON 5

14. Explain why it is better to collide with a soft object than a hard object.

15. What is the difference between passive and active restraint devices?

Critical Thinking

16. Compare and Contrast Explain the relationship between traction and the amount of air in a vehicle's tires.

17. Relate Cause and Effect Describe how speed, sharpness of curve, and your car's load affect how you control your vehicle in a curve.

You're the Driver

18. Identify Which of these three vehicles has the greatest amount of momentum and the lowest center of gravity: a sedan, an SUV, or a truck?

19. Execute How does speed and steering affect a vehicle's ability to roll?

20. Decide You are approaching this curve at 40 mph. To maintain control, when should you adjust your speed?

21. Execute You are driving the yellow car and you've applied your brakes to avoid a head-on collision. Your brakes have locked and you begin to skid. You want to head for the shoulder to avoid trouble. What should you do?

Preparing for the Test

Choose the letter of the answer that best completes the statement or answers the question.

1. If a vehicle increases its speed from 20 mph to 60 mph, its braking distance will increase by
   a. 3 times.
   b. 4 times
   c. 9 times.
   d. 40 times.

Use the art below to answer Question 2.

2. This tire is
   a. bald.
   b. underinflated.
   c. overinflated.
   d. properly inflated.

3. To correct a skid as you turn left in a curve,
   a. brake gently and steer right.
   b. brake gently and steer left.
   c. accelerate quickly and steer toward your target.
   d. release the brake or accelerator, and look and steer toward your target.

4. A vehicle that is driven into a curve tends to
   a. continue in a straight line.
   b. decrease its energy of motion.
   c. increase its speed.
   d. decrease its use of traction.

5. The distance a vehicle travels from the time the driver applies the brakes until the vehicle stops is the
   a. perception distance.
   b. braking distance.
   c. total stopping distance.
   d. reaction distance.

6. What is most likely to happen in rainy weather?
   a. Reaction time will increase.
   b. Reaction time will decrease.
   c. Perception time will increase.
   d. Perception time will decrease.

Use the art below to answer Question 7.

7. During a collision, this driver was protected by wearing a safety belt. What caused the driver to move forward?
   a. friction
   b. gravity
   c. energy of motion
   d. inertia

8. When properly adjusted, a safety belt
   a. fits loosely across the body and tightens during a collision.
   b. fits snugly across the hips and comfortably across the chest.
   c. fits snugly across the upper body and hips.
   d. fits loosely across the hips and snugly across the chest.

drive write

Persuasive Argument About half of the states have a primary safety belt law, which means that law enforcement officers have the right to stop a driver because he or she is not wearing a safety belt. Should all states have a primary safety belt law? Write one or two paragraphs defending your position.

NEGOTIATING INTERSECTIONS

10.1 Searching Intersections

10.2 Determining Right of Way and Judging Gaps

10.3 Controlled Intersections

10.4 Uncontrolled Intersections

10.5 Railroad Crossings

10.6 Roundabouts

KEY IDEA

What skills do you need to approach, enter, and exit the many different types of intersections safely?

YOU'RE THE DRIVER Intersections pose a variety of challenges to drivers. Negotiating intersections requires that drivers are familiar with the kinds of intersections and the various controls used to keep traffic moving safely. If three cars arrived at an intersection at the same time, would you know which driver had the right of way?

lesson 10.1
SEARCHING INTERSECTIONS

OBJECTIVES

- Explain how to identify an intersection.
- Describe the actions to take as you approach an intersection.
- Describe what to do when you have a closed front zone at an intersection.
- Identify the correct way to enter an intersection.

VOCABULARY

- intersection
- point of no return
- safety stop

Intersections are places where roadways meet or cross. Most intersections are simply two roadways crossing in a + or X pattern. Other roads meet to form a T. Where one road divides or two roads join together, intersections form a Y. Sometimes several roadways come together in a circle.

An intersection is one of the most complex situations that drivers encounter. The chance of a collision at an intersection is greater than at any other point on a roadway. Nearly half of all reported crashes and a quarter of all fatal injuries occur at intersections.

One reason for the large number of collisions is the failure of drivers to see and analyze the intersection. You can decrease your chance of collision by searching each intersection and planning a safe path of travel through it. Your IPDE skills and the Zone Control System will give you the tools to approach, enter, and exit safely.

Identifying an Intersection

To identify a safe path of travel, you first need to recognize that you are approaching an intersection. Two clear indicators are traffic lights and crossing traffic. A stationary object in the target area, such as a house or trees, may mean you are coming to a T intersection. Here are some other clues that an intersection is ahead:

- street lights and signs
- roadway markings, such as STOP AHEAD
- stopping or turning traffic
- pedestrians
- rows of fences and mailboxes
- power lines crossing over the street

FIGURE 1

Identify You are approaching this intersection. List all the clues that alert you that this is an intersection.

Approaching an Intersection

After identifying an intersection, look for line-of-sight restrictions, such as large bushes, buildings, signs, or other vehicles. Line-of-sight restrictions can hide other traffic, pedestrians, or animals. If your line of sight is restricted, search that area carefully for any potential problems.

Your goal is to have a clear path of travel through the intersection. You may need to slow, stop, or change lanes to achieve your goal.

12–15 Seconds Ahead   As you approach an intersection, check for traffic controls such as signs or signals. Also look for signs or markings that indicate turn lanes ahead.

Plan a course of action to best solve the restrictions in your line of sight or path of travel. Your decisions should give you the best control of your intended path, which may require you to change lanes. Lane changes are usually not permitted in an intersection. Therefore, you should select the best path of travel before entering the intersection.

Your zone checks should also become more frequent. Search for potential changes that could require you to change speed or direction or to communicate to other users.

4–6 Seconds Ahead   Widen your search pattern to include more information from the right and left of your path of travel. If your front zone is clear, you can keep moving. If not, prepare to stop or change your path of travel.

Keep searching and predicting at 45 degrees to either side, as shown in **FIGURE 3**. Evaluate your left and right zones for other drivers, pedestrians, or line-of-sight or path-of-travel restrictions.

You need sufficient time to identify potential hazards, so be sure to pause briefly as you search. If you move your eyes quickly, you could miss objects as large as a car.

2 Seconds Ahead   As you approach the intersection, you will reach your point of no return . This is the point beyond which you can no longer stop safely without entering the intersection. Under normal conditions, that point is when you are two seconds from the intersection, as shown in **FIGURE 4**.

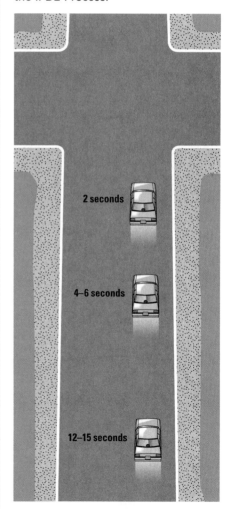

FIGURE 2

These are the three critical locations at which you must use the IPDE Process.

2 seconds

4–6 seconds

12–15 seconds

FIGURE 3
Move your head to see beyond line-of-sight restrictions. Use your searching skills to identify potential hazards in your path of travel.

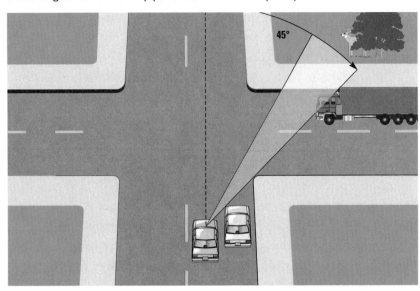

FIGURE 4
Every intersection has a point of no return. Use IPDE when approaching intersections at each different distance.

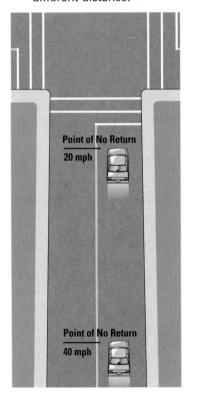

The distance from the point of no return to the intersection depends upon the speed you are going: The faster you are going, the greater the distance.

Deciding to Stop

You may have to stop because there is a red traffic light, a YIELD or STOP sign, or something moving into your intended path. Before braking, check your rear zone. If it is open, cover your brake to be ready in case the condition changes to a closed zone. If it is closed, tap your brake lights to communicate to the driver behind you that you are stopping.

Searching While Stopped   Stop at the legal stop, which could be at a stop line, before the pedestrian crosswalk, or before the intersection. If you do not have a clear line of sight to the right and left, improve your view by moving up to the intersection for a safety stop. In a **safety stop**, your front bumper is even with the curb line or cars parked on the cross street, allowing you to search 90 degrees to the right and left. As you can see in **FIGURE 5**, this position should give you a clear line of sight through the intersection.

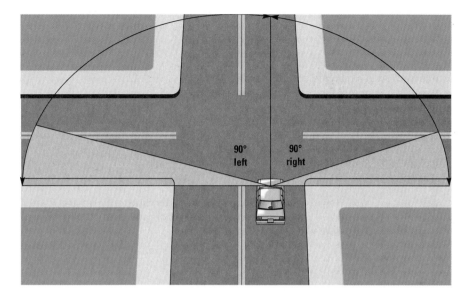

FIGURE 5
After you have stopped, search 90 degrees to your left and right before continuing.

Use your time wisely while stopped. Search for vehicles turning left in front of you and pedestrians entering the street. Remember to pause briefly during your search for time to identify possible conflicts.

Stopping Behind a Vehicle   If there is a vehicle ahead of you, stop where you can see its rear tires touching the pavement. This position will give you sufficient space if you need to drive around the vehicle.

If you have been stopped behind another vehicle, wait two seconds before moving. Use this time to search for red light runners. If the vehicle in front stops suddenly, you will have time to respond.

Entering an Intersection

You may enter an intersection if the traffic light is green. If the intersection has no traffic signals or signs, you may continue if all your front zones are open.

If you have a line-of-sight restriction, make numerous checks to be sure your path is open. You may decide to change your lane position and reduce your speed. This will give you more time to see what is hidden, as well as help others see you.

When turning, your last check should be in the direction of your intended path of travel. You need to know if your intended path is open before you enter an intersection. Looking to your target area while turning will ensure a smooth, controlled turn.

analyzing data

Crashes at Intersections

According to one civil engineer, an intersection is a planned point of conflict on the highway transportation system because it is one of the most complex traffic situations. To control the flow of vehicles and pedestrians, intersections use controls. The types of traffic controls play a role in the number of fatal crashes at intersections. Study the graph before you answer the questions.

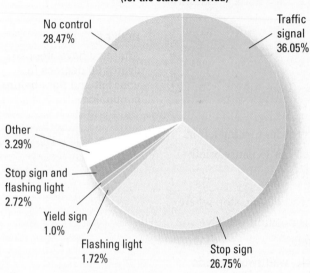

Fatal Crashes at Intersections by Traffic Control (for the state of Florida)

No control 28.47%

Traffic signal 36.05%

Other 3.29%

Stop sign and flashing light 2.72%

Yield sign 1.0%

Flashing light 1.72%

Stop sign 26.75%

1. **Reading the Graph** What is the total percentage of fatal crashes represented by the graph?

2. **Analyzing Data** At which traffic control were the greatest number of fatal crashes? The fewest number of crashes?

3. **Inferring** Suggest a reason for the difference in crashes at a flashing light and at a flashing light with a STOP sign.

4. **Inferring** Suggest a reason why intersections with STOP signs and intersections with no control had about the same percentage of fatal crashes.

5. **Execute** As a driver, what actions can you take to prevent crashes at intersections?

review it 10.1

1. List six clues that indicate that you are approaching an intersection.

2. Which zones should you search when approaching an intersection?

3. Describe what to do when you have a closed front zone at an intersection.

4. What actions should you take when entering an intersection with a line-of-sight restriction?

Critical Thinking

5. **Relate Cause and Effect** Intersections are some of the most dangerous parts of the roadway. What factors cause them to be unsafe? How can driver actions reduce the dangers of intersections?

6. **Predict** You are approaching an intersection on a green light. Your left-front and right-front zones are restricted. Will you be safe using a two-second point of no return? Explain your answer.

IN THE PASSENGER SEAT **Name the Controls** For the next week, with an adult licensed driver, make a list of all the controls at each intersection that you enter. Then note the actions of the other drivers. Did they ignore or obey the controls? Share your observations with the class.

lesson 10.2

DETERMINING RIGHT OF WAY AND JUDGING GAPS

Intersections naturally cause conflict because vehicles are traveling in different directions. You need to know when to yield the right of way. You also need to be able to judge the amount of space and time you will need to enter traffic safely.

What is Right of Way?

The term **right of way** describes the privilege of having immediate use of a certain part of a roadway. You have the right of way only when other drivers give it to you. It is not something you can take.

You will often have to yield, or let others go first. Sometimes you must yield to prevent a collision. At other times, yielding is an act of courtesy. Most of the time, laws determine who should yield the right of way.

Knowing the right-of-way laws will help you make safe decisions. The diagrams in **FIGURES 6 AND 7** show the most common situations. In each situation, the driver in the yellow car is required to yield.

When deciding whether or not to yield, remember:

- Your action should not cause those to whom you should yield to slow, stop, or change their path of travel.

- Traffic signs only show who should yield the right of way. They do not stop traffic for you.

- Do not assume others will always yield to you.

- Many times it is better to yield the right of way even when the law requires the other driver to yield.

 OBJECTIVES

- Define right of way.
- Describe situations in which the driver must yield the right of way.
- Predict how long it takes to cross and join traffic.

 VOCABULARY

- right of way
- gap
- joining traffic

FIGURE 6 YIELDING THE RIGHT OF WAY

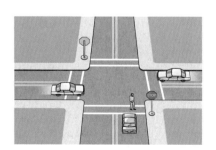 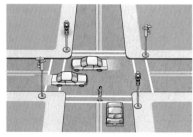

Yield at stop signs to
- pedestrians in or near the crosswalk
- all traffic on the through street

Yield at fresh green lights to
- pedestrians still in the crosswalk
- vehicles still in the intersection

FIGURE 7 YIELDING THE RIGHT OF WAY

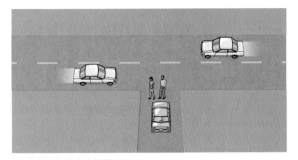

Yield coming from an alley, driveway, or private roadway to

- pedestrians before reaching the sidewalk
- all vehicles on the street (Make two stops.)

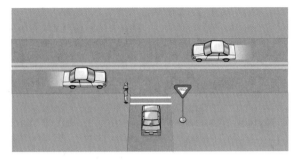

Yield at all YIELD signs to

- all pedestrians in or near crosswalks
- all vehicles on the cross street

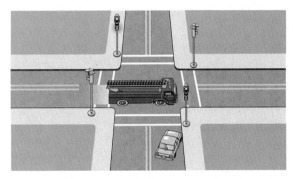

Yield to emergency vehicles

- sounding a siren or using a flashing light (Stop clear of the intersection close to curb. Wait for emergency vehicle to pass.)

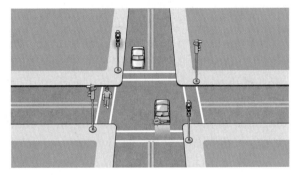

Yield when turning left at any intersection to

- all pedestrians in your turn path
- all oncoming vehicles that are at all close

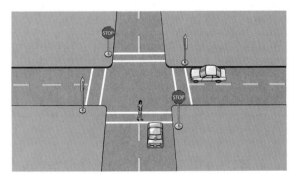

Yield at four-way stops to

- all pedestrians in or near crosswalks
- vehicles that arrive first
- a vehicle from the right if you arrive at the same time

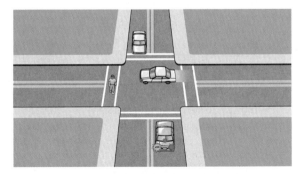

Yield at uncontrolled intersections to

- pedestrians in or near the crosswalk
- any vehicle that has entered the intersection
- a vehicle from the right if you both arrive at the same time

Judging the Size of a Gap

Before entering a street after stopping, you must find a large enough gap in traffic. A **gap** is the distance between two vehicles. You must judge the gap between your vehicle and any approaching vehicles and predict how much time you have to enter or pass through traffic safely.

The size of gap that you need depends on the maneuver you plan to make and the speed of oncoming traffic. As you can see in **FIGURE 8**, it takes more time to turn left or right than to pass through traffic.

Joining Traffic Turning right or left into lanes of other traffic is called **joining traffic**. To join traffic, you must accelerate to the speed of the through traffic without interfering with the flow of traffic. The faster traffic is moving, the larger your gap must be.

To turn right into traffic, you need a larger gap than you do to cross traffic. Turning right and accelerating to 30 mph takes about six seconds.

Turning left to join traffic is more dangerous than turning right. You must cross the path of traffic from the left before entering traffic from the right. Therefore, you need a greater gap to make a left turn.

---- FIGURE 8 **GAP SELECTION FOR CROSSING OR JOINING TRAFFIC** ----

	To Cross Traffic 4–5 Seconds	Turn Right and Join Traffic 6 Seconds	Turn Left and Join Traffic 7 Seconds
20 mph	more than ½ block away	more than ½ block away	more than ⅔ block away
30 mph	more than ⅔ block away	1 block away	more than 1 block away
45 mph	more than 1 block away	more than 2 blocks away	more than 2½ blocks away
55 mph	more than 1½ blocks away	more than 3 blocks away	more than 3½ blocks away

---

review it 10.2

1. What is meant by yielding the right of way?
2. Give six examples of situations in which you must yield the right of way.
3. List two factors that determine how big a gap must be before entering an intersection.

Critical Thinking

4. **Relate Cause and Effect** At an intersection, you see drivers that do not yield the right of way. How can this behavior affect other drivers?

IN THE PASSENGER SEAT **Yield Situations** While riding with a licensed adult driver, make a note each time you find yourself in a yield situation, then describe what actions each driver took. Report your findings to the class.

lesson 10.3
CONTROLLED INTERSECTIONS

 OBJECTIVES

- Describe the correct procedure for entering an intersection controlled by signs.
- Describe the correct action to take at green, yellow, and red traffic lights.
- Explain the procedures for making unprotected and protected left turns and for turning on red.

 VOCABULARY

- controlled intersection
- fresh green light
- stale green light
- unprotected left turn
- protected left turn
- delayed green light

A **controlled intersection** is one that has traffic signs or signals to determine the right of way. Obeying signs and signals helps drivers navigate intersections in an orderly and safe manner.

Controlled Intersections with Signs

You will need to apply your skills for searching and gap selection as you approach and enter controlled intersections.

Two kinds of signs control intersections: STOP and YIELD. At a STOP sign you must come to a full stop at the stop line, crosswalk, or before entering the intersection. At a YIELD sign, slow and yield the right of way to vehicles on the through street.

Controlled Intersections with Signals

As you approach a traffic signal, be sure you are in the correct lane for your path of travel. Then predict if the light is about to change.

In Chapter 2, you learned the meanings of red, yellow, and green lights. Signals can also have a fourth or fifth light, such as a green arrow to allow drivers to turn left.

Fresh Green Light   A light that has just turned green is a **fresh green light**. If you are stopped, don't move until you have checked to be sure that a driver on the cross street is not running a red light.

Stale Green Light   A **stale green light** is a light that has been green for a long time. If a light remains green after you first identify it, be prepared to slow. Check the status of the pedestrian crossing light. If the light is flashing, this is an indication that the light is about to turn yellow, then red.

Yellow Light   When you approach an intersection as the light turns yellow, you must decide whether to stop or proceed. If the light turns yellow before you reach the point of no return, check your rear zone. If it is safe to stop, do so. Otherwise, go through the intersection.

FIGURE 9
Your traffic light is red.
Decide What actions
will you decide to take
when your light turns
green?

Turning left on a yellow light can be very risky. If the light turns red during your turn, waiting drivers can rush into the intersection, creating serious conflicts.

Red Light   When the light is red, you must stop. Be sure to check your rear zone to ensure following cars are slowing too.

Turning Left at Signals

It is often difficult to turn left at intersections with heavy traffic. Before you turn, check to see if the left turn is unprotected or protected.

Unprotected Turns   If a signal-controlled intersection does not have a left-turn light, you must make an **unprotected left turn**. When you turn left, you must yield to oncoming traffic.

Protected Turns   You can make a **protected left turn** when a left-turn signal lets you turn left while oncoming traffic is stopped. A left-turn signal may be a green light or arrow. When the left-turn signal ends, you may be prohibited from making a left turn. If the turn is allowed, respond as you would to an unprotected left turn.

At heavily traveled intersections, a doghouse signal may be used to improve traffic. As you can see in **FIGURE 10**, this signal has five lights, including both a green and yellow left-turn arrow for protected left turns. After the green arrow turns yellow, a solid green light remains, allowing unprotected left turns if there is a safe gap.

A **delayed green light** indicates that one side of an intersection has a green light while the light for the oncoming traffic remains red. A delayed green light allows traffic from one side to turn or go straight before the light for oncoming traffic turns green. Be careful to obey your signal only.

FIGURE 10
This traffic signal is called a "doghouse." The green arrow permits you to make a protected left turn.

FIGURE 11
The opticon camera above this traffic light permits emergency vehicles such as fire trucks to change red lights to green so they can move through traffic quickly.

FIGURE 12
You can turn on red at this intersection. **Identify** Where should you search for vehicles and pedestrians?

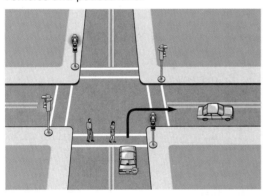

If you are making a protected left turn, watch for the left turn light or arrow to turn yellow, then red, which is your signal to stop. Do not assume you can proceed when oncoming traffic proceeds.

Turns on Red

All states and the District of Columbia permit vehicles to turn right on red. However, some local governments post signs indicating that right on red is not permitted.

Before turning right on red, come to a full legal stop. You must yield the right of way to any approaching vehicle. Also give pedestrians the right of way if they are in the crosswalk or just approaching the crosswalk. Turn into the right lane nearest you.

In some jurisdictions, a left turn on red onto a one-way street may be permitted. Such turns should be made cautiously. Always yield to through traffic and pedestrians before turning.

review it 10.3

1. What two signs are used to control intersections? Briefly describe the correct action to take at each sign.
2. What is the difference between a fresh green light and a stale green light?
3. How does an unprotected left turn differ from a protected left turn?

Critical Thinking

4. **Decide** You are traveling on a two-way street and want to turn left onto a one-way street. Your light is red, but there is no traffic on the one-way street. What action will you take and why?

IN THE PASSENGER SEAT **Right Turn on Red** Search for NO TURN ON RED signs in your community. If you see one, analyze the intersection conditions and decide why the turn is restricted. Compare this intersection to some that permit turns on red. Prepare a report and discuss your findings with your classmates.

UNCONTROLLED INTERSECTIONS

An **uncontrolled intersection** has no signs or signals to regulate traffic. In some intersections, one road is controlled by signs or signals, but the crossing road is uncontrolled. Most uncontrolled intersections are located in areas of light traffic, such as residential areas. In cities, traffic from alleys is often uncontrolled. Although these streets are usually quiet, they can be dangerous because drivers may not be expecting cross traffic or pedestrians.

Sometimes a driver fails to identify that an intersection is uncontrolled. The driver assumes that the other drivers will stop or, on a quiet street, assumes that no one is there. If you do not see a traffic sign or signal, assume that the intersection is uncontrolled. Predict that other traffic will not stop and pedestrians will not see you. Reduce speed and search aggressively. Always be prepared to stop.

 **OBJECTIVES**

- Tell how to identify an uncontrolled intersection.
- Identify the actions to take as you approach an uncontrolled intersection.
- Describe some line-of-sight or path-of-travel restrictions you may encounter at intersections.
- Identify who has the right of way at uncontrolled intersections.

VOCABULARY

- uncontrolled intersection

Using IPDE to Approach an Uncontrolled Intersection

As soon as you identify an intersection, use your search skills to determine if you will have a safe path of travel through the intersection. Refer to **FIGURE 13** as you read how to approach an uncontrolled intersection.

Searching 12–15 seconds ahead will help you identify the uncontrolled intersection early. This is the time to identify if you will have an open or closed path of travel. Predict if you will need to reduce speed or change lane positions. Identify blocked lines of sight and predict if the blockage will remain or change.

-------- FIGURE 13 --------

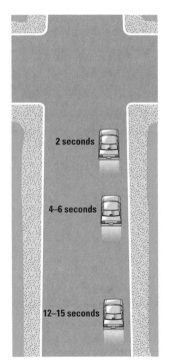

2 seconds

4–6 seconds

12–15 seconds

You should perform a series of steps at each of these three locations before uncontrolled intersections.

By the time you are within 4–6 seconds of the intersection, you should have decided your course of action. Get an update on your rear zone.

When you are 2 seconds from the intersection, you are at your point of no return. Will you continue through the intersection or stop?

Identifying Restrictions

Residential areas typically have parked cars, bushes, trees, or fences that create line-of-sight problems. A tree trunk can be large enough to hide a car, truck, or children playing near the street. If you have a line-of-sight restriction, reduce speed and adjust your lane position to get a better line of sight.

Also watch for path-of-travel restrictions. Search for vehicles intending to make a U-turn in the intersection. Also search for vehicles parked on the street close to the intersection. They create line-of-sight restrictions and path-of-travel restrictions.

Procedures at Uncontrolled Intersections

When two or more vehicles reach the intersection at the same time, the driver on the left must yield to the driver on the right. Yield the right of way to oncoming traffic that reached the intersection first.

When approaching blind intersections, reduce your reaction time by covering your brake. Carefully search your front zones for any potential hazards. Be absolutely sure you have an open path of travel before committing to entering the intersection.

review it 10.4

1. What is an uncontrolled intersection? Why can these intersections be particularly dangerous?
2. What are three actions a driver can take when approaching an uncontrolled intersection?
3. Name four line-of-sight and two path-of-travel restrictions you may encounter at an uncontrolled intersection.
4. Who has the right of way at an uncontrolled intersection?

Critical Thinking

5. **Predict** What might happen if you haven't decided on a course of action when you're within 4–6 seconds of the intersection?

IN YOUR COMMUNITY **Collisions at Intersections** Clip two articles reporting intersection collisions from your local newspaper. Analyze each report to determine which vehicle should have yielded the right of way. Write a summary of your findings. Share your analysis with your classmates.

Where a roadway crosses railway tracks, there is always a danger of collision. Because trains are so massive, their stopping distances will always be longer than those of other vehicles. Trains warn others of their approach, but the driver has the primary responsibility to avoid a conflict. Remember: A moving train always has the right of way.

Active and Passive Crossings

Warning signs and signals are placed near railroad tracks to alert drivers to the possibility of an approaching train. In towns and cities, a round, yellow railroad-crossing sign is posted about 250 feet from the actual crossing. In rural areas, this warning sign is about 750 feet from the crossing. Often a large white X is painted on the roadway before the crossing. Next to the crossing is a **crossbuck**, a large white X-shaped sign, as shown in FIGURE 14.

Crossings that are controlled with electric signals are called **active railroad crossings**. Active crossings often have a crossing gate. When a train is approaching, red lights flash, bells ring, and the crossing gate closes. Make a complete stop. Remain stopped until the lights stop flashing and the gate is raised. When the crossing is clear, proceed cautiously. Never drive around a lowered gate—it is illegal and deadly.

In rural areas, you may encounter **passive railroad crossings**. These crossings do not have flashing red lights or crossing gates. Passive crossings are marked with a crossbuck, a YIELD or STOP sign, and possibly markings on the pavement. You are not warned when a train is coming.

Crossing Railroad Tracks

When you approach railroad tracks, always stop, look, and listen. Expect a train

OBJECTIVES
- Distinguish between passive and active railroad crossings.
- Identify the correct actions to be taken at railroad crossings.

VOCABULARY
- crossbuck
- active railroad crossing
- passive railroad crossing

FIGURE 14

Slow and be prepared to stop at uncontrolled railroad crossings.

to appear at any time. Passenger trains can run early or late, and freight trains do not follow set schedules. A fully loaded freight train may seem far away. Don't be fooled. If you can see the train, it is closer than you think.

Be prepared to stop if you are following a bus or a truck carrying hazardous materials. In most areas, they are required to stop at railroad crossings. Take these precautions when approaching railroad crossings:

- Slow down and be ready to stop. Check traffic to your rear.
- Look both ways as you approach, even if the light is not flashing. The flasher may be broken.

FIGURE 15
Look for multiple-track signs at all crossings.

- Listen for train sounds. Turn off the radio, air conditioner, or heater. Roll down your window if the area is noisy.
- If a train is approaching, stop at least 15 feet from the tracks.
- Wait for the train to pass. Then carefully check for another train approaching. If there are multiple tracks, the number of tracks will be shown on the crossing. Trains may approach from either direction on any set of tracks.
- Drive onto the tracks only when you are sure you have enough space to clear the tracks. Never stop on railroad tracks while waiting for traffic ahead to move.
- Do not shift gears on railroad tracks; your vehicle may stall.

review it 10.5

1. How can you distinguish between an active and a passive railroad crossing?
2. Describe how to search as you approach a railway crossing.

Critical Thinking

3. **Compare and Contrast** Compare the procedures for going through an active railroad crossing with the procedures for going through a passive crossing. Which situation has greater risk? Why?
4. **Apply Concepts** You are preparing to cross a railroad track. The light is flashing but the crossing gate has not come down. Is it legal to cross the tracks now? Is it safe?

IN THE PASSENGER SEAT **Observing Railroad Tracks** When traveling as a passenger, keep a record of all the railroad tracks you cross during one week. Note whether (1) the crossing was actively or passively controlled, (2) a train was approaching or proceeding down the track, and (3) the driver took the appropriate actions when approaching the tracks. Discuss your findings with your class.

Some intersections are designed as circles called **roundabouts**, also called traffic circles or rotaries. Roundabouts do not have traffic signals; instead all vehicles move around a circular pathway in the same direction. Drivers entering the circle are required to yield to circulating traffic. Drivers may use roundabouts to turn right or left, to go straight, or to make a U-turn.

Benefits of Roundabouts

Roundabouts are safer and more efficient than intersections with traffic signals. For this reason, traffic engineers are developing more roundabouts throughout the country.

Why are roundabouts safer? Since all traffic is moving in the same direction, head-on collisions are eliminated. There are no left turns across intersections, so dangerous conflicts are reduced. YIELD signs in roundabouts reduce delays and decrease the level of driver frustration and aggression. Roundabouts are also safer for pedestrians, because pedestrians have to look in only one direction to cross.

Traffic with a high volume of left turns can move through a roundabout more quickly than through a traffic signal. As a result, roundabouts increase the capacity of busy roadways and reduce congestion.

Procedures at Roundabouts

Signs will alert you that there is a circular intersection ahead, as shown in **FIGURE 16**. As you approach, reduce your speed and search for circulating traffic.

Traffic circles are controlled by YIELD and ONE WAY signs. Vehicles traveling in the circle have the right of way. When entering, you must yield to traffic already in the circle.

OBJECTIVES

- Identify how roundabouts benefit drivers and pedestrians.
- Compare the flow of traffic through a traffic circle to that of an intersection with a signal.
- Describe the correct procedures for driving through roundabouts.

VOCABULARY

- roundabout

----- **FIGURE 16 TRAFFIC CIRCLE SIGNS** -----

drive green

Roundabouts Save Energy By reducing the wait at traffic lights, roundabouts reduce fuel consumption and the emission of pollutants. They also eliminate the need for the electricity that would have been used by a traffic light.

All traffic moves counter-clockwise, so vehicles will be coming from your left. Also watch for pedestrians in crosswalks. If there is a vehicle ahead of you, do not stop in the crosswalk.

- If necessary, stop before entering. If the way is clear, you do not need to stop at the entry.
- Select a safe gap and turn right to enter.
- Once you are in the circle, you have the right of way. Even so, be alert to vehicles entering in your right-front zone. Be sure to give large trucks and trailers adequate room to circulate and exit.
- In multiple lane circles, get into the correct lane early. Your lane choice should be based upon your desired exit. Drivers in the right lane may make an immediate exit or travel straight ahead. Drivers in the left and middle lanes can go straight, turn left, or make a U-turn.
- Do not pass or change lanes except to merge into the right lane to exit.
- Signal prior to your desired exit. If you are taking the first right, signal immediately upon entering.
- Never stop in a traffic circle. Continue around the circle until you reach your exit. If you miss your exit, just drive around the circle again until you are able to exit safely.
- When exiting from an inside lane, check the lane next to you and check your blind spot to be sure the outside lane is clear.

review it 10.6

1. State three reasons why roundabouts are safer than intersections with traffic signals.
2. A roundabout is located at the intersection of two roadways. Identify four different paths of travel available to drivers entering the roundabout.
3. In a traffic circle, which vehicle has the right of way? List the actions you should take to enter a traffic circle safely.

Critical Thinking

4. **Decide** You entered a traffic circle and missed your planned exit. What action will you take to get back to your planned path of travel?

IN THE PASSENGER SEAT **Observe Intersections** When riding as a passenger, make a list of any traffic circles in your area. Identify all the signs and lane markings and decide if they clearly identify how to drive through the circle. If you do not find any traffic circles, identify an intersection that you believe would have the greatest safety benefit if it were changed to a roundabout. Report your findings to your class.

CHAPTER 10 REVIEW

Lesson Summaries

10.1 SEARCHING INTERSECTIONS

- Identifying intersections early will prepare you to merge with traffic or go straight through safely.

10.2 DETERMINING RIGHT OF WAY AND JUDGING GAPS

- You must yield the right of way at STOP and YIELD signs, at uncontrolled intersections, and as you enter roadways from alleys and driveways. Emergency vehicles always have the right of way.

10.3 CONTROLLED INTERSECTIONS

- Controlled intersections are regulated by traffic lights or STOP or YIELD signs.

10.4 UNCONTROLLED INTERSECTIONS

- Uncontrolled intersections do not have traffic signs, signals, or markings to manage traffic.
- As you approach an uncontrolled intersection, use the IPDE Process.

10.5 RAILROAD CROSSINGS

- Expect a train at all crossings; check for multiple track signs. If a train is approaching, obey all active crossing controls. At passive crossings, look carefully, listen, and be prepared to stop. Always wait for the train to clear.

10.6 ROUNDABOUTS

- At a roundabout, drivers can make a right or left turn, continue straight ahead, or complete a U-turn.

Chapter Vocabulary

- active railroad crossing
- controlled intersection
- crossbuck
- delayed green light
- fresh green light
- gap
- intersection
- joining traffic
- passive railroad crossing
- point of no return
- protected left turn
- right of way
- roundabout
- safety stop
- stale green light
- uncontrolled intersection
- unprotected left turn

Write the word or phrase from the list above that completes the sentence correctly.

1. An intersection at which traffic signals or signs determine the right of way is called a(n) _____.

2. The _____ is the privilege of having immediate use of a certain part of the roadway.

3. A(n) _____ is the distance between vehicles.

4. An intersection where roads meet in a circle is called a(n) _____.

5. A(n) _____ has no signs or signals to regulate traffic.

6. A traffic light that has been green for a long time is called a(n) _____.

7. A(n) _____ is a sign indicating a passive railroad crossing.

 **STUDY TIP**

To help review the chapter, make a detailed outline of each lesson. Use the lesson titles for your major headings. Under each lesson title, list the red headings as key points and the purple and black headings as subheadings. Add vocabulary and bulleted lists as supporting details.

Checking Concepts

LESSON 1

8. What factors make intersections particularly dangerous?

LESSON 2

9. What action should you take if you arrive at an intersection before a vehicle on your left arrives?

LESSON 3

10. What are the three locations at an intersection where drivers must come to a full stop?

LESSON 4

11. What should you predict when approaching an uncontrolled intersection?

LESSON 5

12. You are stopped at a railroad crossing where a train has just passed. In what direction should you check before you cross the tracks? Why?

LESSON 6

13. When entering a multilane roundabout, what lane should you be in to travel straight through the intersection?

Critical Thinking

14. Infer Explain the difference between a protected left turn and an unprotected left turn.

15. Identify You are driving a car that is approaching an intersection controlled by a STOP sign. You want to turn left. Describe the actions you would take before making the turn.

You're the Driver

16. Predict As you approach an intersection, you see an oncoming car. It does not have a turn signal light on, but its wheels are turned slightly to the left. What do you predict this driver may do?

17. Identify You are 12–15 seconds from an intersection. What should you search for in this range?

18. Execute You are driving the yellow car and approaching an uncontrolled intersection. You and the white car are the same distance from the intersection. What action should you take? Why?

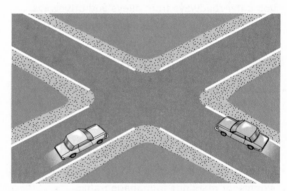

19. Decide You stop at the legal stop at this intersection. Your view is blocked to the right by a large bush. Is it legal to enter the intersection a few feet and stop again? Why or why not?

Preparing for the Test

Choose the letter of the answer that best completes the statement or answers the question.

1. Two vehicles arrive at an uncontrolled intersection from different streets at the same time.
   a. The driver on the right must yield to the vehicle on the left.
   b. The driver on the left must yield to the vehicle on the right.
   c. Both vehicles must stop.
   d. Neither vehicle must stop.

2. Which of the following is required in order to make a protected left turn?
   a. A left green arrow
   b. No oncoming traffic
   c. A left-turn-only lane
   d. A large enough gap

Use the photo below to answer Question 3.

3. This sign means
   a. 4-way intersection.
   b. stop if traffic is approaching.
   c. railroad crossing.
   d. no turns.

4. The gap needed for a left turn is
   a. less than a right turn.
   b. less than crossing traffic.
   c. greater than one block.
   d. greater than a right turn.

5. You have the right of way when
   a. the law says you have it.
   b. you arrive at an intersection first.
   c. other drivers give it to you.
   d. the other driver is on your right.

Use the photo below to answer Question 6.

6. This signal is used to
   a. allow drivers to make a protected or unprotected left turn.
   b. tell drivers when there is a safe gap.
   c. alert drivers that cars are turning left.
   d. protect fire trucks emerging from a fire station.

7. When you see a flashing yellow light at an intersection, you should
   a. yield to all traffic before crossing the intersection.
   b. take the right of way.
   c. stop, then enter the intersection when safe to do so.
   d. stop and wait for it to turn red.

8. When entering a traffic circle, you should
   a. stop and wait until the traffic circle is empty.
   b. yield to circulating traffic.
   c. yield to vehicles entering from your right.
   d. yield to vehicles entering from your left.

drive write

Persuasive Argument Roundabouts have many benefits, but some drivers do not like them. Write one or two paragraphs to persuade drivers of the benefits of roundabouts.

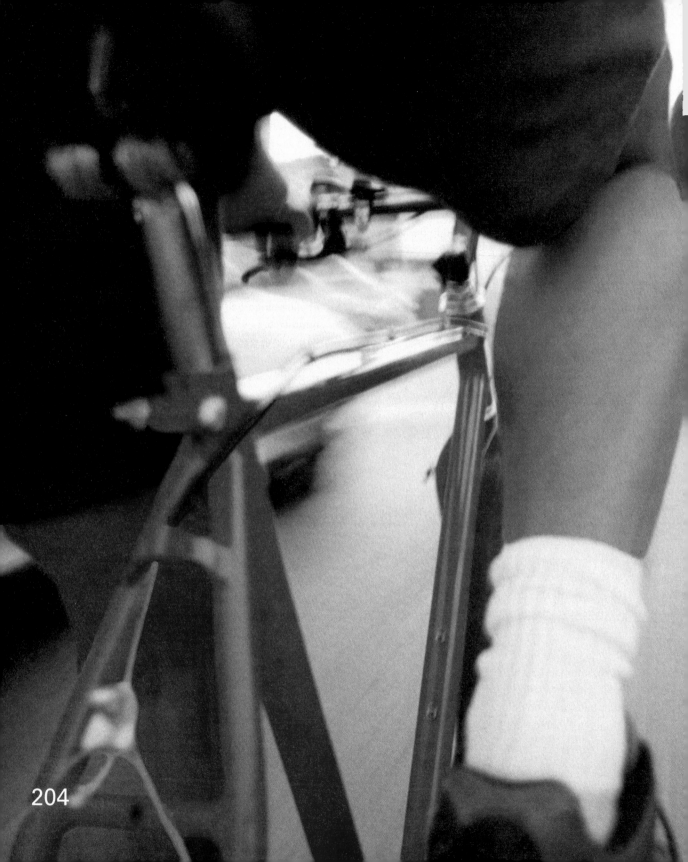

chapter 11

SHARING THE ROADWAY

11.1 Pedestrians

11.2 Bicycles and Mopeds

11.3 Motorcycles and Scooters

11.4 Trucks, Buses, and Emergency and Specialized Vehicles

KEY IDEA

How can drivers help ensure the safety of everyone when sharing the road with other vehicles and pedestrians?

YOU'RE THE DRIVER

Drivers share the roadway with pedestrians and many different kinds of vehicles. Each of these users presents its own particular set of challenges. Do you know the laws regarding cyclists and pedestrians? What should you do when you see the flashing lights of an ambulance?

205

lesson 11.1
PEDESTRIANS

- Identify factors that put pedestrians at risk.
- Explain the correct procedures for interacting with pedestrians in different situations.
- Describe actions that pedestrians can take to ensure their own safety.

VOCABULARY

- jaywalk

FIGURE 1

Pedestrians can often be inattentive to their surroundings. **Identify** What two high-risk behaviors are these pedestrians demonstrating?

Of all roadway users, pedestrians are the most vulnerable. In the United States, collisions injure an average of 1 pedestrian every 8 minutes and kill 1 pedestrian every 108 minutes.

Many pedestrians are not fully aware of traffic laws and signals. The greatest risk of injury is among children and seniors. Children are less visible to drivers and often lack judgment to know when it is safe to cross streets. Seniors may not hear or see well; and some may walk more slowly.

Often drivers fail to see pedestrians, and some pedestrians are careless or in a hurry and take chances on the roadway. Some pedestrians **jaywalk**, or disregard traffic rules and signals. Jaywalkers may cross against a light or dart out from between parked cars. Nearly half of all pedestrian fatalities involve the use of alcohol by the driver or pedestrian.

Protecting Pedestrians

Pedestrians may cross a road anywhere. As a driver, you have a legal and moral obligation to protect them in every situation. If you are alert in situations where they are likely to enter the roadway, you can reduce the risk of conflict. Use the IPDE Process and always be ready to yield to pedestrians. Be particularly alert in the following situations.

Crosswalks Pedestrians have the right of way when crossing within a crosswalk. Marked crosswalks may be located at intersections or mid-block. Collisions often occur in crosswalks when drivers fail to look for pedestrians and pedestrians assume the driver will yield to them.

Some crosswalks are controlled by signals that tell pedestrians when to cross. However, signals may not give enough time for all pedestrians to clear the crosswalk. You must yield until everyone has cleared the crosswalk, even if your light is green.

Intersections   At intersections, many pedestrians are struck just as they step into the street. They often walk into the side of a moving vehicle they do not see. When drivers disregard STOP or YIELD signs, pedestrians are at risk. Before entering an intersection, take a few seconds to search for pedestrians, especially when there are visual obstacles.

Collisions with pedestrians often occur when vehicles are turning left. Because they are concentrating on traffic lights and their turning maneuver, drivers may fail to see the pedestrian. Search carefully for pedestrians before committing to a left turn.

When drivers turn right on red, pedestrians have less opportunity to cross safely. Before turning right on red, always yield to pedestrians who are in or approaching the roadway.

Alleys and Driveways   When approaching a sidewalk from an alley or driveway, expect pedestrians to appear from either direction. If your line of sight is restricted, make two stops. First, stop before the sidewalk and search in both directions. Stop again to look for traffic just before you enter the street.

Business Districts   Business districts typically have heavy traffic and many pedestrians. Both drivers and pedestrians are subjected to many distractions. Drive through business districts safely, searching for pedestrians in crosswalks. Be prepared for jaywalkers who may cross the street mid-block without warning.

Residential Areas   When driving in residential areas, reduce speed and use a lane position with the best visibility. Crosswalks on residential streets are not typically marked. Search for anyone coming from between parked vehicles, such as a child entering a street to retrieve a toy. Sometimes children play games in the street, or use the road for skateboarding or roller skating.

Although joggers are safer on sidewalks and jogging paths, expect to see them on streets and in traffic lanes. Always be ready to slow, steer around, or stop for a jogger.

Reduced Visibility   Most collisions with pedestrians occur at night. When a roadway is poorly lit, it can be a challenge to see a pedestrian, especially one wearing dark clothes. Watch for pedestrians walking along or across the roadway.

----- **FIGURE 2** ----------------------------
Watch for children playing on the street.

FIGURE 3

If you have to walk on roads because there are no sidewalks, be sure to face the traffic.

Rain, snow, and sleet often cause people to be more concerned about protection from weather than protection from traffic. Watch for pedestrians disregarding traffic or crosswalks as they hurry to escape the bad weather.

Pedestrian Responsibilities

We are all pedestrians at one time or another. Be responsible for your own safety as a pedestrian. Expect that drivers may not see you, or that they may not yield the right of way.

- Make yourself visible. If you know you will be out at night, wear light-colored clothing or carry a light, particularly in rural areas.
- Walk on sidewalks if there are any, or walk so you are facing traffic.
- Use crosswalks and obey traffic signals. Do not jaywalk.
- Watch for oncoming traffic every time you cross a street.
- Do not walk into traffic lanes from between parked vehicles.

---

review it 11.1

1. List several reasons why young children and seniors are especially vulnerable as pedestrians.

2. List six situations in which you should be particularly careful to search for pedestrians.

3. As a pedestrian, what steps can you take to ensure your own safety?

Critical Thinking

4. **Predict**   Business districts are full of distractions. List five reasons why drivers or pedestrians might be distracted. How might these distractions affect the actions of pedestrians?

5. **Identify**   You are driving in a hospital zone, searching for a parking space. Describe some high-risk pedestrian behaviors you should search for and explain why.

IN THE PASSENGER SEAT   **Observing Crosswalks**   When riding with another driver, observe how drivers of other vehicles interact with pedestrians. Note pedestrians within crosswalks. Record how many drivers stop for pedestrians and how many do not yield the right of way. Share your observations with the class.

Bicycles and mopeds are popular forms of transportation and recreation. Sharing the road with these small vehicles requires particular attention.

A **moped** is a small, two-wheeled vehicle that can be driven with either a motor or pedals. The word *moped* comes from combining the *mo* in motor-driven with the *ped* in pedal-driven. Like a motorcycle, a moped is powered by an engine and controlled by a hand throttle. Like a bicycle, a moped can be pedaled and can be stopped with a hand brake.

Mopeds have very small engines, with maximum speeds of only 20 to 35 mph. Their small size makes them economical and easy to navigate. But their low power makes it hard for them to keep up with the flow of traffic, so they are vulnerable among larger and faster vehicles. Mopeds are not permitted on high-speed roadways.

Searching for Bicycles and Mopeds

You may encounter bicycles and mopeds almost anywhere you drive. Their small size makes them hard to see, especially at intersections. Their size also makes it difficult to judge their speed and distance—they often appear to be moving much slower than they really are.

Use the IPDE Process to actively search for bicycles and mopeds. Scan widely enough to include the sides of the roadways.

 OBJECTIVES

- Explain why riders of bicycles and mopeds are vulnerable on the roadway.
- Describe how to search for cyclists and how to predict their actions.
- Identify actions drivers can take to help protect cyclists.
- List the guidelines to follow when riding bicycles and mopeds.

 **VOCABULARY**

- moped

FIGURE 4

Because mopeds are small and maneuverable, they can surprise motorists. Always signal well in advance before making a turn or lane change.

Be alert for bicyclists on sidewalks approaching intersections. Predict that they may leave the sidewalk and cross the road in front of you.

Children on bicycles are often difficult to see and can be very unpredictable. Most children do not look for traffic, or know and understand traffic laws. Some children are not able to control their bicycles well. Expect to see children on bicycles around playgrounds, residential areas, and school zones. Search for children riding on sidewalks when you enter or exit driveways, parking lots, and alleys. Reduce speed and select a lane position that gives children on bicycles the most possible space.

Driver Responsibilities

Because mopeds and bicycles are so vulnerable, drivers of larger vehicles have the responsibility to protect them. Give bicycle and moped riders extra space whenever possible. A cyclist may swerve into your path to avoid hazards such as potholes, puddles, storm drains, or gravel on the roadway. Respect their need when they use a whole lane.

Avoid using your horn, which can startle cyclists and cause them to lose control. Allow extra time for them to pass through intersections. Use low-beam headlights at night when mopeds and bicycles are nearby.

Some cities and towns have lanes that are reserved for bicycles. Never park or drive in a marked bicycle lane.

FIGURE 5
The bicyclist is safely using the marked bicycle lane.
Decide   Is the rider of the moped riding legally?

Passing   Do not pass a bicycle if oncoming traffic is near. When it is safe to pass, leave at least one half lane between your vehicle and the bicycle. Leave more if the lanes are narrow. After passing, check your rear zone before returning to your lane.

Turning   Do not make a quick right turn in front of a bicycle or moped. As shown in **FIGURE 5**, the rider may not have enough time or space to avoid you. If there is insufficient space to pass and safely turn right, reduce your speed and let the cyclist pass through the intersection before you.

When turning left, search for bicycles approaching the intersection. Take time to judge the gap and decide whether or not you have enough space to turn left safely.

Backing Out   Check and check again when backing out of a driveway, parking lot, or side street that has line-of-sight restrictions. Reduce risk by parking so you can drive out straight ahead.

Exiting a Parked Car   Bicyclist and moped riders are easily hidden in your blind spots. Before opening your door, check your rear zones for bicyclists. Then open your doors carefully, and check for riders again.

Weather Conditions   Wet and icy roads are especially dangerous for cyclists. Hand-operated brakes do not work well when the wheels are wet, so bicycles may need a greater stopping distance. Share more of the road by increasing your distance from them.

Responsibilities of Cyclists

When riding a bicycle or moped, you must obey all traffic laws, such as STOP signs, traffic lights, and lane markings. To reduce your risk of collision, always ride in a predictably straight line and in the same direction as other traffic, making sure you select lane positions that make you clearly visible. Search intersections, driveways, and parked cars for potential hazards and use hand signals to indicate turns and stops. When riding with others, ride single file. To protect yourself, always wear a helmet, light-colored clothing, and reflective tape. And, of course, you should never wear headphones.

review it 11.2

1. Why are cyclists at risk when sharing the roadway with motor vehicles?

2. Describe at least six areas where drivers should search for bicycles and mopeds.

3. In what ways can you help protect riders of bicycles and mopeds?

4. What actions can cyclists take to increase their own safety?

Critical Thinking

5. **Evaluate**   Many children in your neighborhood ride bicycles. While preparing for a left turn on a street with many line-of-sight restrictions, what action will you take? Explain why.

IN YOUR COMMUNITY   **Safety Features**   Visit several dealers in your area that sell mopeds. Ask the sales people to describe and show you the safety features of various mopeds. Take any free literature that is available. Make a list of the various kinds of mopeds and their safety features. Share your findings with the class.

lesson 11.3
MOTORCYCLES AND SCOOTERS

FIGURE 6 A scooter is similar to a motorcycle, although most scooters require no shifting of gears.

As a licensed driver, you will share the road with motorcycles and scooters. Motorcycle engines can be more powerful than a full-size passenger car and can reach speeds of 100 mph. **Scooters** are generally smaller and less performance-oriented than motorcycles, although some are as large as a mid-size motorcycle. Unlike a motorcycle, scooters have a step-through frame so the rider can sit on the seat like a chair as shown in FIGURE 6.

Operators of motorcycles and scooters have the same rights and responsibilities as those of other motor vehicles. They are expected to obey all traffic laws and rules of the roads.

Riding a Two-Wheeled Vehicle

Riding a motorcycle or scooter is very different from driving a four-wheeled vehicle. Understanding the special needs of scooter and motorcycle riders will help you predict their behavior.

Maintaining balance and traction on a two-wheeled vehicle requires the skillful use of the controls and body position. Motorcycles are less stable at very low speeds than at higher speeds, but higher speeds reduce maneuverability, which can be challenging, especially for new riders.

Like cars, two-wheeled vehicles need traction to accelerate, brake, and turn. A patch of gravel or wet leaves can be a serious hazard for a motorcyclist or scooter rider.

Acceleration and Braking Motorcycles and scooters are capable of amazing acceleration. This acceleration can help them avoid potential hazards, but it can also get them into trouble.

Motorcycles have separate brakes for the front and rear wheels. Most of the stopping power is in the front brake. Locking the front or rear brake can result in loss of control. A skillful rider with good traction and good tires may be able to stop more quickly than a car driver. An inexperienced rider can lose control.

Lane Position A passenger vehicle occupies about six feet of a lane, but a motorcycle occupies only three feet. Even so, riders use every bit of their lane—but not all at the same time.

Riders must adjust their position to get the best visibility and to avoid hazards, such as gravel or potholes. Respect the rider's need and legal right to use their full lane. Never share the lane.

When changing lanes, check your blind spot carefully for motorcycles and scooter riders. Check your rear zone after each lane change.

Using IPDE to Protect Riders

Motorcycle and scooter riders are everywhere, sometimes where you least expect them. Too often, drivers do not identify them in time to prevent a collision. When a motorcycle collides with another vehicle, the driver of the other vehicle is at fault more than 50 percent of the time.

Make a special effort to use the IPDE Process to prevent conflicts. The Identify step is crucial—motorcycles are easily hidden in heavy traffic or by bushes or parked cars alongside the roadway.

Riders are even less visible at night. Many riders wear bright clothing and helmets that will make them more noticeable. Some keep their headlights on at all times to make themselves more visible. Search for reflective materials on a rider's helmet and jacket, especially at night.

Searching at Intersections Most collisions with two-wheeled vehicles occur at intersections. Drivers often misjudge the distance and speed of the oncoming rider, especially at night. Reducing speed as you approach an intersection will give you more time to visually search for motorcycles and scooters.

A blinking turn signal is not an absolute guarantee that the rider is turning.

FIGURE 7 For a motorcycle to turn, the rider must lean into the curve.

FIGURE 8 When passing a motorcyclist, predict that a rider may need to change lanes to avoid risky road conditions. Adjust your lane position if needed.

FIGURE 9
Because they are small,
motorcycles are difficult
to see on the roadway.

FIGURE 9
Because they are small,
motorcycles are difficult
to see on the roadway.

FIGURE 10
On wet roads, motorcyclists can gain
traction by riding in the wheel tracks
of another vehicle.

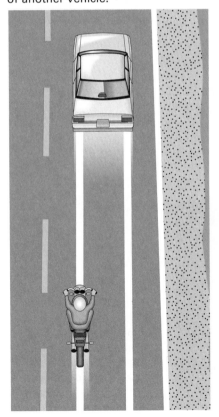

Just as car signals may not automatically cancel, a rider's turn signal may be left on unintentionally. Look for other indications that the rider plans to turn, such as reducing speed, searching the intersection, changing position within a lane, and looking to the left and right.

Turning Right   A motorcyclist turning right is entitled to the entire lane for a new path of travel. The rider may need to change lane position to avoid a hazard, such as gravel.

Multiple right-turning lanes can create a hazard because some drivers move to a different lane during the turn. Watch for riders who are making right turns, too, and stay within your lane.

Turning Left   Drivers often make left turns in front of motorcyclists, leaving little time or space for the rider to avoid a collision. Turning left in front of an oncoming rider is a major cause of rider fatalities.

When you need to turn left, search your left, front, and right zones carefully. Turning onto a multiple-lane, one-way street requires extra alertness. Riders can easily be hidden by larger vehicles. Check for a rider approaching the intersection from the right. Watch approaching riders long enough to determine if the gap is large enough—a left turn onto a two-lane road requires at least seven seconds.

Commit to your left turn only after you are sure you have sufficient time.

When two lanes are reserved for left turns, stay within your lane as you make your turn. A motorcyclist in the left-turn lane next to you will need an entire lane to negotiate his or her own left turn.

Adverse Weather Conditions
When you ride in an enclosed vehicle, you are protected from rain, sun, sleet, wind or hail, but a motorcyclist has limited protection. A rider may have reduced vision, especially if the rider is not wearing a face shield or goggles. Heavy winds can affect a rider's balance. Any time that weather conditions reduce your visibility or traction, be aware that the conditions are much worse for the rider.

Riders who are not wearing proper gear can quickly become chilled and distracted, slowing their perception and reaction time. Increase your space cushion. If possible, move to another lane.

Road Conditions   A rider can quickly lose traction when the road is covered with oil, wet leaves, sand, gravel, or snow. Search for riders who may be riding in these conditions and increase your following distance.

Carrying Passengers   Carrying passengers on a motorcycle or scooter requires skill. Passengers can affect a rider's control if they move around, don't hold onto the rider's waist or handholds, or resist leaning with the rider into a turn. At low speeds, the operator may have difficulty with balance and control.

FIGURE 11

By riding in offset positions, riders provide a full lane to each other. **Predict**   Are these cyclists likely to move within their lanes? Is there room for your vehicle to share this lane?

FIGURE 12
This rider is wearing protective gear and appropriate clothing. **Analyze** Why do you think it is important to wear clothes that are not loose or baggy?

The weight of the passenger will increase the distance needed for acceleration and stopping. Follow at a safe distance and be prepared to change speed or position.

Riding in Groups When two or more motorcyclists travel together, they should ride in an offset position. This gives each individual adequate space for visibility and maneuvering. Give riders in a group their full lane. Don't be tempted to share the lane, even if there appears to be room.

Protective Gear

Riders on scooters and motorcycles are fully exposed to the environment. Riders can reduce or prevent injuries by using **protective gear**, as shown in **FIGURE 12**. Protective gear has two purposes: comfort and protection. Uncomfortable protective gear can create distractions. Inferior gear can reduce protection.

Most states have laws requiring riders to wear helmets. In a collision, helmets are key to saving lives. Helmets also reduce the noise of the wind and help prevent fatigue. Other protective gear includes

- goggles or a face shield—to protect vision
- gloves—to protect hands, increase handlebar grip, and reduce fatigue
- over-the-ankle boots—to protect and support feet and ankles
- sturdy jacket and pants—to protect against the weather and flying objects

analyzing data
Motorcycle Crashes

Motorcycles involved in crashes with vehicles account for over 7,000 collisions each year. These two circle graphs represent the percentages and types of crashes involving motorcyclists by initial point of impact. Study the graphs before answering the questions.

1. **Reading Graphs** What does each section of the graphs represent?

2. **Analyzing Data** What initial point of contact for single-vehicle crashes has the lowest percentage of crashes? The highest percentage?

3. **Relating Cause and Effect** For most collisions involving motorcycles, the initial point of contact was the front of the motorcycle. Suggest factors that may have contributed to this.

4. **Inferring** In multi-vehicle crashes, the right side and the rear have the same percentage of crashes. What do you think accounts for the similarity?

5. **Execute** As a driver, what actions can you take to protect motorcyclists?

Motorcycles Involved in Fatal Crashes* (by initial point of contact)

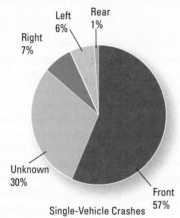

Left 6%
Rear 1%
Right 7%
Unknown 30%
Front 57%

Single-Vehicle Crashes

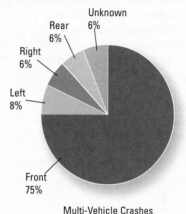

Rear 6%
Unknown 6%
Right 6%
Left 8%
Front 75%

Multi-Vehicle Crashes

* Percents rounded to the nearest whole number

review it 11.3

1. How do a motorcycle's braking and acceleration differ from those of other vehicles?

2. Name five places where you should search for motorcycles and scooters while driving.

3. How does protective gear help riders reduce risk?

4. Identify four situations that can affect the control of a motorcycle or scooter. For each situation, describe the actions a driver can take to reduce the risks to the motorcycle or scooter rider.

Critical Thinking

5. **Compare and Contrast** You are preparing to make a left turn on a multiple-lane roadway with heavy traffic. Which type of vehicle are you least likely to see? Explain how you can effectively search for hazards in this situation.

IN YOUR COMMUNITY **Investigate** Research rules or laws for motorcyclists in your state. Make a list of the rules or laws motorcyclists must follow that are not required of other drivers. Share your findings with the class.

lesson 11.4

TRUCKS, BUSES, AND EMERGENCY AND SPECIALIZED VEHICLES

 OBJECTIVES

- Identify the risks associated with sharing the road with large vehicles.
- Describe how to follow, pass, and meet large trucks safely.
- Describe the precautions you must take when driving near school buses and emergency vehicles.
- Explain how to share the road with specialized vehicles such as recreational vehicles, low-speed vehicles, and snowplows.

 VOCABULARY

- tractor trailer
- no zone
- emergency vehicle
- low-speed vehicle

When you share the roadway with larger vehicles, you must understand and respect their needs. It may be easy to see trucks and buses, but they present greater risks than smaller vehicles.

Sharing the Road with Trucks

There are three primary classifications of trucks: light, medium, and heavy. Service trucks, pickup trucks, and delivery trucks are usually light or medium-weight. Heavy trucks include dump trucks and tractor trailers.

A truck that has a powerful tractor pulling a separate trailer is called a **tractor trailer**. The tractor includes the engine and driver's cab. The most common tractor trailer is the semi-trailer, which has one trailer. In some areas of the country, a tractor may pull as many as three trailers.

Heavy trucks deserve special attention. In a collision, their sheer size puts a car at a disadvantage. Because they are so heavy, these trucks require long stopping distances. In addition, their metal bumpers are high and rigid; they are not equipped with the energy-absorbing bumpers installed on cars. When driving near these vehicles, increase your space cushion to reduce your risk.

Even through most truck drivers practice a high degree of safe-driving behavior, there are times when they suffer from fatigue or loss of sleep. Drivers often face the problem of tight scheduling and drive over long periods of time.

FIGURE 13

Tractor trailers are much heavier than cars. **Predict** Which will have the greater stopping distance, the truck or the car behind the truck?

The No Zone   Drivers of heavy trucks sit high above the road and have an excellent view of the roadway ahead. However, they also have very large blind spots—areas around the truck where your car can disappear from their view. These blind spots are called the **no zone**. As you can see in **FIGURE 14**, the no zone includes areas at the side, rear, and front. The front no zone can extend more than 20 feet.

If you are driving within any part of the no zone, the driver may be unaware of your presence. If you can't see the truck driver in the truck's mirror, the truck driver can't see you. The right-side blind spot is the most dangerous because trucks make wide right turns.

Following Large Trucks   When you follow a large truck, it causes a line-of-sight restriction. Tailgating a truck is like driving down the road with a brick wall directly in front of you. You cannot see what is occurring in front of the truck, so you are relying on the truck driver to be alert and keep the heavy truck under control. If the driver brakes suddenly, you are likely to crash into the truck. Increase your following distance to more than four seconds and stay well out of the rear no zone.

Trucks Making Right Turns   When following large trucks, be aware that they require plenty of space to make a turn. In order to turn right, a truck usually starts by swinging out to the left. Drivers of these vehicles cannot see other drivers directly behind or beside them. Always watch a truck's turn signals and leave plenty of room for the truck to make its turn. Trying to squeeze in between the truck and the curb is an invitation for disaster, as shown in **FIGURE 15**.

Passing and Being Passed   It is safer to pass trucks that are going uphill than trucks that are going downhill. A heavy vehicle will usually lose speed when traveling uphill, and gain speed when going downhill. Passing on a downhill grade can result in a truck quickly moving into your rear zone and tailgating you.

FIGURE 14
Truck drivers have four large blind spots. If you are in a truck's no zone, the driver cannot see you.
Decide   Which is larger, the right or left no zone? Explain why.

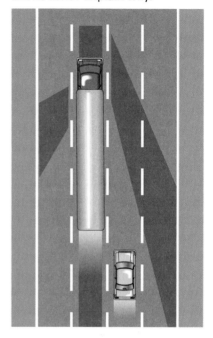

FIGURE 15
To avoid conflict, keep out of the open space to the right of a tractor trailer that is making a right turn.
Identify   Can the truck driver see the car?

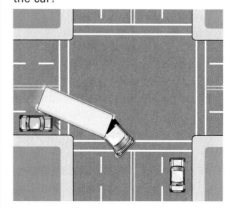

To safely pass a long vehicle, you need more distance. When you are in position to pass, check your front and rear zones and your blind spots. Then signal a lane change. Reduce your risk by using these two good habits when you pass:

- Stay in lane position 2 and complete your pass carefully and quickly. Don't linger in the no zone.
- Signal and return to your lane only after you can see at least one headlight in your rearview mirror. Don't slow down!

Be prepared for increased wind turbulence when passing a truck, or when a truck passes you. Grip the steering wheel firmly. When being passed by a heavy vehicle, move to lane position 3 if conditions permit.

If you pass during rain or snow or when the road is wet, spray from the truck may cover your windshield. If so, increase your wiper speed and use your windshield washer to keep your windshield clear. If necessary, pull over in a safe location and clean your windows.

Meeting a Large Truck   You do not have much room when meeting large trucks on narrow, two-lane roads. When you meet a truck, move to lane position 3. Reduce speed and drive straight toward your target area. Hold the steering wheel firmly because you may encounter a gust of wind as you drive by.

Before you commit to passing or turning left, check your gap and decide how quickly the vehicle is approaching. Large vehicles often appear to be moving more slowly than they really are.

Buses

Although they are not as heavy as tractor trailers, buses also present challenges to other drivers. Like trucks, buses have large no zones and take extra space to turn. They also cause line-of-sight restrictions. When driving behind a bus, increase your following distance to improve your line of sight.

Public Buses   Local transportation buses make frequent stops to pick up and drop off passengers, usually at intersections. On two-lane roads they can slow traffic. Some communities provide special bus lanes to help move traffic. Expect buses to make frequent stops. Be alert for pedestrians rushing to catch a bus or crossing the street after getting off.

School Buses   Because children are often unaware of the dangers of traffic, you have a huge responsibility for driving cautiously near school buses. Watch for bright yellow buses in the morning and afternoon when schools are opening and closing.

Children are at greatest risk of injury around buses that are loading or unloading. Reduce speed around school bus stops. Search for children who are rushing to catch a bus. Be prepared to stop.

You must stop for the flashing red lights on a school bus. Some school buses have amber lights that flash before the red lights begin, or a STOP arm that swings out from the driver's side of the bus, as shown in **FIGURE 16**. When the red lights begin to flash, motorists traveling in both directions must stop before reaching the school bus. All traffic must remain stopped until the flashing red lights are turned off.

Passing a stopped school bus with flashing red lights is a serious offense and can result in a large fine, or even a suspended license. Being patient and cautious will help ensure that children arrive safely.

Emergency Vehicles

Sooner or later, you will hear the sirens or air horns and see the strobe lights of an emergency vehicle. **Emergency vehicles** respond to fires, medical emergencies, rescues, and incidents involving hazardous materials. The driver of an emergency vehicle may disregard traffic signs, speed limits, and the direction of traffic and parking.

Emergency vehicles require immediate action. When an emergency vehicle approaches from any direction, you must yield the right of way. Under normal circumstances, the emergency vehicle will seek to pass you on the left. Help emergency vehicles get to their destination by pulling as far to the right as possible and stop until the emergency vehicle passes. If it is not possible to pull right, stop in a place that is out of the path of the emergency vehicle.

Avoid gawking or rubbernecking. This only adds to congestion and potential conflicts.

FIGURE 16

Children are at greatest risk when they are getting on or off a bus. Vehicles from both directions must stop until the lights stop flashing.

FIGURE 17
LSVs come in a wide variety of designs and types.

Other Specialized Vehicles

In addition to trucks and buses, you share the roadway with a number of other kinds of vehicles. These include low-speed vehicles, snowplows, and farm equipment.

Snowplows and Other Equipment   At different times of the year, you may encounter snowplows, farm vehicles, or equipment used for construction, such as backhoes. These vehicles typically travel very slowly. Manage your space by adjusting your path of travel to gain the best line of sight. When passing, watch for plows or other equipment that are wider than the vehicle itself. Protruding equipment can cause serious harm to you and your vehicle.

Low-Speed Vehicles   Low-speed vehicles (LSVs) include all four-wheeled vehicles (except trucks) with top speeds between 20 and 25 mph. These include golf carts and neighborhood electric vehicles (NEHs). NEHs are growing in popularity, as they require no trips to the gas station, have no emissions, and have lower maintenance requirements. LSVs are not required to have doors or bumpers, but must have a license plate and safety features such as turn signals, windshields, and seatbelts.

When you encounter an LSV, be aware of its low power and lack of protection. Be prepared to adjust your speed and position to avoid conflict.

review it 11.4

1. What is a truck's no zone? Where are the no zones of a large truck located?

2. What precautions should you take when following a large truck?

3. When using school buses, where are children most vulnerable?

4. What should you do when you see an emergency vehicle approaching you from the other side of a two-lane road?

5. What is a low-speed vehicle? What risks do LSVs present to drivers of other vehicles?

Critical Thinking

6. **Apply Concepts**   You are driving during rush hour with many tractor trailers on a four-lane highway. What low-risk driving behaviors will you decide to follow? Explain why.

IN YOUR COMMUNITY   **Interview**   Conduct an interview with someone who drives a truck, bus, or emergency vehicle for a living. Ask how driving the vehicle differs from driving a car. How could the behaviors of other drivers help reduce their risks? Write a report based on your conversation, and share it with the class.

CHAPTER 11 REVIEW

Lesson Summaries

11.1 PEDESTRIANS

- Pedestrians are more vulnerable when drivers make turns and when visibility is reduced.

- Crosswalks may have pedestrian-crossing signals. Marked crosswalks can be located at intersections or mid-block; unmarked crosswalks are typically located in residential areas.

11.2 BICYCLES AND MOPEDS

- Protect bicyclists and moped riders when turning or passing by searching for them and giving them time and space for safe travel.

- Drivers who are passing, turning, or backing should be careful of cyclists, especially children.

11.3 MOTORCYCLES AND SCOOTERS

- The small profile of motorcycles and scooters makes them difficult to see.

- Never attempt to share a lane with a motorcycle or scooter.

- Riders of motorcycles should wear protective gear for safety.

11.4 TRUCKS, BUSES, AND EMERGENCY AND SPECIALIZED VEHICLES

- On a two-lane road, it is against the law to pass a school bus when the warning devices are operating.

- Tractor-trailer trucks have four primary blind spots: directly behind, to the right of the truck, to the left of the truck, and directly ahead.

- Emergency vehicles have the right of way in all conditions and are not required to follow traffic laws.

Chapter Vocabulary

- emergency vehicle
- jaywalk
- low-speed vehicle
- moped
- no zone
- protective gear
- scooter
- tractor trailer

Write the word or phrase from the list above that completes the sentence correctly.

1. Although _____ generally have less-powerful engines than motorcycles, they can accelerate almost as quickly as motorcycles.

2. A small two-wheeled vehicle that can be driven using pedals or a motor is called a(n) _____.

3. A(n) _____ is more friendly to the environment than other motorized vehicles.

4. _____ includes a helmet, boots, jeans and brightly-colored clothes.

5. Drivers of tractor trailers have four blind spots that make it difficult for them to see you. A blind spot is also known as a(n) _____.

6. To cross against the light is to _____.

7. A driver of a(n) _____ can disregard traffic laws when responding to a disaster.

 **STUDY TIP**

Make a list of all the green headings in the chapter, leaving space between the headings. Below each heading, write one or two sentences that explain the heading. Then, refer to the lesson to check the accuracy of the information.

Checking Concepts

LESSON 1

8. What action would you take when a pedestrian is in an unmarked crosswalk?

9. Where are drivers most likely to encounter distracted pedestrians?

LESSON 2

10. In which direction should a driver expect a bicyclist to ride?

11. What driver action can cause a bicyclist to lose control?

LESSON 3

12. How can passengers affect a motorcycle operator's control?

LESSON 4

13. What can a driver expect when being passed by a tractor trailer?

14. What should you do if you are approaching a school bus that has flashing red lights?

Critical Thinking

15. Compare and Contrast Pedestrians and drivers both have responsibilities to stay safe. How do the responsibilities of a pedestrian compare to those of a driver? How do they differ?

16. Relate Cause and Effect According to the NHTSA, the most common initial point of impact for motorcycle collisions is the front. Explain how lane position and making turns can create conditions that cause crashes where the initial point of impact is the front.

You're the Driver

17. Why is it important for drivers of four-wheeled vehicles to use the IPDE Process when encountering two-wheeled vehicles?

18. How might driving behind a truck lead to aggressive behaviors? Identify two aggressive behaviors that might occur in a truck's no zone that could create dangerous situations.

19. Identify Explain the problem with the motorcyclists' position in the traffic lane and how to remedy it.

20. Decide You are driving behind this farm equipment. Is it safe to pass in this situation? Explain your reasoning.

Preparing for the Test

Choose the letter of the answer that best completes the statement or answers the question.

1. Most pedestrian collisions occur
   a. during rush hour.
   b. at marked crossings.
   c. during normal weather.
   d. at intersections.

2. You are driving on a city street and have the green light. A pedestrian begins to cross the street ahead of you. You
   a. should tell the pedestrian to return to the curb.
   b. can drive behind him as he crosses.
   c. must change lanes.
   d. must stop even if the light is green.

3. Mopeds are restricted from
   a. high-speed roadways.
   b. roadways after dark.
   c. rush-hour traffic.
   d. passing other vehicles.

4. Most states require that when a school bus is stopped to load or unload passengers on a two-way street, drivers
   a. in both directions must stop.
   b. should slow and prepare to stop.
   c. in the oncoming lane must stop.
   d. in the same lane must stop.

Use the figure below to answer Question 5.

5. The two motorcyclists are riding in an offset position to
   a. look cool.
   b. maneuver within their lane.

   c. prepare for a left turn.
   d. increase following distance from vehicles ahead.

6. To avoid traction-reducing conditions, motorcycle and scooter riders
   a. reduce speed.
   b. increase speed.
   c. swerve to the left.
   d. change lane position.

Use the figure below to answer Question 7.

7. You are the driver of the yellow car. You are
   a. not in the no zone area.
   b. rushing to get away from the tailgating car.
   c. moving out of the no zone area.
   d. in the largest no zone area.

8. When an emergency vehicle approaches with a siren, you should
   a. stop where you are.
   b. turn off the road.
   c. pull over to the right and stop until it passes.
   d. speed up and get away as quickly as possible.

drive write 🚗

Persuasive Argument   Twenty-nine states do not have a helmet law for bicyclists. The rest of the states require a helmet only for bicyclists who are 17 or younger. Write one or two paragraphs to persuade your senator that all states should have helmet laws for all bicyclists.

chapter 12

DRIVING IN ADVERSE CONDITIONS

12.1 Reduced Visibility

12.2 Reduced Traction

12.3 Other Adverse Weather Conditions

KEY IDEA

What can you do to manage the effects of hazardous weather on your visibility and your vehicle's traction?

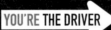

YOU'RE THE DRIVER ▶ Driving in hazardous weather, such as blizzards, heavy thunderstorms, or even rain and fog, requires special skills. The unpredictable nature of drivers in such conditions adds to the driving risk. How can you control your vehicle despite the environmental conditions you'll be driving in?

REDUCED VISIBILITY

OBJECTIVES

- Describe how to use the IPDE Process to manage risks in situations involving poor visibility.
- Explain what you can do to help others see you at dawn and dusk.
- Describe the special techniques you can use for night driving.
- Explain the procedure to use at night when encountering an oncoming driver who fails to use low-beam headlights.

VOCABULARY

- overdriving headlights

Whenever visibility is reduced, drivers need more time to use the IPDE Process and apply Zone Control driving techniques. You can maintain a safe intended path of travel by slowing down to give yourself more time; by scanning in and around your path of travel to the target area; by predicting others will maneuver into your intended path of travel; by deciding to position your vehicle ahead of time with an extra space cushion around it; and by executing driving actions gently to maintain control so others know what you are doing.

Dirty Windows

It's important to keep your windows clean because dirty windows will reduce your visibility.

A simple thing like moisture forming on the inside of your windshield can make the difference between safe, low-risk driving and colliding with another vehicle. When the slightest amount of moisture builds up, turn on your front-window defroster, switch on your rear defogger, or use the air conditioner or heater if it will help. You can always open windows as needed.

Clean all windows and lights ahead of time in bad weather. Keep a

FIGURE 1

Your windshield wipers won't be able to clean the entire windshield. **Evaluate** How would you manage risk in this situation?

close check on any ice, snow, or dirt buildup, especially on headlights and taillights. Stop to clear them by hand.

Even in good weather, clean windows can be a problem. The plastics used in many vehicle interiors can give off vapors that coat the inside of windows over time. Cigarette smoke can create a dirty-window problem as well. By keeping windows clear, you improve your ability to identify, especially at night.

Sun Glare

At times the sun can create severe and blinding glare conditions. Sunglasses and a sun visor can help, but try to avoid looking toward the sun.

By driving with low-beam headlights on all the time, you help other drivers see you. The brightest day will create the darkest shadows. With severe-glare situations and the sun behind you, be prepared for other drivers to miss seeing your signal or even seeing your vehicle.

Low Levels of Light

Low levels of light at night severely limit your ability to use the IPDE Process. Dawn- and dusk-driving situations can also be very dangerous. The low visual contrast between moving vehicles and the driving scene can be deceiving. Again, by always driving with your headlights on low beam, you can help others to see you.

Headlights   Keep these points in mind when driving with your headlights on at night:

- Use high-beam headlights to see further down the road. Also, look beyond your headlights for important information. Only use your high-beam headlights when vehicles are more than one-half mile in front of you.

FIGURE 2

Driving at dawn without headlights can set many traps.
Identify   How would you manage risk if the oncoming driver did not have headlights on?

Switch to low-beam headlights the instant you see the headlights of an oncoming vehicle, the taillights of a vehicle you are approaching, or the taillights of a vehicle that has just passed you. This prevents you from blinding the other driver with your headlights.

- Use low-beam lights in bad weather. In snow, heavy rain, or fog, high-beam headlights will reflect more light back into your eyes; as a result, you will see less.

Meeting Other Vehicles   If an oncoming driver has high-beam headlights on, take the appropriate action based on the following questions:

1. Is the oncoming driver far enough away to respond to you? Briefly flick your headlights from low to high to low to remind the oncoming driver to switch to low-beam headlights. Most new vehicles make this easy by having a flash-to-pass position on their high-beam control switch.

2. Is the oncoming driver closer, and still using high-beam headlights? Slow down, move to lane position 3, and glance at the right edge of the road.

3. Could you be blinded by bright oncoming headlights? Look ahead with frequent quick glances to check oncoming traffic. Do not stare directly into oncoming high-beam headlights.

4. Is it possible you will encounter a hazard to the right after the oncoming vehicle? Be ready to adjust to a new situation beyond the oncoming headlights.

Overdriving Headlights   The term **overdriving headlights** means driving at a speed that makes your stopping distance longer than the

---

FIGURE 3

The oncoming car has its high-beam lights on. **Predict** How might you have to adjust to a new situation beyond the headlights?

distance lighted by your headlights. Make sure you do not overdrive your headlights, especially in bad weather or on a slick road.

In normal driving conditions, use the following steps, known as the 4-second stopping-distance rule, to see if you are driving within the range of your headlights.

1. Pick a fixed checkpoint ahead the instant the checkpoint appears in the area lit by your headlights, as shown **FIGURE 4**.

2. Count off four seconds: "one-thousand-one, one-thousand-two, one-thousand-three, one-thousand-four."

3. Check your vehicle's position. When you have just reached your fixed checkpoint, you can assume your stopping distance on dry pavement is within the range of your headlights.

Visibility and Weather

Adverse weather can increase the risk of being unable to see your surroundings and be seen by other drivers. The best way to reduce the level of risk is to postpone driving until the weather clears. If you must drive in fog, rain, or snow, remember that with reduced visibility comes an increased level of risk.

Fog When your headlights shine into fog, light is reflected back by water particles in the air, making it harder for you to see. If you use high-beam headlights, your ability to see is reduced even further. Always use low-beam headlights in fog, as shown in **FIGURE 5**.

Fog also reduces your ability to judge distances. Oncoming vehicles may be closer than you think. Avoid trouble by slowing and increasing the space cushion around your vehicle.

Thick fog, even heavy industrial smoke, can be very dangerous. Before entering fog or heavy smoke, be prepared to slow or park safely off the side of the road.

---FIGURE 4---

The stop sign is five seconds away. **Decide** Are you overdriving your headlights?

---FIGURE 5---

In fog, other vehicles may be closer than you perceive.

If you stop at the side of the roadway, use your hazard lights to warn others that you are stopped. To be even safer, park in a rest area or parking lot.

Rain   Heavy rain reduces your ability to see and be seen. Keep your windshield clear by using your wipers and your defroster on if your windows fog. Make sure your low-beam headlights are on, as shown in **FIGURE 6**.

Many states require low-beam headlights to be on, when wipers are on. Reduce your speed. If the rain is so heavy that you cannot see well, be prepared to pull off the road and sit out the storm in a safe location, using your hazard flashers.

Snow   Wind-driven snow can reduce your vision, cover roadway markings, and make steering more difficult. Be prepared to slow and steer carefully. Heavy snow can block your rear window, reducing visibility. Slush or ice also can build up on your windshield wipers. If snow, slush, or ice build up, pull off the roadway and clean it off. Also, clear your headlights, taillights, and other parts of your vehicle as needed.

Use low-beam headlights when it snows, day or night. Reduce your speed to maintain control and to give others time to respond to you. If snow covers the road, closing your right-front zone, do not crowd the center of

FIGURE 6 Just like fog, heavy rain reduces your ability to see and be seen. **Apply Concepts** How would you manage risk if you were the driver?

the road by moving to lane position 2. This action has the effect of narrowing the road and could lead to a head-on collision.

Of course the best way to stay safe is to try to delay travel until roads and weather improve.

FIGURE 7 Blizzard conditions reduce visibility. **Execute** What special actions would you need to take in this situation?

review it 12.1

1. What actions should you take when using the IPDE Process in limited-visibility situations?

2. What steps can you take to help others see you at dawn and dusk?

3. When should you use low-beam headlights at night?

4. What should you do if an oncoming driver fails to use low-beam headlights?

Critical Thinking

5. **Apply Concepts** How would you try to alert an oncoming driver to turn on the headlights?

6. **Relate Cause and Effect** Why are high-beam headlights not as effective as low-beam headlights in increasing a driver's visibility in fog or snowy conditions?

IN THE PASSENGER SEAT **Turn on Those Lights!** How common is it for drivers in your community to have their headlights off in reduced-lighting situations? When riding as a passenger during times of reduced lighting, keep track of how many drivers do not have their headlights on when they should. Keep records for at least five different days and report your findings to the class.

lesson 12.2
REDUCED TRACTION

 OBJECTIVES

- Describe what happens to traction during rain and snow.
- Identify the steps to take to avoid hydroplaning.
- Describe how to correct an understeer skid situation.
- Explain how to use the controlled-braking technique.

 VOCABULARY

- hydroplaning
- rocking
- skid
- understeer situation
- oversteer situation
- fishtail
- controlled braking

Traction allows your tires to grip the road so that you can control your vehicle. Rain, snow, ice, sand, and other materials can limit your traction. Reduced traction can create high-risk driving situations.

Wet Roadways

Rain-slick roads can create a problem for any driver. You can avoid trouble by knowing the right actions to take ahead of time.

Rain   When rain starts to fall, it mixes with dust and oil on the road. This mix can make the road very slippery, until more rain washes the mixture away.

Any amount of rain will reduce the traction needed to start, stop, and steer the vehicle. Reduce speed to make better use of limited traction on wet roads.

Hydroplaning   When a tire loses road contact by rising up on top of water and no longer has contact with the road, **hydroplaning** occurs. Hydroplaning is caused by a combination of standing water, speed, and tire condition. The deep tread of new, properly inflated tires will cut through the water and grip the road. But even with good tires, hydroplaning can occur at speeds of 35 mph, in water as little as 1/12-inch deep. Tires that are bald or under inflated can start to lose their grip and hydroplane at less than 35 mph. Slushy snow in standing water also increases the risk of hydroplaning.

FIGURE 8

Any standing water is a risk to drivers. **Decide** What action should be taken to avoid hydroplaning *before* driving through the water?

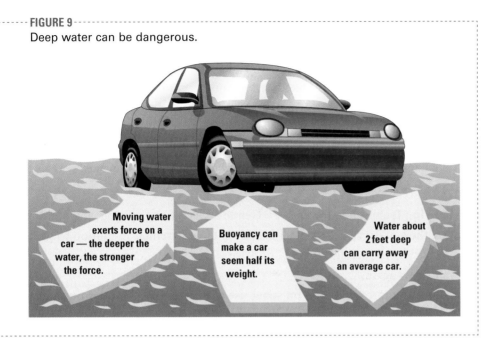

FIGURE 9
Deep water can be dangerous.

Moving water exerts force on a car — the deeper the water, the stronger the force.

Buoyancy can make a car seem half its weight.

Water about 2 feet deep can carry away an average car.

If you must drive through standing water, reduce speed and use properly inflated tires with good tread to avoid hydroplaning.

Deep Water   If you don't know the depth of the water ahead, do not drive through it. If you must drive through deep water, use the following steps:

1. Estimate water depth by watching other vehicles and looking at objects such as fire hydrants, fence posts, and parked vehicles. **If there is even a slight possibility of the water coming up to the bottom of your vehicle, do not enter the water.**

2. If the water is just over the rims of your tires, drive slowly in low gear. Avoid driving on a soft shoulder. Try to drive on the higher center of the road.

3. When driving at a low speed through water, apply a light brake pressure with your left foot to build friction and create heat on your brake pads. This heat will help dry your brakes and keep them working.

4. After leaving the water, squeeze your brake pedal lightly to see if your brakes are working normally. If your vehicle pulls to one side or does not slow, drive for a short distance while applying a light brake-pedal pressure with your left foot to help dry your brakes.

DID YOU KNOW?

Floods cause more deaths than any other weather condition, and 60 percent are vehicle related.

Snow

Different types of snow can produce different levels of traction. When fresh snow falls at low temperatures, traction can be fairly good. When traffic packs the snow at places like intersections, traction can be reduced. In subzero weather, even the moisture from vehicle exhaust can freeze into dangerous ice on the pavement.

Temperatures at or just below the freezing point (32°F or 0°C) can create dangerous traction situations. The combination of snow, slushy water, and ice can make for extremely slippery surfaces.

Driving Techniques for Snow   Gentle acceleration, steering, and braking are the keys to vehicle control in snow. Put your vehicle in motion by gently squeezing the accelerator. If your drive wheels slip, release your accelerator and start again.

To improve traction on snow, use all-season tires. To improve traction even more, many states allow the use of tire chains at certain times. Chains are placed over the tread on the tires to increase traction.

Rocking   Often you can move your vehicle out of deep snow, mud, or sand by driving forward a little and then back a little. By repeating this sequence, you can work your way out. This technique is called **rocking** a vehicle. Check your owner's manual to make sure this procedure will not hurt your transmission. If it is okay, follow these steps:

1. Straighten your front wheels as the driver in **FIGURE 10** has done.
2. Gently accelerate forward. Do not spin your wheels.
3. Let up on your accelerator. Pause just long enough to let the engine slow. Shift to REVERSE and gently move backwards. Let up on your accelerator and shift to DRIVE to move forward.
4. Continue this back-and-forth movement until your vehicle has cleared tracks that are long enough to drive out.

--------- **FIGURE 10** ---------

Evaluate   Why are gentle control actions needed to rock your vehicle?

Ice

Be especially alert if temperatures drop below freezing and it is raining. These conditions are just right for snow, ice, and sleet. Predict the worst when ice begins to form.

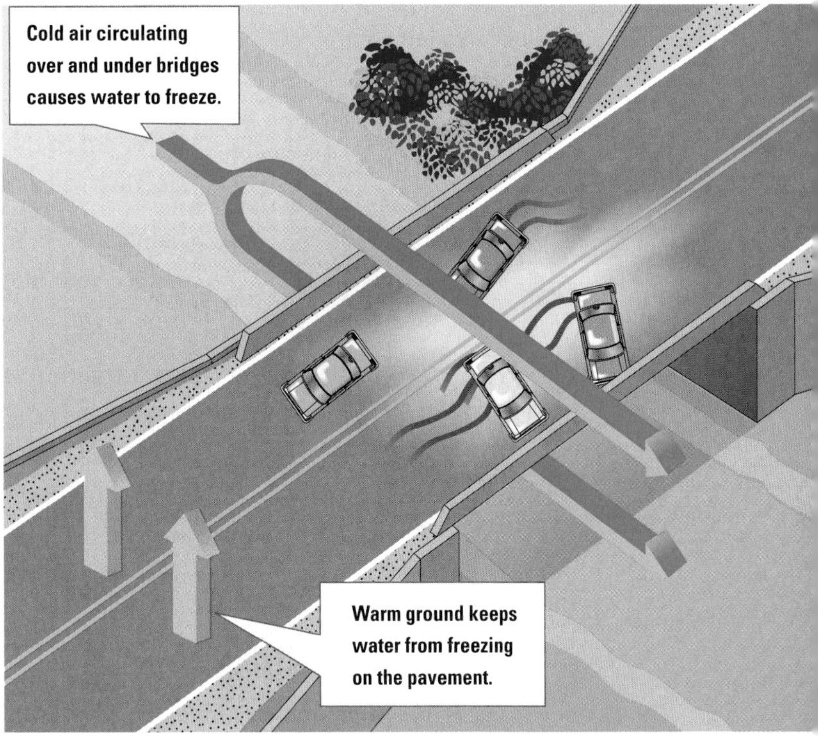

Temperatures will change the amount of traction you will have on ice. If the temperature of ice warms from 0°F to 32°F, your traction will be cut in half.

Squeeze your brakes lightly to check your traction in icy areas. Only do this at low speeds away from traffic. Slow gradually if your vehicle starts to slide.

Windows and windshield wipers can also ice up in severe weather. If your defroster cannot keep your windshield clear, pull out of traffic and clear it manually. It might be best not to drive at all.

If you must drive, be extra alert for these icy situations:

FIGURE 11   Ice forms on bridges and overpasses first.

Cold air circulating over and under bridges causes water to freeze.

Warm ground keeps water from freezing on the pavement.

Ice on Bridges   Bridge roadways tend to freeze before other roadway surfaces. Cold air circulates above and below the roadway on bridges and overpasses, as shown in **FIGURE 11**.

Black Ice   Be alert for "black ice" that forms in thin sheets, which can be extremely hard to see. Be extra careful for this type of ice in winter mountain situations.

Ice in Tire Tracks   Snow can pack down into ice in the normal driving tracks, especially at intersections. Avoid these slippery tracks by moving a little to the right in lane position 3 to use the unpacked, less-slick portion of your lane.

Other Reduced-Traction Situations

Braking distance will always increase in low-traction situations. Slow early and then be ready to slow even more.

Gravel roads and loose gravel on a road's surface will affect your control.

Gravel Roads   Loose gravel on roads can act like marbles under your tires and cause skids. Well-packed wheel paths usually form on heavily traveled gravel roads. Drive in these paths for better traction and control. If you need to move out of the wheel paths, slow down, and hold your steering wheel firmly.

Leaves   Wet leaves on the road can decrease traction and reduce your stopping and steering control. Slow ahead of time if you see wet leaves on the pavement.

Construction Areas   Construction trucks and other equipment can leave mud, dirt, or sand on the road. Slow, steer gently, and obey workers' directions. Be especially careful for workers and construction drivers who do not see you. Use an extra space cushion to protect them. In many states, traffic fines double in construction zones.

Skidding

In extreme reduced-traction situations, your tires may lose all or part of their grip on the road and **skid**. Skidding can happen on any surface while you are braking, accelerating, or steering.

Construction zones can create hazardous roadway conditions. **Identify**   What are some factors that could affect your traction in this road construction area?

In addition to slowing ahead of time, early detection is one of your best defenses to control skidding. Look ahead to see your target well down the road. The instant you see your vehicle is not traveling in your intended path of travel toward your target, you need to start correcting the skid. If you wait until you feel your vehicle skidding, you may not be able to correct the skid in time to avoid trouble.

Loss of Traction   If you know and can execute the correct response when your tires lose traction and you start to skid, you will be able to control the situation more quickly. In all loss-of-traction situations, remember that a locked or spinning wheel provides no traction or steering control. Keep applying the correct driver inputs and responses and don't give up trying to correct a skid.

Loss of Traction to Power Wheels   You are at a stop sign and the road is slippery with hard packed snow and ice. As you accelerate to pull away from your stopped position, you notice your power wheels are spinning. What should you do?

In this situation, simply release your accelerator and allow the spinning tires to stop spinning and regain traction.

If you are driving a front-wheel-drive vehicle and apply too much power, the vehicle will likely just sit there while your front wheels spin. If you are driving a rear-wheel-drive vehicle, the rear wheels will slip and spin, and there will be a slight tendency for the rear end to slide out.

Loss of Traction to Front Wheels   You are in a residential area and turning. Your car is not turning as quickly as you want it to turn. The front wheels are sliding straight ahead. What should you do?

In this situation, your front wheels do not have enough traction for your vehicle to turn as it should. This is known as an **understeer situation**.

To correct the loss of traction, ease off the accelerator. By doing so you allow more weight to the front, which should help provide more traction to your front wheels. In order for the vehicle to respond to your steering, the front wheels need to have traction.

Loss of Traction to Rear Wheels   Imagine you're driving at 50 mph when a dog suddenly runs into your lane. You brake hard, turn the wheel, and feel your rear end sliding out. This is known as an **oversteer situation**, a skid situation in which a vehicle's rear end tends to slip out or **fishtail**.

---FIGURE 14---

Two examples of a car skidding off target (represented by the yellow circle).

If your vehicle skids off target to the right, steer back toward your target area by turning the wheel to the left.

If your vehicle skids off target to the left, steer back toward your target area by turning the wheel to the right.

FIGURE 15
Correcting a fishtailing skid

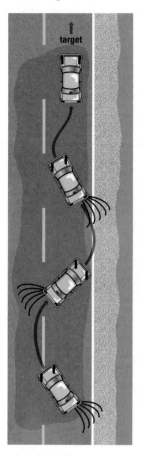

In this situation, when you hit the brakes a transfer of weight suddenly occurs. Weight is moved from the rear wheels and shifted to the front. This puts the vehicle out of balance. Then, when you turn the steering wheel sharply, the out-of-balance vehicle starts to go out of control, as the rear end begins to slide out.

In rear-wheel-drive vehicles when an oversteer situation occurs, you do not want to apply more power to the sliding wheels. Antilock braking and stability control systems help minimize fishtailing. Here are actions you should take:

1. Release your accelerator or brake. With manual transmission, depress your clutch pedal.

2. Steer quickly and precisely in the direction your vehicle needs to go, as shown in **FIGURE 14**. On a straight road, steer for your target and intended path of travel. Be careful not to overcorrect for the skid by steering too much.

3. The rear end of your vehicle probably will continue to fishtail after you have corrected the initial skid. Steer and countersteer in the direction your vehicle needs to go. As your speed drops, your control will increase. Look at **FIGURE 15** to see how you can provide precise, smooth, continuous steering actions to correct a fishtail.

A key to avoiding oversteer situations is maintaining your vehicle's balance. If you feel the rear end slide out, let up on the gas pedal, focus on your target area, and steer toward that target down your intended path of travel.

Keep in mind that although rear-wheel-drive vehicles have a tendency to oversteer, and front-wheel-drive vehicles tend to understeer, each type of vehicles can experience both conditions.

Controlled Braking

Too much braking in a panic stop can lock your wheels, causing a skid and loss of steering control.

Use **controlled braking** to reduce your speed as quickly as possible while maintaining steering control of your vehicle. Controlled braking is a technique of applying your brakes to slow or stop quickly without locking your wheels. Follow these steps to use controlled braking.

1. With the heel of your foot on the floor, let the ball of your foot press your brake pedal. You must press hard enough to slow your vehicle rapidly without locking your wheels.

2. If your wheels lock and your vehicle skids, ease up on your brake pedal just enough to let your wheels start rolling.

3. Keep using this squeeze–relax a little–squeeze process until you stop.

Using just the right amount of pressure is the hardest part in controlled braking situations. To overcome this problem, most new vehicles are equipped with an antilock braking system (ABS). An ABS-equipped vehicle uses a computer to prevent its wheels from locking—even in an emergency stop. If your vehicle has an ABS, just press the brake pedal as hard as you can in an emergency. You may feel little pulses through the brake pedal or hear the ABS at work. Don't let up on the brake pedal; maintain firm pressure until you stop. Also remember, ABS vehicles will allow you to steer and brake at the same time. *They will not enable you to stop in a shorter distance.*

FIGURE 16 shows how far a typical vehicle travels before stopping when braking at a speed of 20 mph. Notice the difference that different tires and road surfaces can make.

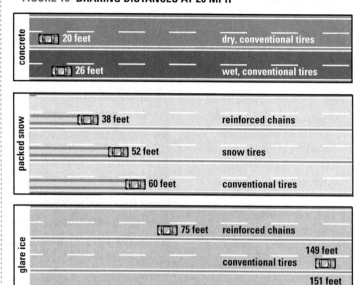

FIGURE 16 BRAKING DISTANCES AT 20 MPH

concrete
- 20 feet — dry, conventional tires
- 26 feet — wet, conventional tires

packed snow
- 38 feet — reinforced chains
- 52 feet — snow tires
- 60 feet — conventional tires

glare ice
- 75 feet — reinforced chains
- 149 feet — conventional tires
- 151 feet — snow tires

review it 12.2

1. How do rain and snow affect a vehicle's traction?
2. How does hydroplaning affect vehicle control?
3. How do you know if you are experiencing an understeer situation?
4. How can a driver attain maximum controlled braking in a vehicle that is not equipped with ABS?

Critical Thinking

5. **Relate Cause and Effect** Explain why tires with poor or little tread can cause a vehicle to be less fuel efficient.

6. **Apply Concepts** Explain why front-wheel-drive vehicles are less likely to experience situations in which the rear end slides out.

IN YOUR COMMUNITY **On the Skids** Identify a busy intersection in your community and observe traffic after a fresh snow or rainstorm. Watch vehicles approaching the intersection and identify how many vehicles were able to stop without skidding and how many experienced a skid situation when attempting to stop. Report your findings to your class.

lesson 12.3
OTHER ADVERSE WEATHER CONDITIONS

 OBJECTIVES

- Explain how to maintain control of your vehicle in windy conditions.
- List precautions for driving in extremely hot or cold weather.
- Describe what to do to maintain vehicle control during winter driving.

 VOCABULARY

- exhaust pipe

Extreme weather conditions can make routine driving very difficult. Other adverse conditions such as wind, extreme temperatures, and winter weather may also affect the control you have while driving.

Wind

Strong winds can reduce your vehicle control and push lightweight vehicles out of the lane or even off the road. Just remember to keep a balanced grip on the steering wheel and be ready to make steering corrections for crosswinds.

Sometimes a passing truck can produce a strong blast of wind. To maintain control, be ready to slow a little, move to lane position 3, and apply extra steering to the left just to keep moving in your intended path of travel.

In the unlikely event you are in an area where tornadoes are spotted, be ready to act. The last place you want to be in a tornado is in a car. If you see a tornado, stop, get out of your vehicle, and lay down in a ditch or under a bridge.

----- FIGURE 17 -----

It's a very windy day and the wind is moving from your left to right. **Predict** What should you expect to occur once the truck on the left has completely passed you?

Hot Weather

Your vehicle is designed to operate in a wide range of temperatures. It has a cooling system to help it warm up in winter and stay cool in the summer. But in extreme conditions, problems can develop.

Your temperature light or gauge indicates when your engine is too hot. When this happens, turn off your air conditioner. It may be uncomfortable, but you might also be able to cool your engine by turning on your heater. If the engine temperature warning light stays on, stop and park in a safe place to let the engine cool. Once cool, check the coolant level in your cooling-system surge tank. Never remove the radiator cap on a hot engine because the hot liquid inside can scald you. If needed, refill and repair your cooling system.

Cold Weather

Very cold weather creates problems for vehicles.

Be Alert for Exhaust Leaks

Carbon monoxide gas is created when your engine runs. This gas is color-less, odorless, and deadly. Even a small exhaust leak can be dangerous. When driving, always have a source of fresh air coming into your vehicle—even if you have to open a window a little. If you are stuck in snow with your engine running, make sure your **exhaust pipe**, or tailpipe, is not blocked, as the woman in **FIGURE 18** is doing.

Do Not Race a Cold Engine
Racing a cold engine will increase wear on it. Do not run a cold engine at high speeds.

Do Not Set Your Parking Brake
Ice or slush stuck to the underside of your vehicle can freeze your parking brake when you park your vehicle. In these conditions, use your automatic transmission PARK gear, or the REVERSE gear with a standard transmission.

Tips for Smooth Winter Driving

Winter driving will test the best of your IPDE driving skills. The extra effort you make to maintain an adequate line of sight is worth it. The following tips will help make winter driving a smooth process:

Look and Listen for Traffic Reports
Be alert to television and radio reports about collisions, road repairs, and bad weather. You also can take advantage of Internet sources.

FIGURE 18
The woman is checking the exhaust pipe before she gets in the car. **Analyze** Why is it a good idea to clear deep snow away from your tailpipe?

drive
green

Idling When warming your vehicle in cold weather, avoid excessive idling. Excessive idling can overheat a vehicle's engine, waste fuel, and add air pollution.

FIGURE 19
Be sure to clear your windows, roof, hood, trunk, headlights, and taillights of snow and ice.

Keep Windows Clear   Remove snow and ice before driving as the driver in **FIGURE 19** is doing. Don't forget to clean your headlights and taillights. You want to see and be seen; you do not want snow to blow off and block your vision or become a hazard to vehicles behind you.

Respect Lower Speeds   Travel with the flow of traffic, but always maintain control of your vehicle.

Keep a Safe Following Distance   Allow six, seven, or more seconds of following distance just to make sure you have room.

Try to Keep Moving in Snow   If you must be out in a blizzard, be alert for drivers who are stalled, disabled, or moving extremely slowly. Try to avoid getting stuck behind them. Slow down and maneuver to avoid others and to keep moving. The energy of motion created by your moving vehicle can help carry you through snowy situations.

Use a Lower Gear on Slippery Roads   Use a lower gear to maintain control on ice or snow. Remember to keep moving to avoid getting stuck.

Avoid Cruise Control   Do not use cruise control on slippery roads. The system could cause you to lose control.

review it 12.3

1. What actions must you take to maintain vehicle control in strong winds?
2. What can you do to cool an overheated engine?
3. Why should you try to keep moving at low speeds in heavy snow?

Critical Thinking

4. **Relate Cause and Effect**   Explain why driving under an overpass in extremely windy conditions can affect vehicle control.

5. **Predict**   You're on an interstate and following a large semi-tractor trailer with a lot of snow on top of its trailer. What potential hazard might this pose to you? What could you do to minimize risk in a situation like this?

IN THE PASSENGER SEAT   **Losing Traction**   Your friend is driving to school when it starts to snow heavily. Because you're late for class, she begins to speed up and starts to skid. What would you say to your friend to help her control the skid?

CHAPTER 12 REVIEW

Lesson Summaries

12.1 REDUCED VISIBILITY

- When visibility is poor, slow down, allow extra space, and actively scan and search.
- Proper use of high- and low-beam headlights helps drivers see better and prevents blinding—or being blinded by—oncoming drivers.
- Driving with your headlights on helps others see you, especially at dawn and dusk.

12.2 REDUCED TRACTION

- Whenever the road surface is wet or snow-covered, traction is reduced.
- When a vehicle's tires rise on top of standing water, the tires lose traction and the vehicle does not respond to steering.
- Understeer and oversteer conditions, if not quickly corrected, can put a vehicle out of control.

12.3 OTHER ADVERSE WEATHER CONDITIONS

- Strong side winds can cause your vehicle to shift lane positions. Driving in windy conditions requires constant steering corrections to maintain lane position.
- Extreme temperatures place demands on vehicles' heating and cooling systems, and often cause vehicles to overheat.
- Snow can adversely affect a driver's vision and a vehicle's traction.
- Greater vehicle control can be maintained on snow- and ice-covered roads by accelerating, steering, and braking gradually and gently.

Chapter Vocabulary

- controlled braking
- exhaust pipe
- fishtail
- hydroplaning
- overdriving headlights
- oversteer situation
- rocking
- skid
- understeer situation

Write the word or phrase from the list above that completes the sentence correctly.

1. A(n) _____ results when a vehicle loses part or all of its grip on the road.

2. _____ is a technique that can be applied when trying to move your vehicle out of deep snow.

3. The action of a vehicle's rear end sliding out to a side is called a(n) _____.

4. _____ is a technique of reducing your speed as quickly as possible while maintaining control of your vehicle.

5. Driving at a speed where the stopping distance of your vehicle is longer than the distance you can see with your headlights is called _____.

6. _____ occurs when a tire loses road surface contact and rises on top of water.

7. It is a(n) _____ when your front tires begin to plow and your vehicle is not responding, or not responding as quickly as it should, to a steering input.

✓ ✓ ✓  **STUDY TIP**

Make a Poster Draw a diagram illustrating an understeer situation, along with a description. Your partner will create a similar poster for an oversteer situation. Share your posters and discuss the accuracy of both the drawings and the descriptions.

Checking Concepts

LESSON 1

8. How do you apply the IPDE Process to manage risks in bad weather?

9. What can you do to help others see you at dawn and dusk?

10. What special driving techniques can you use for night driving?

LESSON 2

11. What happens to traction during rain and snow?

12. What steps can you take to avoid hydroplaning?

13. How do you correct an understeer skid in a front-wheel-drive vehicle?

14. How do you use controlled braking in a vehicle without ABS?

LESSON 3

15. How can you control your vehicle in windy conditions?

16. What precautions can you take for driving in extremely hot or cold weather?

17. What should you do to maintain vehicle control during winter driving?

Critical Thinking

18. **Evaluate** Why would a vehicle have more traction on snow at very cold temperatures than at warmer temperatures?

19. **Compare and Contrast** What advantage do vehicles with ABS provide to drivers for maintaining maximum vehicle control that non-ABS-equipped vehicles don't offer?

You're the Driver

20. **Decide** A heavy snowfall is occurring and traffic is heavy. Vehicles are in your lane, both ahead of you and behind you. What actions will you need to take to minimize risks ahead of and behind you?

21. **Execute** You are out on a rural road and it is raining. The road you are on has worn tire tracks in your lane, and there is standing water in the tracks. What can you do to avoid losing traction?

22. **Identify and Execute** What actions are needed to control your vehicle in this skid situation?

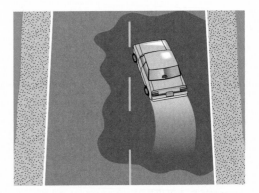

23. **Decide and Execute** In this winter situation, what precautions should you take when approaching the bridge?

Preparing for the Test

Choose the letter of the answer that best completes the statement or answers the question.

1. What does hydroplaning involve?
   a. ice and snow
   b. fog
   c. compacted gravel
   d. standing water

2. Where would icy conditions most likely first appear?
   a. on an overpass
   b. in an underpass
   c. in a roundabout
   d. at the exit of a tunnel

Use the art below to answer Question 3.

3. When you see this sign when driving in the rain, what action should you take?
   a. Turn on your headlights.
   b. Slow down.
   c. Turn off your radio.
   d. Turn on your flashers to warn vehicles behind of possible hazards ahead.

4. How do sliding wheels on snow or ice affect a driver's ability to control the vehicle?
   a. greater traction and greater steering control
   b. less traction and greater steering control
   c. the same as sliding on loose gravel
   d. ABS doesn't affect a driver's control of the vehicle.

5. ABS systems do not
   a. provide steering capabilities while applying hard brake pressure.
   b. create a pulsing sensation.
   c. make a strange sound.
   d. assure a shorter stopping distance than locked wheels.

6. When should high-beam headlights be used?
   a. during daylight hours so others see you
   b. when driving in a tunnel
   c. at night when alerting an oncoming driver that they do not have their headlights on
   d. at night when you need more light to see and no oncoming traffic is—or headlights are—visible

7. Which of the following is most likely to provide the best traction while traveling at 35 mph?
   a. a polished concrete road when it is snowing and sleeting
   b. a snow-covered roadway with a temperature of 27°F
   c. a loose gravel–covered roadway with snow falling and a temperature of 32°F
   d. a vehicle with poor tread on a snow-covered road

drive write

Safe Driving Tips Get a group of four students together to develop a series of Safe Driving Tip articles for submission to a local newspaper or your school newspaper. Identify at least four adverse driving conditions. Have each person take one condition and write a short article about it. Remember to develop and submit articles that are seasonally appropriate.

HANDLING EMERGENCIES

13.1 Vehicle Malfunctions

13.2 Driver Errors

13.3 Roadway Hazards

13.4 Collisions

13.5 Insurance

KEY IDEA

Sometimes, even the best drivers meet unexpected situations. Do you know how to handle emergency conditions?

Vehicle malfunctions, driver errors, and roadway hazards can cause emergencies. In all cases, you must be prepared to act quickly to avoid or minimize a collision. Do you know what to do in an emergency and what steps to take if you are involved in a collision?

lesson 13.1

VEHICLE MALFUNCTIONS

 OBJECTIVES

- List actions to take if a tire fails.
- List the proper steps to follow if the brakes fail.
- Describe what to do in case of engine or steering failure.
- Explain what to do in case of loss of forward vision and vehicle fires.

 VOCABULARY

- blowout
- compact spare
- brake fade
- forward vision

Proper maintenance can prevent most vehicle malfunctions. When your vehicle gives you any warning signs, promptly make the necessary repairs.

Vehicle equipment can sometimes malfunction without warning. A sudden malfunction can create an emergency. If you are prepared for an emergency, you will greatly reduce the risk of harm to people and property.

Tire Failure

Tires wear more quickly due to unfavorable driving and poor maintenance conditions. Abrupt braking and sharp steering shorten tire life. Bumps, potholes, and poor roadway surfaces add to tire stress and can cause sudden damage to tires. Unbalanced wheels and poor alignment can cause tires to wear unevenly. Underinflation and overinflation also cause tire wear.

Tire Blowout   A **blowout** occurs when a tire loses air pressure suddenly. A blowout might occur if the tire hits an object on the roadway or a pothole. Most blowouts, however, occur because a driver fails to maintain proper tire pressure. Older and badly worn tires are more likely to blow out.

When a front tire blows out, the vehicle quickly pulls in the direction of the deflated tire. You must focus on getting the vehicle back on target by steering firmly *against* the pull of the vehicle. A left-front tire blowout is especially dangerous, since the vehicle may pull toward the lane of oncoming traffic.

When a rear tire blows out, the back of the vehicle can fishtail. Handle a rear blowout just as you would a skid.

1. Grip the steering wheel firmly.

2. Ease up on the accelerator to slow the vehicle. Do not brake because it can cause the vehicle to swerve.

3. Check the traffic situation as you gain control of the vehicle.

FIGURE 1

If a left-front tire blows out, the vehicle might pull toward oncoming traffic.
Execute   What actions would you take to avoid a car with a blowout that was moving into your path of travel?

FIGURE 2 Many spare tires are called "50-50" tires. This means that the vehicle should not be driven over 50 mph or more than 50 miles on the spare tire.

4. Drive off the roadway slowly, braking gently.

5. Turn on hazard flashers. Drive slowly until you find a safe location to stop.

Changing a Tire   Even if you are an auto club member or your car insurance provides free roadside assistance, you should know how to change a tire. Tire-changing instructions are included in the owner's manual for your vehicle. Always refer to the owner's manual before changing a tire.

The most dangerous aspect of having a flat tire on the road is finding a safe place to change it. You can drive a short distance at a slow speed to get as far off the road as possible.

Replace or repair the flat tire as soon as possible. If your spare tire is a temporary or **compact spare**, such as shown in **FIGURE 2**, drive on it only as necessary under the manufacturer's conditions for use.

Brakes

The brake system is set up such that two systems are actually in place: one for the front wheels and one for the back wheels. If both braking parts fail at the same time, your foot brake will have no braking power at all; however, this rarely happens.

FIGURE 3 The brake warning light signals a problem with your braking system that needs immediate attention.

Total Brake Failure   Total brake failure rarely happens. However, if it does happen, stay calm and follow these steps:

1. Pump the foot brake pedal. Pumping might temporarily restore enough brake-fluid pressure to slow or stop your vehicle. You will know after three or four pumps if your brakes are going to hold.

2. Downshift to a lower gear. This uses the braking power of the engine to slow.

3. Pull and hold the parking-brake release lever out or hold the parking-brake button at OFF. Apply the parking brake. You can quickly release the parking brake for a moment if the vehicle begins to skid.

4. Search for a safe place to steer toward. As a last resort, rub the wheels against a curb to reduce speed. If a collision is unavoidable, steer for a sideswipe rather than colliding head-on into something solid.

When brakes overheat, they can lose effectiveness. This condition, called **brake fade**, occurs after continuous hard braking. To regain full braking ability, stop the vehicle and let the brakes cool.

Driving through water can temporarily reduce your brakes' effectiveness. Gently brake with your left foot as you drive through and leave the water. Friction will help generate heat to dry your brakes. Test them after leaving the water to be sure they work normally.

FIGURE 4 If your engine fails, turn on the hazard flashers, move safely off the roadway, and raise the hood to signal that you need help. If you have a cell phone, call for help. Be sure to stay away from any traffic.

Engine Failure

Usually you have very little warning that your engine is going to sputter or stop. With a stalled engine, you can still steer your vehicle. Follow these steps if your engine stops suddenly:

1. Shift to NEUTRAL when the engine first sputters or stops.

2. Begin moving out of traffic to the nearest shoulder. Turn on the hazard flashers. Do not brake.

3. Try to restart the engine while you are moving. If the engine starts, shift into a forward gear and proceed. If it does not start, move onto the shoulder or to the curb, if possible. Steering will be harder when power is lost by engine failure. Try again to start the engine.

If your vehicle becomes disabled in a risky situation, such as along a highway or around a curve, set flares or other warning devices to alert other roadway users.

Stalling on Railroad Tracks **If a train is approaching in either direction, abandon the vehicle immediately. Get away from the tracks as far as you can.**

FIGURE 5 Running toward the train helps you avoid injury from any flying debris.

If a train is not approaching, you can try to restart the vehicle. If you cannot restart the engine, have passengers leave the vehicle. Have one passenger watch for trains and ask others to help you. Before you push the vehicle off the tracks, put your car into NEUTRAL.

Overheated Engine Sometimes even a well-maintained engine overheats in hot weather or in stop-and-go traffic. Driving up long hills with the air conditioner on also can cause overheating. The temperature light or gauge warns you when the engine overheats.

Take these steps if your engine overheats:

1. Turn off the air conditioner and turn on the heater to draw heat away from the engine. You might be uncomfortable, but this will lower the engine temperature.

2. During stops, shift to NEUTRAL. Press the accelerator gently to speed up the engine slightly.

3. If the temperature light stays on or if the gauge points to hot, move to a safe place. Stop, turn off the engine to let the engine cool. Do not add water to the radiator until the engine has cooled. Steam can escape and cause severe burns.

Total Steering Failure

Total steering-system failure seldom occurs but is extremely serious when it does occur. If your steering fails completely, immediately communicate the emergency by using your horn and hazard flashers. Try to stop as quickly and as safely as possible. Lift your foot from the accelerator. Do not brake unless a crash is imminent because braking could cause the vehicle to skid. If you must brake, brake forcefully to reduce your speed.

You can hold the parking brake release and use a quick, on-off action. Try to shift into a lower gear.

Power-steering failure occurs when the engine dies, when the power-steering fluid level is low, or when a drive belt slips or breaks. The steering mechanism still works, but you must exert more effort to steer.

Loss of Forward Vision

When headlights fail, when the hood flies up, or even when your wind-shield gets splashed with dirt, your driving view, or **forward vision**, is obstructed. If you have lost forward vision, you must act promptly to regain your driving view. Immediately check your rear zone to see if it's safe to stop quickly.

The more aware you are of your targeting path before you lose forward vision, the better control you will have. A common cause of loss of forward vision happens when a windshield gets splashed with snow, slush, or mud. If this happens, hold your steering wheel steady and quickly turn on the wipers.

If you are driving at night and your headlights flicker, immediately put your right turn signal on to illuminate the path you need to travel as you move to the right shoulder of the road. You can also try the dimmer switch, parking lights, and hazard flashers, as some circuits might still work. If so, use parking or hazard lights to help you drive off the roadway to a safe location.

Once you're off the road, use a flashlight to check fuses or fuse clips. If necessary, replace or reseat the fuse before proceeding.

FIGURE 6

If you anticipate that your windshield will get splashed, turn on the windshield wipers so your forward vision stays clear.

Vehicle Fires

Vehicle fires are dangerous. A fire can involve fuel, oil, grease, ordinary combustibles, electrical equipment, or a combination of sources. Notify the fire department of any vehicle fires.

Most vehicle fires start in the engine. If your car suddenly starts to smoke:

1. Quickly steer the vehicle off the roadway to a safe, open area. Stay away from buildings and service stations. Turn off the ignition.

2. Have passengers move at least 100 feet away from the vehicle.

3. Even if you see flames around the hood, leave the hood closed and do not try to put out the fire. Move away from the vehicle while you wait for the fire department. The fuel tank could explode.

A passenger-compartment fire is usually caused by a carelessly handled match or burning tobacco product. Pull off the roadway immediately. Use water or a fire extinguisher and make sure the fire is completely out. Upholstery fires often restart, sometimes even hours later.

Fire is possible in any collision where the engine compartment is smashed. In the case of a collision, turn off the ignition and get passengers out and away from the vehicle.

review it 13.1

1. As a driver, what can you do to minimize the risk of tire failure?

2. Why is it important not to brake if you have total steering failure?

3. What actions should you take if your steering fails?

Critical Thinking

4. **Relate Cause and Effect** An approaching train traveling at high speeds may appear to be moving slower than it actually is. How could this affect a driver's decision to abandon the car on the tracks?

5. **Apply Concepts** Why do you think it's important to shift into NEUTRAL when your car's engine stops?

IN THE PASSENGER SEAT **Practice Changing a Tire** When riding with a licensed driver, arrange for the driver to stop in a paved parking area. After reading the owner's manual on how to change a flat tire, go through the process as if the tire were flat. Report on your experience to the class.

Driver errors cause most emergencies. Errors due to inexperience, distractions, lack of attention, and poor decisions can create driving emergencies. In addition, any driver can be trapped in an emergency situation by another driver.

Developing the right response to emergency situations can be a critical part of your total driving task. The instant you approach or find yourself in an emergency situation, you need to be prepared to take the right actions to avoid conflict.

Off-Road Recovery

Your actions to recover your lane of travel depend on the number of wheels off the road and what's ahead of you. In any situation where your wheels are off the road, you must know how to get back on the road safely.

Four Wheels Off the Road   If you are forced completely off the road, turning your steering wheel sharply in order to try and jerk your car back on the road could cause your car to roll over.

The SUV in **FIGURE 7** has all four wheels off the road. Since the vehicle is on a soft-turf surface and the **grade**, or slope, is away from the road, this driver should move slowly up to the road. After making sure there is no oncoming traffic, the driver can move back into the normal lane of travel.

Two Wheels Off the Road   When your two right wheels drop off the right side of the road, make sure your hands are firmly positioned at the 9:00 and 3:00 positions on your steering wheel. Then:

1. Steer toward your target while holding your car halfway on the road. Both your front-right and right-rear tires should be the same distance from the edge of the road.

OBJECTIVES
- Explain how to get back on the road if four wheels are off the road.
- List the steps necessary to return to the road when two wheels are off the road
- Explain when to use an emergency swerve.

VOCABULARY
- grade

FIGURE 7
The driver veered off the road.
Decide   How should the driver of the SUV correct this problem?

2. If there is no conflicting traffic and the road is straight and clear ahead, simply slow your car by letting up on the accelerator and braking very gently if needed.

3. When your speed has dropped to 10 mph or less, turn your steering wheel slightly (3–5 inches) to the left.

4. When your right-front tire touches the edge of the road, get back on the road by turning your steering wheel to the right 3–5 inches.

Once you're in your lane, resume a normal speed. If there is heavy traffic and the side of the road is wide, firm, and smooth, you can bring your car to a stop completely off the road and wait for traffic to clear before returning to the road.

Off-Road and Obstruction Ahead   If your two right wheels drop off the road and there is an obstruction like a telephone pole ahead, you will have to act quickly. Even though you follow the same steps as when two wheels are off the road, at higher speeds, precision steering is very important.

You must position your car so that it straddles the road drop-off. Then, without reducing speed, make your first turn to the left. Do not jerk the steering wheel. The instant your right-front tire contacts the edge of the road, turn to the right and focus all your attention on your target area. You must not hesitate in getting your car pointed toward the target area to avoid crossing into an oncoming lane of traffic.

Emergency Swerving

No matter how careful you are, you may find yourself in a position where your only maneuver to stay safe is to swerve sharply. The driver of the yellow car in **FIGURE 9** has been driving too fast for traffic conditions and too close to the car ahead.

FIGURE 8

The yellow car is approaching the intersection.
Decide   Should the driver of the yellow car—while traveling at 35 mph—stop or swerve?

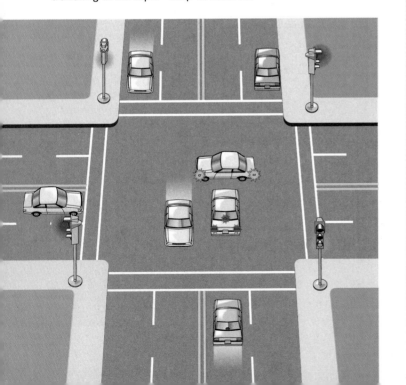

Remember that at 40 mph or faster, you can swerve into an open-right zone in a shorter distance than you would need to brake to a stop.

The amount of time a driver has to respond is controlled by his or her speed and distance. The faster a driver travels and the shorter the distance to an obstacle, the less time the driver will have to respond.

FIGURE 9

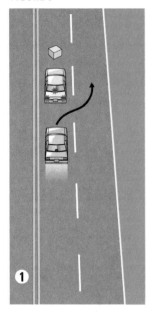

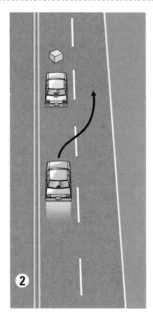

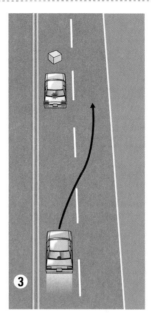

① You must swerve sharply around a close object.

② When the object is farther away, swerve less sharply.

③ The swerve is less sharp at a greater distance.

review it 13.2

1. When two wheels are off the road, why do you think it's important to keep your hands at the 9:00 and 3:00 positions?

2. Why is it important to steer toward your target area if your wheels drop off the road?

Critical Thinking

3. **Relate Cause and Effect** What driver, vehicle, or environmental conditions could make swerving an acceptable action?

4. **Infer** Why do you think you should swerve into an open-right zone rather than brake to a stop if you're traveling at 40 mph?

IN YOUR COMMUNITY **Research** Investigate the number and kind of crashes in your community that were due to driver error. Then suggest how each crash might have been prevented. Share your findings with the class.

lesson 13.3
ROADWAY HAZARDS

OBJECTIVES
- Describe how to reduce vehicle damage caused by potholes.
- Explain what to do if you enter a curve too fast.
- Tell how to escape from a vehicle that is sinking in water.

VOCABULARY
- air pocket

Unusual and unexpected roadway hazards can cause you to lose control of your vehicle. Driving into deep water, going around sharp curves, and encountering objects on the roadway can result in emergency situations.

Roadway Hazards

Be aware of the condition of a roadway surface and objects that may end up in lanes of traffic. You need to be aware of their potential impact on your vehicle. You also need to anticipate how other drivers ahead and alongside of you might react to roadway hazards.

Potholes in the Roadway   Potholes can develop as water collects in cracks in the roadway. The water can freeze and thaw, causing the cracks to expand. As vehicles drive over these water-filled cracks, they break up the roadway even more.

Potholes often have sharp edges that can severely damage tires. You can lose control of your vehicle—and severely damage it—if you hit a pothole at a fast speed.

Watch for potholes and avoid hitting them whenever possible. Drive carefully around or straddle a pothole. Stay in your own lane and check front zones as you try to avoid potholes in the roadway.

If you must drive through a pothole, slow down to prevent tire damage. By driving slowly, you can better keep control of your vehicle.

Objects on the Roadway   An object on the roadway creates a hazard, whether it is an object, leaves, an animal, or even a pedestrian.

First check traffic, and then decide whether to steer around, brake, straddle, or drive over the object. Choose to straddle the object only if your vehicle can clear it and you cannot safely steer around it. Avoid swerving left across the center line because you could encounter other traffic. Drive over an object only as a last resort.

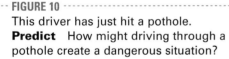

FIGURE 10
This driver has just hit a pothole.
Predict   How might driving through a pothole create a dangerous situation?

Driving Around a Sharp Curve   You should always enter a curve with care and caution. Driving too fast in a curve is dangerous because you can lose control easily. Take these actions if you enter a curve too fast:

1. Brake gently as soon as you realize your problem. If you are not yet in the curve, brake more firmly. If you are already in the curve, apply the brakes but do not lock the wheels. Antilock brakes and electronic stability control systems will help you in this type of situation.

2. About halfway through the curve, look to your target area and accelerate gently to help stabilize your vehicle.

FIGURE 11

The standard warning sign may not indicate exactly how sharp the curve is. Also, the warning sign might not have an advisory speed sign.

Vehicle in Deep Water

Never attempt to drive through deep water on the roadway. Turn around or take another route. However, if your vehicle goes into deep water:

1. Open the window that is the farthest from the water. Power windows might short circuit in water, so open these windows immediately, before the water level rises.

2. Unfasten your safety belt. Check your passengers and have them unfasten their safety belts.

3. Exit promptly through the open window.

If the windows will not open, attempt to exit through a door. Do not panic if the door is slow to open. Pressure will equalize as water enters your vehicle. You then can open the door.

If your vehicle is totally submerged underwater, some air will be trapped for a brief time toward the highest point of the vehicle creating an **air pocket**. During nighttime conditions, the location of the air pocket will tell you in which direction to swim to reach the surface. Try to get a full breath or two of air while locating a window or door that is facing up. Open the window or door and leave your vehicle.

drive green

Beginning in 2008, all new cars in the United States must have a tire pressure system to tell a driver when a tire is low. This saves tires, increases traction, and improves mileage.

FIGURE 12
You see a box in the middle of the road. **Decide** Should you steer around, brake, or straddle the object?

review it 13.3

1. How do potholes increase driving risk?
2. Why is it important to keep your wheels from locking if you enter a curve driving too fast?
3. Explain how you would escape a vehicle that is sinking in deep water.
4. How can you minimize damage to your vehicle caused by driving on a road with potholes?

Critical Thinking

5. **Reasoning** Explain how a pedestrian can become a hazard to a driver, and what actions to take to keep control of the vehicle.

6. **Relate Cause and Effect** How can you as a driver keep the roads free of hazards?

IN YOUR COMMUNITY **Dangerous Street Conditions** Take the time to identify the sections of roads in your community that are in need of repair. Present your findings to the public works department and ask them what needs to be done to solve this problem. Report your findings to the class.

Most drivers encounter "near miss" situations or actual collisions during their lives. If you know how to react to an emergency situation in advance, you can avoid or lessen the effects of a collision.

Collisions

If a collision is about to occur, you can minimize the effects by keeping control of your vehicle. Any change of speed or direction that lessens the impact will help. Steer for something "soft" if you leave the roadway. Look for bushes or an open field, and avoid objects such as trees and parked vehicles. Immediately get yourself and passengers out and away from your vehicle if there is a chance of another vehicle colliding with yours.

Head-On Collision   A **head-on collision**—in which the front ends of two vehicles collide—produces the greatest force of impact of any collision. As a result, serious injuries or death are more likely to occur in this type of collision than in any other. If you are threatened with a head-on collision:

1. Maintain vehicle control. Brake hard, but do not lock the wheels. Slowing lessens the force of impact and gives the other driver space and time to recover control.

2. Blow the horn and flash the headlights. These actions might alert an impaired driver. Continue braking and move to the right if the driver does not heed your warning.

3. Steer right toward the shoulder. Do not steer left. The other driver likely will try to steer back into the proper lane. Prepare to drive entirely off the roadway to the right, if necessary.

OBJECTIVES

- Explain how to avoid or minimize head-on, side-impact, and rear-end collisions.
- List the immediate steps and the follow-up steps to take if a collision occurs.

VOCABULARY

- head-on collision
- rear-end collision
- side-impact collision

FIGURE 13
A driver has moved into your path of travel. **Execute**   What should you do if you believe that you can't avoid a head-on collision?

Rear-End Collision   You are at greater risk for a **rear-end collision**—in which the front of one vehicle hits the rear of another—at an intersection. Checking your rearview mirror may give you the time and space to avoid being hit from behind. What can you do if you checked your rearview mirror as you slowed for a stop and saw a vehicle closing in on you quickly?

Take these actions if you are threatened with a rear-end collision:

1. Tap your brakes as you are slowing. This may alert the driver behind you.

2. Check your front zones for open space and be prepared to move to an open-front zone if you think the driver will not stop in time.

3. If a collision is unavoidable, release your brakes just before the collision occurs. This may soften the impact. Brake immediately after the collision to avoid sliding into another traffic lane.

Checking your rearview mirror, maintaining a 3-second following distance, and stopping so that you see the tires of the vehicle ahead are good habits. These actions often can help you avoid being hit from behind.

FIGURE 14

The driver of the white car might find it difficult to avoid being hit.
Predict   What can the driver of the white car do to minimize the effects of a collision on the passengers?

Side-Impact Collision   To avoid or lessen the effect of a **side-impact collision**—in which the front of one vehicle hits the side of another—brake or accelerate quickly. Do whichever seems more likely to lessen the collision impact. Blow the horn to alert the other driver, and change lanes or swerve into the space vacated by the entering vehicle. Be aware of the constantly changing traffic situation around you.

If You Have a Collision

If you collide with another vehicle, a pedestrian, or someone's property, you are legally required to follow specific procedures depending on your state's laws.

Stop Immediately.   Failure to stop is a serious offense. Move your vehicle to the side of the road. Do not leave your vehicle where it can block traffic unless it is too damaged to be moved. Turn off the ignition.

If you damage a parked vehicle even slightly, try to find the owner. If you cannot, write your name, address, and phone number on a note. Leave the note under a windshield wiper. Notify the police.

Aid the Injured.   **Never move an injured person unless there is danger of fire or another collision.** Send for paramedics if anyone is seriously injured. Administer basic first aid for injuries such as severe bleeding or shock only if you have completed a certified first-aid course.

Prevent Further Damage.   Warn oncoming traffic with flares or reflectors placed at least 100 feet ahead of and behind the collision site (500 feet away in high-speed traffic). If you do not have such devices, another person might stand in advance of the site and direct vehicles around the collision. Do not put yourself or others in danger while directing traffic.

Call for Police.   You must call the police if anyone is injured or killed. Some states require you to call the police for any collision, even if no personal injuries are evident.

Once police arrive, provide accurate facts. Never argue about who was to blame, and never admit blame. Stay at the scene until all information has been recorded. Take your vehicle to a repair shop for any necessary repairs. Depending on your insurance, you may need two repair estimates. Keep all bills.

Exchange Information.   Get and provide the following information from other drivers involved in the collision: names, addresses, driver's license numbers, license plate numbers, and insurance company names and addresses. Note the names and addresses of passengers, the positions in which they were sitting, and the extent of their injuries. Getting and giving this information is your responsibility.

File Necessary Reports.   Each state requires drivers involved in a collision to file a written report if someone is killed or injured, or if property damage exceeds a set amount. Some states require that a report be filed within 24 hours of the collision.

You must also produce proof of financial responsibility by showing a card that lists your current insurance coverage, or a bond card. Finally, notify your insurance agent promptly. If you fail to do this within the time-frame specified in your policy, the company might refuse to pay your claim.

review it 13.4

1. How can you reduce the impact of a head-on collision? A side-impact collision? A rear-end collision?

2. What steps should you take immediately if you are involved in a collision?

3. What additional steps should you take following a collision?

Critical Thinking

4. **Relate Cause and Effect**   Why do you think rear-end collisions occur most frequently at intersections?

5. **Apply Concepts**   Using cell phones to dial 911 to report emergencies is a relatively new procedure. How does dialing 911 help you?

6. **Reasoning**   If you're involved in a collision, what actions could you take even before help arrives?

IN YOUR COMMUNITY   **Emergency Response**   In many traffic crashes, it is the medical response team that makes the difference between life and death. Visit a local fire station or an independent ambulance service and interview a paramedic. Ask how they respond to and provide immediate care for individuals injured in a traffic crash. Report your findings to the class.

If you are involved in a collision, you may find that the largest expense of owning a vehicle is paying for damages you cause. Every state has a **financial responsibility law**, which requires you to prove that you can pay for damages you cause that result in death, injury, or property damage.

Vehicle Insurance

Insuring your vehicle is a financial responsibility. You buy insurance from a company by paying a **premium**, a specified amount of money for coverage over a specified period of time. A **policy** is a written contract between you—the insured—and the insurance company. A policy includes the terms and conditions of insurance coverage.

There are many different kinds of insurance. **Liability insurance** covers others when you are at fault in a collision. It provides compensation to the third party involved.

Your **collision insurance** provides coverage to pay the costs of repair or replacement of your vehicle, minus the deductible. A **deductible** is the amount you agree to pay towards the repair or replacement of your vehicle.

Because of the backlog and long delays in litigation cases coming to trial, some states have no-fault insurance. Although no-fault insurance works differently from state to state, generally people involved in collisions recover losses and expenses associated with the collision directly from their own insurance company—regardless of who is at fault.

OBJECTIVES

- Explain financial responsibility law.
- List three factors that affect the cost of insurance.

VOCABULARY

- financial responsibility law
- premium
- policy
- liability insurance
- collision insurance
- deductible

-----FIGURE 15-----

Top Five Most Expensive and Least Expensive Cities for Automobile Insurance, 2007					
Rank	Most Expensive	Average Annual Auto Premiums	Rank	Least Expensive	Average Annual Auto Premiums
1	Detroit, MI	$5,072	1	Eau Claire, WI	$869
2	Philadelphia, PA	3,779	2	Norfolk, VA	954
3	Newark, NJ	3,381	3	Raleigh, NC	966
4	Los Angeles, CA	3,027	4	Bismarck, ND	989
5	Hempstead, NY	2,764	5	Burlington, VT	1,001

As of June, 2007.
Source: Runzheimer International.

VEHICLE INSURANCE

TYPE OF INSURANCE	COVERAGE	COVERAGE INCLUDES	MINIMUM COVERAGE	INFORMATION
Bodily-injury liability	Pays claim against owner if someone is killed or injured and owner is at fault.	Hospital and doctor bills Legal fees Court costs Loss of wages	Each state normally specifies minimum: $10,000-$30,000 for one person $20,000-$100,000 for several persons	Required in most states. Minimum coverage required is often too low to cover costs. Needed by all vehicle owners.
Property-damage liability	Pays claim against owner if property of others is damaged and owner is at fault.	Other car and possessions in vehicle. Damage to house, telephone pole, and traffic lights and signs, etc.	States normally specify minimum coverage: $5,000-$25,000	Required in many states. Needed by all vehicle owners.
Uninsured motorist* and underinsured motorist	Pays for injuries to you and your passengers in case of a hit-and-run crash or a collision with an uninsured or underinsured motorist.	Hospital and doctor bills Legal fees Court costs Loss of wages Does not cover property damage.	Minimum is usually the same as bodily-injury liability.	Required in most states. Needed by all vehicle owners. Uninsured or underinsured driver must be at fault for coverage to apply.
Collision	Pays the cost of repairing or replacing owner's vehicle when owner is at fault or when owner cannot collect from person at fault.	Repair or replacement of any vehicle driven by the owner or with the owner's permission	Covers depreciated value of vehicle, usually with a $100-$500 (or more) deductible payment to reduce the cost of the premium.	Important for new or expensive vehicles. When value of vehicle no longer justifies the cost of this insurance, this coverage can be dropped.
Comprehensive	Pays cost of repairing or replacing the owner's vehicle from damage not caused by a collision.	Fire Theft Flood Wind Earthquake Storm Riots Vandalism	Covers depreciated value of vehicle, usually with a $100-$500 (or more) deductible payment to reduce the cost of the premium.	Important for new or expensive vehicles. When value of vehicle no longer justifies the cost of this insurance, this coverage can be dropped.
Medical-payment	Pays medical costs for you and your passengers injured in any collision, regardless of fault.	Generally pays all immediate medical costs and generally does not include wage loss.	Ranges from $1,000-$10,000 or more per person.	This insurance does not require a legal process to determine fault, while bodily-injury coverage usually does.
Towing	Pays labor cost of towing or minor repair to disabled vehicle.	Dead battery Out of gas Flat tire Crash, regardless of cause or fault	Usually pays the amount validated by the towing company. Typically does not cover parts or fluids.	Good to have. Not needed if owner belongs to automobile club with towing service.

*Note that uninsured-motorist insurance covers collision-related injuries only, not property damages. Some states allow insurance companies to offer uninsured-motorist, property-damage insurance.

Insurance Rates

A number of factors determine the cost of your insurance. Data on different factors are reviewed and statistics developed. Rates are then established based on the statistics. Factors upon which statistics are based and rates determined include:

▶ **Driving Record**   Drivers with a certain number of convictions for moving violations and collisions pay higher premiums because they are at a higher risk for collisions.

▶ **Age**   Younger drivers have a proportionally higher number of collisions; thus, they have higher premiums. Older, more experienced drivers have fewer moving violations and are involved in comparatively fewer collisions. A principal driver is a person who will drive a certain vehicle most often. A person under the age of 25 listed as the principal driver of a vehicle could pay as much as four times more than an older driver.

▶ **Miles Driven**   The more miles a vehicle is driven on a regular basis (usually annual), the greater the premium. This is because the vehicle is exposed to the possibility of a collision the more it's on the road.

▶ **Driver's Gender**   Male drivers tend to pay higher premiums. Historically, statistics have shown that men drive more and have more collisions, and their crashes tend to be more severe than those involving female drivers.

▶ **Marital Status**   Married drivers statistically have fewer collisions than unmarried drivers.

▶ **Type of Vehicle**   Sports cars, some vans, and sport utility vehicles tend to be stolen or vandalized often and cost more to repair.

▶ **Address**   Traffic density in urban areas increases the potential for collisions. Therefore, drivers who live in rural areas tend to pay less for insurance than those who live in larger metropolitan areas.

▶ **Driver's Claim Record**   Higher and more frequent claims, especially for comprehensive and collision coverage, will usually result in a higher premium. In some cases, the insurance company may simply cancel your policy.

DID YOU KNOW?

Reduced Premiums   Most insurance companies reward low-risk drivers with reduced premiums. Premiums are reduced for drivers who have maintained good grades in school, and in some cases, have successfully completed an approved driver-education program; who have had no claims or convictions for three years; and who have vehicles with certain safety features like airbags and anti-theft devices.

analyzing data

According to the Insurance Institute for Highway Safety, in 2005, nearly 2,000 teenagers aged 16 to 17 died in motor vehicle crashes. Many teens in the U.S. drive to and from school, and many crashes occur during these peak, on-road hours. Study the graph before you answer these questions.

1. **Reading Graphs** What does each line represent?

2. **Analyzing Data** During which two hours of the day during the summer did the most collisions occur? Which two hours of the day during the school year have the fewest collisions?

3. **Inferring** Suggest one or two reasons for the increase of deaths during the school year?

4. **Relating Cause and Effect** During the school year, most teenagers were involved in crashes on Friday and the fewest were involved in crashes on Sunday. What risk factors do you think contribute to this difference?

5. **Execute** As a driver, what actions can you take to reduce the number of crashes?

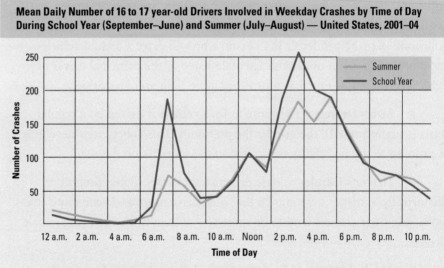

Mean Daily Number of 16 to 17 year-old Drivers Involved in Weekday Crashes by Time of Day During School Year (September–June) and Summer (July–August) — United States, 2001–04

review it 13.5

1. Describe what financial responsibility laws require.

2. What is the purpose of automobile insurance?

3. What are the main factors that determine the premiums charged for automobile insurance?

Critical Thinking

4. **Analyze** If you're involved in a crash, you should see a doctor, contact the police and file a report, and find out the legal consequences. Which of these actions do you think is most critical and why?

IN YOUR COMMUNITY **Research** Visit a local insurance agent and ask what the laws in your state require for insurance. Then ask what insurance plans the company has for drivers like you. You may find that things like good grades or being on your parents' policy will be important. Share your findings with the class.

CHAPTER 13 REVIEW

Lesson Summaries

13.1 VEHICLE MALFUNCTIONS

- Engine failures include a flooded engine, an overheated engine, and an engine fire.
- A total brake failure is, and needs to be treated as, an extreme emergency.
- Rain, sleet, fog, and even headlights that fail cause loss of forward vision.

13.2 DRIVER ERRORS

- Driving completely or partially off-road is a dangerous situation.
- Even though you maintain a space cushion around your car, you might be challenged by another driver. Knowing how to safely stop or swerve around a car ahead can avoid a crash.

13.3 ROADWAY HAZARDS

- Normal roadway problems like potholes or debris in the road can cause damage to your car.
- Driving in water can create dangerous conditions you need to avoid.

13.4 COLLISIONS

- If a collision happens, taking immediate action can help reduce the consequences.

13.5 INSURANCE

- Every state has a financial responsibility law that drivers must follow.
- There are different types of auto insurance. The cost of insurance is based on the state you live in and by the kind of insurance you choose.

Chapter Vocabulary

- air pocket
- blowout
- brake fade
- collision insurance
- compact spare
- deductible
- financial responsibility law
- forward vision
- grade
- head-on collision
- liability insurance
- policy
- premium
- rear-end collision
- side-impact collision

Write the word or phrase from the list above that completes the sentence correctly.

1. When the brakes on a car overheat, your car may experience a condition called _____.

2. The slope of a road is called its _____.

3. An insurance policy that includes _____ enables an at-fault driver to pay for harm or damages done to others.

4. The amount you agree to pay first as a result of a car crash is called the _____ amount in an insurance policy.

5. When a tire loses pressure suddenly, you have a(n) _____.

6. Another name for your driving view is _____.

 STUDY TIP

Role Play Pair with a classmate. One of you should say the name of an emergency situation from this chapter and see how quickly the other student can list the actions to take.

Checking Concepts

LESSON 1

7. Explain how to respond to a blowout.

8. How can you compensate for steering failure?

LESSON 2

9. Explain why it might be a better decision to swerve around a stopped car in front of you than to brake?

LESSON 3

10. What is the best way to avoid a pothole while staying in your lane?

LESSON 4

11. What is the first rule to remember when trying to reduce the effects of a collision?

12. What is the first step to take if you are in a crash?

LESSON 5

13. What is the most important type of car insurance you should buy?

14. List four factors that can change your insurance premium.

Critical Thinking

15. **Evaluate** Driver education teaches drivers how to respond in extreme situations that require quick action. How does knowing how to respond give drivers a better chance to avoid hazardous situations?

16. **Predict** If a driver is surprised by a fading brake situation, how long do you think it will take the driver to take the right actions to regain control?

You're the Driver

17. **Execute** Your vehicle has just been in a collision with another vehicle. What steps should you take immediately? What steps should you take after help arrives?

18. **Decide** Explain how potholes and debris on a roadway add risk to the driving task.

19. **Identify** The driver in the photo cannot stop in time to avoid hitting the bicyclist. What actions should the driver take?

20. **Decide** You are driving at 30 mph and approaching the stop sign ahead when your brakes fail. What should you do?

Preparing for the Test

Choose the letter of the answer that best completes the statement or answers the question.

1. To stop in an emergency situation when your car does not have ABS brakes, you should
   a. pump your brakes.
   b. slam on your brakes.
   c. apply hard, steady pressure without locking up your wheels.
   d. slam on your brakes so you lock up all the wheels.

2. When a car with bright headlights comes toward you at night, you should
   a. allow other drivers to pass.
   b. look below the lights.
   c. look toward the right edge of your lane.
   d. none of the above

3. When driving in adverse conditions, the proper speed to travel is
   a. the posted speed limit.
   b. 55 mph.
   c. 65 mph.
   d. only as fast as it is safe to drive.

Use the art below to answer Question 4.

4. When you see this sign without a gate or signal, you should
   a. assume the track is clear and move forward slowly.
   b. move closer to the vehicle ahead of you.
   c. pay attention and use good judgment.
   d. all of the above

5. Always leave extra space in front of you when
   a. the weather is hazardous.
   b. someone is following you too closely.
   c. you are following a motorcycle.
   d. all of the above

6. You should drive on the shoulder to pass a car
   a. only if the vehicle ahead of you is turning left.
   b. under no circumstances.
   c. when the shoulder is wide enough.
   d. with caution and an adequate shoulder.

7. If you are involved in a traffic collision, you must report it
   a. if someone is injured.
   b. if there is excessive property damage.
   c. no matter who is at fault.
   d. all of the above

8. If you drive faster than other vehicles on a road with one lane in each direction and continually pass the other cars, you will
   a. get to your destination faster and safer.
   b. increase your chances of running off the road.
   c. prevent traffic congestion.
   d. create a risky situation for yourself and other drivers.

drive write 🚗

Express a Point of View   More and more cities are starting to use high-tech equipment to record and charge drivers with traffic violations. Crashes at these sites are reduced, yet some people think this type of enforcement is unfair and violates their privacy rights. Write a short statement presenting your opinion on using high-tech devices to monitor driving behavior.

274

chapter 14

DRIVING IN CITY TRAFFIC

14.1 Adjusting to City Traffic

14.2 Following and Meeting Traffic

14.3 Managing Space in City Traffic

14.4 Special City Situations

KEY IDEA

What special driving skills will you need for city traffic?

YOU'RE THE DRIVER

Fast-moving, tightly-packed city traffic will put your driving abilities to the test. Pedestrians often act unpredictably, tailgaters can hit you from the rear, and the doors of parked cars may open suddenly. How can you navigate safely through the city?

lesson 14.1

ADJUSTING TO CITY TRAFFIC

OBJECTIVES

- Name two factors that can make driving difficult in city traffic.
- Describe how to use the IPDE Process for city driving.

VOCABULARY

- traffic density

Once you are comfortable making basic maneuvers and using the IPDE Process, you will be ready to start driving in city traffic. City driving will test your best abilities.

Traffic Complexity

When you drive on a little-used rural road in good weather at a moderate speed, you probably will encounter few critical hazards. However, driving in heavy, fast-moving city traffic is different and more challenging. **Traffic density**, or the number of vehicles you meet per mile, is heavier in cities, and city hazards can quickly block your path of travel. In city driving, you may have to respond to several close hazards and possible conflicts at the same time.

As you drive, remember it takes time to use the IPDE Process. You will have to contend with many situations involving closed zones and line-of-sight restrictions. If you cannot increase the distance between your vehicle and a hazard, you must change your lane position, slow, or stop to give yourself time to solve the conflict.

FIGURE 1

The number of city hazards can vary dramatically.

Decide Why does the photo on the right pose more hazards?

Using the IPDE Process

In heavy city traffic, you need to focus your attention on driving to avoid conflicts and distractions. You might see other drivers using cellular phones. You also will see aggressive drivers who needlessly increase the risk in a situation by challenging other drivers. In some situations, aggressive drivers who are cut off or being followed too closely may become so angry that they try to retaliate in some way. This kind of violent behavior or road rage is a criminal offense. In these situations, be cool and drop back. Give the angry, distracted, or absent-minded driver distance. You can control these situations by avoiding them.

As you drive, focus on the IPDE Process in these ways:

- **Identify**   Be vigorous in using your visual skills. Look well ahead to your target area. Check your searching ranges to make sure your front zone is open and you have time to spot things like a line-of-sight restriction.

- **Predict**   Predict possible points of conflict quickly and gain valuable time to respond.

- **Decide**   Always be ready to communicate or adjust your vehicle position by changing speed and using distance effectively.

- **Execute**   Be ready to use your vehicle's controls to make smooth low-risk maneuvers in traffic.

drive green

Tire Monitor   Remote-control key fobs are now being made that let you check the fuel and pressure on each tire before you get in your car. By monitoring your tire pressure, you can maintain good gas mileage.

---

review it 14.1

1. What two factors can make city driving difficult?

2. How can you best use the IPDE Process in city driving?

Critical Thinking

3. Relate Cause and Effect   Distractions are a leading cause of crashes. How can distractions become dangerous in city driving?

4. Predict   In some cities, rush-hour traffic can cause traffic jams and angry drivers on a regular basis. What are some things you can do to avoid getting trapped in rush-hour traffic?

IN THE PASSENGER SEAT   **Observe Traffic**   As a passenger, you can be a big help to the driver, especially in situations with high-density traffic. When riding in the city, record how you helped the driver follow directions, provided an early alert to important line-of-sight restrictions, and helped the driver avoid distractions. With your list, make a quick report to your class.

FOLLOWING AND MEETING TRAFFIC

 OBJECTIVES

- Describe how to use a 3-second following distance.
- Describe how you can safely manage a tailgater.
- List the steps to take to avoid conflicts with oncoming traffic.

 VOCABULARY

- 3-second following distance
- tailgate

You need to maintain ample space between your vehicle and possible hazards in all driving environments. Managing the distance between your vehicle and the vehicle ahead is the first step.

Following Traffic

An adequate following distance lets you see further ahead, lets others see you better, gives you more time to use IPDE, and puts you in a better position to avoid a front-end collision.

3-Second Following Distance A **3-second following distance** provides a safe distance from the vehicle ahead in most normal driving situations. Use the steps in **FIGURE 2** to measure your 3-second following distance.

This 3-second technique works well at all speeds for measuring a normal following distance. A 3-second following distance only protects you from colliding with the vehicle you are following. It is not the total stopping distance you need to avoid hitting a stationary object.

Increase your following distance to more than three seconds if driving conditions are not ideal.

FIGURE 2 3-SECOND FOLLOWING DISTANCE

Step 1: Pick a fixed checkpoint on the road ahead. Road marks or shadows make good fixed checkpoints.

Step 2: When the vehicle ahead of you passes your checkpoint, count: "one-thousand-one, one-thousand-two, one-thousand-three," for your 3-second count.

Step 3: If the hood of your vehicle does not reach the fixed reference point, you have an adequate following distance. If not, slow and add more distance.

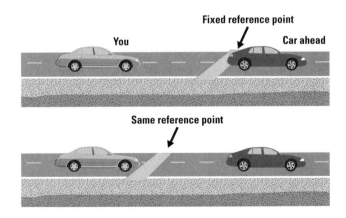

Stay Alert The 3-second rule is only one technique to use when following other vehicles. Also look over, through, and around the vehicle you are following. You can even see the reflection of brake lights on wet pavement by looking under the vehicle ahead. Be alert for brake lights. Always try to anticipate what the driver ahead is likely to do in response to a changing zone condition.

Be alert in areas where sudden stops can occur, in particular at intersections where drivers may have to stop for traffic or pedestrians, in lanes next to parked vehicles, and business driveways with high-volume traffic.

Tailgaters

You are in a high-risk situation when someone **tailgates**, or follows too closely. A tailgater is a hazard because if you have to stop suddenly, the tailgating driver can hit you from the rear. Tailgating drivers often think they can save time or make other drivers go faster. Neither is true.

Managing Tailgaters If you are being tailgated, take these actions to avoid being hit from the rear.

- Increase your following distance to at least four seconds. If you must slow or stop, you can do it more slowly and give the tailgater more time to respond.

- Move slightly to the right. This helps the tailgating driver see traffic further ahead.

- Signal early for turns, stops, and lane changes. Flash your brake lights ahead of time to warn a tailgater that you plan to slow or stop. Slow sooner to make a gradual stop.

- In extreme situations, change lanes or pull out of traffic to avoid the tailgater.

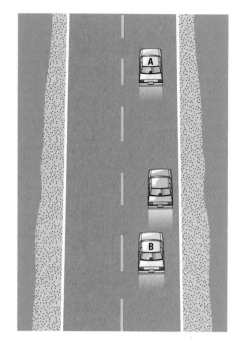

FIGURE 3 The driver of the yellow car has added tailgater protection by using a following distance longer than three seconds.

FIGURE 4 Ahead of you are two cars. The driver directly ahead has moved slightly to the right. **Infer** How does this help keep the driver safe?

FIGURE 5 You are driving a car approaching this intersection. **Predict** What do you predict the driver of the blue car might do?

Meeting Traffic

If a driver crosses the center line, you must react instantly. Knowing how to identify and predict, and how to respond to this type of situation before it becomes dangerous may give you enough time to avoid a collision.

Avoiding Conflicts If a vehicle comes toward you, take these actions to avoid a collision.

- Slow until the other driver can return to the normal lane. You can also slow so that you meet the other driver at a point where there is room to pass.

- Turn on or flash your headlights and blow your horn.

- If your right-front zone is open, move to the right to give the oncoming driver more room. Swerve sharply to an open space on the right if needed.

review it 14.2

1. Why do you think three seconds is used as a normal following distance?

2. What are two examples of reference points you can use for measuring your following distance?

3. How do tailgaters cause potential conflict to the driver ahead?

4. How can you avoid a conflict with an oncoming vehicle in your lane?

Critical Thinking

5. **Relate Cause and Effect** If you cannot see enough ahead of a truck in front of you, how can you adjust your distance in seconds?

6. **Apply Concepts** What are some examples of driving conditions in which a 3-second following distance would not be enough?

IN YOUR COMMUNITY **Research** Find out how many crashes in your community were a result of rear-end collisions, and the causes. Then try to find out how many rear-end collisions and their causes happened in your state. Compare your results, and note the top three reasons for rear-end collisions in both your community and the state. Make a graph to show your results and share your findings with the class.

lesson 14.3
MANAGING SPACE IN CITY TRAFFIC

When driving in city traffic, you must respond to a wide variety of situations. Unfamiliar streets, line-of-sight restrictions, narrow lanes, and high-density traffic all make your driving task difficult. To manage these situations, you will need to use your best skills combined with a positive, alert attitude.

How far ahead should you look while driving in the city? In addition to looking around your vehicle, look ahead one block or more. By looking far ahead into your target area to protect your path of travel, you will be able to identify zone problems in time to adjust your speed and/or position.

Approaching Traffic Signals

Look at your target area to detect traffic signals. By doing so, you will have more time to respond. If the light is red, slow and be ready to stop. If the signals on your street are synchronized to work together, you should be able to drive at or near the speed limit for several blocks as lights turn green.

OBJECTIVES
- Describe how far ahead you should look in city traffic.
- Tell how to cover the brake.
- Explain how to select the proper lane for driving.

VOCABULARY
- cover the brake
- ride the brake
- overtake

FIGURE 6

By maintaining a following distance of three or more seconds, you can identify and predict possible points of conflict. You also will be able to better manage the distance between your vehicle and the truck ahead.

The truck creates a line-of-sight restriction ahead because you are tailgating.

The view of the road ahead is visible with three or more seconds of following distance.

FIGURE 7 The flashing DON'T WALK signal warns that your green signal is about to turn yellow.

FIGURE 8 You are approaching this intersection.
Decide Could you stop before the light turns red?

If the light is green when you first see it, predict it will change soon. Watch for a DON'T WALK pedestrian signal that has started to flash, like the one in **FIGURE 7**, or a pedestrian countdown signal number below 10 seconds. These signals warn you that the light is stale, or about to change, and you will have to decide if you have time to drive through the intersection safely before the light turns yellow. Your decision will depend on your distance to the intersection and your speed.

Never speed up to get through a green light before it changes. At any speed, you will reach a point-of-no-return, or a point where you must start braking if you are going to stop before the intersection.

Covering the Brake You can maintain a normal speed if you are driving into a stable, hazard-free traffic situation. In other situations, such as the one in **FIGURE 9**, you might have to stop quickly. To get ready to stop, you need to **cover the brake**. Take your foot off the accelerator, and hold it over the brake pedal. You can use this technique whenever you sense a possible conflict. This could cut your reaction time and help you avoid a collision.

When you cover your brake, make sure not to rest your foot on the brake pedal, or **ride the brake**. When you do so, your brakes heat up and wear faster. In addition, your brake lights stay on, confusing drivers behind you. Only flash your brake lights to warn drivers behind you when you know you are going to slow or stop.

FIGURE 9
Be ready for doors to
open at the last second.
Apply Concepts How
can covering the brake
help in a situation like
this one?

Take these actions to identify and respond to the risk of parked
vehicles:

- Cover your brake and move left in your lane to lane position 2.
- Look for drivers through the windows of parked vehicles.
- Be alert for the parked vehicles' brake lights, exhaust, or wheels
  turned out.
- Lightly tap your horn if needed.
- Be ready to stop or swerve. Swerve only if your left-front zone is open.

While driving past parked vehicles, watch for doors that might open
unexpectedly. Try to drive at least one car door's width away from parked
vehicles. Otherwise, reduce speed.

Adjusting Speed   Blending into traffic is one of the most common city driving skills you will need. Use these techniques to select your best driving speed:

- Drive with the traffic flow.
- Stay within the speed limit.
- Adjust speed and position ahead of time for other drivers who might
  block your way.

DID YOU KNOW?

Mass Transit   Before
pollution and global
warming were serious
concerns, London was
forced to deal with
crippling traffic jams.
In the mid-1800s, the
world's first subway
system was designed
and built in London.
Today, subways carry
millions of passengers
daily in cities around
the world.

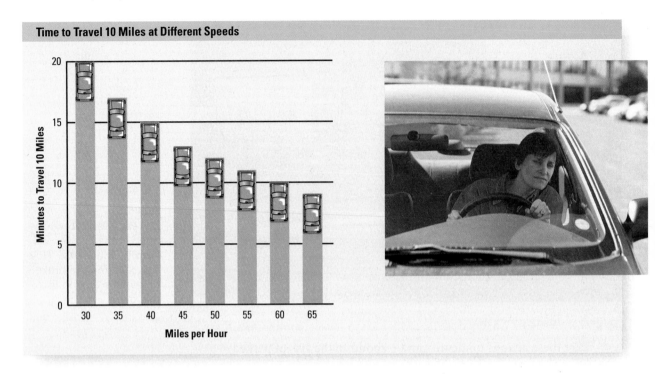

Time to Travel 10 Miles at Different Speeds

FIGURE 10 Look at the graph to see how much time you save by driving 5 mph faster for 10 miles. **Draw Conclusions** Is driving faster worth it?

Selecting the Best Lane

When driving in multilane traffic, you will use different lanes at different times. Select the lane with the smallest number of hazards.

The left lane is usually for faster traffic. But at times, traffic can be held up by drivers waiting to turn left. These left-turning drivers can be a problem when only two lanes are going in your direction. If your street has multiple lanes going your way, choose the lane where the traffic flow is smoothest.

Lane Positioning Use these techniques to position your vehicle in multi-lane city traffic:

- Increase your following distance to more than three seconds in heavy traffic.

- Adjust your speed and lane position as needed to stay out of other drivers' blind spots.

- Move to another lane if your front zone closes.

- Once you start driving in a lane, try to stay in that lane.

Overtaking and Passing   Passing in a city can be dangerous. You must be alert for pedestrians, cross traffic, signals, and an endless number of line-of-sight restrictions.

At times, you might decide to **overtake**, or pass, a vehicle ahead. If you must overtake another moving vehicle on a two-lane, two-way street, make sure you can do so safely and legally. It is illegal to pass at intersections or over double-yellow center lines.

To overtake another vehicle, use the lane-changing procedure and drive past the slower-moving vehicle. Signal briefly and return to your lane when both headlights of the vehicle you have passed appear in your inside rearview mirror.

Special Traffic Lanes   To help move rush-hour traffic, many cities now have special lanes for buses and carpool drivers. Drivers who travel alone must use the regular, more-crowded, slower lanes. By riding together in High-Occupancy Vehicle (HOV) lanes, people save time and fuel, reduce pollution, and reduce parking problems.

FIGURE 11
Through traffic should use the center lane to avoid slowdowns or stops.

review it 14.3

1. Why should you look ahead when driving in city traffic?

2. Explain how to cover your brake and when you should do it.

3. How do you select the best lane on a multilane street?

Critical Thinking

4. **Compare and Contrast**   How much time can a driver save on a 20-mile trip by increasing speed from 30 mph in 5 mph increments?

Use the table in **FIGURE 10** to calculate the amount of time saved for each speed.

IN THE PASSENGER SEAT   **Observing Traffic**   With a licensed, adult driver, over the period of a week, count the number of times the driver covered the brake. Also, note the situations that caused the driver to cover the brake. Report your findings to your class.

SPECIAL CITY SITUATIONS

OBJECTIVES

- Describe the procedure for turning left or right from a one-way street.
- Explain how to warn a driver who is driving the wrong way on a street.

VOCABULARY

- blind intersection

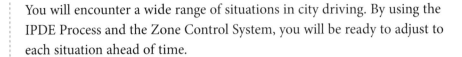

You will encounter a wide range of situations in city driving. By using the IPDE Process and the Zone Control System, you will be ready to adjust to each situation ahead of time.

Driving on Two-Way Streets

Most city roadways are two-way streets with one lane going in each direction. Other streets have two or more lanes going in the same direction.

Many city intersections do not have traffic controls. You cannot be sure what other drivers will do as you approach an uncontrolled or **blind intersection**, in which your view of traffic on an intersecting road is impeded.

Some intersections have special left-turn lanes. If you turn left at an uncontrolled intersection, you must yield to oncoming traffic.

Driving on One-Way Streets

One-way streets can move a greater volume of traffic with fewer conflicts than two-way streets. Generally, one-way streets are less congested than two-way streets, so fewer conflicts occur.

Identifying One-Way Streets   When you come to an unfamiliar street, first determine if it is a one-way street. Look to see if a ONE WAY sign is posted or if all moving traffic and parked vehicles point in the same direction. You might also see broken white lines that separate lanes and traffic signs facing the same direction. (If you are driving on a street and the signs are facing the other way, you probably are going the wrong way on a one-way street.)

FIGURE 12   You are approaching this intersection. **Identify** What two clues identify this as a one-way street?

Entering One-Way Streets   To make a left turn onto a one-way street, position your vehicle in the nearest left lane. Make a sharp left turn into the nearest lane going left. Signs are used to alert you when your street is about to become a one-way street.

If you plan to drive on a one-way street for a distance, try to avoid a lane that is next to parked vehicles. A parked vehicle could pull out and close your front zone. Each parked vehicle creates a line-of-sight restriction. If a center lane is available, use it to reduce possible conflicts.

When you plan to turn, position your vehicle ahead of time. Move into the right or left lane at least one block before your turn.

Leaving One-Way Streets   To turn left from a one-way street, position your vehicle in the far left lane ahead of time. To turn right, position your vehicle in the far right lane ahead of time. Complete your turn by entering the nearest lane going your way.

On some one-way streets, the outside lane may be for turns only. On other one-way streets, you can turn into a multilane street from more than one lane. Road markings or overhead signs will direct you.

You will need to adjust when a one-way street turns into a two-way street. Your left lane might end. Signs or lights will warn you when a one-way street is about to change to a two-way street.

FIGURE 13   To turn right onto a one-way street, turn from the far right lane into the first available right lane.

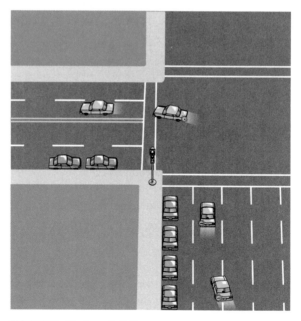

FIGURE 14   To turn left from a one-way street, turn from the far left lane to the first available lane going left.

FIGURE 15

This street is too narrow for you to maneuver. If you cannot move left, be prepared to stop.

Unexpected Situations on Crowded Streets   If you encounter a vehicle headed the wrong way on a one-way street, slow, steer right, and sound your horn. If you have time, flash your headlights to warn the other driver.

If a vehicle suddenly emerges from an alley, as shown in **FIGURE 15**, slow down and cover your brake to maintain a safe path of travel. If necessary, let traffic clear before you move ahead.

When driving on city streets, you should maintain a continuous, orderly visual search pattern. Even though drivers may have a green light, they are required to stop for pedestrians.

Angle or parallel parking is allowed on most streets. If you must drive close to parked vehicles, be alert for possible conflicts. At the first hint of movement from a vehicle or pedestrian, slow, stop, or move to another lane.

More and more communities have turned to traffic engineers to keep residential speeds lower. Roadway features used to manage traffic include speed bumps, or little humps one must drive over; special islands that force drivers to slow; and traffic circles. Research has demonstrated that roundabouts can improve traffic flow and cut crashes leading to injuries by up to 75 percent.

review it 14.4

1. What lanes should you use when making a right or left turn from a one-way street?

2. What should you do if another driver approaches you from the wrong direction on a one-way street?

Critical Thinking

3. **Apply Concepts**   If you wanted to convince your community to convert a one-way street to a two-way street, what arguments might you use?

4. **Relate Cause and Effect**   If traffic speeds are too high on a one-way street in a residential community, what can traffic engineers do to slow traffic?

IN YOUR COMMUNITY   **Research**   Identify a street in your neighborhood that is very congested. On a sheet of paper, design roadway feature(s) to improve the traffic flow. This might include one-way streets or traffic signals. Share your design with the class.

CHAPTER 14 REVIEW

Lesson Summaries

14.1 ADJUSTING TO CITY TRAFFIC

- Traffic density is one of the main factors that makes city driving hazardous. The number and proximity of vehicles and pedestrians are always a challenge for drivers.

14.2 FOLLOWING AND MEETING TRAFFIC

- The 3-second following distance provides a safe distance from the vehicle ahead of you.

- To manage a tailgating driver, you can move slightly right and increase your following distance. In extreme situations, you can pull out of traffic and let the other driver go ahead.

- Meeting an oncoming car in your lane requires immediate action. To avoid a crash, slow, signal the other driver, and—if your right-front zone is open—move right.

14.3 MANAGING SPACE IN CITY TRAFFIC

- Looking well ahead is the first step to use in managing space in city traffic.

- If you approach a high-risk driving situation, cover your brake to cut your reaction time.

- To help keep traffic moving, you need to select the correct lane for driving.

14.4 SPECIAL CITY SITUATIONS

- To identify one-way streets, look for ONE WAY signs or parked vehicles pointing in the same direction.

- To warn another driver who is driving the wrong way on a one-way street, slow, move as far right as you can, and sound your horn.

Chapter Vocabulary

- 3-second following distance
- blind intersection
- cover the brake
- overtake
- ride the brake
- tailgate
- traffic density

Write the word or phrase from the list above that completes the sentence correctly.

1. The term _____ can be used to describe the volume of traffic on a road.

2. _____ can be used to measure the space between two cars moving in the same direction on a two-lane road.

3. When you _____, you follow another car too closely.

4. When drivers are not sure what is going to happen next, they can _____ to cut their reaction time.

5. When you rest your foot on the brake pedal, you _____.

6. It is illegal to _____ another vehicle in an intersection or if there is a double yellow line.

7. A tall hedge or wall at a corner could create a _____.

 STUDY TIP

Question Headings Rephrase each green heading in the chapter as a question to ask your partner. For example, you might ask, "What does traffic complexity mean?" and "How do you use the IPDE Process in city driving?" for lesson 1. Take turns asking and answering questions with a partner.

Checking Concepts

LESSON 1

8. What are two main factors that make city driving more dangerous?

9. Why is it important to understand the relationship between time, distance, and speed?

LESSON 2

10. Why is it important to pick a high-visibility fixed checkpoint when measuring your following distance?

11. What are the advantages of using a following distance of three seconds or more?

12. What are the best ways to manage a tailgating driver?

LESSON 3

13. How can you improve your line of sight when following a large truck?

14. Why are pedestrian crosswalk signals important to drivers?

LESSON 4

15. Describe how to turn from a one-way street onto a two-way street.

16. How should you respond to another car coming toward you in your lane?

17. Why would a driver in front of you stop when the signal light ahead turns green?

Critical Thinking

18. **Relate Cause and Effect**   How does riding the brake create hazards for other drivers?

19. **Analyze**   How do traffic engineers help keep communities safe?

You're the Driver

20. **Decide**   You are following a driver who seems lost and is tailgating the car ahead of him. Even though you have a 3-second following distance and have identified a possible problem ahead, how can you help avoid trouble?

21. **Execute**   As you approach an intersection, the DON'T WALK sign begins to flash but the light is still green. What should you do before deciding whether to drive through the intersection or to stop?

22. **Predict**   What can you do to alert this oncoming driver and avoid trouble?

23. **Identify**   What clue do you have to indicate this is not a stale green light?

Preparing for the Test

Choose the letter of the answer that best completes the statement or answers the question.

1. When you see a "Roadwork Ahead" sign, you should
   a. brake and be prepared to stop.
   b. slow down and look for the roadwork.
   c. look straight ahead.
   d. look to the right.

2. When you see a flashing yellow light at an intersection, you should
   a. yield to all traffic before crossing the intersection.
   b. stop then enter the intersection when safe to do so.
   c. slow down and cross the intersection carefully.
   d. proceed since other traffic must always yield.

3. Which of the following statements about blind spots is true?
   a. They are eliminated if you have one outside mirror on each side of the vehicle.
   b. Large trucks have bigger blind spots than most passenger vehicles.
   c. Blind spots can be checked by looking at your inside rearview mirror.
   d. Blind spots cannot be eliminated by turning your head.

4. You may legally block an intersection
   a. when you entered the intersection on the green light.
   b. during rush-hour traffic.
   c. under no circumstances.
   d. when other drivers are blocking the intersection.

5. You may cross a double yellow line to pass another vehicle if
   a. there is a solid yellow line on the far left edge of the road.
   b. the line on your side of the double yellow line is broken.
   c. there is a solid yellow line on the right edge of the road.
   d. the line on the other side of the double yellow line is broken.

Use the photo below to answer Question 6.

6. You're driving alone and see this sign ahead. You should
   a. get into a different lane.
   b. move to the left side of your lane.
   c. increase your following distance to four seconds.
   d. be ready to reduce speed.

Use the photo below to answer Question 7.

7. You are driving at the posted speed limit. Most of the other vehicles are driving 70 mph or faster. You may legally drive
   a. 70 mph or faster, to keep up with the speed of traffic.
   b. between 65 and 70 mph.
   c. no faster than 65 mph.
   d. slower than 65 mph, to try to make other traffic slow down.

drive write 🚗

Hazards City traffic presents many challenges to managing time and space as you drive. Write one or two paragraphs about two specific hazards drivers in city traffic face and how you would manage those hazards to stay safe.

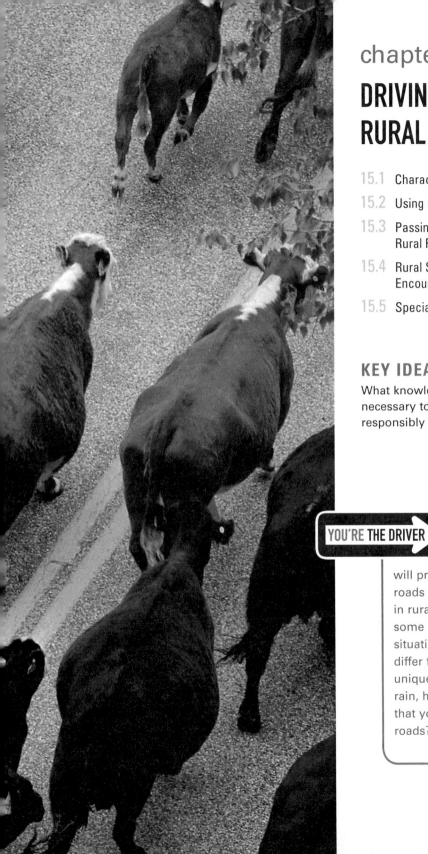

chapter 15

DRIVING IN RURAL AREAS

15.1   Characteristics of Rural Driving

15.2   Using Basic Skills in Rural Areas

15.3   Passing and Being Passed on Rural Roads

15.4   Rural Situations You Might Encounter

15.5   Special Driving Environments

KEY IDEA

What knowledge and skills are necessary to drive safely and responsibly in rural areas?

YOU'RE THE DRIVER

Even if you live in the city, you will probably drive on rural roads at some point. Driving in rural environments presents some unique and challenging situations. How does this road differ from a city street? What's unique about the roads, terrain, hazards and vehicles that you'll encounter on rural roads?

lesson 15.1
CHARACTERISTICS OF RURAL DRIVING

OBJECTIVES

- Describe rural roadways.
- Describe factors to consider when selecting a safe speed.
- Identify traffic controls and how they help inform, warn, and regulate drivers on rural roads.
- List roadside hazards common in rural driving.

VOCABULARY

- graphics

Rural roads comprise nearly 80 percent of all the roadway mileage in our country. They also account for 40 percent of the vehicle miles traveled and nearly 61 percent of our nation's traffic fatalities. Wide-open spaces and less traffic are common characteristics of rural roads, but don't assume that conflicts won't occur. As statistics show, rural driving has its challenges.

Rural Roadways

Rural roads are constructed of many different types of materials. Some are paved and others are not. Shoulders can be wide or narrow, paved or gravel. Road surfaces may be smooth or in very poor condition.

Lack of adequate lighting can make visibility difficult at night. Trees and other foliage can also restrict one's line of sight on sunny days or during evenings, casting deceptive shadows.

Safe Speed

Determining a safe speed is critical for safe rural driving. Speed affects your line of sight, stopping distance, and vehicle control, and the amount of damage and injury suffered in the event of a collision.

Many rural roads have a speed limit of 55 mph or more. Depending on conditions, lower speeds may be posted. There is a difference between safe speeds and posted speeds. Posted speeds are the maximum legal speeds allowed under ideal conditions. When conditions are not ideal, a slower speed is safer. Other roadway users, inclement weather, hills, and the surface conditions of the roadway determine safe speeds. Never drive faster than conditions allow.

FIGURE 1

Driveways, side roads, and entrances to fields may be difficult to identify. **Identify** Did you see the vehicle waiting to pull out onto the road?

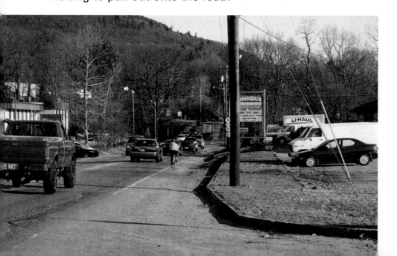

Traffic Controls

Traffic controls—signs, signals, and lane markings—direct, regulate, inform, and warn drivers. Traffic controls provide advance information and warning of hazards that you cannot yet identify, major intersections ahead, passing conditions, unusual or hazardous conditions (curves, shoulders, animal crossings), and traffic channeled into reduced space.

Most warning signs use **graphics** or pictures. They alert drivers of hazardous conditions. In **FIGURE 2**, why do you think the warning sign is placed where it is? Hills can block your line of sight, your view of the situation ahead, and your path of travel. Paying attention to warning signs will help you reduce your speed well in advance.

Traffic controls can be complex, especially at intersections where rural highways cross. Identify them early to avoid conflicts.

Roadside Hazards

Use the road conditions to determine a safe driving speed. Older, less-traveled rural roads are often narrow and not maintained as well as more traveled rural roads. Roads may have potholes or other damage that affect your ability to control your vehicle.

Shoulders may be soft, narrow, and uneven with the edge of the roadway. Deep ditches may be present just inches from the shoulder.

Trees, shrubs, or snow piles created by plows can restrict your line of sight. These conditions also make it difficult for drivers trying to enter the roadway to see you and other traffic. Be alert; drivers could turn into your path of travel without warning.

FIGURE 2
Many drivers assume that they are less likely to crash on a rural road. **Identify** Can you see the intersection ahead?

review it 15.1

1. What are three roadway conditions commonly found in rural driving?
2. What factors should you use to help select a safe speed when driving on rural roads?
3. List three examples of common rural roadside hazards.

Critical Thinking

4. **Decide** The road ahead is wet with standing water in the left tire track of your lane. A tractor just pulled into traffic and is picking up speed; mud is flying off its rear tires. You are closing in and cannot see around the tractor. What should you do, and why?

IN THE PASSENGER SEAT **Observe Rural Roadway Surfaces** While traveling on some of the different rural roads in your area, take note of the different types of materials that the roads are made of. Report your findings to your class.

lesson 15.2
USING BASIC SKILLS IN RURAL AREAS

 OBJECTIVES

- Explain how IPDE and Zone Control should be applied in rural driving.
- Explain the appropriate steps to use to safely handle curves, hills, and intersections.
- Identify rural situations that require greater following distances.
- Describe characteristics of multilane rural highways and explain how to safely enter them.

 VOCABULARY

- advisory speed sign
- median

Don't be fooled by a seemingly quiet rural scene. It can quickly change with little warning. Remember, whenever and wherever you drive, you will encounter risks. However, as you learned in Chapter 5, by properly applying IPDE and Zone Control driving techniques, you empower yourself to better manage the level of risk.

Applying IPDE and Zone Control

Rural driving typically involves driving at higher speeds than in urban driving situations. The faster you drive, the less time you have to identify and respond to sudden hazards in your path of travel. At higher speeds, you increase the risk of losing control in situations that demand quick responses.

While traveling on rural roads, there are many ways your zones can become closed. To best apply IPDE and Zone Control, you must control your speed. The slower your speed, the more time you have to solve problems. One or two additional seconds can make a great difference in your ability to successfully apply the IPDE Process and manage space.

Maintaining vehicle control at higher speeds is more difficult than at lower speeds. It takes longer to stop, and excessive braking or steering can result in a skid and loss of vehicle control. Assess road conditions and the amount of traction available, and adjust your speed accordingly. Drive at a speed at which you know you will be able to brake and steer your vehicle without losing control.

-------- FIGURE 3 --------
Can you identify points of conflict in this situation?

FIGURE 4
You should search
12–15 seconds ahead
in this situation.
Identify What four
warning signs were you
able to identify?

Visual Search Pattern

You should apply the orderly visual search pattern technique in rural areas
where your 12–15-second visual lead covers more area because of the
higher speeds.

Whenever possible, in open areas, extend your visual lead. You may
find that in some situations you are able to establish a visual lead of up to 30
seconds. The greater your visual lead, the more time you will have to identify and safely respond to hazards and unexpected situations.

Curves, Hills, and Intersections

Rural roads have some common characteristics such as hills, curves, and
intersections. Knowing these characteristics beforehand can help you handle them safely while driving.

Curves Rural roads typically have many curves. When a driver has difficulty handling a curve, it is typically the result of having too much speed on
the approach to the curve. Before approaching a curve, you likely will notice
a yellow warning sign that warns of the potential hazard ahead. These signs
often are located 250 to 700 feet before the curve, depending on the posted
speed limit. A warning sign for a curve is yellow with a black arrow showing
the direction of the curve. The sharper the curve of the arrow, the sharper the
actual curve ahead.

FIGURE 5   You are approaching this curve.
Execute   What should you do to safely handle this curve?

Curve warning signs often have smaller yellow rectangular **advisory speed signs** just below the main sign. Advisory speed signs provide suggested maximum travel speeds under ideal conditions for the curve ahead. Advisory speeds are usually lower than the posted speed limit for other sections of the roadway.

Follow the recommended speeds, and when conditions are less than ideal, use a slower speed. Remember that natural forces work to push your vehicle to the outside of the curve. At higher speeds, these forces are even greater.

When you approach a curve, follow these steps:

1. See the curve in your target area.
2. Check your rear zone.
3. Check your left-front zone for oncoming traffic.
4. Check your right-front zone to determine if it is open or closed to your line of sight and path of travel.
5. Stay in or get into lane position 1.
6. If the curve is sharp, lightly apply your brakes and hold until the midpoint of the curve before you turn the steering wheel.
7. As you get closer to the curve, look in the direction the road curves. See if your path of travel is open.
8. Once you are beyond the midpoint of the curve, begin to accelerate gently if conditions allow.
9. Identify and evaluate your new target area, steer toward that target area, and search ahead for possible zone changes.

Hills   Hills are not normally marked, unless they have steep slopes. Hills restrict your line of sight because you cannot see what is on the other side. As you approach the crest of a hill, slow down and use lane position 1. At night, look at the crest of the hill for light, since this can indicate an approaching vehicle. If needed, use lane position 3 to provide more space between you and any oncoming vehicle.

Intersections   Rural intersections can vary. Some may have traffic lights; others just STOP signs. Identifying intersections early will help you anticipate possible problems and give you extra time to deal with them.

Most rural intersections have a side road intersecting a main road. The side road usually has a STOP sign. Often, tall crops, trees, or bushes create line-of-sight restrictions.

Driveways should be treated like intersections but may be very difficult to identify, especially at night. Look well in advance to identify signs of driveways ahead such as loose gravel spilling onto the main road; reflectors marking a driveway; or mailboxes at the edge of, or immediately across from, a driveway.

FIGURE 6
You are driving behind this car and closing in. **Decide**   Will you pass or not?

Following Traffic

Although traffic is usually not very heavy on rural roads, you will come upon other vehicles. Since speeds are greater, always maintain a safe following distance of three or more seconds. When conditions are less than ideal, increase your following distance.

Maintaining a following distance of more than three seconds gives you a better view of traffic and conditions ahead and allows you to keep a more open front zone. This extra cushion of space gives you more time to use IPDE and Zone Control. Use greater following distances when being tailgated, driving on a steep downhill slope, or following a motorcycle.

Driving on Multilane Roads

Some rural roads have multiple lanes that travel in the same direction and higher posted speed limits. However, unlike interstate roads, they may have intersections instead of exit and entrance ramps. Some intersections may have a two-lane road crossing a four-lane road; others may involve two major multilane roads that cross.

Multilane Roadways with Center Lines   Many multilane rural roads have only a yellow line (dashed or solid) separating high-speed traffic moving in opposite directions. You should never cross a solid yellow line except

FIGURE 7

A median safely separates lanes of traffic that move in opposite directions.

FIGURE 7

A median safely separates lanes of traffic that move in opposite directions.

to make a left turn or clear an obstacle blocking your lane because the danger of a head-on crash is very high.

Divided Roadways   All divided roads have traffic moving in opposite directions separated in some way. The division may be a guardrail, fence, or a **median**, as shown in **FIGURE 7**. A median is an area of ground or concrete separating traffic moving in opposite directions. A median can be from a few inches wide to several feet wide.

When you have to cross a multiple-lane road, cross each half as if you were crossing a one-way street. If a large enough median crossover area exists, move into it and if traffic from the right dictates that you stop, stop in your own lane, just to the right of the center of the median crossover area. If you need to turn left after stopping, remember you'll be entering the nearest lane, which is the fastest lane of traffic moving in the direction you want to go. You will need to look for a large enough gap to enter this lane safely. Look for at least a 6–8 second gap.

Lane Selection   When driving on a multilane roadway, always try to drive in the right-hand lane, unless signs indicate otherwise. The left lane is usually for passing or for preparing for a left turn. In some states, it is even illegal to drive in the left lane unless you are passing.

Turning at Intersections   When leaving a multilane roadway, turn right from the right lane. When making a left turn, turn from the left lane nearest the center line or median strip.

Some multilane roads have special turn lanes. When preparing to turn, check your rearview mirror for possible conflicts in the rear zone. Signal your intention to turn early, at least five seconds before the actual turn.

Signaling early gives vehicles behind you a chance to adjust their speed and position to minimize conflict. If turning left, wait with your wheels straight until you start your turn. If you are hit from behind, you will not be forced into oncoming traffic.

If you see a vehicle approaching you from behind very fast and believe it may not be able to stop in time, do not make your turn. Instead, accelerate quickly and go straight ahead if the conditions of the intersection allow you to. If you are hit from behind, it is better to be moving in the same direction as the vehicle striking you than to be stopped.

Entering a Multilane Road   Follow these procedures if you are on a side road and wish to enter a multilane roadway:

- To turn right, check traffic to the left, ahead, and to the right of your target area. Make certain the left, front, and right zones are open. Enter the nearest right lane as you turn. Look and steer toward your target and accelerate to the prevailing speed. If a lane change left is needed, do so only after you complete your turn, clear the intersection, and attain the prevailing speed.

- Left turns require larger gaps than right turns. First, make certain you have checked left, front, and right zones. When it is safe, cross the lanes on your side of the roadway. Choose a time when no traffic is approaching from your right in the far left lane of the road you will be turning into. Then turn into the nearest lane. Accelerate more quickly to the prevailing speed than you would for a right turn.

Entering the roadway from a driveway is similar to entering from a side road and presents similar problems. Oncoming drivers may not see you because of line-of-sight restrictions. Although drivers may have advanced warnings of intersections ahead, driveways rarely have warning signs.

review it 15.2

1. How should IPDE and Zone Control be applied in rural driving?

2. List the steps you should take in handling a curve.

3. What are two situations that would require you to establish a greater following distance when driving in a rural area?

4. What are the steps to take for making a left turn onto a multilane rural highway?

5. **Apply Concepts**   You are at a STOP sign on a side road that intersects a multiple-lane highway. You want to continue going straight. The median has a large enough crossover area to accommodate two vehicles side-by-side. Where should you position yourself in the median?

6. **Compare and Contrast**   How is crossing a multilane roadway without a median area large enough for cars to pull into similar to crossing a multilane highway with a large median? How is it different?

IN YOUR COMMUNITY   **Research**   Choose a rural area, in your county or township or near where you live. Find out what law enforcement agencies are responsible for this area. Arrange an interview with a representative from each agency, and find out what factors cause most crashes in the rural area. Write a brief report summarizing your findings and be prepared to report your findings to your class.

PASSING AND BEING PASSED ON RURAL ROADS

OBJECTIVES

- List the steps for passing on two-lane rural roads and multilane roads.
- List situations where passing should never be attempted.
- Describe the actions to take when being passed.

VOCABULARY

- prohibited

WHAT WOULD YOU SAY?

Safe Passing Your friend is driving in the center lane of a three-lane highway. There are slower vehicles ahead in both the left and center lanes. What would you say to your friend if she wanted to pass?

Passing on a two-lane road carries a higher level of risk than passing on a multilane road. When you pass on a two-lane rural road, you will be in the same lane as oncoming traffic for a short period of time. Use the IPDE Process and the Zone Control System to help lower your risk when passing.

Passing

Passing is a three-stage process. The three stages are the decision stage, the preparation stage, and the execution stage.

Deciding to Pass   In situations where you want to pass a vehicle, you should scan ahead to see if there are any turns. Before you start a passing maneuver, you must first assess the situation and then decide when to pass. You must ask yourself: Is it worthwhile? Is it legal? and Is it safe?

Consider passing only if you can answer yes to all three questions. Remember, the major responsibility for passing safely rests with the driver who is passing.

Preparing to Pass   If you believe the vehicle ahead of you will be turning, delay passing and maintain a minimum following distance of three or more seconds. If you've answered yes to all three questions above, follow these steps in preparing to pass:

1. Check all roadway signs and markings to be sure it is legal to pass.
2. While maintaining a following distance of three seconds or more, look ahead to your target area to make certain it is safe to pass.
3. If there are no conflicts ahead, get into the ready position (a two-second following distance), and then get into lane position 2.
4. Check roadway conditions. Is there anything that might cause the vehicle ahead to swerve left?
5. Check your rearview mirror for possible conflicts in your rear zone. Delay passing if your rear zone is closing because of another vehicle rapidly approaching from behind.

6. Glance over your left shoulder to make certain no vehicles are in your blind spot.

7. Check the oncoming traffic lane again to be sure there are no vehicles approaching and that you have enough space to safely pass. Oncoming vehicles must be at least 30 seconds away. You will need 10–15 seconds to complete your pass. **If in doubt, do not pass.**

8. Check ahead for driveways and side roads. Make sure no traffic will be entering the roadway ahead.

After you have made certain that the path you will take is clear, you are ready to pass. If you identify a problem, slow down and re-establish a safe following distance. Repeat the steps again to prepare to pass. In time, these steps will become a habit.

Executing a Pass   When executing a pass on a two-lane road, follow these steps:

1. Move from your following distance position (3 or more seconds) to your ready position, which is 2 seconds behind the vehicle you intend to pass.

2. When it is safe to pass, signal left to prepare for your lane change, and check over your left shoulder to make sure no vehicles are in your blind spot.

3. Change lanes smoothly and accelerate at least 10 mph faster than the vehicle you are passing. However, all passing should be done within the speed limit.

4. Make a final evaluation. Provided you have not passed the vehicle, you can change your mind if any conflicts to your front zone exist 20–30 seconds ahead. If your front zone is clear, continue to accelerate to proper speed.

5. Maintain your speed until you can see at least one of the headlights of the vehicle you are passing in your rearview mirror.

6. Signal for a right lane change, and return smoothly to the right lane. Do not slow down.

7. Cancel your turn signal and adjust your speed and lane position.

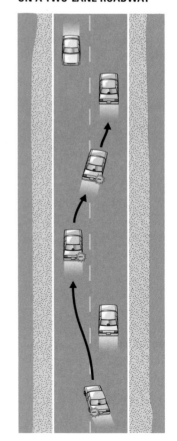

FIGURE 8   EXECUTING A PASS ON A TWO-LANE ROADWAY

FIGURE 9 Drivers in the right lane must not pass, as they are unable to see vehicles coming over the hill. **Identify** How is this indicated by the road markings?

FIGURE 10 Passing at or near an intersection is dangerous and illegal. A driver turning from the crossroad might enter your lane.

Passing on Multilane Roads You need to be cautious on a multilane highway with only a center line to separate traffic. Check all lanes going in your direction before you pass on a multilane roadway to make sure your path of travel is clear.

Generally, all passing should be done in the left lane. Passing on the right is illegal in many states. However, it sometimes becomes necessary to use the right lane to pass a vehicle. Remember the procedures for passing and follow them every time you pass.

No-Passing Situations

No-passing situations are marked by solid yellow lines, as shown in **FIGURES 9 AND 10**. Signs can also mark no-passing zones. Rectangular white signs on the right side of the road will indicate DO NOT PASS; yellow pennant-shaped signs are on the left side of the road and indicate a NO PASSING ZONE. Passing is illegal and unsafe when your line of sight is restricted, your front zone is closed, or cross-traffic is present, even if no warning signs or lines are present.

No Passing on Uphill Roards

Passing is not allowed within 700 to 1,000 feet of the top of a hill. Notice that the driver of the yellow car in **FIGURE 9** has too great a restricted line of sight to pass safely.

No Passing at Intersections

Passing is illegal within 100 feet of an intersection. Slow down when approaching an intersection.

Other No-Passing Situations There are other situations where passing is **prohibited**, or illegal, in some states or should not be attempted. For example, you shouldn't pass

- within 100 feet before a railroad crossing;
- on a two-lane bridge or underpass; on curves, where your line of sight is so restricted you cannot see around the curve;
- when the vehicle ahead is traveling at or near the speed limit;
- in fog, rain, snow, or anytime your line of sight is restricted;
- when several vehicles are ahead of you. You should pass only one vehicle at a time.
- when you cannot complete a pass before the start of a no-passing zone;
- any time oncoming traffic is too close; and
- when you will be stopping or turning soon.

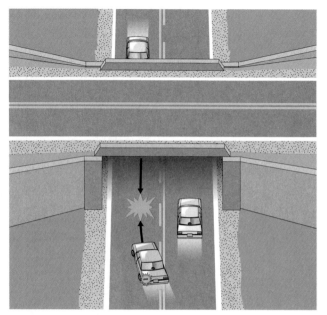

FIGURE 11 Do not pass on bridges and near underpasses, since they might not have shoulders to provide escape areas.

Being Passed

If you are the passing driver, you have the majority of the responsibility for passing safely. However, you also have responsibilities when being passed.

You must be aware that another vehicle is passing, even when the driver of the vehicle fails to properly warn you. Check your mirrors often to identify vehicles approaching from the rear.

When another vehicle passes, it may help to move to lane position 3. By doing so, you provide an extra space cushion and provide the passing driver with a better view ahead.

FIGURE 12 **Evaluate** Why is passing illegal in both lanes around this curve?

If the passing driver is having a difficult time trying to pass, slow down to help that driver. Intentionally speeding up while being passed is illegal. Only speed up when the driver has decided not to pass and drops back. This will quickly open a space behind you.

FIGURE 13

review it 15.3

1. What steps do you need to take when preparing to pass a vehicle ahead if you've already determined there are no conflicts from any vehicle behind?

2. When is it safe to return to your lane after passing a vehicle?

3. What are some situations in which you should never pass?

4. What can you do to help another driver who is passing you?

Critical Thinking

5. **Decide** You notice that a large tractor pulling a hay wagon has pulled out of a field and into your lane about 20 seconds ahead. You are driving 55 mph and closing fast. What actions should you take? Why might passing

in this situation be more difficult than passing just a car?

6. **Evaluate** Accelerating when being passed to prevent someone from passing you is rude as well as illegal. However, in what type of situation might rapid acceleration be an appropriate response when a vehicle is attempting to pass? Explain why.

IN THE PASSENGER SEAT **Observe Passing Situations** As a passenger, observe other vehicles passing over the course of a week. For each situation, determine if the pass was safe or unsafe and the reasons why. Create a chart summarizing the passes you observed. What percentage of passes did you determine were safe and prudent passes? Report and discuss your findings with your class.

In rural areas, you may encounter vehicles, animals, and situations that you do not encounter on city streets. Apply the same driving techniques in rural areas that you would in urban areas. For example, in a rural area you would respond to a tractor pulling a plow the same way you would respond to a large truck or bus in the city. By applying IPDE and Zone Control techniques whenever you drive, you will maximize your ability to predict and identify conflicts and solve problems.

Slow-Moving Vehicles

A **slow-moving vehicle** is one that is unable to travel at highway speed, such as tractors and other large farm machinery.

The sooner you can identify such vehicles ahead of you, the more time you have to respond. The vast difference in speeds between an approaching vehicle and a slow-moving vehicle ahead of it often causes conflicts between vehicles in rural areas.

When driving at a higher speed, you will rapidly close in on a slow-moving vehicle. If you find yourself closing to less than 3 seconds, be aware that you may have a problem. Slow down and prepare to pass when it is safe to do so. Get into the 2-second ready position for passing. If you decide not to pass, re-establish at least a 3-second following distance.

Most slow-moving vehicles are required to have a red and orange triangle sign mounted on them, such as the one in **FIGURE 14**. These signs help other vehicle operators identify slow-moving vehicles more quickly.

OBJECTIVES

- Explain how to safely deal with slow-moving vehicles.
- Explain precautions to take when encountering animals on or along the roadway.
- Describe two actions you can take to allow hazards to separate when meeting oncoming traffic.
- Explain steps to take to safely deal with hazards posed by railroad crossings.

VOCABULARY

- slow-moving vehicle

FIGURE 14
The vehicle ahead has closed your front zone. **Decide** What following distance should you maintain and why? What lane position should you get into and why?

Animals

Animals can be a problem on rural roads. They can easily become frightened and dart out into your path. Each year, millions of dollars in property damage occur when animals and motor vehicles collide. In some areas, livestock such as cattle occasionally wander onto roadways. In other areas of the United States, wild animals such as deer, elk, and moose present the biggest hazard for vehicle collisions.

Hitting a large animal can result in damage to your vehicle and serious injury or death to you, your passengers, and the animal. In areas where large wild animals are common, reduce your speed and search a much wider area than usual. If you see one animal, anticipate the presence of more. In addition, many animals are most active in the evening and at night when it is more difficult to see them.

If you happen to observe one or more animals crossing the road, stop well in advance. Be patient and wait until it is clear to proceed. Do not get out and attempt to hurry any stragglers across the road. You are much safer in your vehicle.

When a smaller animal suddenly appears in your front zone, you may be tempted to brake hard or swerve. Be careful not to risk a more serious collision by trying to avoid the animal.

Meeting Oncoming Traffic

Meeting traffic on two-way roads can be dangerous. Very little space separates you from oncoming traffic. With traffic moving at higher speeds, a head-on collision can cause serious damage, injury, or death.

If you identify an oncoming vehicle, check your right-front zone for an alternate path of travel and for line-of-sight restrictions. Try to adjust your timing so that the oncoming vehicle will approach you when you have the fewest hazards in your right-front zone.

Separate the hazards in or next to your path of travel. Adjust your speed to deal with only one hazard at a time. In most situations slowing down is your best option. Imagine the hazard is a narrow bridge, as in **FIGURE 15**. By slowing down and letting the approaching vehicle clear the hazard first, you separate the hazards.

Meet where the most space is available. When you must meet oncoming traffic, try to select a location where you have an open right-front zone to move into if you need to swerve to avoid conflict.

If you are meeting a line of vehicles, slow down and move into lane position 3 to provide a little more space between you and the approaching vehicles.

Oncoming drivers may cross into your lane on rural roads for several reasons such as a blowout or hitting or swerving to avoid a pothole, animal, or other debris on the road.

Meeting Slow-Moving Vehicles   When you see a slow-moving or stopped vehicle in your left-front zone, check to the rear of the vehicle for a passing vehicle. The passing driver may not see you. If you are applying the IPDE Process, you will check your right-front zone and move into lane position 3, or onto the road shoulder if necessary. If you do not have an open zone, slow enough to create space for yourself or the passing driver.

Meeting at Night   Be alert when driving at night. You need to be aware of vehicles in the distance. Keep your windshield clean.

At night, headlights shining over the crest of a hill can warn you of an approaching vehicle. If you have your high beams on, switch them to low beam anytime you are within 500 feet of an approaching vehicle. Do not look directly into the headlights of approaching vehicles; you could be temporarily blinded, especially if their high beams are on. Glance instead to the right edge of the road. There is often a white line to help you maintain position in your lane.

Railroad Crossings

Many railroad crossings do not have complete controls (flashing lights and gates). In rural areas, trains travel at high speeds. Be alert for railroad-crossing warning signs. Slow and check left and right before crossing. Never cross a railroad crossing until you know it is absolutely safe to do so. Remember, when a vehicle and a train collide, the train always wins.

---- **FIGURE 15** --------
You've run into two hazards in your path of travel.
Execute   What actions should you take in order to let the hazards separate?

analyzing data

Railroad Crossing Crash Data

Each year, thousands of vehicle-train incidents are reported. The table shows numbers of reported incidents, injuries, and deaths reported to both the Federal Railroad Administration (FRA) and the Federal Transit Administration (FTA).

1. **Reading the Table** What are the six different categories of data the table displays?

2. **Analyze the Data** What year was the worst in terms of number of events? What year was the worst in terms of people killed?

3. **Calculate** Based on the data in the table, what is the annual average of total events, fatalities, and injuries?

4. **Infer** Why might the FRA report so many more incidents than the FTA?

5. **Execute** What actions can you take to better ensure that you, as a driver, never become a statistic that gets reported on a table like this?

Highway-Rail at Grade Crossing Incidents per Year									
Year	FRA events	FRA killed	FRA injured	FTA events	FTA killed	FTA injured	Total events	Total killed	Total injured
2006	2,918	368	1,010	95	7	154	3,013	375	1,164
2005	3,053	358	1,015	95	8	160	3,148	366	1,175
2004	3,076	372	1,091	107	9	76	3,183	381	1,167
2003	2,977	334	1,035	66	4	68	3,043	338	1,103
2002	3,077	357	999	112	1	76	3,189	358	1,075

review it 15.4

1. As a driver, what do you need to do to safely pass a slow-moving vehicle?

2. What actions can you take to avoid conflict with an animal you spot ahead along the roadway?

3. Describe two actions you can take to separate hazards when meeting traffic.

4. What can you do to avoid conflicts at rural railroad crossings?

Critical Thinking

5. **Evaluate** You scan ahead and notice that there is a large, very slow-moving combine ahead with its flashers on. It takes up all of your lane and part of the oncoming lane. There are wheat fields on both sides of the roadway. What should you be anticipating?

6. **Compare and Contrast** How might dealing with a coyote in the road ahead be different from dealing with a rabbit? How might your actions be similar?

IN YOUR COMMUNITY **Research** Deer-vehicle crashes are common in many states. However, deer are only one type of animal involved in crashes with motor vehicles. What agency or organization is responsible for removing animal carcasses along the rural roads where you live?

Driving through mountains and deserts can challenge your patience, energy, and skills. Make certain your vehicle is in good working condition. Adhere to the speed limits and warning signs. Be particularly aware of your vehicle's gauges while driving.

Mountain Driving

Mountain driving presents more problems and special situations than driving in flatter areas. The effects of gravity are constantly at work. Gravity will make your vehicle go faster when going downhill and slow your vehicle when going uphill.

Mountain roads often zigzag across a mountain with a series of sharp turns called **switchbacks**. A switchback bends sharply in the opposite direction. In **FIGURE 16**, the sign warns of a switchback ahead.

Driving Up a Mountain You should accelerate steadily when driving uphill to maintain speed because gravity pulls your vehicle downhill. If the slope is steep, you might need to downshift to a lower gear. An automatic transmission vehicle will downshift by itself. On extremely steep inclines, when extra power is needed, you may need to manually shift an automatic transmission vehicle into a lower gear (LOW 1 or LOW 2).

When you can't see around a curve, reduce your speed, move into lane position 1, and tap your horn. Evaluate your path of travel through the curve. An oncoming vehicle could cross into your lane because it has built up too much downhill speed before the curve. Driving too fast is a leading cause of collisions in the mountains.

OBJECTIVES
- Describe special safety precautions for mountain driving.
- Describe special safety precautions for desert driving.

VOCABULARY
- switchbacks
- pull-out areas
- runaway vehicle ramps

FIGURE 16

At the switchback ahead the road reverses direction.
Identify and Decide   What actions should you take?

FIGURE 17
Some mountain roads have areas along the side of the road for vehicles to safely pull over and stop.

FIGURE 18
This runaway vehicle ramp helps drivers of large vehicles to get out of traffic safely when their brakes fail. **Evaluate**   What are two safety components of this ramp?

Loaded trucks, recreational vehicles (RVs), and vehicles pulling trailers move more slowly up mountain roads. Follow these vehicles at their speeds and maintain at least a 4-second following distance. Some mountain roads have locations called **pull-out areas** where an additional right lane is provided for slower-moving vehicles. When slower-moving vehicles move into such lanes, faster-moving vehicles can safely pass and proceed.

Driving Down a Mountain   When driving down a mountain road, downshift before you start traveling downhill. Never coast downhill; the vehicle will speed up and you might lose control.

Adjust your speed with an occasional use of the brakes. Do not ride your brakes. Doing so can overheat them and make them fade. If you are braking often, shift to a lower gear; your transmission can help slow you down and reduce the need to brake. Finally, keep your speed low enough to maintain control and stay in your lane.

Large vehicles can experience serious brake problems going downhill, especially on long, steep grades. Some mountain roadways have **runaway vehicle ramps**, as **FIGURE 18** shows. These provide a place for vehicles, especially large trucks, to safely get out of traffic and stop when their brakes are no longer effective.

Weather in the Mountains   Fog, snow, and ice can make mountain driving even more difficult. Some mountain roads become blocked with excessive snow. Weather conditions can change suddenly in the mountains. Before driving, call the highway department or state police hotline or tune your radio to frequencies that update travelers on weather and road conditions. These frequencies are often identified on blue driver-service signs along the side of the road.

To drive in some mountain areas in winter, vehicles should be equipped with snow tires and/or tire chains. Know the conditions and requirements before driving in the mountains in winter.

Effects of Altitude on Drivers   High altitudes can affect drivers, causing shortness of breath, faster heartbeat, and headache, especially if they are not accustomed to living at high elevations.

Lower amounts of oxygen at higher altitudes can reduce concentration and cause drowsiness. These effects can be worse for tired drivers. Do not drive if you feel these effects or are tired.

Effects of Altitude on Vehicles   The thin mountain air can affect your vehicle's engine. Climbing power is reduced. Acceleration can become sluggish. The temperature of the water in your radiator may increase significantly and could cause overheating. If your air conditioner is on, turn it off.

Check your gauges and warning lights often. If the engine temperature light comes on, safely pull over and stop to let the engine cool. Turning on your heater may help remove some of the heat built up in the engine.

Engines can get extremely hot during mountain driving. When you shut off your engine, vapor lock occurs. The engine will not start because the fuel cannot be pumped in a gaseous state. Allow the engine to cool. Then try restarting it.

If you do a lot of mountain driving, have your vehicle serviced regularly for maximum performance.

safe
driving tip

Rockslides   Mountains often have falling rock zones. Be especially alert for falling rock or boulders in the road in these zones. Be prepared to stop suddenly or swerve.

Desert Driving

Desert driving is hard on the driver, the car, and the roadway. Always prepare yourself and your vehicle for driving in desert climates.

Effects of Heat on Drivers   Intense daytime heat can cause great stress on you when driving long distances. The sameness of the scenery can lull you into a false sense of security. Intense glare from the sun can reduce your vision.

To help reduce the effects of driving in a hot desert, you should wear good quality sunglasses to help reduce the effects of sun glare, plan more frequent stops, change drivers often, and carry plenty of water.

Effects of Heat on Vehicles   Extensive desert driving requires more frequent vehicle service. Battery fluids should be checked daily if the battery is not self-contained. Radiator fluids should be checked at every fuel stop.

CAUTION: *Never remove a radiator cap from a hot radiator.* The steam and hot fluid could burn you. Check the fluid level in your radiator recovery tank. If you must check the level in the radiator, wait until your engine cools.

Check tire pressure regularly; it will increase as you drive. Do not reduce the tire pressure below the lowest recommended pressure. A tire with low air pressure will run hotter, which could result in tire failure.

FIGURE 19
Visibility can be limited in a sandstorm. **Analyze** Why should you use low beams when driving in a sandstorm?

The Desert Roadway   Well-designed highways with gentle curves on flat terrain invite higher speeds. Some desert roadways have speed limits of 75 or 80 mph. Be careful of sandy roadside shoulders; your wheels could sink quickly into the sand if it is not firm and compacted. If you need to pull over, make sure the location you select is firm and out of traffic.

Sandstorms and Dust Storms   Windy conditions in deserts often create visibility problems. Avoid driving in sandstorms or dust storms. If you encounter such a storm, slow immediately and find a safe place to pull over. Turn off your headlights and turn on your hazard flashers. Wait in your vehicle until the storm passes.

If you must drive, go slowly. Use your low-beam headlights to help see and be seen. As soon as possible after the storm, have your oil, oil filter, and air filter changed. Dirt particles from the storm that remain in your fuel injection system and engine oil can cause excessive engine wear and damage.

Flash Floods   A flash flood is a sudden, unexpected rush of water from heavy rain. A flash flood can develop very quickly. This condition is especially dangerous in the desert because the ground washes away easily and there is no soil to absorb runoff. If you encounter a flash flood, seek higher ground immediately and wait for the water to recede. Stay away from creeks or natural drainage areas.

review it 15.5

1. What safety precautions should you take when driving in mountains?
2. What safety precautions should you take when driving in deserts?

Critical Thinking

3. **Apply Concepts** Why is it safer for a downhill driver to yield to an uphill driver in narrow mountain roadway situations?

4. **Relate Cause and Effect** Why should you remain in your vehicle if forced to stop in a dust storm?

IN YOUR COMMUNITY **Use Technology** Use the Internet to find current road conditions on mountain roads (either in your state or another state). Discuss the conditions and the precautions or special actions you would take if you were driving in those conditions.

CHAPTER 15 REVIEW

Lesson Summaries

15.1 CHARACTERISTICS OF RURAL DRIVING

- Rural roads are constructed of many different materials. Shoulders are often made of gravel and can be quite narrow.
- Rural roads may have hazards such as potholes and uneven or soft shoulders.

15.2 USING BASIC SKILLS IN RURAL AREAS

- Drivers should use IPDE and Zone Control techniques in rural situations.
- Before a curve, slow down and make all traffic checks behind and ahead.
- Some situations require more than a 3-second following distance.

15.3 PASSING AND BEING PASSED ON RURAL ROADS

- There are three major stages in passing: deciding to pass, preparing to pass, and executing the pass.
- Drivers should never attempt to pass when approaching a hill, while in a curve, or when in an intersection.
- When being passed, maintain or reduce your speed. Never accelerate to keep a person from completing a pass.

15.4 RURAL SITUATIONS YOU MIGHT ENCOUNTER

- Follow the same rules as you would in the city for passing slow-moving vehicles.
- Be aware of the hazards posed by animals near roadways. To separate hazards, adjust your vehicle speed and position.

15.5 SPECIAL DRIVING ENVIRONMENTS

- In mountain or desert driving, be sure to check your brakes and cooling system.
- Extreme heat, sun glare, dust storms, and flash floods are hazards for driving in the desert.

Chapter Vocabulary

- advisory speed sign
- graphics
- median
- prohibited
- pull-out areas
- slow-moving vehicle
- switchbacks
- runaway vehicle ramps

Select the word or phrase from the list above that correctly completes the sentence.

1. A(n) _____ is a place on a mountain road for vehicles to safely get out of traffic when their brakes are not effective.
2. The warning signs posted on a curve with suggested speeds for ideal conditions are called _____.
3. _____ are usually additional lanes on a mountain road for slower-moving vehicles.
4. The strip of ground separating traffic moving in opposite directions on a roadway is called a(n) _____.
5. A vehicle unable to travel at highway speeds is referred to as a(n) _____.
6. A(n) _____ is a location in the mountains where the road bends sharply in the opposite direction.

STUDY TIP

Make color flashcards of different warning signs common to rural driving. Work with a partner to test each other on the meaning of each sign.

Checking Concepts

LESSON 1

7. How does the construction of rural roads differ from that of city streets?

8. What are some typical rural driving hazards?

LESSON 2

9. What are two critical driving actions a driver needs to take before entering a curve?

10. How should IPDE and Zone Control driving techniques be applied in rural situations?

LESSON 3

11. What are the three stages of passing?

12. What are some of the critical steps in each stage of passing?

LESSON 4

13. How do large, slow-moving vehicles create some challenging driving situations?

14. If you are approaching a narrow bridge and there is an oncoming vehicle, what actions should you take to allow the hazards to separate?

LESSON 5

15. What are some challenges of mountain driving?

16. How is driving in the desert different from driving in other environments?

Critical Thinking

17. Relate Cause and Effect   Why do you think rural collisions account for a majority of U.S. highway deaths?

18. Predict   What should you do when driving in an area that has animal warning signs?

You're the Driver

19. Identify   It is nighttime and you are driving uphill in a rural area. What should you look for? What actions could you take to avoid or reduce potential conflicts?

20. Predict   You are driving at night when you spot a deer on your left. It stays still as you approach. What actions should you take? How do you predict the deer will respond?

21. Identify   What hazards do you see in the scene below? Which zones are open? What would you do to avoid the hazards?

22. Decide   The driver behind you is attempting to pass you. What are three visual clues that should help the driver with the decision to pass?

Preparing for the Test

Choose the letter of the answer that best completes the statement or answers the question.

1. Posted speed limit signs indicate
   a. the safest speeds possible in any condition.
   b. minimum speeds under ideal conditions.
   c. maximum speeds under ideal conditions.
   d. suggested speeds that legally may be exceeded.

2. Which of the following provides information and warnings about a driving situation ahead?
   a. medians
   b. road shoulders
   c. posted speed limits
   d. traffic controls

Use the art below to answer Question 3.

3. When you see this sign, you should
   a. stop at the sign and look right, left, and right again before proceeding across the tracks.
   b. start listening and looking left and right to see if any trains are coming.
   c. begin passing any slow-moving vehicles so that you will have a clear view of the railroad tracks.
   d. accelerate so that you can get across the railroad tracks quickly.

4. When passing a vehicle on a two-lane highway, it is safe to pull back into your lane when
   a. the vehicle you passed lowers its high beams to low beams.
   b. your rear bumper is even with the front bumper of the vehicle you are passing.
   c. you can see the front-left headlight of the vehicle you are passing in your rearview mirror.
   d. you can see both headlights of the vehicle you are passing in your left sideview mirror.

Use the art below to answer Question 5.

5. When you see the sign above, it means
   a. if you turn right at the intersection ahead you will soon come to an intersection with a gravel road.
   b. if you turn left at the intersection ahead you will soon come to a railroad crossing.
   c. if you proceed straight at the intersection ahead you will soon come to a railroad crossing.
   d. if you turn right at the intersection ahead you will soon come to a railroad crossing.

6. Solid yellow lines on a roadway indicate
   a. no passing situations.
   b. conditions are favorable for passing.
   c. you must pass with caution.
   d. hazards in the roadway.

7. After driving through a desert and encountering a lot of blowing dust and sand, you should
   a. rotate your tires.
   b. replace your windshield.
   c. check your spare tire for proper air pressure.
   d. change your vehicle's oil, oil filter, and air filter.

drive write

Animals on the Roadway Each day hundreds of animals are struck by motor vehicles on rural roadways. Collect information about collisions with deer, moose, and elk on U.S. roadways. Write a report comparing the numbers of vehicle collisions with these different animals and the amount of damage to vehicles.

chapter 16

DRIVING ON HIGHWAYS

16.1   Classification of Highways

16.2   Entering Controlled-Access Highways

16.3   Strategies for Driving on Highways

16.4   Exiting Controlled-Access Highways

16.5   Highway Problems and Features

KEY IDEA

How can you manage risk when entering, driving on, and exiting multi-lane highways?

The skills necessary for low-risk driving on multi-lane highways are different from those you need for driving in city or rural traffic. Do you know the best way to merge with traffic? Do you know what to do if a vehicle is following too closely?

lesson 16.1
CLASSIFICATION OF HIGHWAYS

 OBJECTIVES

- Explain the difference between highways that have fully-controlled access and those that have non-controlled access.

- Describe the three kinds of highways that are located in each state.

- Describe four different types of highway interchanges.

 VOCABULARY

- controlled access
- interchange
- grade elevation
- non-controlled access

Even though highway driving is actually safer than driving on city streets or rural roads, it is more stressful on drivers because traffic moves much faster. To be a low-risk driver on highways, you need to learn skills that keep you safe as you enter, drive on, and exit highways. Safe driving demands that you manage visibility, time, and space expertly.

Three Classifications of Highway Systems

In the United States, there are three classifications of highways: the Interstate Highway System, the U.S. Highway System, and the State Highway System. Some states also have county highways, which have the same characteristics as state highways.

Names and design features for highways vary. For example, sometimes freeways are called expressways, or expressways are called freeways, though they have different design features.

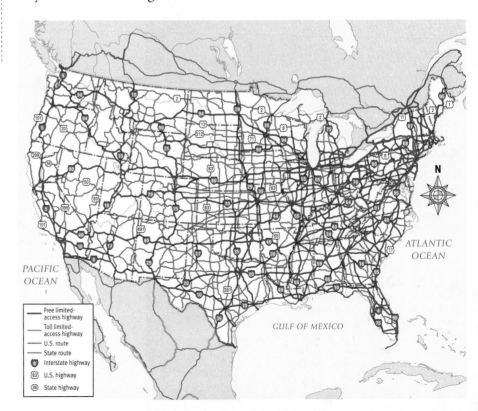

FIGURE 1 The United States has 46,726 miles of highways that make up the Interstate Highway System.

Interstate Highway System The greatest system of controlled-access freeways is the Interstate Highway System. The design features of the Interstate System require every access to be a fully **controlled access**, which means that vehicles can enter and leave only at designated interchanges. **Interchanges** are places where drivers can cross over or under traffic as well as enter or leave the freeway.

There is a uniform standard for signs for interstates. The Interstate highway sign is a red, white, and blue shield, as shown in **FIGURE 2**.

Freeways are major multi-lane divided highways designed for high speeds. They have at least two travel lanes going in opposite direction with adequate shoulders. Traffic is separated by **grade elevation**, which means that bridges and tunnels are used to direct traffic over or under other travel lanes.

Without traffic lights or STOP signs, the freeway is able to accommodate a larger volume of traffic and reduce the potential for high-speed rear-end crashes.

Freeways can have tolls. The word *free* in freeway refers to the fact that traffic can flow freely without traffic lights.

Expressways Other controlled-access highways that have similar characteristics as freeways are turnpikes, parkways, super-highways, and expressways. The difference in the characteristics of freeways and expressways, as defined by the federal government, is that an expressway may have **non-controlled access** rather than fully-controlled access. This means that expressways could have traffic lights, intersections, and driveways where traffic is able to enter or leave the expressway.

Traffic entering or exiting at slower speeds than the traffic flow creates a dangerous situation, especially for distracted drivers. If you look to your target area and predict that there could be a traffic light, or a vehicle entering from a side road, you will have ample time to adjust your speed and control the traffic to the rear. If you are distracted and suddenly confronted with stopped traffic ahead, you would be at great risk of rear-ending the vehicle ahead or of being rear-ended by others.

Turnpikes and Parkways Turnpikes and freeways are very similar in design features. *Turnpike* was used to designate a toll road. However, many

---

FIGURE 2

The even numbered routes run east and west with the lowest numbered routes beginning in the south.

The odd numbered routes go north and south with the lowest numbers beginning on the west coast.

FIGURE 3 Parkways may have some rest areas, but commercial buildings such as stores or office buildings are prohibited.

of the highways classified as turnpikes no longer charge tolls, or have been absorbed into the Interstate highway system.

Parkways were some of the earliest controlled-access highways. Commercial traffic and billboards are prohibited on parkways. Because many parkways have a STOP sign at the end of the entrance ramp and no acceleration lane, a driver may have to accelerate from a full stop directly into a travel lane of the parkway. Some parkways may have traffic lights to accommodate crossing traffic, which can create a dangerous situation for parkway drivers who do not search to the target area. However, some of the most scenic highways in the United States are parkways.

U.S. Highways   The U.S. highway system was the first highway network that connected states. Most of the state highways and U.S. highways have non-controlled access, which allows drivers to enter and leave the highway from any point. There are intersections with traffic controls to separate crossing traffic, which makes traveling slower and more dangerous than being on a controlled-access freeway.

State Highways   The state highway system is a network of highways existing within the boundaries of a state. Many of these highways are narrow two-lane roadways in rural areas. However, some state highways may be expressways and others may be controlled-access freeways.

Freeway Interchanges

The four most common types of freeway interchanges are cloverleaf, diamond, trumpet and all-directional interchanges. The names of the interchanges are based on their shapes.

FIGURE 4 A cloverleaf interchange has a series of entrance and exit ramps that resemble the outline of a four-leaf clover. This type of interchange enables drivers to proceed in either direction on either highway.

FIGURE 5 A diamond interchange is used when a road that crosses a busy highway has little traffic.

FIGURE 6 A trumpet interchange is used where one highway forms a T-intersection with a freeway.

FIGURE 7 An all-directional interchange is used in complicated intersections with high-volume traffic. From this interchange, traffic is channeled in many different directions.

review it 16.1

1. Explain why knowing the difference between a fully-controlled access highway and a non-controlled access highway helps to make you a low-risk driver.

2. Explain the differences between interstate, U.S., and state highways, and their numbering systems.

3. Explain how each type of interchange helps to keep traffic moving.

Critical Thinking

4. **Infer** How does understanding the numbering system on route markers help you to be a safe driver?

5. **Reasoning** Do you think parkways require greater attention to the driving task than driving on a freeway? Explain your reasoning.

IN THE PASSENGER SEAT **Cause and Effect** As a passenger on any highway of the interstate highway system, list some of the advantages of the highway that you notice compared to local streets and roads. Then explain the effect the advantage has for drivers. For example, you might list that the curves are gradual and banked, which means you can drive at higher speeds without loss of traction.

ENTERING CONTROLLED-ACCESS HIGHWAYS

Any plans for driving on any controlled-access highway should include a travel plan, regardless of the length of the trip. For short trips, know the name, route, or number for both the entrance and exit you will use. For long-distance trips, plan stops for food, fuel, and rest.

Controlled-Access Entrances

Before you enter any highway, make sure you are using the correct entrance ramp. Many drivers have mistakenly tried to enter a freeway by using an exit ramp. To help prevent this error, red and white signs are posted saying WRONG WAY or DO NOT ENTER.

There are three parts to a controlled-access entrance, as shown in FIGURE 8. The **entrance ramp** provides access to the highway and the opportunity to search for a merge area. Many drivers make the mistake of driving too quickly on the entrance ramp. Driving more slowly provides time to evaluate zone conditions and to select a gap in the traffic flow, which allows you to slip into the gap or hole without causing drivers behind you to brake. If you do an adequate search while you are on the entrance ramp, you will be able to predict between which vehicles you should merge. You can then accelerate so that you will be at the same speed as the traffic flow when your merge area is next to you.

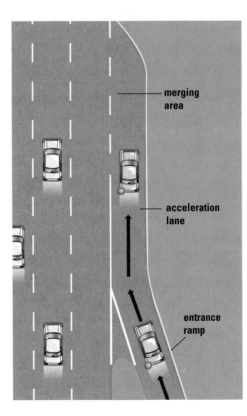

merging area

acceleration lane

entrance ramp

FIGURE 8
CONTROLLED-ACCESS ENTRANCE

The **acceleration lane** provides an area where you can speed up in order to match the speed of the traffic flow you're entering.

The **merging area** is the space in a travel lane of the highway that is parallel to the acceleration lane, where you will be joining the traffic flow.

Entrance Problems

Entrances to controlled-access highways require special attention because they have the highest risk for crashes. **FIGURE 10** shows the number of deaths as a result of drivers who mistakenly entered an exit ramp. Short entrance ramps, short acceleration lanes, and high dividing walls contribute to entrance problems.

FIGURE 9

Some entrance ramps have high walls blocking traffic, which makes it more difficult to see the gap in time to accelerate to the proper speed. Using the outside mirror can give you a view of approaching traffic.

The Entrance Ramp If you make an error and enter the wrong entrance ramp, continue onto the highway and drive to the next exit. **Never back up on an entrance ramp or on a freeway.**

When other vehicles are on the entrance ramp, adjust your speed to establish 3 or more seconds of space. Begin looking immediately for a gap or hole in traffic. If you have a closed front zone, reduce your speed to give the vehicle in front more time to enter. Check your rear zone and do not slow down or stop suddenly.

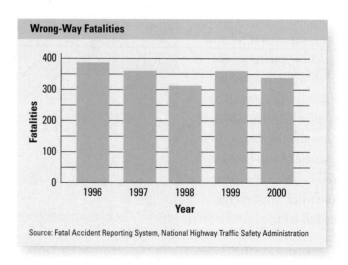

Wrong-Way Fatalities

Source: Fatal Accident Reporting System, National Highway Traffic Safety Administration

FIGURE 10

The more space you have from the vehicle in front of you, the better opportunity you will have to accelerate into a safe merge area.

When the entrance ramp and acceleration lane are short, it can be difficult to time entry into a merge area. When you are on the entrance ramp, check the outside mirror and look to the left for a merge area.

Where there is no acceleration lane, find a **hole in traffic**—an empty space between traffic clusters—for a point of entry. This will give you enough space to get on the highway from a stopped position without causing another car to brake.

Some entrance ramps have a **ramp meter**, which is a set of traffic signals—red and green only—to control traffic flow onto the highway.

Acceleration Lane   During rush hours, the number of vehicles entering the freeway will alter the speed and space you need to enter. If entrances have very short acceleration lanes, slow down to provide the best opportunity to merge. Otherwise, you will be forced to reduce your speed or come to a stop while on the acceleration lane, which creates a highly dangerous situation.

Make every effort to enter a highway without stopping. A driver behind you might be looking for a gap and not see that you are stopped. If you must stop, flash your brake lights to warn drivers behind you and try to reduce your speed gradually so that you'll be able to accelerate when you get a gap.

If you run out of room, you are in an emergency situation. Wait for a large, safe gap or hole. Signal and accelerate quickly while staying in lane position 3, which will give an approaching vehicle an opportunity to pass by you without incident. **Never stop in a travel lane of the highway!**

Merging Problems   Adjusting your speed is critical to timing a smooth entrance into traffic. A closed front zone may cause you to reduce your speed and select a new gap. Accelerate to reach traffic speed. Check your rear zone and establish lane position and a safe following distance.

Left-Entrance Ramp   Some entrance ramps are located on the left of the highway, which creates a high-risk situation. Checking fast-moving traffic over your right shoulder can be more difficult than checking to your left. Use your right-outside mirror before

FIGURE 11
At a ramp meter, you must wait for the green light before entering the highway. Even with the green light you are still responsible for performing a safe merge.

FIGURE 12
Entering a freeway from the left can be more difficult than entering from the right. The acceleration lane merges into the far-left lane of traffic. Since this lane is usually used for high-speed traffic, the potential for conflict is greater than when you enter from the right.

FIGURE 13

making a blind-spot check. You might have difficulty seeing a motorcyclist or a very small car. Signal early as you look for a gap. When you see a gap, accelerate, and merge into the traffic lane.

Steps for Entering

Before you begin entering a highway, make sure the entrance is the one you want and that there are no red and white WRONG WAY or DO NOT ENTER signs, as shown in **FIGURE 13**. Look for a ramp meter and be prepared to stop if it is red.

Once on the entrance ramp, take these steps:

1. Check your front and rear zones. Do not accelerate until you are in the acceleration lane and have selected a gap or hole.

2. When your vehicle is at a 45-degree angle to the highway, signal, and make quick glances through your left outside rearview mirror and over your left shoulder to find a gap in traffic. While looking in your left-outside mirror, move your head about 8 inches forward and slightly away from the mirror to get a better view of traffic.

3. Once you are in the acceleration lane, decide between which vehicles you will enter. Increase your speed to time a smooth merge.

4. As you enter the merging area, adjust your speed to match the traffic flow.

5. Once on the highway, cancel your signal and adjust to the speed of traffic.

6. Position your vehicle with 3 or more seconds of following distance.

review it 16.2

1. Describe the actions that help you merge smoothly while in the acceleration lane.

2. Describe a situation on an entrance ramp that might prevent you from safely merging.

3. Why is the correct speed important on the entrance ramp?

4. Why is it important to look for a hole in traffic?

Critical Thinking

5. **Analyze** What special problems does an entrance ramp with a line-of-sight restriction present for drivers?

6. **Compare and Contrast** Compare your actions when entering a highway that doesn't have an acceleration lane with a highway that does have one.

IN YOUR COMMUNITY **Research** Visit your local fire department or police station and find out how many crashes that were reported took place on or near entrance ramps. Then find out how many crashes at entrance ramps happened across your state. Find out the time of the crash, the type of highway, and the type of ramp. Make a graph comparing the data. Share your graph with the class.

Once you are on the highway, stay alert as you adjust to the constantly changing traffic scene. Search to your target area to use the IPDE Process and Zone Control System to manage space.

Applying the IPDE Process and Zone Control

Highway driving makes using the IPDE Process and Zone Control easier than driving on two-lane roads because there are more opportunities to search farther ahead and there are fewer variations of highway designs to change your intended path of travel.

Identify   Interstate highways are designed to give drivers a long sight distance. However, higher speeds and multiple lanes require you to get the visual information farther ahead. You also need to identify closed front zones early. Never allow yourself to become trapped between two large vehicles.

Be aware of distracted drivers who may be talking on cellular phones or reading a map. Always take the best lane position and maintain proper following distance in order to stay clear of those drivers.

Predict   A predictable traffic flow is a safety feature of highways. However, you must search ahead to your target area to watch for slower traffic or for drivers changing lanes. Anticipate closed zones and points of conflict at entrances. In construction areas, predict that traffic will move slowly or stop.

Decide   The driving speeds on highways demand that you make quicker decisions. Last-second decisions and driving adjustments can quickly change your safe path of travel into a dangerous one, and may close one or more zones. Interchanges, in particular, create potential-collision areas because of the various speeds of drivers who are entering and exiting the highway.

 OBJECTIVES

- Explain how to apply the IPDE Process on the Interstate Highway System.
- Explain the advantages of a 3 or more second following distance.

 VOCABULARY

- reversible lane
- high-occupancy toll (HOT) lane
- common speed

Driving on high-density highways such as this is difficult because of the challenges drivers face in managing visibility, space, and time.
Predict How can you manage visibility, space, and time driving on highways?

Execute   Execute your decisions smoothly. Signal early for every maneuver and maintain 3 or more seconds of following distance. When passing, or when a vehicle is passing you, use a lane position that will give you the greatest amount of separation space. This will provide an escape path for vehicles, if needed, and minimize the road spray splashed on your windshield during wet road conditions. It will also decrease the wind buffet caused by passing trucks.

Lane Choice

Generally, it is safer to drive in the right lane and pass on the left. Reserve the center and left lanes for drivers who are passing and for faster traffic.

When traffic is heavy in the right lane, especially at entrance ramps during rush hour, use the center or left lane to avoid conflicts in the far right lane. Large trucks and vehicles towing trailers are restricted from using the left lane on many interstate highways. Avoid driving between two large vehicles.

Part of your decision of lane choice is based on information from signs, signals, and roadway markings. You are better able to maintain a safe path of travel and avoid sudden last-second decisions if you know your destination, read signs and roadway markings, and think ahead to your target area.

Often, several overhead signs are posted at the same place. Scan the signs quickly to get the information you need to continue in a safe path. An overhead sign with a yellow panel indicates the exit lane. All traffic in this lane must exit.

Reversible Lanes   Traffic lanes where traffic can travel in either direction depending on certain conditions are called **reversible lanes**. These lanes are often used during commuter hours where traffic in and out of a city is heaviest. By using reversible lanes, traffic authorities can make most efficient use of traffic lanes.

While reversible lanes are good for opening more lanes to traffic, they can also be deadly. Distracted drivers account for many head-on crashes, so to help to eliminate them, some reversible lanes use retractable cones, vertical yellow markers, or a movable physical concrete to create a barrier when certain lanes are closed. Some highways use overhead signal lights, as shown in **FIGURE 15**, to indicate when it's safe to use a reversible lane.

FIGURE 15

Overhead signal lights use an arrow or an X to indicate open and closed lanes.

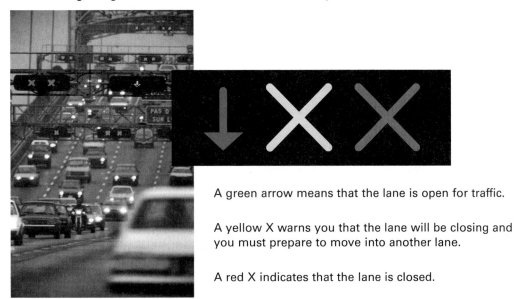

A green arrow means that the lane is open for traffic.

A yellow X warns you that the lane will be closing and you must prepare to move into another lane.

A red X indicates that the lane is closed.

Many highways have High-Occupancy Vehicle (HOV) lanes for buses and vehicles that have two or more occupants. Some highways have **high-occupancy toll (HOT) lanes**, which allow drivers to pay a fee in order to drive in an HOV lane with only one person in the vehicle.

Speed Limits   The posted speed limit sign indicates the maximum speed the driver of a passenger vehicle may travel under ideal weather and traffic conditions.

The minimum speed limit is the lowest legal speed you can drive under ideal conditions.

Driving too slowly can be very dangerous in fast-moving traffic and can cause rear-end collisions. Use the far right lane when you are driving at or under the minimum speed limit.

When you drive in areas with no posted speed limit, follow the last sign you saw. Always drive at the speed that is safe and prudent for the weather and roadway conditions.

If you drive at the **common speed**, the speed used by most drivers, you can better blend with traffic. Sometimes the common speed is above

FIGURE 16   Some signs post special speed limits for different times of day and type of vehicle.

the maximum speed limit. Resist the temptation to increase your speed to keep up with the faster vehicles. Drivers who exceed the common speed are likely to weave in and out of traffic to pass other vehicles are dangerous to other drivers.

Blind Spots   Remember that you have blind spots in both your left-rear and right-rear zones. Check these zones often and be alert for other drivers who may pass you. Avoid driving in anyone's blind spots, especially truck drivers' blind spots.

Tailgating   Vehicles that follow you too closely, or tailgate, can put you in a dangerous situation. To stay safe, encourage tailgaters to pass you by reducing your speed gradually. However, do not reduce your speed if heavy traffic prevents tailgaters from passing.

If a driver continues to tailgate, change lanes when it is safe to do so. Frequently check your rear zones to keep awareness of any tailgaters.

Changing Lanes

Avoid changing lanes too often. Unnecessary weaving from one lane to another can lead to a collision.

Changing lanes on a highway is more complicated when three or more lanes of traffic are moving in the same direction. Potential conflicts are created when two drivers head for the same space at the same time from opposite sides after passing a vehicle, as shown in **FIGURE 17**.

Remember that some highways have entrance ramps on the left as well as on the right. If you are driving in the left lane while approaching a left entrance, check your right-rear zone to see if you will have an open zone to move into.

Lanes are often closed for construction and road repair. When you see in your target area that a lane is closed, check to find an alternate lane.

It is both illegal and hazardous to use the shoulder or median as a driving lane when traffic is backed up. Drivers who drive illegally on the shoulder are also preventing emergency vehicles from having an open path of travel.

Passing and Being Passed

Passing other vehicles on an interstate is usually safer than passing on a two-lane highway because the traffic you are passing is going in the same direction. With a median separating you from oncoming traffic on an interstate, a head-on collision is not a threat. However, highway speeds and a high volume of traffic demand concentration along with the use of the IPDE Process and Zone Control System when passing.

Before you pass, evaluate the zone you are entering, and signal your lane change. Be sure to check the blind-spot area to the left or right as necessary.

Passing on the left is best; however, passing on the right is permitted in some states. Passing on the right is dangerous because it is less expected, and drivers' peripheral vision is less effective than their central vision. When passing another vehicle, use the procedure for making a lane change to the left. After passing, return to your original lane.

When you are being passed, be aware of the position of the vehicle that is passing you. If the vehicle is too close to your side, move to lane position 2 or 3 to gain better separation. Continue to check the position of the vehicle passing you. If you want the vehicle to pass you more quickly, reduce your speed. Never increase speed while being passed.

Interstate highways provide the safest roadways per miles of driving. However, due to the high speed limits, they also account for the greatest number of fatalities per crash. Although highways are safer than other roadways, tired drivers, stalled vehicles, construction workers, and aggressive drivers combine to present hazards and potential conflict.

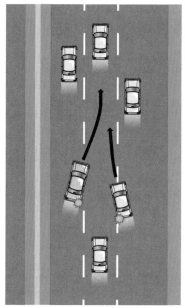

FIGURE 17
Conflict can occur when two drivers head for the same space at the same time.

safe
driving tip

Passed Again If you are continually being passed on the right, it may mean that you are driving too slowly and that you should move to the lane on your right when it is safe to do so.

analyzing data

Licensed Drivers Every year, there are changes in the number of licensed drivers in different age groups. This chart shows how many drivers there were of different ages in 1996, 2001, and 2006. Study the chart before answering these questions.

1. **Reading Graphs** What does each color on the graph represent?

2. **Reading Graphs** About how many licensed drivers aged 60–64 were there in the U.S. in 2001?

3. **Calculating** Which age group had the greatest increase in number between 1996 and 2006?

4. **Analyzing Data** Which age group had the most licensed drivers in 1996? Which had the most in 2001, and in 2006?

5. **Making Judgments** Why do you think the age group with the most licensed drivers changed during the three years measured?

Licensed Drivers in the United States

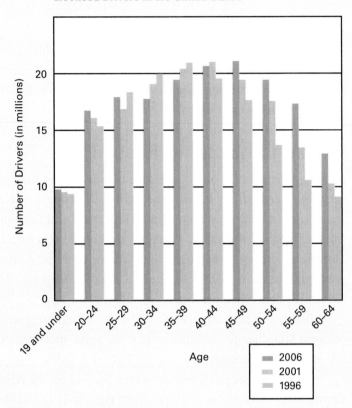

---

review it 16.3

1. How is using the IPDE System on interstate highways different from using it on other roadways?

2. Why is it important to identify reversible lanes?

3. How does using the 3-or-more second rule when following a vehicle help you to be a low-risk driver?

Critical Thinking

4. **Infer** Explain how drivers who tailgate put other drivers around them in a high-risk situation.

IN THE PASSENGER SEAT **Pass or Be Passed** With an adult licensed driver, watch for cars that are passing you or that you pass. Record the distance traveled, your speed, and the number of times that you were passed and the number of times you passed a vehicle. Were there certain times of the day that you were passed more frequently than you were the one doing the passing? Record your data and share it with the class.

EXITING CONTROLLED-ACCESS HIGHWAYS

Leaving a highway safely requires planning and skill. Plan for your exit as early as possible. Search to the target area, and when you see the sign for your exit, move into the lane designated by the sign.

Most exits provide a **deceleration lane**—an added lane where it's safe to slow your vehicle without blocking the vehicles behind you. Try not to decelerate until you are out of the travel lane and in the deceleration lane.

The deceleration lane leads into the **exit ramp**—the ramp leading off the highway. The posted ramp speed limit indicates the recommended speed for negotiating the exit safely. Pay close attention to the exit-ramp speed because a low speed may indicate that the exit leads into a sharp curve. Remember, if you miss the exit you want, go on to the next exit. Never stop or back up if you go past your exit.

 OBJECTIVES

- Describe three possible exiting problems.
- Explain how to apply the IPDE Process to exiting a freeway.
- List the steps for exiting a freeway.

 VOCABULARY

- deceleration lane
- exit ramp

Applying the IPDE Process at Exits

Use the IPDE Process as you search well ahead to the target area.

1. Identify the green guide signs that show the distance to your exit.

2. Identify any potential weave pattern before you reach your exit.

3. Identify closed and open zones.

4. Predict actions of other drivers who might be using the same exit.

5. Decide on the best speed and lane position before getting in the deceleration lane.

6. Execute your maneuver smoothly and blend with slower traffic.

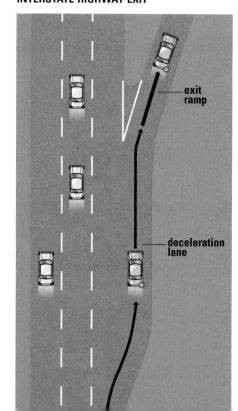

FIGURE 18
INTERSTATE HIGHWAY EXIT

exit ramp

deceleration lane

FIGURE 19 On some highways, one lane is used as the exit and entrance, which means that drivers' paths may cross on the lane. Exiting traffic should merge behind entering traffic since entering traffic is accelerating.

Even though leaving a highway should be a smooth operation, problems can occur. Be alert and ready to adjust to any potentially hazardous situations. If the ramp is backed-up, check your rear zone, flash your brake lights, and begin to reduce speed. Check your rear zone again to make sure traffic is slowing. If traffic is not slowing, try to pass the exit area smoothly. Rather than joining the overflow and risking a rear-end collision, go past the exit and drive on to the next exit.

Steps for Exiting

Exiting a highway has special risks. In order to avoid last-second decisions and sudden moves, identify your exit and the exit ramp speed at least one half mile before the exit. Predict a stop at the end of the exit ramp, as there is likely to be a traffic control device. Be alert when entering traffic on a local highway or street after leaving the highway. Expect two-way traffic, pedestrians, intersections, and the need for lower speeds. Once you've made the decision to exit, execute the following actions.

1. Check front and rear zones for traffic.
2. Signal and move into lane position 3 for right-side exits. Change only one lane at a time. Do not slow down until you are in the deceleration lane.

FIGURE 20

3. Move into the deceleration lane.

4. Turn your signal off and tap your brake lights to warn drivers behind that you are slowing. Slow gradually and keep 3 or more seconds of space ahead. Check your own speed, and adjust to the posted speed limit.

5. Check your speed frequently and check for line-of-sight and path-of-travel restrictions affecting your targeting path.

Some highways may have short deceleration lanes, so you will have to slow down more quickly. As you enter the deceleration lane,

- judge the length of the lane,
- identify the exit-ramp speed,
- check your speed and,
- most importantly, check traffic behind you.

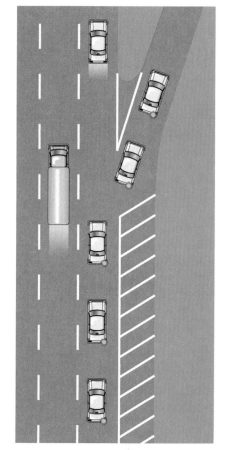

FIGURE 21 Traffic can back up from an exit ramp onto the highway. Ramp overflows are most likely to occur during rush hour traffic.

review it 16.4

1. Explain what to do if your exit lane has an overflow.

2. Explain how you apply the IPDE Process when you exit an interstate.

3. Why should you look one-half mile ahead before exiting an interstate highway?

Critical Thinking

4. Infer Why is it important to avoid last-second decisions when exiting an interstate highway?

IN YOUR COMMUNITY **Research** Driving with an adult licensed driver, take note of the posted speed limits at various highway exits and the kind of highway you're exiting. Compare your data to find any connection between exit speed limits and types of highway. Report your conclusions to the class.

lesson 16.5
HIGHWAY PROBLEMS AND FEATURES

 OBJECTIVES

- Explain how highway hypnosis and velocitation create risk for drivers.
- Explain what to do if you need to pull your car over to the shoulder.
- Explain the risks associated with toll plazas and how you can reduce them.

 VOCABULARY

- highway hypnosis
- velocitation
- beltway
- spur

Safe Driving

Some of the problems associated with driving on the interstate highway system are caused by drivers or other vehicles. In addition, construction zones and toll plazas present their own risks.

By being alert to possible problems and knowing how to react, you'll have the skills that will make you a low-risk driver.

Drivers   Staying alert on highways can be a problem when you travel long distances at a steady speed or are tired. You can be lulled into an inattentive drowsy state known as **highway hypnosis**. Drivers who fail to recognize their own fatigue, or even ignore it, pose a high-risk to themselves and to other drivers.

When you first notice that your attention is less focused or that your eyelids want to close, stop at the next exit for a safe place and take a brief nap, or stretch or exercise before continuing. Do not drive any further if you feel that you're too tired to continue.

Hours of driving at freeway speeds can fool you into thinking your vehicle is moving slower than it actually is, causing you to drive too fast unknowingly. This condition, called **velocitation**, can be especially hazardous while you are approaching a curve of the exit ramp. Look at the suggested speed limit for the ramp and check your speedometer to be sure you're traveling at the posted speed.

Disabled Vehicles   Whether you see a vehicle stopped on the shoulder or if your vehicle needs to pull over, be alert for potential conflicts. At first sign of trouble with your vehicle, check rear zones, signal, and move as far as possible away from traffic. Turn on your hazard flashers. If the vehicle is not far off the road, get everyone out and stand to the rear side of the vehicle as far away from traffic as possible. **Never stand in the highway to direct traffic.** When it is safe to do so, raise the hood and tie a white cloth to the antenna or door handle.

If you remain in a disabled vehicle, lock all doors. Keep your safety belts on and place your head against the head restraint.

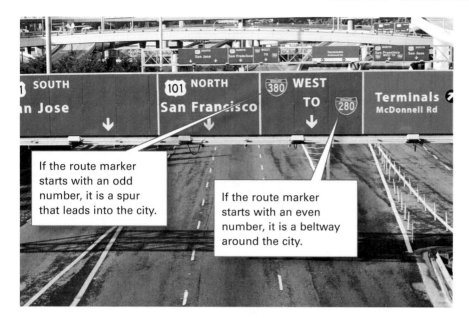

FIGURE 22 A three-digit route identifies beltways and spurs.

This will protect you in the event that a vehicle crashes into you. If you have a cellular phone, call for help. Ask anyone who stops to assist you to go to a phone and call for help. Never get into a stranger's vehicle.

Roadways

Watch for orange construction signs and be prepared to slow as soon as you identify the first one. Early warning construction signs with blinking lights indicate the construction-zone speed limit. Reduce your speed and follow the directions of the person directing traffic.

Belts and Spurs   As you approach a major city you may have an option to take a **beltway**, or loop around the city, or a **spur**, or branch going into a city.

Toll Plazas

Toll plazas, where you pay a fee for the use of the highway, are hazardous environments for drivers. While stopping, and until there are at least two or three vehicles stopped to your rear, continue to monitor the rearview mirror every few seconds. If you see a vehicle approaching fast in the rear, tap your brake lights repeatedly to get the driver's attention.

Electronic tolls, as shown in **FIGURE 23**, are becoming more common. As you approach the toll plaza there will be signs showing which lanes to use. Sometimes there is a bypass lane that is separate from the toll plaza.

FIGURE 23 Electronic tolls make highway driving more convenient and reduce congestion because drivers don't have to stop to deposit coins.

review it 16.5

1. Explain why it's dangerous to drive on a highway for extended periods of time without a break.

2. Explain why it's important to check your speed at exit ramps.

3. Explain how you can reduce the risks drivers face at toll plazas.

Critical Thinking

4. **Relate Cause and Effect** What might happen if a driver fails to notice the beginning symptoms of highway hypnosis?

5. **Infer** How does a disabled vehicle on the shoulder of the highway pose a risk for other drivers?

IN THE PASSENGER SEAT **Know Your Routes** While driving on a highway with a licensed adult, make a list of all the highway route signs you see and identify them as freeways, U.S. highways, state or county highways, loops or spurs. Later check with the legend on a map to see if you identified the routes correctly.

CHAPTER 16 REVIEW

Lesson Summaries

16.1 CLASSIFICATION OF HIGHWAYS

- In the United States, there are three classifications of highways: the Interstate Highway System, the U.S. Highway System, and State Highway System.
- Freeways require controlled-access interchanges. Traffic is separated by grade elevation.
- An expressway may have non-controlled access, which means that they could have traffic lights or intersections.

16.2 ENTERING CONTROLLED-ACCESS HIGHWAYS

- Controlled-access highways have an entrance ramp, an acceleration lane, and a merging area.
- Factors such as short entrance ramps, short acceleration lanes, and high dividing walls contribute to entrance problems.

16.3 STRATEGIES FOR DRIVING ON HIGHWAYS

- Higher speeds and multiple lanes of freeways require you to get the visual information farther ahead.
- Search ahead to your target area for slower traffic or for drivers changing lanes.
- Reversible lanes can be deadly if you are not attentive.

16.4 EXITING CONTROLLED-ACCESS HIGHWAYS

- Most exits provide a deceleration lane where it's safe to slow your vehicle without blocking the vehicles behind you.

16.5 HIGHWAY PROBLEMS AND FEATURES

- Watch for orange construction signs, and be prepared to slow as soon as you identify the first one.
- As you approach a toll plaza, be aware of signs for the correct lane to use.

Chapter Vocabulary

- acceleration lane
- beltway
- common speed
- controlled access
- deceleration lane
- entrance ramp
- exit ramp
- grade elevation
- high-occupancy toll (HOT) lanes
- highway hypnosis
- hole in traffic
- interchange
- merging area
- non-controlled access
- ramp meter
- reversible lane
- spur
- velocitation

Write the word or phase from the list above that completes the sentence correctly.

1. The space between traffic clusters is called a(n) _____.

2. A(n) _____ is often used during commuter traffic to make more efficient use of traffic lanes.

3. Some entrance ramps have a(n) _____ to control traffic entering the highway.

4. Most U.S. highways have _____, which allow drivers to enter or leave the highway from any point.

5. _____ are places where drivers can cross over or under traffic as well as enter or leave the freeway.

6. Some highways have _____, which allow drivers to pay a fee in order to drive in an HOV lane with only one person in the vehicle.

Checking Concepts

LESSON 1

7. What problems should you be prepared for when entering a parkway?

LESSON 2

8. How should you manage speed to best be able to find a gap to merge into?

LESSON 3

9. Why is it generally safer to travel in the right lane of a freeway?

10. How do you know whether you can travel in a reversible lane?

LESSON 4

11. Why is it a good practice to tap your brake lights when exiting a highway?

LESSON 5

12. What actions should you take as soon as you detect a mechanical problem with your vehicle while in the center lane of the freeway?

Critical Thinking

13. **Compare** Compare traveling from Maine to Florida on I-95 and U.S. 1. Driving on which route would consume more time, more fuel, and have greater risk?

14. **Contrast** Explain how entering a freeway is different from entering a highway.

15. **Analyze** Why is being in the correct lane position especially important for highway driving?

You're the Driver

16. **Decide** You are in the far left lane and several vehicles have passed you on the right. What does this tell you and what should you do?

17. **Identify** What key factors contribute to safe driving on freeways?

18. **Predict** What unsafe practice is the driver of the yellow car following? What options does this driver have to improve the situation? How might the tailgater affect the yellow car driver's decision?

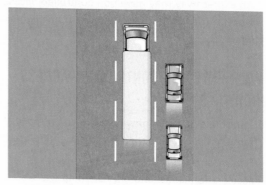

19. **Execute** What is the driver of the car required to do when driving through the construction zone?

Preparing for the Test

Choose the letter of the answer that best completes the statement or answers the question.

1. Which of the following highways have similar features?
   a. freeways, expressways, interstate highways
   b. freeways, U.S. routes, state highways
   c. interstate highways, county routes, U.S. routes
   d. U.S. routes, state routes, expressways

Use the photo below to answer Question 2.

2. Which highway system is most likely to have one of these?
   a. freeways   **c.** interstate highways
   b. expressways   **d.** turnpikes

3. A freeway interchange does not have
   a. a bridge or tunnel.
   b. crossing traffic separated by grade elevation.
   c. entrance ramps and acceleration lanes.
   d. an exit ramp meter to control exiting traffic.

Use the photo below to answer Question 4.

4. You are traveling south on an Interstate highway, and want to enter another freeway to travel in an easterly direction. Which of the following statements is true?
   a. You will go over or under the bridge before exiting.
   b. You will make a left turn off the highway.

   c. You will not have any potential weave patterns from other traffic.
   d. You can expect a traffic light at the end of the exit ramp.

5. Which of the following statements is true?
   a. A gap and hole in traffic means the same thing.
   b. A gap in the traffic flow will give you more time to enter.
   c. A hole in traffic is space between traffic clusters.
   d. There will be larger space within a gap than there is in a hole.

6. The far left lane of a freeway should be used
   a. for trucks, buses and other commercially licensed drivers.
   b. only for passing. Once the pass is completed, the lane should be vacated.
   c. if you want to practice the 3-second following distance.
   d. only by commuters with three or more occupants in the vehicle.

7. Which of the following statements is *not* true?
   a. Passing and being passed is safer on a freeway than on a U.S. Highway.
   b. There is less chance for head-on crashes on Interstates than on state highways.
   c. Expressways always have controlled access.
   d. Freeways always have controlled access.

---

drive write

History of the Interstate Research the history of the interstate highway system in the United States. In one or two paragraphs, summarize your findings, including beginning and end dates, cost, and how route numbers were assigned.

344

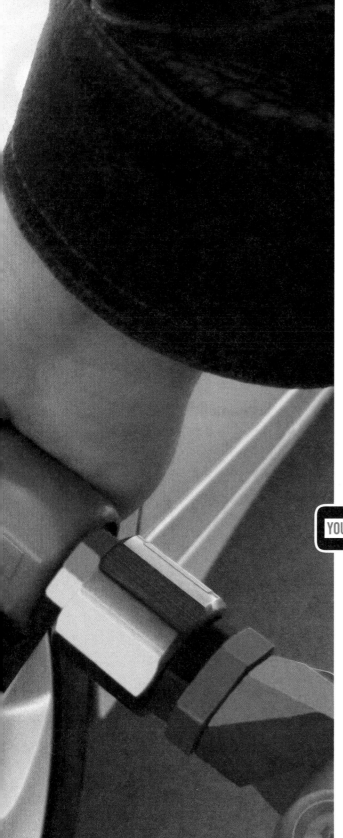

chapter 17

BUYING AND MAINTAINING A VEHICLE

17.1 Buying a Vehicle

17.2 Preventive Maintenance

17.3 Fuel Efficiency, Recycling, and Security Systems

KEY IDEA

Before you buy your first vehicle, how will you decide what the best car is for you and where will you find information about maintaining your vehicle?

 **There** are many responsibilities that go along with vehicle ownership. After buying a vehicle, you will have years of maintenance and repairs to ensure your vehicle is kept in safe, efficient operating condition. Where can you find information about vehicle safety and security systems?

BUYING A VEHICLE

OBJECTIVES

- Identify questions to be answered before deciding to buy.
- Identify three safety features available in new vehicles and explain their function.
- Describe the advantages and disadvantages between buying a new and used vehicle.

VOCABULARY

- budget
- Variable Ride-Height Suspension

Buying a vehicle is one of the most expensive purchases a person will make. In order to make the best decision about which kind of car to buy, you should consider your driving needs, your budget, and the vehicle's safety features and record. With the ongoing awareness of the effects of driving on the environment, you can buy vehicles that are environmentally friendly, too.

The Cost of Ownership

As you think about buying a car, you will need to consider how much money you have to spend, or your **budget**. When considering your budget, you must understand the real cost of owning a vehicle. The purchase price is just the beginning of your cost. In addition to the purchase price, you will have the immediate cost of auto insurance, registration fees, and state vehicle stickers. Depending on your driving needs, you will also have to consider the cost of gasoline, oil, tires, preventive maintenance, and repairs. If you take out a loan to buy the car, you will have a monthly loan payment as well.

Evaluate Your Driving Needs

Once you've determined your budget, you should evaluate your needs for buying a car. Vehicles can range in size and weight from small compact cars to large SUVs, and all other types in between.

Ask yourself:

- What kind of driving will I do: local, long distance, towing a trailer?
- How many miles will I drive each year?
- How many passengers or how much cargo will I need to carry?
- What safety features do I want?
- How long will I expect to keep the vehicle?
- Will it fit in my parking area?

Fuel efficient

More cargo room

More passenger room

FIGURE 1 Evaluate your needs before deciding which kind of vehicle to buy.

Generally, heavier SUVs and full-size sedans will provide better protection in a crash than smaller vehicles. However, because of their higher centers of gravity, SUVs roll more frequently than full-size sedans. Compact and sport type vehicles with a short wheelbase will skid more easily and more violently than full-size vehicles.

Know the Safety Features

As technology improves, vehicles are becoming safer every year, with microprocessors and sensors that provide more control and protection. Vehicles made before 2000 may not have improved safety features.

Electronic Stability Control (ESC) With an ESC, drivers have more control during extreme steering maneuvers or on slippery roads. The sensors recognize when a vehicle starts to oversteer or understeer, then automatically apply the brake to one or more wheels to get the vehicle back on target.

FIGURE 2

Side-Impact Air Bags Curtain and tubular air bags deploy downward from the vehicle's roof rail, protecting the heads of vehicle occupants. Combination air bags deploy from the side of the seat, protecting the head and chest.

Tire Pressure Monitoring System (TPMS) Underinflation is a leading cause of tire failure. Starting September 2007, federal regulations required all new vehicles to have a TPMS.

The TPMS uses sensors with a dashboard warning light that alerts drivers when one or more tires are significantly underinflated.

FIGURE 3 A beeper sounds when an object is close and beeps faster as the object gets very close.

Back Up Camera A rear video camera, as shown in **FIGURE 3**, gives the driver a wide angle view of much of the rear area that is usually hidden.

Lane Departure Warning When the sensors detect a vehicle is drifting from the lane, a lane departure warning sounds. These systems use radar, infrared sensors, or a camera to read the lines on the road, and vehicle speed sensors to determine drifting over the line.

Variable Ride-Height Suspension (VRHS) Depending on conditions such as vehicle speed and terrain, the **Variable Ride-Height Suspension** raises or lowers the ride height of the vehicle while it is in motion. During off-road driving at lower speeds, the vehicle adjusts to ride higher to allow increased ground clearance. During on-road driving at higher speeds, the vehicle will adjust to ride lower to the ground. The vehicle riding lower by several inches has a lower center of gravity and is less likely to roll over in a crash.

New or Used Vehicle?

As a smart consumer, you need to know the advantages and disadvantages of buying a new and a used vehicle.

Advantages Buying a new vehicle gives you a sense of security with a written warranty for repairs or parts replacement over a given period of time. Financing can be up to seven years. A new vehicle has more safety features, requires less maintenance, and has more easily obtainable replacement parts. When the loan is paid off, the remaining years of service can reward you with substantial savings.

A used or pre-owned vehicle, on the other hand, will have a lower purchase price and will probably be cheaper to operate. Used cars are typically cheaper to insure, and they won't be affected by the quick depreciation that new cars experience. A well-maintained used vehicle can have many years and miles of useful service.

Disadvantages The minute you drive your new vehicle off the dealership's lot, its value declines and will continue to decline during the first few years. Your insurance premium will probably be higher as will taxes and vehicle registration. After the loan is paid off, the vehicle will have aged over that period of time.

A pre-owned vehicle may not have a warranty or service records. Replacement parts may be difficult to find and records of previous damages may be unavailable. You will need to pay for a thorough inspection by a certified mechanic. A used vehicle will not have the advanced safety features offered by a new vehicle.

In fact, a used vehicle may give you the best value. Armed with your budget and research, prepare a checklist before you start your search. **FIGURE 4** shows an example of a checklist. What would you look for when checking each of the items in this checklist?

Before you make any decision, however, it's best to comparison shop. The Internet offers sites with information about the most fuel-efficient vehicles, safety features, and which vehicles have the worst repair rates. Many websites provide studies and reports, and articles that cover a variety of consumer information. In addition, some websites provide crash test and rollover ratings with a five star system and information about defects, recalls, or how to file a complaint.

FIGURE 4

Used Vehicle Inspection Checklist		
Inspection Items	**YES**	**NO**
Outside Checks		
No signs of damage		
Tires same size and brand, same tread		
No fluid leaks		
Trunk has spare tire, jack, lug, wrench		
When bounced, all 4 corners respond same		
Inside checks		
Seats and upholstery in good condition		
All controls and accessories work		
No odor or source known		
Warning and alert lights work		
Under the Hood Checks		
No radiator or hose leaks		
Belts not frayed		
Fluid levels maintained		
No battery corrosion		
Performance		
Engine starts easily every time		
Accelerates, brakes smoothly with power		
When steering, doesn't pull to one side		
Steering wheel is centered when going straight		
Turns sharply without noises, rubbing		

review it 17.1

1. Identify what you must know before deciding on a vehicle to buy.
2. Describe five safety features available in new vehicles.
3. Describe one advantage of buying a new vehicle and a used vehicle.

Critical Thinking

4. **Analyze**   Explain how the cost of fuel affects the cost of buying a car.

IN YOUR COMMUNITY   **Compare and Contrast**   Visit a new-car dealership and compare two new cars of different models. Find the fuel economy rating of each car, then estimate how much it would cost to drive each vehicle for one year based upon the current price of gas in your area, and driving 10,000 miles. Prepare a report on your findings explaining which vehicle you would prefer to purchase and why.

lesson 17.2
PREVENTIVE MAINTENANCE

 OBJECTIVES

- Identify three parts of a battery's electrical system.
- Explain how cooling and lubricating systems protect your vehicle.
- Name four parts to a vehicle's control system.
- Identify the three tire ratings that are part of the Uniform Tire Quality Grading System.

 VOCABULARY

- electronic control module
- catalytic converter
- muffler

Your vehicle consists of systems that need routine care and preventive maintenance to keep it running smoothly and efficiently. A car needs day-to-day attention, as well as periodic servicing as recommended by your owner's manual. The two most important systems are the power systems that create power so your vehicle can run and the control system that gives you control of the brakes, steering, suspension, and tires.

There are different engine types and drive systems, such as rear-wheel, front-wheel and all-wheel drive. No matter what type of engine or drive system you have, when the CHECK ENGINE or SERVICE ENGINE SOON warning light comes on, as shown in FIGURE 5, be sure to check your owner's manual immediately and call a certified automotive technician.

Maintaining Power Systems

All modern vehicles have an **electronic control module** (ECM), a computer located in the engine compartment that controls your engine's efficiency. A large number of electronic devices and sensors work with the ECM. The sensors tell the ECM when to make adjustments to keep your vehicle running. The ECM constantly tests how the sensors and components are operating, because they must be in sync to function properly.

In addition to the ECM, new vehicles have an on-board diagnostic system that uses a standardized series of digital trouble codes to give owners and automotive technicians quick access to identify and fix malfunctions.

Fuel and Emission Systems   Electronic direct fuel injection systems have replaced carburetors in newer cars. Fuel injection systems deliver just the right amount of fuel, resulting in higher performance with lower fuel consumption.

To remove the burned exhaust gas, the exhaust valve opens and high pressure expels burned gas with a violent force through the tail pipe. **Catalytic converters** are used in the exhaust system to reduce the levels of nitrogen oxides, which the sun heats into smog.

FIGURE 5
Check Engine Light

The emission control system is an integral part of the engine and must not be tampered with or disconnected. This is especially true on vehicles with computerized engine controls.

The **muffler** reduces the noise from combustion sounds in the engine. Over time, rust causes holes and the muffler will sound loud.

Lubrication and Cooling Systems   Oil, grease, or other substances are used to lubricate moving parts to reduce damage from heat caused by friction. Changing the oil is the key to keeping your vehicle in good running condition. Your owner's manual will give you a schedule for when to replace the oil and check other parts that need lubrication, either by miles or time period.

Low oil pressure can quickly damage your engine. If the oil pressure warning light comes on while driving, pull safely off the road, turn off the engine, and wait for the engine to cool. Replace the oil immediately.

Low coolant levels can cause your engine to overheat. Check and replace low coolant levels when the vehicle is cold. Don't spill coolant on the ground; if you do, clean it up thoroughly because coolant is very toxic to animals. Check your owner's manual for service intervals.

Excessive heat can destroy the engine, so proper lubrication and cooling keeps your vehicle's systems operating at peak performance.

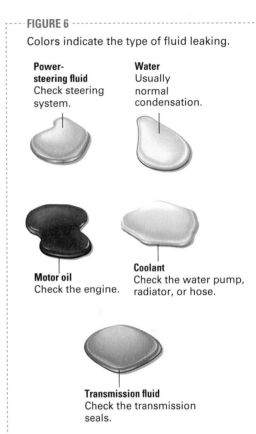

FIGURE 6

Colors indicate the type of fluid leaking.

Power-steering fluid Check steering system.

Water Usually normal condensation.

Motor oil Check the engine.

Coolant Check the water pump, radiator, or hose.

Transmission fluid Check the transmission seals.

Maintaining the Control Systems

Several different systems and components make up your vehicle's control system. Steering, brakes, tires, and the suspension systems are what give you control as well as safety and comfort.

Steering System   Problems with power steering can occur gradually or overnight. You may notice that turning the steering wheel is more difficult, especially when parking. There may be excessive "play" when the steering wheel moves more than normal to complete a maneuver. Check with an automotive technician immediately before driving any further if you experience any problems steering.

Brake System There are two types of brakes: disk brakes on the front wheels, and either disk or drum brakes on the rear wheels. Power brakes and anti-lock brakes have become standard on most vehicles. If the brake or anti-lock brake warning light stays on after starting the engine or when driving, have your vehicle serviced immediately.

The parking brake is mechanical and a separate rear wheel brake system. Properly adjusted parking brakes should hold a vehicle on a hill. When the parking brake is rarely used, the brake cable can get corroded and lock. By using the parking brake regularly, the cables stay clean and functional.

Regularly maintain your brakes by checking the brake fluid level and having your brakes checked on an annual basis or whenever you notice a problem. Good brake maintenance could save your life.

Tires It is important to understand tires and ensure your vehicle is equipped with the proper tires for safety and control. Federal laws require tire manufacturers to place standardized information on the sidewall of all tires. This information identifies and describes the characteristics of the tire and the identification number for safety standard certification in the event of a recall, as shown in **FIGURE 7**.

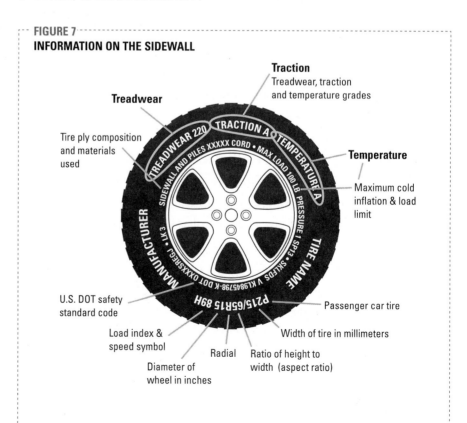

FIGURE 7
INFORMATION ON THE SIDEWALL

The federal government requires all passenger car tires sold in the United States to follow the Uniform Tire Quality and Grading (UTQG) Standards to help consumers compare different tires for treadwear, traction performance, and temperature resistance.

▶ **Treadwear** The higher the grade (60-500), the longer the tread should last.

▶ **Traction** Ratings are based on the tire's ability to stop on wet concrete or asphalt. The higher the grade (AA down to C), the better the traction.

▶ **Temperature** Ratings A-C (A is highest) are an indication of a tire's resistance to heat. Underinflation, excessive speed, or overloading can cause more heat buildup, which leads to tire failure.

Tires become unsafe when the tread is down to 1/16 of an inch and the wear bars are seen. You can quickly determine if your tires have enough tread by looking at the built-in treadwear indicators, as shown in **FIGURE 8**.

To prolong the life of your tires, have them rotated, aligned, and balanced as recommended in your owner's manual.

FIGURE 8

Notice the wear bar. Narrow bands appear across the tread.

Suspension System The suspension system provides steering stability and maximizes the friction between the tires and road surface. Suspension systems absorb road bumps so passengers can ride in comfort. The shock absorbers or strut assembly unit is located at each wheel to control hard bouncing and keep the tires on the road. When a vehicle bounces more than usual, or you see uneven tire wear, have the suspension checked. Check your owner's manual for servicing.

Electrical Systems Every car today contains a rechargeable 12-volt battery. The car battery powers everything electrical, including the engine's control computer, the ignition system, the radio, and the headlights. There are two types of batteries: sealed and non-sealed; many do not need maintenance. Keep the battery cables tight and free of corrosion, especially where the terminals connect to the battery. Use gloves and eye protection when working on a battery; the strong acid fluid can cause severe injury.

safe driving tip

Lincoln Penny To quickly check the condition of your tire tread, put a penny in the tread with Lincoln's head upside down, facing you. You need new tires if you can see the top of Lincoln's head.

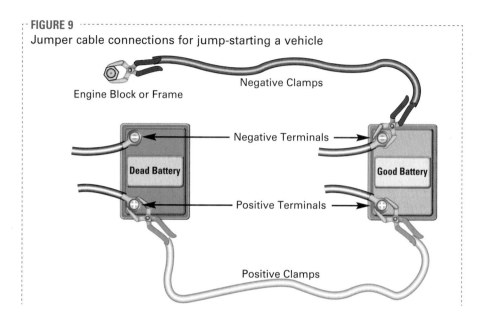

FIGURE 9
Jumper cable connections for jump-starting a vehicle

Engine Block or Frame

Negative Clamps

Negative Terminals

Dead Battery

Good Battery

Positive Terminals

Positive Clamps

If you turn the ignition key while in PARK or NEUTRAL and the starter makes no sound, it usually indicates a dead battery. Before jump-starting your vehicle or using it to jump-start another vehicle, check your owner's manual. Some new vehicles have specific instructions or prohibit jump-starting, so read the owner's manual carefully before attempting to jump-start a car.

When connecting jumper cables directly from battery to battery, be sure that the jumper cables are connected as shown in **FIGURE 9**.

Your lights not only help you see, but also help others see you. Check your headlights, taillights, backup lights, and turn signals often. Check the instrument panel to be sure the turn signal light is flashing when you activate the signal. Check your owner's manual for the correct replacement bulb. Your CHECK ENGINE lights can turn on because a bulb is malfunctioning.

Static Electricity Static electricity can spark a fire or explosion, so drivers need to be careful. Static electricity can build up when you exit and re-enter a vehicle, especially in dry or cold conditions. Static electricity is also discharged when you open the fuel cover, then touch the nozzle or pump before refueling. A new static charge can be picked up when you

FIGURE 10 When you see this light, you can still drive, but turn off any unneeded electrical devices such as the radio, and avoid starting the engine more than necessary. Drive your car to a repair shop as soon as possible to avoid getting stranded.

get back into the vehicle after starting to refuel. You need to discharge the electricity by touching any metal surface before touching the nozzle because that static charge can transfer to the nozzle and possibly cause a flash fire.

Here are some tips for safe refueling:

- If you're at a self-service gas station, do not leave your vehicle's fueling point.

- Do not go back into your vehicle when refueling, regardless of whether you use the nozzle's hold-open latch or not.

- If you must re-enter your vehicle while refueling, discharge the static electricity by touching a metal part of the outside of your car away from the filling point before touching and removing the gas nozzle.

FIGURE 11

Any kind of fire at a fueling station is extremely dangerous because of the amount of fuel nearby. This fire is a result of static electricity igniting fuel during refueling.

review it 17.2

1. What two systems protect your vehicle from heat and wear?

2. How does maintaining the steering system, brakes, tires, and the suspension help you stay safe?

3. Identify the three tire ratings that are part of the Uniform Tire Quality Grading Standards.

4. A good suspension system makes driving more comfortable. How does a suspension system that needs servicing affect your ability to be a safe driver?

Critical Thinking

5. **Evaluate** What could happen if you fail to maintain your vehicle's control systems?

6. **Analyze** Why is it important to check the information on your tires' sidewall?

IN THE PASSENGER SEAT **Dead Battery** Your friend turns the key in the ignition of his car and there is no sound. You tell your friend that the battery is probably dead. While you're waiting for help, explain to your friend how to jump-start a dead battery.

lesson 17.3
FUEL EFFICIENCY, RECYCLING, AND SECURITY SYSTEMS

 OBJECTIVES

- List five techniques for fuel-efficient driving.
- List two vehicle fluids and five vehicle parts that can be recycled.
- Explain how a keyless system works and how it can give you access to your vehicle.
- Describe five ways that satellites can make your driving safer.

 VOCABULARY

- alternative fuel

Advancements in design and technology have changed the way our vehicles look and perform. Today's vehicles are designed and built for greater fuel efficiency. The way you drive can also improve fuel efficiency.

Fuel-Efficient Vehicles

Automobile manufacturers continue to design vehicles that save gas without compromising performance. Hybrids combine the benefits of gas engines with electric motors that operate in unison or independently. The energy from the wheels turns the motor, which functions as a generator that converts energy normally wasted when coasting and braking into electricity. This energy is stored in the battery until needed.

The electric motor provides power for accelerating, passing, or climbing a hill, which allows a smaller, more efficient engine to be used. The engine is controlled by an automatic system that shuts the engine off when the vehicle comes to a stop and restarts the engine when the accelerator is pressed.

FIGURE 12 Hybrid models are available in all types of vehicles, giving consumers greater choices when shopping for fuel-efficient vehicles.

Maximize Fuel Efficiency

Even though modern vehicles are more fuel efficient, you can take additional actions to get the best fuel efficiency for your vehicle. By keeping periodic track of your gas mileage using the steps in **FIGURE 13**, and comparing your data, you will know if you're getting the most miles per gallon or if your car needs servicing.

Control Speed   For most cars, the maximum fuel efficiency is between 40 and 60 mph. If you drive at 70 mph, you will get 2–4 fewer miles per gallon over the duration of your trip. Slamming on the accelerator or brakes will increase the need for fuel and cause excessive wear on your brakes.

Warm the Engine   Most modern fuel injected vehicles need only 30 seconds to warm up and go.

Lighten Load   Reduce the load you carry in your vehicle.

Reduce Idling   Excess idling wastes gas. Turn off the engine if you won't be moving for a few moments.

Reduce Drag   Having your windows down creates aerodynamic drag and can decrease fuel economy by up to 10 percent. Rooftop carriers and rear racks increase drag. A clean car can reduce drag by up to 12 percent.

FIGURE 13
HOW TO CALCULATE MILES PER GALLON

Calculate Miles Per Gallon (MPG)
✓ Fill the gas tank
✓ Record the odometer reading and reset the odometer or trip meter to zero
✓ Drive until you have a 1/2-full fuel tank
✓ Record the number of gallons it took to refill the tank
✓ Again, record the odometer or trip meter reading
✓ Subtract the first odometer reading from the second to obtain miles driven
✓ Divide number of miles driven by the number of gallons of fuel used to refill the tank
Total is miles per gallon (mpg)

Alternative Fuels

Alternative fuels come from resources other than petroleum and are reducing our dependence on imported oil. **FIGURE 14** shows available alternative fuels and how they are produced.

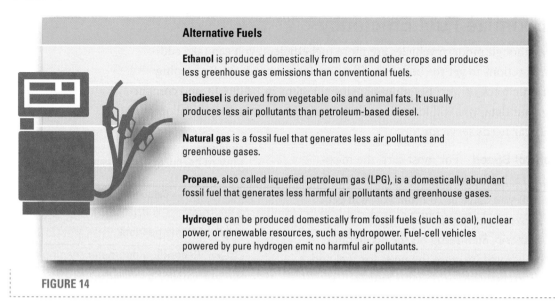

Alternative Fuels

Ethanol is produced domestically from corn and other crops and produces less greenhouse gas emissions than conventional fuels.

Biodiesel is derived from vegetable oils and animal fats. It usually produces less air pollutants than petroleum-based diesel.

Natural gas is a fossil fuel that generates less air pollutants and greenhouse gases.

Propane, also called liquefied petroleum gas (LPG), is a domestically abundant fossil fuel that generates less harmful air pollutants and greenhouse gases.

Hydrogen can be produced domestically from fossil fuels (such as coal), nuclear power, or renewable resources, such as hydropower. Fuel-cell vehicles powered by pure hydrogen emit no harmful air pollutants.

FIGURE 14

Recycling

According to the Federal Government, the oil from just one oil change is enough to contaminate a million gallons of fresh water. Commercial motor oil and transmission fluid are toxic substances that can cause injury or death when ingested, inhaled, or touched.

Motor oil can be recycled, providing a valuable form of energy that helps our economy by reducing the need to refine new oil. To recycle used motor oil and transmission fluid, take them to a service station, recycling drop-off location, or household hazardous waste collection site.

Cars are also recycled through dismantling, crushing, shredding, and resource recovery. Cars have usable parts and components that include batteries, wheels and tires, steering columns, fenders, radios, engines, starters, transmissions, alternators, select plastic parts, glass, foams, catalytic converters, and other components.

Security Systems

Over a million vehicles are reported stolen every year. Vehicle theft can be deterred with a variety of security systems. New vehicles come with factory-installed security systems; others can be installed after purchase.

The automotive industry has developed a wide variety of ways to protect you and your vehicle, such as computer chips, wireless technology, voice recognition commands, radio transmitters and satellites.

FIGURE 15

Motor Vehicle Theft, Top Ten U.S. Metropolitan Areas, 2005			
Rank	Metropolitan Statistical Area	Vehicles Stolen	Rate (1)
1	Modesto, CA	7,071	1,418.80
2	Las Vegas/Paradise, NV	22,465	1,360.90
3	Stockton, CA	7,586	1,167.30
4	Phoenix/Mesa/Scottsdale, AZ	41,000	1,103.50
5	Visalia/Porterville, CA	4,257	1,060.20
6	Seattle/Tacoma/Bellevue, WA	33,494	1,057.60
7	Sacramento/Arden-Arcade/Roseville, CA	20,268	1,005.00
8	San Diego/Carlsbad/San Marcos, CA	28,845	983.90
9	Fresno, CA	8,478	978.11
10	Yakima, WA	2,212	965.54

(1) Ranked by the rate of vehicle thefts reported per 100,000 people based on the 2000 Census.
Source: National Insurance Crime Bureau.

These systems make it easier to enter your vehicle, protect it from theft, and get you help when you need it.

Keyless Entry   A keyless entry is a wireless remote control. It can open the door, start or disable the engine, pop the trunk open, activate the alarm, and may have a panic button.

A key fob in your pocket can have a chip that recognizes you and lets you enter and start the vehicle by touching a power button.

Theft Prevention   A bar that locks the steering wheel in place is a simple system; however, more sophisticated systems are available.

Sensors for Security   Some alarm systems use sensors that activate if

- a door, the trunk, or the hood is opened
- the car is moved
- a window is broken
- someone tries to load your vehicle onto a tow truck

Interior motion sensors will deter a "smash and grab" break-in by sounding the horn and an alarm, and by flashing lights.

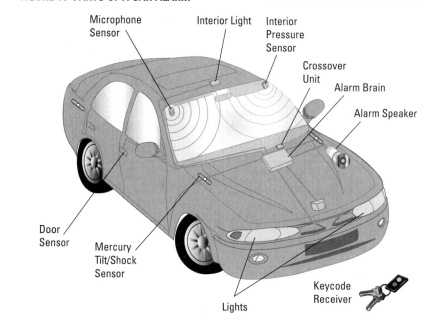

FIGURE 16 **PARTS OF A CAR ALARM**

Microphone Sensor

Interior Light

Interior Pressure Sensor

Crossover Unit

Alarm Brain

Alarm Speaker

Door Sensor

Mercury Tilt/Shock Sensor

Lights

Keycode Receiver

Satellite Systems   A satellite can find a vehicle within hours, offer hands-free voice commands, get you emergency assistance and traffic reports, unlock your door, and give directions to a destination. You can also get weather and natural disaster crisis information and be warned of natural emergencies. Security and anti-theft systems may reduce your insurance premium, so check with your agent before buying.

review it 17.3

1. What actions can you take to reduce fuel consumption?

2. List two vehicle fluids and five vehicle parts that can be recycled.

3. Describe how a keyless system works.

4. How is a satellite system a good means of security for your car?

Critical Thinking

5. **Compare and Contrast**   How is a hybrid different from a gasoline-powered car?

6. **Analyze**   Apart from the security systems mentioned, what other actions can you take to keep your car safe from being stolen?

IN YOUR COMMUNITY   **Recycling**   Visit your local recycling center and find out where and how drivers can recycle car-related materials. For example, where can drivers go in your area to recycle used motor oil and transmission fluid? What might you do with a non-working car that cannot be repaired? Report your findings to the class.

CHAPTER 17 REVIEW

Lesson Summaries

17.1 BUYING A VEHICLE

- Buying a vehicle requires careful planning and preparation to select the type of vehicle that will fit your budget and needs.

- Find out about all the new safety features available and purchase the safest vehicle you can afford.

- Compare the advantages and disadvantages of purchasing a new vehicle or used vehicle.

17.2 PREVENTIVE MAINTENANCE

- Today's vehicles are controlled by computers with electronic devices and sensors.

- A vehicle's lubricating and cooling systems keep all of the moving parts moving and cool down the engine or transmission. Frequent oil changes keep your vehicle in good shape.

- Your vehicle's emission system is important in reducing pollution.

- The vehicle's control system contains the steering, brakes, tires, and suspension systems. Careful maintenance can mean the differences between safety and high-risk driving.

17.3 FUEL EFFICIENCY, RECYCLING, AND SECURITY SYSTEMS

- Modern vehicles have improved fuel efficiency. Drivers can maximize efficiency by using good fuel-saving driving habits.

- Almost every component of a vehicle can be recycled, which saves energy.

- Satellites, computer chips, sensors, and wireless technology have all reduced the risk of having your vehicle stolen or damaged.

Chapter Vocabulary

- alternative fuel
- budget
- catalytic converter
- electronic control module
- muffler
- Variable Ride-Height Suspension

Select the word or phrase from the list above that correctly completes the sentence.

1. A(n) _____ is used in the exhaust system to reduce harmful emissions.

2. Before you buy a car, you need to know your driving needs and your _____.

3. All new cars have a(n) _____ that controls the engine's efficiency.

4. A(n) _____ reduces the noise from the sounds of the engine.

5. The _____ automatically adjusts a car's distance from the ground.

6. We can reduce our dependence on foreign oil by using _____.

✓ ✓ ✓  **STUDY TIP**

Use Technology   Search the Internet for every new-vehicle safety feature you can find. Make a list of the features with a definition of each.

Checking Concepts

LESSON 1

7. Explain what is meant by the real cost of owning a vehicle?

8. How do new safety features help you to stay safe and be a low-risk driver?

9. How does the electronic stability control help keep you safe?

LESSON 2

10. Should you ever disconnect or try to repair the electronic control module yourself? Explain your answer.

11. Are all leaks from a vehicle a sign of a serious problem? Explain your answer.

12. What can happen to your engine if the coolant level is low?

13. Why is it important to pull over when the oil-pressure warning light comes on?

LESSON 3

14. What are three actions you can take to maximize fuel economy?

15. What are the advantages of recycling motor oil?

16. How can wireless technology help protect your vehicle?

17. What can be used to prevent a thief from hot wiring your vehicle?

Critical Thinking

18. **Reasoning** Explain why a hybrid is considered to be a fuel-efficient vehicle.

19. **Apply Concepts** As a driver, how can a penny help to keep you safe?

20. **Apply Concepts** Why is it important to attach jumper cables correctly?

You're the Driver

21. **Decide** You are shopping for new tires for your car when the salesperson offers you a bargain on used tires. Is the bargain really a good deal?

22. **Decide** Your engine needs to be replaced. Is purchasing a rebuilt engine a good idea? Explain your answer.

23. **Identify** In this photo, the drivers are jump-starting a dead battery. What is the correct procedure for connecting the cables?

24. When the driver applies the brakes, the car pulls to the right. What might this indicate about the car's braking system?

Preparing for the Test

Choose the letter of the answer that best completes the statement or answers the questions.

1. If a car drove 320 miles and used 10 gallons of gas, the miles per gallon is
   a. 28 mpg.
   b. 30 mpg.
   c. 32 mpg.
   d. 34 mpg.

2. A hybrid vehicle stores its energy in the
   a. battery.
   b. motor.
   c. gas tank.
   d. generator.

Use the art below to answer Question 3.

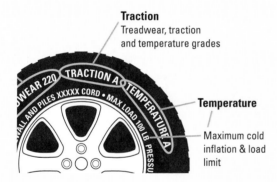

Traction
Treadwear, traction and temperature grades

Temperature

Maximum cold inflation & load limit

3. The tire marking for the temperature rating indicates the tire is
   a. lowest quality.
   b. medium quality.
   c. unrated.
   d. highest quality.

4. One advantage of purchasing a new vehicle is
   a. that gas is cheaper.
   b. the years of service you get after it's paid for.
   c. a lower insurance premium.
   d. that depreciation is minimal the first few years.

5. One advantage of a used car is
   a. greater fuel efficiency.
   b. gas is cheaper.
   c. lower insurance premiums.
   d. guaranteed parts replacement.

Use the art below to answer Question 6.

6. When you see this light on your dashboard, it means
   a. one of your tires is underinflated.
   b. it's time for a routine check by a technician.
   c. you need to add oil.
   d. the coolant level is too low.

7. You should select a certified automotive technician because
   a. it's cheaper and quicker.
   b. they do not use computers and sensors.
   c. they use computers and sensors.
   d. batteries are not sealed.

8. After planning and comparison shopping, a used vehicle passes your tests. The next thing you should do is
   a. buy it immediately.
   b. have a friend test drive it.
   c. buy it only if a warranty is offered.
   d. have a technician make a final check of the vehicle.

drive write

Persuasive Argument Many communities require quick oil-change businesses to accept used motor oil and/or filters from the public. Should this be a requirement? Explain your reasoning.

chapter 18

PLANNING YOUR TRAVEL

18.1 Environmental Concerns

18.2 Local Travel

18.3 Long-Distance Travel

18.4 Special Vehicles and Trailers

KEY IDEA

What are some important details you should consider before driving in your community or taking long trips in a recreational vehicle?

YOU'RE **THE DRIVER**

You planned a camping trip to a national park for a family vacation. What are some trip-planning resources you can use? How does this long trip compare to driving around town?

lesson 18.1
ENVIRONMENTAL CONCERNS

OBJECTIVES

- Describe how vehicles affect the ozone layer and the environment.
- Explain how drivers can reduce the effects of driving on the environment.

VOCABULARY

- On-Board Diagnostic (OBD) system

Transportation is the largest single source of air pollution and accounts for roughly 25 percent of the total energy used in the United States. Almost every vehicle that uses gasoline or diesel fuel creates engine exhaust resulting in air pollution. Additionally, some vehicle parts and fluids contain substances hazardous to our environment. Unless properly disposed of, these harmful substances can leech into the ground, killing wildlife and polluting water sources. As an owner and driver of a vehicle, you must know what you can do to help protect and preserve our environment.

The Environment and Vehicles

The ozone layer is a section of the earth's atmosphere that absorbs most of the sun's harmful ultraviolet (UV) radiation. When a car produces exhaust, it also produces chemicals that deplete the ozone layer, thus reducing Earth's natural defenses against the sun's harmful UV rays.

Over the years, design improvements have resulted in smaller average amounts of harmful exhaust emissions. As vehicles age, the amount of pollution they produce typically increases, which is why it's so important to maintain your vehicle's emissions control.

CFCs   Air conditioners in most motor vehicles manufactured before 1994 use a refrigerant called CFC-12, also known as Freon. When Freon is allowed to escape and enter the ozone layer, it attacks and degrades the ability of this layer to absorb harmful UV rays. Although new vehicles now use an alternative refrigerant, it is important to realize that many older cars are still in operation, and therefore these harmful chemicals must still be contained and disposed of properly.

On-Board Diagnostic (OBD) Systems

Beginning in 1996, all new light-duty cars and trucks were equipped with a system that monitors the engine's major components, which also includes emissions controls. This computer-based **On-Board Diagnostic (OBD) system** provides owners with a diagnostic tool for recognizing malfunctions, and also stores important information about the problems.

DID YOU KNOW?

Passenger vehicles account for approximately 40 percent of U.S. oil consumption and about 20 percent of all carbon dioxide emissions.

Repair technicians use this stored information to diagnose and fix vehicle problems.

Drivers Can Help Keep up with routine vehicle maintenance and watch for your CHECK ENGINE light. When possible, use public transportation, walk, carpool or ride a bike. Shop by phone, mail or Internet and combine your errands into one trip. Make responsible choices such as:

- Drive 55 mph instead of 65 mph to improve gas mileage by about 15 percent.
- Inflate tires properly to improve gas mileage by about 3 percent.
- Receive maintenance checks and engine tune-ups regularly (especially the spark plugs).
- Repair all vehicle leaks promptly.
- Fill the gas tank during cooler evening hours to minimize evaporation.
- Avoid spilling gas and do not "top off" the tank. Always be sure to replace the gas cap tightly.

FIGURE 1

This circle graph shows the means of transportation that Americans took to and from work in 2005.

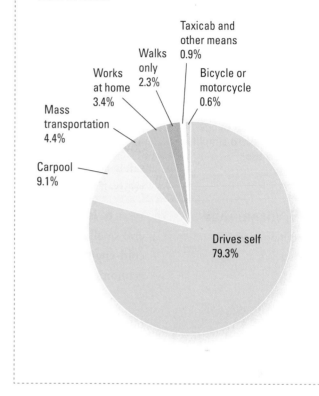

review it 18.1

1. Explain how increasing fuel efficiency can protect the environment.
2. Identify four actions drivers can take to reduce pollution.

Critical Thinking

3. **Apply Concepts** Why do you think the federal government set emissions control standards for all new vehicles?

IN YOUR COMMUNITY **Research** At any fast-food restaurant in your neighborhood, watch at least ten cars as they drive through the drive-through lane. Record how much time it takes each vehicle to enter the lane and receive its order. Are you surprised by the amount of time each car spends idling? Share your findings with your class.

lesson 18.2
LOCAL TRAVEL

OBJECTIVES

- Identify two questions you should ask yourself before making a short trip.
- Describe two things you can do to simplify a short trip.

VOCABULARY

- routine check

Most of your driving will be short, local trips. Careful planning will not only cause less pollution, but will also save you time, fuel and money.

Before You Drive

A short trip can be as simple as driving to a neighborhood store or to a downtown restaurant. No matter where you're going, you want to arrive safely and on time. To minimize pollution and save time and money, ask yourself the following two questions before any short trip:

▶ **Is This Trip Needed?**   If you must drive, try to combine several small trips into one. By combining trips, you reduce travel time and cold-engine time, resulting in less wear on your vehicle and increased fuel economy.

▶ **Do I Have Enough Time?**   It is very difficult and often dangerous to try to make up time as you drive. Always allow extra time for delays caused by bad weather or heavy traffic.

FIGURE 2 Use good driving habits to save fuel and reduce pollution.

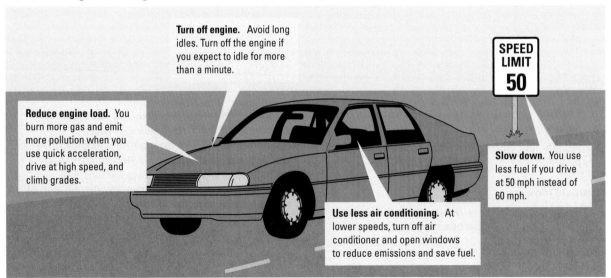

Turn off engine. Avoid long idles. Turn off the engine if you expect to idle for more than a minute.

Reduce engine load. You burn more gas and emit more pollution when you use quick acceleration, drive at high speed, and climb grades.

SPEED LIMIT 50

Slow down. You use less fuel if you drive at 50 mph instead of 60 mph.

Use less air conditioning. At lower speeds, turn off air conditioner and open windows to reduce emissions and save fuel.

Planning Process

Even if your trip involves only a few miles, you should make travel plans in advance so that your trip doesn't turn into a problem situation. By preparing your vehicle and knowing your route and destination, your trip will be smooth, efficient, and economical.

Each time you fill your vehicle's fuel tank, make a **routine check** of tire pressure, level of coolant, and windshield-washer fluid level so that it becomes a habit. By following the tips shown in **FIGURE 2**, you can save fuel on every trip.

Write down directions and have a map to avoid getting lost. If you have a passenger, ask for help in identifying street names, directions, and addresses.

Listen to local weather and traffic reports before your trip. These reports can help you avoid traffic jams or alert you to any adverse weather conditions.

FIGURE 3
You can help plan the route as a passenger.

review it 18.2

1. Explain why you should consider the time and purpose of a trip before getting in your car.
2. How does planning your trip in advance help save time and money?

Critical Thinking

3. **Apply Concepts** If you have a list of errands you must complete, would it be better to do each item in a separate trip or to combine them into one trip? Why?

IN YOUR COMMUNITY **Research** Find out all the kinds of public transportation between your home and a local movie theater and library. Find out the transportation stops, fares, and the distance you may need to walk to get to your destinations. Present your findings to the class, including ideas on how to increase the efficiency of public transportation.

lesson 18.3
LONG-DISTANCE TRAVEL

 OBJECTIVES

- Explain how a GPS receiver can help you find your destination.
- Explain how to use the index and legend on a map.
- List the steps necessary to prepare your vehicle for a long trip.
- List ways to prepare yourself for long-distance travel.

 VOCABULARY

- Global Positioning System
- legend
- index

A well-planned trip can be a satisfying, memorable experience. To ensure a safe and problem-free trip, you must know how to plan and be familiar with different trip-planning resources. While planning your trip, you must consider the number of miles you want to travel each day, the roadways you want to use, construction zones, weather, and your need for overnight accommodations.

Electronic Resources

Global Positioning System (GPS)   Since 1994, a network of mapping and navigation satellites known as the **Global Positioning System** has been orbiting Earth. The satellites transmit radio signals that can be received by GPS receivers, which are factory installed on some models or can be installed as an accessory after purchase.

The Global Positioning System can calculate your exact position anywhere on Earth. The GPS receiver can also map out a route to a destination. By simply entering your destination you will receive real-time directions, with a map and your current location on the screen. Even if you make a wrong turn or detour, the GPS will automatically calculate a new route to your planned destination.

Internet   A number of websites are available to help you plan a long trip. After entering the address of your starting location and ending destination, the website will produce a map and turn-by-turn directions. With added tools such as distance calculators and links to various trip-related needs, the Internet has become a convenient tool to plan a trip.

Print Resources

Print resources include maps, guidebooks, and telephone directories. You can find resources for planning a trip at auto clubs, state tourism offices, and bookstores.

FIGURE 4

Some GPS receivers can be programmed to find scenic routes or points of interest. Some have advanced features like voice activation and color maps.

Maps One of the most valuable trip-planning tools is an up-to-date map. Maps include a **legend** that explains the markings and symbols used on the map. The legend includes types of highways and roads, symbols for cities and towns, points of interest, and a mileage scale to determine how far you will travel. Maps also include an **index**, an alphabetical list of cities or roads with alphanumeric coordinates used for finding the city or road on the map. The index may include airports, bodies of water, and historical areas. State maps will have enlarged detail maps of select major cities in the corners of the map.

▶ **Using the Index** Locations are identified by a letter and a number, as shown in **FIGURE 5**. A map has numbers at the top and at the bottom, and letters along the sides. Find the point at which a letter and number meet to see the location of that site on the map.

▶ **Calculating Distances** State and regional road maps include mileage markers, which give mileage between towns, junctions or interchanges. The number between any two mileage markers represents the distance in miles between those two points. If you are trying to determine the distance between two points that includes more than one marked section, simply add the mileage listed in each section to get the total distance in miles.

Vehicle Preparation

Preparation of your vehicle is essential to ensuring a safe trip. Familiarize yourself with your vehicle and any maintenance procedures you will encounter on the road, such as checking the oil level and changing a flat tire. Be sure you pack all the necessary items you'll need for emergencies or hazardous weather.

Vehicle Check Avoid service problems while traveling by having your vehicle serviced at least a week before you take a long trip. Inform the technician that you are going on a long trip and be sure that your brake system, the exhaust, and the steering/suspension system are checked to be sure that everything is in working order. Check all fluids such as oil, engine coolant, power-steering fluid,

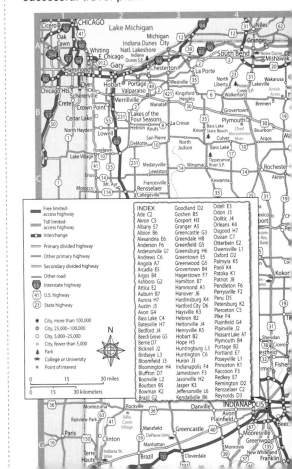

FIGURE 5
A map is a necessary part of any successful travel plan.

brake fluid, and windshield-washer fluid. Be sure that the headlights, turn signals, mirrors and windshield wipers are working properly, and don't forget to check your spare tire and keep a tire gauge in your vehicle.

▶ **Emergency Equipment**   Long-distance travel requires special equipment for use in emergencies. Be sure to pack the following items as you prepare your vehicle for the trip:

- extra oil, antifreeze, and windshield-washer fluid
- an unused, easily operated A-B-C-type fire extinguisher
- first-aid kit, flares or reflectors, and a flashlight
- jumper cables or battery charger and spare fuses
- a pair of mechanic's gloves, and basic tools such as an adjustable wrench, screwdriver, and pliers

▶ **Winter-Driving Equipment**   If your trip takes you into remote or mountain areas in winter weather, you will want to pack these additional items:

- blankets, sleeping bags, and additional warm clothing
- tire chains or all-weather tires with good tread
- plenty of water and non-perishable, no-preparation food, such as energy bars, granola, nuts, dried fruit
- a window ice scraper and small shovel
- tow line and sand bags for extra traction

▶ **Weight Check**   Because added weight affects the fuel efficiency and performance of your vehicle, the best rule to keep in mind when loading a vehicle is to go light. Added weight will increase your fuel consumption. Exceeding your vehicle's maximum weight load may contribute to vehicle instability. If you must travel with a heavy load, be prepared to:

- Use the highest recommended tire pressure listed in your owner's manual, but be careful not to overinflate.
- Load heavy items in the trunk toward the front.
- Avoid loading and securing luggage on the roof. The luggage will raise the vehicle's center of gravity, and in an

FIGURE 6

Tire chains can help improve traction on snow or ice.

emergency maneuver, could create excessive instability that may be uncontrollable.

Personal Preparation

Now that you have planned your trip and prepared your vehicle, you need to be sure that you pack all necessary personal items. A good way to organize your personal items is to make a checklist, as shown in **FIGURE 8**, so you won't forget anything essential.

In order to arrive safely and on time, it is important to stay alert and aware of your surroundings while driving. Practice these safe-driving behaviors while on any trip, whether down the street or to another state:

- Do not drive when you are tired. You will be less prepared to handle emergency situations.
- When possible, drive during the day. Night driving is more dangerous due to low visibility.
- Take regular breaks every two hours and get out of the vehicle to stretch. Rotate drivers regularly if possible.
- Keep fresh air circulating in the vehicle at all times.
- Eat light and frequently; large meals consisting of fatty foods can cause drowsiness.
- Maintain your focus on driving. If you need to consult a map or make a call, pull over at a rest area or gas station.

FIGURE 7 Secure all loose items either with a tie or in the vehicle's trunk or cargo area.

- - - **FIGURE 8** -

Checklist			
coins for tolls	✓	phone numbers	
maps		hotel	✓
travel guides	✓	emergency	✓
extra keys	✓	cell phone	
		battery charger	

★ map skills

Maps have more information than just routes. In addition to showing interstate, federal, and state highways, maps can show you scenic routes, toll roads, and secondary roads. Use the legend and map below to answer the following questions.

1. Which interstate highways are shown on the map?

2. Will you have to pay a toll to use Highway 95?

3. If you wanted to take an interstate highway across the Everglades, which would you take?

4. To drive along the Atlantic coastline, what state highway can you use?

5. **Compare and Contrast** List two ways to go from Miami to Tampa using highways. Which would you choose? Why?

review it 18.3

1. How would you explain how to use a map's index?

2. Why is exceeding your vehicle's weight load dangerous?

3. How is preparing your vehicle related to low-risk driving?

Critical Thinking

4. **Apply Concepts** You are going on a long trip with your family. The car is packed and ready to go, but you notice that the luggage is on the roof of the car and there are several loose items inside the vehicle. Explain how you would repack the car and why.

IN THE PASSENGER SEAT **Mileage** As you drive with a friend or any experienced driver, follow your route on a map. Calculate the mileage using the mileage markers on the map. How does your calculation compare with the mileage on the odometer? Are there any markers along the route that are shown on the map?

SPECIAL VEHICLES AND TRAILERS

Driving a recreational vehicle, using a rental truck, and pulling a camping trailer are examples of special vehicles and trailers. You will have to use additional precautions when driving these vehicles because of their large size.

Recreational Vehicles

A vehicle equipped for vacations and extended travel is called a **recreational vehicle**, or RV. These vehicles are usually equipped with beds, bathrooms, and kitchens. A camper on a pickup truck, a trailer, and a motor home are all examples of recreational vehicles.

Driving an RV is different than driving a passenger vehicle or pickup truck because of its size and weight. An RV is larger, heavier, and harder to maneuver than a four-door passenger car. Therefore, there are special considerations you must take when driving a recreational vehicle.

Limited Vision   Your vision is limited in recreational vehicles, since you do not have a rear window. Refer to the No Zone diagram on page 219 for the visual limitations typical in an RV. RVs usually have larger side mirrors that increase the view to the sides of the vehicle. You can see from the narrow field of visibility how important it is for RV drivers to pay attention to their surroundings and drive cautiously.

Backing   Although newer RVs may have rearview cameras to help you see when backing up, you must pay extra attention to your surroundings. Whenever possible, avoid backing. Instead, drive around the block or turn around in a large, open parking lot. If you must back the vehicle, get another person to stand beside and behind the vehicle to guide you.

Maneuvering   A recreational vehicle is much heavier and less maneuverable than the average passenger vehicle. It will take longer to accelerate, slow down, and make turns.

OBJECTIVES

- Explain how maneuvering a special vehicle is different from maneuvering a passenger vehicle.
- Describe the special equipment needed when pulling a trailer.

VOCABULARY

- recreational vehicle
- trailer hitch
- safety chain

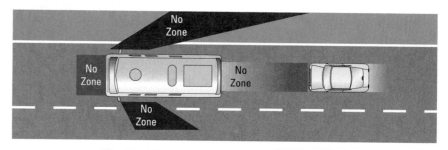

FIGURE 9
When driving a large vehicle such as an RV, pay special attention to what's behind you.

Crosswinds   Large vehicles are more difficult to control in high winds. During windy conditions, it is wise to slow down or stop because the vehicle can be affected by the wind. Be ready to make steering adjustments. Under extremely windy conditions, some roadways may close temporarily to large vehicles such as RVs and trailers.

Remember Your Size   Hitting an overhead object like a low, drive-through ceiling can cause extensive damage. Observe posted maximum clearance signs whenever you are in a parking lot or garage. Check your routes for height and weight restrictions on bridges and tunnels.

Following Distance   Because RVs are heavy, your safe following distance is also longer than that of a smaller car. You must be at least four seconds behind other vehicles to provide enough stopping distance. Larger following distances will allow more time for you to use the IPDE Process.

Fatigue   Driving a recreational vehicle, especially for the first time, requires more attention while driving than other vehicles. In order to stay alert and attentive at all times, plan frequent stops at rest areas and points of interest.

Trailers

Pulling a trailer puts an additional stress on your tow vehicle. The extra weight will further affect the maneuverability of the vehicle and increase the time it takes to respond to emergency situations. Before heading out on public roads, find a safe location such as a vacant parking lot to get a feel for how your RV handles with a trailer attached. In order to operate an RV with a trailer safely, you must know how to attach and load the trailer, as well as how to drive safely with an additional load.

Equipment   To pull a trailer safely, you will need a piece of equipment used to connect a trailer to a vehicle, called a **trailer hitch**. You will also need larger side mirrors on both sides of your vehicle and a chain that ensures the connection of a trailer to a trailer hitch, also known as a **safety chain**.

Pre-Departure Equipment Check   Before any trip involving a trailer, be sure to check the brakes, lights, and drive train; the tire pressure on the vehicle and on the trailer; and the safety chain. Also be sure that the brake lights, turn signals, and license-plate lights are functioning properly.

Load   Whenever you're loading a trailer, place the heavy items over the trailer's axle. If the load is more than 1,000 pounds, you must get a trailer equipped with special brakes. Make sure that about 10 percent of the trailer's loaded weight is on the trailer's hitch. Secure the load with ropes or tie-down straps.

Towing Techniques   When towing a trailer, remember that it will take twice as long to pass, stop, accelerate, and turn. Observe these guidelines when towing a trailer:

- Increase your following distance to four or more seconds.
- Travel at or below the posted speed limit.
- Make wide, slow turns at curves and corners.
- Slow down whenever approaching a turn or a bend in the road.
- If your trailer starts to sway or "fishtail," steer straight toward your target with your foot off the accelerator. Once the trailer is under control, brake gently to reduce speed.
- Allow at least twice the normal stopping and passing distance.
- Use a low gear when going up or down steep hills.
- Be ready to slow or adjust steering for crosswinds.
- Never allow passengers to ride in or on the trailer.

Backing   When backing, place your hand on the bottom of the steering wheel as shown in **FIGURE 10**. If you cannot see where you are backing with your mirrors, have someone outside to the rear to help guide you. If you are having trouble, pull straight forward to realign the vehicle and trailer and start again.

FIGURE 10 Backing a trailer requires more patience and space.

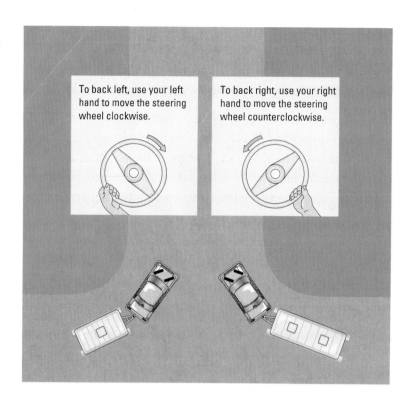

To back left, use your left hand to move the steering wheel clockwise.

To back right, use your right hand to move the steering wheel counterclockwise.

review it 18.4

1. Describe how a recreational vehicle's size affects your field of vision.

2. Summarize the driving guidelines for towing a trailer.

Critical Thinking

3. **Analyze** Explain why large vehicles and trailers often have more than just four wheels and tires.

4. **Compare** How is driving a large tractor trailer similar to driving an RV?

5. **Evaluate** Why is it important to rest often while driving an RV or other large vehicle?

IN THE PASSENGER SEAT **Safe Following Distance** Make a table with three columns: "1-2 seconds," "2-4 seconds," and "more than 4 seconds." For the next week, as you drive with an experienced driver, observe the following distance of tractor trailers, RVs, or any large vehicle behind any passenger car. Make a check in the appropriate column after you have determined the following distance. In general, are drivers of large vehicles maintaining safe following distances? Report your findings to the class.

CHAPTER 18 REVIEW

Lesson Summaries

18.1 ENVIRONMENTAL CONCERNS

- Air pollutants, such as CFCs from automobile air conditioners, are eroding the ozone layer.

18.2 LOCAL TRAVEL

- Before driving, consider whether the trip is necessary and whether or not you have enough time.
- Know your route and destination before heading on a trip, and try to combine daily errands into one trip to save time and fuel.

18.3 LONG-DISTANCE TRAVEL

- Using satellites, the Global Positioning System can pinpoint your exact location on Earth.
- Maps are an essential component of any long-distance trip.
- Before any long trip, check brakes, exhaust, steering, engine, and accessory systems.

18.4 SPECIAL VEHICLES AND TRAILERS

- Special care must be taken when driving RVs such as motor homes and trailers.
- Special vehicles have a limited range of visibility to the side of and behind the vehicle. The increased size and weight of a special vehicle also make it harder to turn back and maneuver in an emergency.
- Because special vehicles take longer to stop, increase your following distance to four or more seconds.
- In order to drive an RV with a trailer safely, you must know how to attach and load the trailer.

Chapter Vocabulary

- Global Positioning System
- index
- legend
- On-Board Diagnostic (OBD) system
- recreational vehicle
- routine check
- safety chain
- trailer hitch

Write the word or phrase from the list above that completes the sentence correctly.

1. A(n) _____ explains the markings and symbols used on a map.

2. You can find an alphabetical list of cities or towns in the _____ of a map.

3. The _____ is a network of mapping and navigation satellites.

4. A large vehicle equipped for vacations and extended travel is called a(n) _____.

5. A(n) _____ is a piece of equipment used to connect a trailer to a vehicle.

6. A device that ensures the connection of a trailer to a trailer hitch is called a(n) _____.

7. Technicians use information stored in the _____ to learn about malfunctions in the vehicle.

✓✓✓ **STUDY TIP**

Flash Cards Create a set of flash cards for all of the vocabulary from the chapter. Work with a partner to test your knowledge of the vocabulary.

Checking Concepts

LESSON 1

8. Why do owners of older cars have to be especially careful about environmental concerns?

9. How does an On-Board Diagnostic system in a vehicle help protect the environment?

LESSON 2

10. What effect does driving with a cold engine have on fuel efficiency?

11. Why is it important to do a routine check of the tire pressure, coolant level, and windshield-washer fluid level when you fill your fuel tank?

LESSON 3

12. How can you use a map's legend to plan your travel?

13. What is a GPS receiver and how can it help you find a destination?

14. How can the Internet help you with trip planning?

15. Explain why vehicle preparation is important.

LESSON 4

16. Describe how driving a special vehicle is different from driving a passenger vehicle.

17. Why is it important to distribute weight in a trailer?

18. What systems do you need to check before pulling a trailer?

Critical Thinking

19. Evaluate   Describe driving habits that can conserve fuel and help reduce air pollution caused by vehicles.

20. Relate Cause and Effect   How does following distance affect the number of highway collisions per year?

You're the Driver

21. What routes would you take to get from Seattle to Duvall? How many miles is it? What other routes are available?

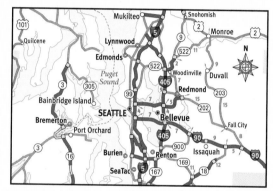

22. Execute   If you were pulling a trailer on this road and the trailer began to fishtail, what actions would you take?

Preparing for the Test

Choose the letter of the answer that best completes the statement or answers the question.

1. Drivers can help reduce air pollution by
 a. properly inflating tires.
 b. braking less.
 c. topping off the gas tank.
 d. driving at night.

2. All vehicles on the road
 a. create the same amount of pollution.
 b. have On-Board Diagnostic systems.
 c. are required to be tested for fuel efficiency.
 d. require safety chains when driving.

3. The best time to travel is
 a. when school is out.
 b. when interstates are open.
 c. during rush-hour traffic.
 d. when traffic is light.

Use the art below to answer Question 4.

4. The legend on a map
 a. tells who created the map.
 b. explains markings and symbols.
 c. lists the names of all cities on the map.
 d. tells the story of how maps were invented.

5. To prepare for a long trip, you should
 a. have your vehicle serviced before the trip.
 b. pack equipment for emergency situations.
 c. have a variety of coins for tolls.
 d. all of the above

6. When driving a special vehicle, you must
 a. keep an eye on your rearview mirror.
 b. expect the vehicle to stop quickly when braking.
 c. be prepared to react to emergency situations.
 d. drive as fast as possible.

Use the art below to answer Question 7.

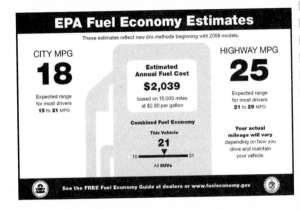

7. The number of miles you can expect to drive on a single gallon of gas should
 a. be the same under all conditions.
 b. change depending on how and where you drive.
 c. change depending on how you maintain your vehicle.
 d. both b and c

8. When backing while turning with a trailer,
 a. keep your eyes on the rearview mirror.
 b. steer using the top of the steering wheel.
 c. use the bottom of the steering wheel.
 d. use both hands at the 9:00 and 3:00 positions.

drive write

Persuasive Argument Transportation is the single largest source of air pollution in the United States. Do you believe the federal government should set fuel-efficiency standards for vehicles? Write one or two paragraphs explaining your position.

glossary

a

acceleration lane lane that permits drivers entering an expressway to accelerate to the speed of expressway traffic (p. 325)
carril de velocidad carril que permite a los conductores que entran a una autopista acelerar hasta alcanzar la velocidad del tránsito de la autopista

active railroad crossing a crossing controlled with electric signals, often having a crossing gate (p. 197)
cruce ferroviario activo cruce controlado con señales eléctricas, que frecuentemente tiene barreras de paso a nivel

active restraint device restraint device that you have to engage (p. 175)
dispositivo de sujeción activa dispositivo de sujeción que se tiene que accionar

advisory speed signs provide suggested maximum speeds for sharp curves and other special situations (p. 298)
señales de advertencia sobre la velocidad indican la velocidad máxima sugerida en las curvas pronunciadas y otras situaciones especiales

aggressive driving driving without regard for the safety of others (p. 107)
manejo agresivo conducir sin tomar en consideración la seguridad de los demás

air pocket air trapped in the highest point of a vehicle for a brief time after it is completely submerged underwater (p. 262)
bolsa de aire aire atrapado en el punto más alto de un vehículo durante un breve período de tiempo después de haberse sumergido completamente en el agua

alcoholism an addiction to alcohol (p. 131)
alcoholismo adicción al alcohol

alternative fuel fuel not based on petroleum, reducing dependence on imported oil (p. 357)
combustible alternativo combustible que no es derivado del petróleo y reduce la necesidad de depender de petróleo importado

angle parking parking the vehicle diagonally to the curb (p. 71)
estacionarse en ángulo aparcar el vehículo en diagonal al bordillo

antilock braking system (ABS) computer-controlled braking system that keeps the wheels from locking if the driver brakes hard (p. 47)
sistema de frenado con antibloqueo sistema de frenado controlado por computadora que evita que las ruedas se bloqueen si el conductor frena con fuerza

auditory distraction a sound that diverts the driver's attention from the driving task (p. 151)
distracción auditiva sonido que distrae la atención del conductor de su tarea de conducir

b

beltway a highway that loops around a city (p. 339)
carretera de circunvalación carretera que circunda una ciudad

biomechanical distraction any mechanical act not specifically related to driving that is performed by a driver (p. 151)
distracción biomecánica cualquier acción mecánica realizada por un conductor que no está relacionada específicamente con el manejo

blind intersection an intersection in which your view of traffic on an intersecting road is impeded (p. 286)
intersección ciega intersección donde no se puede ver el tránsito de la carretera que cruzarás

blood alcohol concentration (BAC) amount of alcohol in the blood expressed as a percentage of alcohol in the bloodstream (p. 131)
concentración de alcohol en la sangre (alcoholemia) cantidad de alcohol en la sangre expresada como porcentaje de alcohol en el flujo sanguíneo

blowout a sudden loss of tire air pressure while driving, as when a tire is punctured and loses all its air at once (p. 169)
reventón de llanta pérdida repentina de la presión del aire de una llanta mientras se conduce un vehículo, como sucede cuando una llanta es perforada y pierde todo su aire de golpe

brake fade loss of braking effectiveness caused by the brakes overheating after continuous hard braking (p. 252)
pérdida de frenos pérdida de la eficacia del frenado causada por un sobrecalentamiento de los frenos después de frenar continuamente con fuerza

braking distance distance your vehicle travels from the time you apply the brake until your vehicle stops (p. 174)
distancia de frenado distancia que recorre el vehículo desde el momento en que se acciona el freno hasta que el vehículo se detiene

braking point the point at which the brakes begin to work and slow the vehicle (p. 55)
punto de frenado el punto en el cual los frenos comienzan a funcionar y disminuyen la velocidad del vehículo

budget the amount of money you have to spend (p. 346)
presupuesto cantidad de dinero disponible para gastar

C

carbon monoxide colorless, odorless, tasteless gas contained in the exhaust fumes of gasoline engines (p. 120)
monóxido de carbono gas incoloro, inodoro e insípido contenido en los gases de combustión de los motores a gasolina

catalytic converter part of a vehicle's emission system that converts harmful gases into less harmful gases and water (p. 350)
convertidor catalítico parte del sistema de emisión de gases de un vehículo que convierte los gases dañinos en gases menos perjudiciales y en agua

center of gravity point around which an object's weight is evenly distributed (p. 170)
centro de gravedad punto alrededor del cual el peso de un objeto está distribuido uniformemente

central vision the portion of your field of vision which you can see clearly; this is a 10-degree cone-shaped area directly ahead (p. 113)
visión central la parte de tu campo de visión que puedes ver claramente; es un área directamente frente a tus ojos que tiene la forma de un cono de 10 grados

chronic illness an ailment that lasts over a period of years (p. 122)
enfermedad crónica dolencia que dura un período de años

closed zone space not open to you because of a restriction in your line of sight or intended path of travel (p. 83)
zona cerrada espacio al que no se tiene acceso debido a una restricción en la línea de visión o en el recorrido previsto de desplazamiento

clutch mechanism in a manual transmission vehicle that enables a driver to shift gears (p. 57)
embrague en un vehículo de transmisión manual, mecanismo que le permite a un conductor cambiar de marcha

cognitive distraction occurs when the driver is lost in thought or daydreaming (p. 151)
distracción cognitiva ocurre cuando el conductor está perdido en sus pensamientos o sueña despierto

collision contact between a vehicle and another object, whether or not the object is moving (p. 8)
colisión contacto entre un vehículo y otro objeto, que puede estar inmóvil o en movimiento

collision insurance provides coverage to pay the costs of repair or replacement of your vehicle from a collision (p. 267)
seguro contra choque ofrece cobertura para cubrir los gastos de reparación o para reemplazar su vehículo menos el deducible aplicable

color blindness an inability to distinguish colors (p. 114)
daltonismo incapacidad de distinguir los colores

common speed speed used by most drivers on an expressway (p. 331)
velocidad usual velocidad utilizada por la mayoría de los conductores en una autopista

compact spare a temporary spare tire (p. 251)
llanta de auxilio llanta de auxilio provisional

compromise space reduce risk by giving as much space as possible to the greater of two or more hazards (p. 95)
ceder espacio reducir el riesgo dando tanto espacio como sea posible al mayor de dos o más peligros

controlled-access refers to a highway that vehicles can enter and exit only at interchanges (p. 321)
acceso controlado relativo a una autopista donde los vehículos pueden entrar o salir sólo en los intercambios viales

controlled braking reducing speed as quickly as possible while maintaining steering control of your vehicle (p. 240)
frenado controlado reducir la velocidad tan rápidamente como sea posible manteniendo el control de la dirección del vehículo

controlled intersection intersection at which traffic signals or signs determine the right of way (p. 192)
intersección controlada intersección en la cual hay semáforos o señales de tránsito que determinan el derecho de paso

convex mirror a mirror curved outward, like the exterior of a ball, allowing a wider view of the side and rear of a vehicle (p. 64)
espejo convexo espejo curvado hacia afuera, como la parte exterior de una pelota, que permite una visión más amplia del costado y de la parte posterior de un vehículo

cover the brake take your foot off the accelerator and hold it over the brake pedal to be ready to brake quickly (p. 282)
cubrir el freno sacar el pie del acelerador y mantenerlo sobre el pedal del freno con el fin de estar listo para frenar rápidamente

crossbuck large white X-shaped sign located beside an uncontrolled railroad crossing (p. 197)
cruz ferroviaria señal grande y blanca en forma de X colocada junto a un cruce ferroviario no controlado

cruise control device that lets you maintain your desired speed without keeping your foot on the accelerator (p. 42)
control de crucero dispositivo que te permite mantener la velocidad deseada sin mantener el pie sobre el acelerador

d

deceleration lane expressway lane used to slow your vehicle without blocking vehicles behind you (p. 335)
carril de desaceleración carril de una autopista utilizado para disminuir la velocidad de un vehículo sin cerrar el paso a los vehículos que vienen detrás

decide third step of the IPDE Process in which the driver selects the best actions as well as when and where to take them to avoid conflicts (p. 92)
decidir tercer paso del Proceso IPDE, en el cual el conductor escoge las acciones más apropiadas, así como también cuándo y dónde llevarlas a cabo para evitar conflictos

deductible amount an insurance policyholder agrees to pay toward vehicle repair or replacement (p. 267)
gasto deducible cantidad que un asegurado acuerda pagar para reparar o reemplazar un vehículo

delayed green light indicates that one side of an intersection has a green light while the light for the oncoming traffic remains red (p. 193)
luz verde retardada indica que un lado de una intersección tiene luz verde mientras que la luz del semáforo para el tránsito que viene en dirección contraria permanece roja

depressant drug that can slow down the central nervous system (p. 135)
agente depresivo droga que puede disminuir la actividad del sistema nervioso central

depth perception ability to judge distance between yourself and other objects (p. 114)
percepción de profundidad capacidad para juzgar la distancia entre uno mismo y otros objetos

designated driver person who decides ahead of time not to drink alcoholic beverages and is appointed to drive others who do drink (p. 133)
conductor designado persona que decide con anticipación no tomar bebidas alcohólicas y es designado para conducir el automóvil que llevará a otras personas que sí beben alcohol

disability a diagnosed physical or mental impairment that interferes with or prevents normal achievement in a particular area (p. 119)
discapacidad alteración diagnosticada, física o mental, que entorpece o impide el desarrollo normal de las actividades propias de un ámbito en particular

distracted driving occurs when an event, person, activity, or object draws a driver's attention away from the driving task (p. 150)
manejo distraído ocurre cuando un suceso, una persona, una actividad o un objeto atrae la atención de un conductor distrayéndolo de la tarea de conducir

dram shop laws state laws that provide liability to a person who serves alcoholic beverages to an intoxicated or underage individual (p. 137)
leyes sobre la responsabilidad del establecimiento de venta de bebidas alcohólicas leyes estatales que atribuyen responsabilidad civil a una persona que sirve bebidas alcohólicas a un individuo ebrio o menor de edad

driver inattention when a driver's awareness and focus drift to anything other than the driving task (p. 150)
distracción del conductor cuando la atención y la concentración de un conductor se desvían hacia otra cosa que no es la tarea de conducir

driving under the influence (DUI) or **driving while intoxicated (DWI)** an offense for which a driver can be charged in all states if the driver's blood-alcohol concentration is above 0.08 (p. 138)
conducir bajo la influencia de alcohol y/o drogas o **conducir en estado de ebriedad** un delito por el cual un conductor puede ser acusado en todos los estados si la concentración de alcohol en su sangre es superior a 0.08

e

electronic control module (ECM) a computer in the engine compartment that controls engine efficiency (p. 350)
módulo de control electrónico computadora ubicada en el compartimento del motor que controla la eficiencia del motor

emergency vehicle a vehicle that responds to fires, medical emergencies, rescues, or incidents involving hazardous materials (p. 221)
vehículo de emergencia vehículo que responde en caso de incendios, emergencias médicas, rescates o accidentes con presencia de sustancias tóxicas

emotion strong feeling such as anger, fear, and joy (p. 106)
emoción sentimiento intenso, tal como el enojo, el miedo y la alegría

energy of motion kinetic energy or the energy an object has because it is moving (p. 165)
energía motriz energía cinética o la energía que tiene un objeto al estar en movimiento

entrance ramp ramp leading onto an expressway (p. 325)
rampa de entrada rampa que lleva a una autopista

euphoria false sense of well-being developed as a result of alcohol or drug consumption (p. 129)
euforia sensación falsa de bienestar surgida como consecuencia del consumo de alcohol o drogas

execute fourth step of the IPDE Process, in which a driver performs proper vehicle control responses to avoid possible conflicts (p. 92)
ejecutar cuarto paso del Proceso IPDE, en el cual un conductor lleva a cabo las respuestas adecuadas de control del vehículo para evitar posibles conflictos

exhaust pipe also called the tailpipe; the pipe from which exhaust gases are released (p. 243)
tubo de escape también llamado simplemente escape; el tubo desde el cual se liberan los gases de combustión

exit ramp ramp leading off an expressway (p. 335)
rampa de salida rampa que conduce fuera de una autopista

f

field of vision all the area a person can see while looking straight ahead (p. 84)
campo de visión toda el área que puede ver una persona cuando mira directamente hacia adelante

field sobriety test series of on-the-spot, roadside tests that help an officer detect impairment of a driver suspected of DUI or DWI (p. 138)
prueba de sobriedad en el sitio serie de pruebas llevadas a cabo al costado de la carretera que ayudan a un oficial de policía a detectar la incapacidad para manejar de un conductor bajo sospecha de hallarse bajo la influencia de drogas o en estado de ebriedad

financial responsibility law law that requires you to prove that you can pay for collision damages you cause that result in death, injury, or property damage (p. 267)
ley de responsabilidad financiera ley que requiere que pruebes que puedes pagar por los daños del choque que ocasiones, cuyo resultado sea la muerte, heridas o daños a la propiedad

fishtail sliding of the rear of a vehicle from side to side (p. 239)
derrapar deslizamiento hacia los lados de la parte traera de un vehículo

fixed costs the purchase price of your car, licensing fees, insurance, and other costs that do not vary with the amount of driving you do (p. 9)
costos fijos el precio de compra del carro, los pagos por la licencia de conducir, el seguro y otros costos que no varían con la cantidad de millas que recorras

flashing signal traffic signal that alerts drivers to dangerous conditions or tells them to stop (p. 29)
semáforo intermitente semáforo que alerta a los conductores sobre condiciones peligrosas o les indica que se detengan

force of impact force with which one moving object hits another object; varies according to speed, weight, and distance between impact and stop (p. 175)
fuerza de impacto fuerza con la cual un objeto en movimiento golpea a otro objeto; varía según la velocidad, el peso y la distancia entre el impacto y el cese del movimiento

forward reference point a reference for the point in a maneuver when steering should begin (p. 71)
punto de referencia anticipado una referencia para el punto en el cual debe comenzar una maniobra al volante

forward vision your driving view through your windshield (p. 255)
visión delantera la vista que se tiene a través del parabrisas cuando conduces

4–6-second range area where you will be traveling during the next 4 to 6 seconds, and where you get the final update of how you are controlling your intended path of travel (p. 83)
alcance a los 4-6 segundos área que recorrerás durante los siguientes 4 a 6 segundos y donde obtienes la actualización final de tu desempeño en el control del recorrido deseado

fresh green light light that has just turned from red to green (p. 192)
luz verde reciente luz que acaba de pasar de rojo a verde

friction the force of resistance that acts between materials moving past one another, which keeps tires from sliding on the road (p. 166)
fricción fuerza de resistencia que actúa entre los materiales cuando entran en contacto y se rozan entre sí, la cual evita que las llantas se deslicen en la carretera

fringe vision the part of your peripheral vision that is closest to your central vision and helps you monitor zone changes (p. 113)
visión marginal parte de tu visión periférica que está más cerca de tu visión central y te ayuda a controlar los cambios en la zona

g

gap a vacant space between vehicles (p. 191)
espacio lugar vacante entre vehículos

gawking staring at a crash scene (p. 157)
permanecer curioseando quedarse observando en la escena de un choque

glare recovery time time your eyes need to regain clear vision after being affected by glare (p. 115)
tiempo de recuperación del resplandor tiempo que los ojos precisan para recobrar una visión clara después de haber sido afectados por un resplandor

glare resistance ability to continue seeing when looking at bright lights (p. 115)
resistencia al resplandor capacidad de continuar viendo cuando se miran luces brillantes

global positioning system (GPS) a network of 24 satellites used by vehicle navigation systems to pinpoint a vehicle's location (p. 370)
sistema de posicionamiento global (SPG) red de 24 satélites utilizados por los sistemas de navegación de los vehículos para determinar la ubicación de un vehículo

grade the slope of a surface, such as the side of a road (p. 257)
cuesta la pendiente de una superficie, tal como el costado de un camino

grade elevation bridges and tunnels are used to direct traffic over or under other travel lanes (p. 321)
elevación a nivel puentes y túneles utilizados para dirigir el tránsito por encima o por debajo de otros carriles de circulación

graduated driver licensing program program requiring young drivers to progress through a series of licensing stages with various restrictions (p. 11)
programa graduado para obtener licencia de conducir programa que requiere que los conductores jóvenes progresen a través de una serie de etapas con diferentes restricciones para obtener su permiso de conducir

graphics pictures used on warning signs (p. 295)
gráficas imágenes utilizadas en las señales de advertencia

gravity force that pulls all things to earth (p. 165)
gravedad fuerza que atrae todas las cosas hacia la Tierra

ground viewing making quick glances to the roadway in front of your vehicle (p. 86)
observación del camino dar vistazos rápidos a la carretera que está enfrente del vehículo

guide sign sign that gives directions, distance, services, points of interest, and other information (p. 25)
señal vial señal que da direcciones, indica la distancia, los servicios, los puntos de interés y otros datos

h

head-on collision a collision between the front ends of two vehicles (p. 263)
choque frontal choque entre los extremos delanteros de dos vehículos

high-occupancy toll (HOT) lane a high-occupancy vehicle lane on which single-occupant vehicles can travel by paying a fee (p. 331)
carril para ocupación alta con peaje carril para vehículos ocupados por varios pasajeros en el cual los vehículos con un único ocupante pueden viajar pagando un peaje

high-occupancy vehicle (HOV) lane a lane reserved for buses and carpools with at least two or three passengers (p. 35)
carril para vehículos con ocupación alta carril reservado para autobuses y carros compartidos con al menos dos o tres pasajeros

highway hypnosis drowsy or trancelike condition caused by concentration on the roadway ahead and monotony of driving (p. 338)
hipnosis de carretera condición de somnolencia o de confusión causada por la concentración en la carretera que se extiende por delante y por la monotonía del manejo

highway transportation system (HTS) complex system made up of roadway users, vehicles, and roadways (p. 4)
sistema de transporte por carreteras sistema complejo constituido por los usuarios de las carreteras, los vehículos y las carreteras

hole in traffic an empty space between traffic clusters (p. 327)
hueco en el tránsito un espacio vacío entre aglomeraciones de tránsito

hydroplaning occurs when a tire loses road contact by rising up on top of water (p. 234)
hidroplaneo ocurre cuando una llanta pierde contacto con el la carretera al elevarse sobre el agua

i

identify first step in the IPDE Process, in which the driver locates potential hazards (p. 82)
identificar primer paso del Proceso IPDE, en el cual el conductor reconoce peligros potenciales

illegal *per se* law state laws that make it illegal to drive with a given blood alcohol concentration or with certain drugs in one's body (p. 137)
ley de ilegalidad per se leyes estatales que hacen que sea ilegal conducir con una concentración dada de alcohol en la sangre o habiendo ingerido ciertas drogas

implied consent law states that anyone who receives a driver's license automatically consents to be tested for blood-alcohol content and other drugs if stopped for suspicion of drug use while driving (p. 137)

ley de consentimiento implícito indica que cualquier persona que recibe una licencia de conducir consiente automáticamente en someterse a pruebas para determinar el contenido de alcohol y de otras drogas en la sangre si es detenido bajo sospecha de uso de drogas al manejar

index a list of cities, roads, or other places of interest on a map, with alphanumerical coordinates for finding them (p. 371)

índice lista de ciudades, carreteras u otros lugares de interés en un mapa, con coordinadas alfanuméricas para hallarlos

inertia the tendency of an object at rest to stay at rest, and of an object in motion to stay in motion (p. 164)

inercia la tendencia de un objeto que está en estado de reposo a permanecer en reposo y de un objeto en movimiento a permanecer en movimiento

inhibitions inner forces of personality that restrain or hold back impulsive behavior (p. 129)

inhibiciones fuerzas internas de la personalidad que dominan o reprimen un comportamiento impulsivo

interchange a place where drivers can cross over or under traffic, as well as enter or leave a freeway (p. 321)

intercambio vial lugar donde los conductores pueden cruzar por encima o por debajo del tránsito, así como entrar a una autopista o salir de ella

international signs traffic signs that use symbols instead of words (p. 26)

señales internacionales señales de tránsito que utilizan símbolos en lugar de palabras

intersection a place where roadways meet or cross (p. 184)

intersección lugar donde las carreteras se encuentran se cruzan

IPDE Process organized process of seeing, thinking, and responding that includes the steps of identifying, predicting, deciding, and executing (p. 7)

Proceso IPDE proceso organizado de observar, pensar y responder que incluye los pasos de identificar, predecir, decidir y ejecutar

j

jaywalk pedestrian action taken with disregard for traffic rules and signals (p. 206)

cruzar imprudentemente acción de un peatón realizada sin tomar en consideración las reglas y las señales de tránsito

join ... (p. 191)

unirse al tr... right or left into lanes of other vehicles de otros vehícul... derecha o a la izquierda en los carriles

k

key fob a hand-held remote con... vehicle's doors (p. 49) for locking and unlocking a

mando en llavero un dispositivo de co... abrir y cerrar los seguros de las puertas de un...moto manual para

l

lane signal signal, usually overhead, that tells whether a lane can or cannot be used at a specific time (p. 29)

semáforo de carril semáforo, usualmente colocado en lo alto, que indica si un carril puede usarse o no en un momento específico

legend chart that explains the markings and symbols used on a map (p. 371)

leyenda tabla que explica las marcas y los símbolos utilizados en un mapa

liability insurance provides compensation for damages to a third party for which the insured is legally obligated to pay; covers others when you are at fault (p. 267)

seguro de responsabilidad civil contra terceros provee una indemnización por los daños ocasionados a un tercero que el asegurado está legalmente obligado a pagar; cubre a otros cuando la falta es tuya

line of sight distance you can see ahead in the direction you are looking (p. 83)

campo visual distancia hasta donde puedes ver, en la dirección a la que estás mirando

low-risk driving constantly monitoring other vehicles and roadway users without assuming they will do what they should (p. 7)

manejo de bajo riesgo controlar constantemente a los demás vehículos y a los otros usuarios de la carretera sin suponer que harán lo que deben

low-speed vehicle (LSV) a mail truck, golf cart, or other four-wheeled electric-powered vehicle that operates at low speeds (p. 222)

vehículo de baja velocidad una camioneta de correo, un carrito de golf u otro vehículo eléctrico de cuatro ruedas que se desplaza a baja velocidad

m

maneuver a driving action (p. 9_)
maniobra acción de manejo

median area of ground or _ _arating traffic moving in opposite directions (p. 300)
mediana o faja divis __ntral área de tierra o de cemento
que separa el tráns_ _ _ desplaza por carriles de dirección
contraria

merging are_ _ _tch of roadway at the end of an acceleration lane
_r an exp__ _ _ay where vehicles join the flow of traffic (p. 325)
_rea de _onfluencia en una autopista, tramo que se halla al final
de un_arril de aceleración donde los vehículos entran a la circulación
del tránsito

minimize a hazard reduce the possibility of conflict by putting
more space between your vehicle and the hazard (p. 94)
minimizar un riesgo reducir la posibilidad de conflicto al abrir más
espacio entre tu vehículo y el riesgo

mirror's blind spot area that rearview mirrors cannot show (p. 45)
punto ciego de un espejo área que los espejos retrovisores no
pueden mostrar

momentum the tendency of an object in motion to stay in motion
(p. 165)
ímpetu la tendencia de un objeto en movimiento a permanecer en
movimiento

moped two-wheeled vehicle that can be driven with either a motor or
pedals (p. 209)
ciclomotor vehículo de dos ruedas que puede manejarse con un
motor o con pedales

muffler device that reduces the noise from combustion sounds in the
engine (p. 351)
silenciador del tubo de escape dispositivo que reduce el ruido
proveniente de los sonidos de la combustión en el motor

n

night blindness not being able to see well at night (p. 115)
ceguera nocturna no poder ver bien de noche

no zone large blind-spot areas where truck drivers cannot see other
vehicles (p. 219)
zona muerta grandes áreas de puntos ciegos donde los conductores
de camiones no pueden ver a los demás
vehículos

non-controlled access refers to a highway in which traffic can
enter or leave at any point, not just at interchanges (p. 321)
acceso no controlado relativo a una autopista en la cual el
tránsito puede entrar o salir en cualquier punto, no sólo en los
cruces o intercambios viales

nystagmus involuntary jerking of the eyes as a person gazes to the
side (p. 139)
nistagmo oscilación espasmódica involuntaria de los ojos cuando
una persona mira al costado

o

odometer device on the instrument panel indicating the total number
of miles the vehicle has been driven (p. 47)
odómetro aparato colocado en el panel de instrumentos
que marca la cantidad total de millas que ha recorrido el vehículo

On Board Diagnostic (OBD) system a computer-based tool for
recognizing and storing information about malfunctions (p. 366)
sistema de diagnóstico a bordo instrumento computarizado
que permite reconocer y almacenar información sobre las fallas en el
funcionamiento

open zone space where you can drive without a restriction to your
line of sight or intended path of travel (p. 83)
zona abierta espacio donde puedes conducir sin restricciones hacia
tu línea de visión o siguiendo el recorrido deseado

operating costs vehicle-related costs that vary depending on the
amount of driving you do, such as costs for fuel, oil, and tires (p. 9)
costos operativos costos relacionados con el vehículo que varían
dependiendo de la cantidad de millas que recorres, tales como los
costos de combustible, aceite y llantas

operating while impaired (OWI) _see_ **driving under the
influence**
operar estando incapacitado _ver_ **conducir bajo la
influencia de alcohol o drogas**

orderly visual search pattern process of searching critical areas
in a regular sequence (p. 83)
patrón de búsqueda visual sistemática proceso de buscar
áreas críticas siguiendo una secuencia regular

overdriving headlights driving at a speed that makes your stopping distance longer than the distance lighted by your headlights
(p. 230)
marcha que excede los faros delanteros conducir a una
velocidad que hace que tu distancia de frenado sea mayor que la
distancia iluminada por tus faros delanteros

oversteer situation the result of turning the steering wheel too much (p. 239)

situación de sobreviraje la consecuencia de girar excesivamente el volante

overtake pass the vehicle ahead (p. 285)

adelantar o rebasar pasar el vehículo que va adelante

over-the-counter (OTC) medicine drug that can be obtained legally without a doctor's prescription (p. 135)

medicamento sin receta droga que puede obtenerse legalmente sin la prescripción de un médico

p

parallel parking parking the vehicle parallel to the curb (p. 71)

estacionamiento en paralelo estacionar el vehículo paralelo al bordillo

passive railroad crossing a crossing without flashing lights or a crossing gate (p. 197)

cruce ferroviario pasivo cruce que no tiene luces intermitentes ni barreras

passive restraint device restraint device, such as an air bag or an automatic seatbelt, that works automatically (p. 175)

dispositivo pasivo de sujeción dispositivo de sujeción, tal como una bolsa de aire o un cinturón de seguridad automático, que funciona automáticamente

pedestrian signal signal used at heavy traffic intersections that tells pedestrians whether they should walk or wait (p. 30)

semáforo para peatones semáforo utilizado en las intersecciones de tránsito intenso que indica a los peatones si deben pasar o esperar

peer education process in which young people help other young people make decisions and determine goals (p. 144)

educación en grupo proceso en el cual los jóvenes ayudan a otros jóvenes a tomar decisiones y determinar metas

peer influence internal force created out of a desire to be accepted by others (p. 141)

influencia del grupo fuerza interna surgida a partir del deseo de ser aceptado por los demás

peer pressure external force from others of a similar age (p. 141)

presión del grupo fuerza externa proveniente de otras personas de edad similar

perception distance distance your vehicle travels during perception time (p. 173)

distancia de percepción distancia que recorre tu vehículo durante el tiempo de percepción

perception time length of time you take to identify, predict, and decide to brake for a hazard (p. 173)

tiempo de percepción lapso de tiempo que te toma identificar, predecir y decidir frenar ante un peligro

peripheral vision area a person can see to the left and right of central vision (p. 113)

visión periférica área que puede ver una persona a la izquierda y a la derecha de su visión central

permanent disability a disability that cannot be cured or improved (p. 121)

discapacidad permanente discapacidad que no puede curarse ni mejorarse

perpendicular parking parking the vehicle at a right angle to the curb (p. 71)

estacionamiento perpendicular estacionar el vehículo en ángulo recto al bordillo

personal reference point an adaptation of a standard reference point to one's own vehicle (p. 71)

punto de referencia personal adaptación de un punto de referencia estándar al vehículo propio

pitch a tilting motion from front to back (p. 171)

cabeceo un movimiento oscilante de adelante hacia atrás

point of no return point beyond which a driver can no longer stop safely without entering the intersection (p. 185)

punto sin retorno punto más allá del cual un conductor ya no puede detenerse con seguridad sin entrar en la intersección

policy a written contract between you and an insurance company (p. 267)

póliza un contrato escrito entre una persona y una compañía aseguradora

predict second step of the IPDE Process, in which the driver anticipates possible conflicts (p. 88)

predecir segundo paso del Proceso IPDE, en el cual el conductor anticipa posibles conflictos

premium specified amount of money paid to an insurance company for insurance coverage over a specified period of time (p. 267)

prima cantidad específica de dinero que el asegurado paga a una compañía aseguradora por su póliza de seguros durante un período determinado de tiempo

prescription medicine that can be purchased legally only when ordered by a doctor (p. 135)

medicamento de venta bajo receta droga que puede comprarse legalmente sólo con una prescripción médica

prohibited against the law (p. 305)
prohibido contrario a la ley

projectile a flying object that could be a hazard to a driver or passengers (p. 155)
proyectil objeto arrojadizo que podría ser un riesgo para un conductor o para los pasajeros

protected left turn left turn made on a left-turn light, green arrow, or delayed green light while oncoming traffic is stopped (p. 193)
giro a la izquierda protegido vuelta a la izquierda realizada con luz verde de giro, una flecha verde o una luz verde retardada mientras el tránsito que viene en sentido contrario está detenido

protective gear items a motorcyclist wears to protect head, eyes, and body (p. 216)
equipo de seguridad artículos que usa un motociclista para protegerse la cabeza, los ojos y el cuerpo

pull-out area additional right lane on narrow mountain roadways for slower-moving vehicles (p. 312)
calzada de incorporación carril derecho adicional en las carreteras de montaña estrechas destinado a los vehículos de marcha más lenta

---

r

ramp meter a set of traffic signals—red and green only—used to control traffic flow onto a highway (p. 327)
semáforos de ramal de enlace un conjunto de semáforos (sólo de luz roja y verde) utilizados para controlar la circulación del tránsito que entra en una autopista

reaction distance distance your vehicle travels while you react (p. 174)
distancia de reacción distancia que recorre el vehículo mientras reaccionas

reaction time length of time you take to execute your action (p. 174)
tiempo de reacción el tiempo que te toma ejecutar una acción

rear-end collision a collision in which the front of one vehicle hits the rear of another (p. 264)
colisión de impacto trasero choque en el cual la parte delantera de un vehículo impacta la parte trasera de otro

recreational vehicle large vehicle such as a motor home, a trailer, or a camper on a pickup truck, used mainly for vacations and extended travel (p. 375)
vehículo de recreo vehículo grande, tal como una caravana, un remolque o una autocaravana remolcada por una camioneta, utilizado principalmente para viajes largos y vacaciones

reference point a part of the outside or inside of the vehicle, as viewed from the driver's seat, that relates to some part of the roadway (p. 71)
punto de referencia parte externa o interna del vehículo, tal como se ve desde el asiento del conductor, que se relaciona con alguna parte de la carretera

regulatory sign sign that controls traffic (p. 20)
señal reglamentaria señal que controla el tránsito

reversible lane a lane in which traffic can travel in either direction, depending on conditions, often used during commuter hours (p. 330)
carril reversible carril en el cual el tránsito puede desplazarse en una u otra dirección, dependiendo de ciertas condiciones, utilizado frecuentemente durante las horas pico

ride the brake resting your foot on the brake pedal while driving (p. 282)
montar el freno conducir con el pie puesto sobre el pedal del freno

right of way privilege of having immediate use of a certain part of a roadway (p. 189)
derecho de paso privilegio de usar inmediatamente cierta parte de una carretera

right-turn-on-red turning right when the red signal is on, permitted at most intersections (p. 28)
giro a la derecha en rojo girar a la derecha cuando el semáforo está en rojo, permitido en la mayoría de las intersecciones

risk in driving, the possibility of having a conflict that results in a collision (p. 4)
riesgo al conducir, la posibilidad de tener un conflicto que produzca una colisión

risk factor anything that can increase the possibility of a collision (p. 80)
factor de riesgo cualquier cosa que pueda aumentar la posibilidad de una colisión

road rage driving with the intent to harm others (p. 107)
violencia vehicular conducir con la intención de perjudicar a otros

roadway marking marking that gives you a warning or direction (p. 33)
marcas en la carretera marcas que indican una advertencia o una dirección

roadway user a person who uses the HTS by walking, driving, or riding (p. 4)
usuario de autopista persona que utiliza el sistema de carreteras caminando, conduciendo o andando en bicicleta

rocking repeating the sequence of driving forward a little and then back a little to move your vehicle out of deep snow, mud, or sand (p. 236)

balanceo repetir la secuencia de mover el vehículo hacia delante y hacia con el fin de sacarlo de la nieve profunda, el lodo o la arena

roundabout a circular intersection, also called a traffic circle or rotary (p. 199)

glorieta una intersección circular, también llamada pista circular o rotonda

routine check inspection done habitually, such as checking your tire pressure, coolant level, and windshield-washer fluid level every time you fill your fuel tank (p. 369)

inspección de rutina inspección realizada habitualmente, tal como verificar la presión de aire en las llantas, el nivel del refrigerante y el nivel del líquido para el limpiaparabrisas cada vez que llenas el tanque del combustible

rubbernecking looking around a crash scene with curiosity (p. 157)

curiosear observar la escena de un choque con curiosidad

rumble strip a short section of grooved or corrugated roadway, used to warn drivers of a need to reduce speed or stop (p. 36)

sección corrugada sección corta de carretera corrugada o con surcos, utilizada para advertir a los conductores de la necesidad de reducir la velocidad o detenerse

runaway vehicle ramp place on mountain roads for vehicles to safely get out of traffic when their brakes are not effective (p. 312)

rampa de frenado en los caminos de montaña, lugar para que los vehículos salgan de la circulación con seguridad cuando sus frenos han perdido efectividad

S

safety chain backup link used in case a trailer hitch fails (p. 377)

cadena de seguridad cadena adicional utilizada en caso de que falle el enganche del remolque

safety stop a stop in which the front bumper is even with the curb line or cars parked on the cross street, allowing the driver to search 90 degrees to the right and left (p. 186)

parada de seguridad una parada en la cual el parachoques delantero está al nivel de la línea del bordillo o de los carros que están estacionados en la intersección, lo cual le permite al conductor maniobrar 90 grados a derecha e izquierda

scanning glancing continually and quickly with very brief eye fixations through your orderly visual search pattern (p. 85)

examinar el área mirar continua y rápidamente fijando la vista brevemente según tu patrón de búsqueda visual sistemática

scooter vehicles that are generally smaller and less performance oriented than motorcycles (p. 212)

motoneta vehículo generalmente más pequeño y destinado a un rendimiento menor que las motocicletas

semi-automatic transmission a manual transmission in which the clutch is replaced with electronics that allow the driver to shift gears using the shift lever (p. 58)

transmisión semiautomática transmisión manual en la cual el embrague se reemplaza con dispositivos electrónicos que permiten al conductor cambiar de velocidad utilizando la palanca de cambios

shared left-turn lane lane on a busy street that helps drivers make safer mid-block left turns into business areas from a center lane (p. 35)

carril de giro a la izquierda compartido carril de una calle transitada que ayuda a los conductores a girar con seguridad a la izquierda a mitad de la cuadra para entrar a áreas comerciales desde un carril central

shift indicator device that shows the gear positions of an automatic transmission (p. 43)

indicador de cambio dispositivo que muestra las posiciones de las velocidades en una transmisión automática

shift lever device used to select a gear (p. 42)

palanca de cambio dispositivo utilizado para escoger una velocidad

side-impact collision a collision in which the front of one vehicle hits the side of another (p. 265)

choque con impacto lateral colisión en la cual la parte delantera de un vehículo impacta contra el costado de otro vehículo

skid when tires lose part or all of their grip on the road (p. 238)

derrapar cuando las llantas pierden parcial o totalmente su adherencia al suelo

slow-moving vehicle vehicle unable to travel at highway speed (p. 307)

vehículo de marcha lenta vehículo que no puede desplazarse a la velocidad de la autopista

space cushion open area around a vehicle consisting of adequate following distance between it and the vehicles ahead and behind, plus swerve paths to left and right (p. 93)

área de protección área libre alrededor de un vehículo que consiste en una distancia de seguimiento adecuada entre ese vehículo y los que están adelante y atrás, además de las trayectorias de viraje a izquierda y derecha

speed bump a raised portion of the road, designed to make drivers slow down (p. 36)

badén porción elevada de la carretera, destinada a que los conductores disminuyan su velocidad

speed smear   occurs when objects off to your sides become blurred and distorted as your speed increases (p. 116)
distorsión de velocidad   ocurre cuando los objetos que pasas se vuelven borrosos y distorsionados a medida que aumentas la velocidad

spur   a branch of a highway that goes into a city (p. 339)
ramal   brazo de una autopista que entra en una ciudad

stale green light   light that has been green for a long time (p. 192)
luz verde suspendida   luz que ha estado verde durante largo tiempo

standard reference point   point on the vehicle typical for most drivers (p. 71)
punto de referencia estándar   punto de referencia del vehículo utilizado generalmente por la mayoría de los conductores

stimulant   drug that speeds up the central nervous system (p. 136)
estimulante   droga que acelera las funciones del sistema nervioso central

switchbacks   turns in a road that bend sharply in opposite directions (p. 311)
zigzags   vueltas en una carretera que se curvan de manera pronunciada en direcciones opuestas

synergistic effect   the multiplied effect of drugs taken at the same time as each other or alcohol (p. 136)
efecto de sinergia   el efecto multiplicado de las drogas ingeridas juntas, al mismo tiempo, o con alcohol

---

t

tachometer   device that indicates the engine revolutions per minute (RPM) (p. 47)
tacómetro   aparato que indica las revoluciones del motor por minuto (RPM)

tailgate   to follow another vehicle too closely (p. 279)
conducir pegado al carro de delante   seguir a otro vehículo demasiado cerca

target   stationary object that appears in the distance in the center of the path you intend to occupy (p. 52)
blanco   objeto inmóvil que aparece a la distancia en el centro del curso que intentas seguir

target area   section of roadway where the target is located and the area to the left and right of the target (p. 83)
área del blanco   sección de la carretera donde está ubicado el blanco y el área a la izquierda y a la derecha del blanco

target area range   space from your vehicle to the target area (p. 83)
alcance al área del blanco   espacio desde tu vehículo hasta el área del blanco

temporary disability   a disability that can improve and clear up (p. 119)
discapacidad temporal   discapacidad que puede mejorar y curarse

3-second following distance   a safe following distance between your vehicle and the one ahead, which would take three seconds to cross at your current speed (p. 278)
distancia de seguimiento de 3 segundos   distancia de seguimiento segura entre tu vehículo y el que va adelante, al que alcanzarías en tres segundos a tu velocidad en ese momento

total stopping distance   distance your vehicle travels while you make a stop (p. 173)
distancia de detención total   distancia que recorre el vehículo al detenerse

traction   a form of friction that enables the tires to grip the roadway surface (p. 166)
tracción   forma de fricción que permite que las llantas se adhieran a la superficie de la carretera

tractor trailer   truck that has a powerful tractor that pulls a separate trailer (p. 218)
camión con remolque   camión que tiene una tracción poderosa y remolca a otro vehículo

traffic density   the number of vehicles you meet per mile (p. 276)
densidad del tránsito   número de vehículos que encuentras por milla

traffic signal   any signal used to control the movement of traffic (p. 27)
señal de tránsito   cualquier señal utilizada para controlar la circulación del tránsito

trailer hitch   a piece of equipment used to connect a trailer to a vehicle (p. 377)
enganche del remolque   pieza utilizada para conectar un remolque a otro vehículo

transmission   mechanism in a vehicle that delivers power from the engine to the drive wheels (p. 57)
transmisión   mecanismo de un vehículo que transmite la energía desde el motor hasta las ruedas de tracción

tread   outer grooved surface of a tire that grips the road (p. 166)
banda de rodamiento   superficie exterior corrugada de una llanta que se adhiere a la carretera

tunnel vision having a field of vision of 140 degrees or less (p. 113)
visión de túnel tener un campo de visión de 140 grados o menor

turnabout maneuver for turning your vehicle around to go in the opposite direction (p. 68)
giro completo maniobra para girar el vehículo totalmente con el fin de ir en la dirección opuesta

12–15-second range area you will be traveling in during the next 12 to 15 seconds, and where you need to identify changes in your path of travel (p. 83)
alcance de 12 a 15 segundos área que recorrerás en los siguientes 12 a 15 segundos y en la que debes identificar los cambios que haya en tu recorrido

---

u

uncontrolled intersection intersection that has no signs or signals to regulate traffic (p. 195)
intersección sin señalización intersección que no tiene señales ni semáforos para regular el tránsito

understeer situation the result of not turning the steering wheel enough (p. 239)
situación de giro de baja resolución consecuencia de no girar el volante lo suficiente

unprotected left turn left turn made at a signal-controlled intersection without a special left-turn light (p. 193)
giro a la izquierda desprotegido giro a la izquierda en una intersección controlada por señales sin un semáforo especial con luz verde

---

V

Variable Ride-Height Suspension (VRHS) a suspension that raises or lowers the ride height of the vehicle while it is in motion, depending on conditions such as vehicle speed and terrain (p. 348)
suspensión de altura variable durante el manejo suspensión que eleva o baja la altura del chasis del vehículo mientras está en movimiento, dependiendo de ciertas condiciones, tales como la velocidad del vehículo y el terreno

vehicle balance the distribution of a vehicle's weight on its tires as they contact the ground (p. 170)
equilibrio vehicular la distribución del peso de un vehículo sobre sus llantas cuando entran en contacto con el suelo

velocitation condition of unconsciously driving too fast as a result of driving for long periods at high speeds (p. 338)
hipnosis de velocidad estado en el que se maneja demasiado rápido inconscientemente, como consecuencia de manejar durante largos períodos de tiempo a alta velocidad

visual acuity the ability to see things clearly, both near and far away (p. 112)
agudeza visual capacidad de ver objetos claramente, tanto cercanos como lejanos

visual distraction a sight that causes you to take your eyes off the roadway ahead (p. 151)
distracción visual divisar algo que te hace quitar los ojos de la carretera al frente

---

W

warning sign sign that alerts you to possible hazards and road conditions (p. 23)
señal de advertencia señal que advierte sobre posibles peligros y sobre las condiciones de la carretera

wheel lock-up occurs when the brakes are applied with such force that the wheels stop turning and the tires begin to slide (p. 55)
bloqueo de las ruedas lo que ocurre cuando se frena con tanta fuerza que las ruedas dejan de girar y las llantas comienzan a derrapar

---

z

zero tolerance law law stating it is illegal for persons under the age of 21 to drive with any measurable amount of alcohol in the blood (p. 137)
ley de tolerancia cero ley que establece que es ilegal que las personas menores de 21 años manejen con una cantidad cualquiera de alcohol en la sangre

zone one of six areas of space around a vehicle that is the width of a lane and extends as far as the driver can see (p. 82)
zona una de las seis áreas del espacio alrededor de un vehículo que tiene el ancho de un carril y se extiende hasta donde alcanza tu vista

Zone Control System organized method for managing the space—or six zones—around your vehicle (p. 7)
Sistema de control de zonas método sistemático de manejar el espacio (o las seis zonas) alrededor de tu vehículo

index

a

AAA Foundation for Traffic Safety, 152
Acceleration control, 54
Acceleration lane, 325, 327
Acceleration of motorcyclists, 212
Accelerator, 42, 54
Accidents. *See* Collisions
Active railroad crossings, 197
Active restraint device, 175
Adjustable steering position, 42
Adverse conditions, 215
   driving in, 227–244
   reduced traction in, 234–241
   reduced visibility in, 228–233
   weather as, 211, 242–244
Advisory speed limit, 22
Advisory speed signs, 298
Aggressive driving, 107
   behaviors in, 118
Aging, 121–122
Air bags, 176–177
   frontal, 176
   head protection, 347
   side, 177
   warning light for, 48
Air conditioner, 46, 254, 366
Air pocket, 262
Alcohol, 128–134
   being stopped by police, 140
   blood alcohol concentration (BAC) and,
     131–134
   combining drugs with, 136
   driving ability and, 128–129
   impairment by
     controlling, 132–133
     levels of, 138
     tests for, 138–139
   penalties for conviction, 139
   physical effects of, 131
   reducing driving risks, 133
   traffic laws governing use of, 137–140
Alcoholism, 131
All-directional interchange, 324
Alleys, 207
**Alliance Against Intoxicated Motorists
  (AAIM),** 144
All ways stop sign, 21
Alternative fuels, 357–358
Alternator warning light, 46
Altitude, effects of, 313
**American Automobile Association
  (AAA),** 107
Anger while driving, 107–108

Angle parking, 71–74
   leaving space, 72
Animals
   inside vehicle, 154
   outside vehicle, 156
   in rural driving, 308
Antilock braking system (ABS),
  55, 241
   light for, 47
Anxiety, driving and, 108
Arrows, 29
Attitude, effects of, 312–313
Auditory distractions, 117, 151

b

Backing, 65
   into driveway on right side, 69
   of recreational vehicles, 375
   of trailer, 377–378
Back-up camera, 348
Back-up lights, 97
Balance of vehicle, 171
Basic driving maneuvers, 66
   entering traffic flows, 66–67
   lane changes, 68
   making right and left turns, 67
   signaling, 66
   turning vehicle, 68–70
Basic vehicle operation, 41–58
   controls, 42
   devices for safety, communication, and
     comfort, 44–46
   instrument panel, 46–48
   shift indicator positions, 43–44
Being passed, passing and, 333
Beltway, 339
Bicyclists, 209–210
Biodiesel, 358
Biomechanical distractions,
  151
Black ice, 237
Blind spots, 332
Blood alcohol concentration (BAC),
  131–134
Blowout, 169
Blurred vision, 130
Body movement, 98
Brake fade, 252
Brake lights, 97
Brake pedal, 42
Brakes, 251–252
   covering the, 282
   parking, 42, 51, 243, 352
   riding the, 282–283

Brake system, 352
   antilock, 55, 241
   warning light for, 47
Braking
   constant pressure, 55
   controlled, 240–241
   by motorcyclists, 212
   total failure in, 252
Braking control, 55
Braking distance, 174
   factors that affect, 174
   in low-traction situations, 237
Braking point, 55
Bridges, ice on, 237
Budget, 346
Buses, 220–221
Business districts, 207. *See also* City

c

Carbon monoxide, effects of, 120–121
Carjacker, 50
Catalytic converters, 350
Cell phones, 117, 152–153
Center lines, multilane roads with, 300
Center of gravity of vehicle, 170
Central vision, 113
CFC-12, 366
Chemical testing, 138
Child passenger safety, 177
Chronic illnesses, 122
Cigarette smoke, 229
City
   adjusting to traffic in, 276–277
   driving on one-way streets in, 286–288
   driving on two-way streets in, 286
   managing space in traffic, 281–285
Closed zone, 83
Cloverleaf interchange, 323
Clutch, 57
Clutchless manual transmission, 58
Cognitive distractions, 151
Cold weather, 243
Collisions, 8, 263–266
   aiding injured in, 265
   avoiding, 280
   calling for police, 265
   controlling force of impact, 175–178
   costs of, 9
   in crosswalks, 206
   exchanging information in, 265–266
   filing necessary reports in, 266
   head-on, 263
   insurance for, 267–268
   at intersections, 188

motorcycle, 217
with pedestrians, 207
preventing further damage, 265
rear-end, 264
scenes of, as distractions, 157–158
side-impact, 265
stopping immediately after, 265
trucks in, 218
vehicle fire in, 256
while backing, 73
Color blindness, 114
Common speed, 331–332
Communication, decisions in, 93–94, 97
Compact spare, 251
Compromise space, 95
Computerized traffic lights, 28
Constant braking pressure, 55
Construction, areas of, 24, 238
Controlled-access, 321
entering highways, 325–328
exiting highways, 335–337
Controlled braking, 240–241
Controlled intersections, 192
with signals, 192–193
with signs, 192
**Controlled steering, hand positions
for,** 52
Control speed, 96–97
Control systems, maintaining, 351–355
Convex mirrors, 64
Cooling systems, 351
Cooling-system surge tank, 243
Covering the brake, 282
Crashes. *See* Collisions
Crossbuck, 197
Crosswalks, 206–207
Crosswinds, 376
Cruise control, 42, 244
Crush zones, 178
Curves
forces in, 171–172
in rural areas, 297–298
sharpness of, 172, 261
warning signs for, 297–298
Cyclists, 209–210. *See also* Motorcyclists
responsibilities of, 211

d
Damage, preventing further, 265
Dawn-driving situations, 229
Deceleration, 96
Deceleration lane, 335
Deciding
in changing direction, 93

in changing speed, 92–93
in IPDE Process, 7, 81, 92–94, 277, 329
in stopping, 186–187
Decisions, making responsible, 143–144
Deductibles, 267
Deep water, driving in, 235, 252, 261–262
Defogger, rear, 228
Defroster, 46
Delayed green light, 193–194
Depressants, 135–136
Depth perception, 84, 114, 130–131
Deserts, 313–314
Designated driver, 133
Diamond interchange, 323
Direction, deciding to change, 93
Dirty windows, 228–229
Disabilities, 119
permanent, 121–122
temporary, 119–121
Disabled vehicles, 338
Distances
calculating, 371
fog in ability to judge, 231–232
Distractions
animals and insects, 154
classifications, 151
distracted driving, 150
driver inattention, 150
eating or drinking while driving, 154
inside vehicle, 152–155
loose objects, 155
managing, 149–158
outside vehicle, 156–158
passengers, 155
vehicle equipment or controls, 153–154
Divided roads, 300
DON'T WALK signals, 30
Door before opening, 49
Double lines, 32
**Drag, reducing, in maximizing fuel
efficiency,** 357
Dram shop laws, 137
Drinking while driving, 154
Driver-contributed factors, 80
Drivers
education of, 12–13
effects of altitude on, 312–313
effects of condition of, 105–122
effects of heat on, 313
errors of, 257–258
emergency swerving, 258–259
off-road recovery, 257–259
inattention of, 150

responsibilities of, with mopeds and
bicycles, 210–211
Driver's license, 11–13
Driveways, 207, 299
backing into, 69
backing out of, 211
Driving
aggressive, 107
alcohol and, 128–131
anger while, 107–108
animals in rural, 308
desert, 313–314
effect of attitude on, 312–313
evaluating your needs, 346–347
getting ready, 49–50
on highways, 320–340
kinds of drugs and, 135–136
meeting oncoming traffic, 308–309
mountain, 311–313
on rural multilane roads, 299–301
on one-way streets, 286–288
physical senses and, 112–118
railroad crossings in rural, 309
responsibilities of, 8–10
slow-moving vehicles in rural, 307
on two-way streets, 286
Driving risk, 6
reducing, 133
Driving under the influence (DUI), 138
Driving while intoxicated (DWI), 138
Drowsiness, fatigue as cause of, 119
Drugs. *See also* Medicines
combining, 136
kinds of, and driving, 135–136
Dusk-driving situations, 229
Dust storms, 314

e
Eating while driving, 154
Electrical systems, 353–354
Electricity, static, 354–355
Electronic Control Module (ECM), 350
Electronic resources, 370
Electronic Stability Control (ESC), 347
Electronic tolls, 339–340
Emergencies, handling, 249–269
Emergency equipment, 372
Emergency swerving, 258–259
Emergency vehicles, 221
Emission control system, 351
Emotions
controlling, 110–111
effect of, on driving, 106–110
IPDE Process and, 108–109

Emotions (*cont.*)
mental effects of, 106
passengers and, 109
physical effects of, 106–107
Energy-absorbing bumpers, 178
Energy of motion, 165
Engine
failure of, 253–254
overhead, 254
starting, 51
temperature of, in desert driving, 313
warming, in maximizing fuel efficiency, 357
Engine revolutions per minute (RPM), 47
Entrance ramp, 325–328
Environment, vehicles and, 366–367
Environmental responsibilities, 9
Environment-contributed factors, 80
Equipment
emergency, 372
vehicle, 153–154
winter-driving, 372
Ethanol, 128, 358
Ethyl alcohol, 128
Euphoria, 129
Excitement, driving and, 108
Executing in IPDE Process, 7, 81, 95–98, 330
Exhaust emissions, 366
Exhaust leaks, 243
Exit ramp, 335
Expressways, 321
Eye contact, 98
Eye-hand coordination, 6

f --

Fatigue, 119, 218
in driving recreational vehicles, 376
Field of vision, 84, 113
Field sobriety testing, 138–139
Financial responsibilities, 9
laws on, 267
producing proof of, 266
Fires
as distraction, 157–158
vehicle, 256
Fishtailing, 239–240
Fixed costs, 9
Flash floods, 314
Flashing signals, 29
Fog
driving in, 231–232
in mountain driving, 312
Following distance
for recreational vehicles, 376
in rural areas, 299

Footprint, 166–167
Force of impact, 175
Forces in curves, 171–172
Forward reference point, 71
Forward vision, 255
4-way stop sign, 21
Four wheels off the road, 257
Freeway interchanges, 323–324
Freon, 366
Fresh green light, 192
Friction, 166
Fringe vision, 113
Frontal air bags, 176
Front wheels, loss of traction to, 239
Front-window defroster, 228
Fuel(s), alternative, 357–358
Fuel efficiency, 356
effect of weight on, 372
maximizing, 357
Fuel gauge, 46
Fuel symbol, 48
Full-privilege license, 12

g --

Gap, judging size of, 191
Gawking, 157
Getting ready to drive, 49–50
Glare, 115, 229
Glare recovery time, 115–116
Glare resistance, 115
Global Positioning System (GPS), 370
Grade, 257
elevation of, 321
Graduated driver licensing program, 11–12
Gravel roads, 238
Gravity, 165, 172
energy of motion and, 164–165
Green arrows, 29
Green light, 27
fresh, 192
stale, 192
Ground viewing, 86–87
Groups, riding motorcycles in, 216
Guide signs, 25

h --

Hallucinogens, 136
Handicapped parking, 35, 122
Hand-over-hand steering, 52–53
**Hand positions for controlled
steering,** 52
Hand-to-hand steering, 53
Happiness, driving and, 108
Hazard flashers, 45, 97, 314

Hazard lights, 231–232
Hazards
minimizing, 94
separating, 94–95
Headlights, 97, 229–230
failure of, 255
in fog, 231–232
high-beam, 229
low-beam, 229, 230, 232–233
overdriving, 230–231
Head-on collision, 263
Head protection airbags, 347
Head restraints, 44, 178
analyzing, 50
Hearing, 116
Heat, effects of
on drivers, 313
on vehicles, 313
Heater, 46
High-beam headlights, 229
High-beam indicator, 48
High-occupancy toll (HOT) lanes, 331
High-occupancy vehicle (HOV) lanes,
34, 35, 285
Highway driving, 320–340
entering controlled access, 325–328
exiting controlled access, 335–337
IPDE process and zone control in, 329–330
problems and features, 338–339
roads, 339
toll plazas, 339–340
Highway hypnosis, 338
Highways
classification of, 320–324
driving on, 320–340
exit ramps on, 34
interstate, 320, 321
**Highway Transportation System
(HTS),** 4–5, 82
Hills
parking on, 74
in rural areas, 298
Hole in traffic, 327
Horn, 45, 98
Hot weather, 242–243
Hydrogen, 358
Hydroplaning, 234–235

i --

Ice
black, 237
on bridges, 237
in mountain driving, 312

reduced traction in, 236–237
in tire tracks, 237
Identifying in IPDE Process, 7, 81, 82–85, 277, 329
Idling, reducing, in maximizing fuel efficiency, 357
Ignition and starter switch, 51
Illegal *per se* **laws,** 137
Impairment
  controlling, 132–133
  levels of, 138
  tests for, 138–139
Implied consent laws, 13, 137
Index, 371
Inertia, 164–165
Information, exchanging after collision, 265–266
Inhibitions, 129
Injured, aiding, in collision, 265
Insects in car, 154
Inside rear-view mirror, 44, 64
Instrument panel, 46–48
Insurance, 267–270
  collision, 267
  liability, 267
  no-fault, 267
  rates, 269
  vehicle, 267–268
Interchanges, 321
  freeway, 323–324
Intermediate license, 11
International signs, 26–27
Internet, 370
Intersections
  approaching, 185–186
  controlled, 192–194
  crashes at, 188
  deciding to stop, 186–187
  entering, 187
  identifying, 184
  no passing at, 305
  in rural areas, 299
  searching, 184–188, 213
  turning at, 300–301
  uncontrolled, 195–196
Interstate highways, 320, 321
Intoxilyzer, 138
IPDE Process, 7
  in city traffic, 277
  deciding in, 7, 81, 92–94, 277, 329
  emotions and, 108–109, 110
  executing in, 7, 81, 95–98, 330
  at exits, 335–336

in highway driving, 329–330
identifing in, 7, 81, 82–85, 277, 329
managing risk with, 79–100
need for time and practice, 100
predicting in, 81, 88–91, 277, 329
in protecting motorcyclists, 213–216
putting, into action, 99–100
risk factors in, 80
in rural areas, 296
in searching for bicycles and mopeds, 209–210
in searching intersections, 184
selective seeing in, 85–88
selective use of, 99
traffic flow in, 94–95
in uncontrolled intersections, 195–196
in winter driving, 243–244
Isopropanol, 128
Isopropyl alcohol, 128

j --

Jaywalking, 206
Joining traffic, 191
Judgment, effects of alcohol on, 129

k --

Key fob, 49
Keyless entry, 359

l --

Lane(s)
  acceleration, 325, 327
  change in width of, 87
  changing, 332–333
  deceleration, 335
  express, 331
  making changes in, 68
    in intersection, 185
  markings for, 295
  motorcyclists and, 212–213
  reversible, 330–331
  selection of, 284–285, 300
Lane choice, 330–332
  changing lanes, 332–333
  passing and being passed, 333
Lane departure warning, 348
Lane positioning, 284
Lane signals, 29
Laws, 8
  dram shop, 137
  financial responsibility, 267
  illegal *per se,* 137
  implied consent, 13, 137
  natural, 163–178

traffic, governing use of alcohol, 137–140
zero tolerance, 137
Learner's permit, 11
  passing visual acuity test, 112
Leaves, 238
Left, backing, 65
Left angle parking, 71–73
Left-entrance ramp, 327–328
Left side, driveway on, 70
Left-turn arrows, 29
Left turns
  in entering multilane highway, 301
  by motorcyclists, 214–215
  protected, 193
  on red, 28
  at signals, 193–194
  unprotected, 193
Legal drinking age, 147
Legal responsibilities, 8
Legend, 371
Liability insurance, 267
Light, low levels of, 229–231
Light switch, 45
Line of sight, 83
  restrictions on, 196
Load, 172, 377
  lightening, in maximizing fuel efficiency, 357
Local travel, 368–369
Long-distance travel, 370–373
  personal preparation in, 373
Loose objects as distraction, 155
Low-beam headlights
  in bad weather, 230
  in rain, 232
  in snow, 232–233
  sun glare and, 229
Lower gears, 44
Low levels of light, 229–231
Low-risk driving, 7
Low-speed vehicles (LSVs), 222
Lubrication, 351

m --

Maneuvers, 99
  basic driving, 66–70
  of recreational vehicles, 375
Manual transmission, 57–58
Maps, 371, 374
Marijuana, 136
Mass transit, 284
Median, 300
Medicines. *See also* Drugs
  effects of, 120

Medicines (*cont.*)
over-the-counter, 135
prescription, 135
Mental skills in driving task, 6
Merging area, 325
Merging problems, 327–328
Methanol, 128
Methyl alcohol, 128
Midblock U-turn, 69
Minimum speed limit, 22
Mirrors
blind spot of, 45
checking and adjusting, 50
convex, 64
inside, 44, 50, 64
outside, 44–45, 64
rearview, 44, 50
usage of, 64–65
Momentum, 165
Mopeds, 209–210
**Mothers Against Drunk Driving
(MADD),** 144
Motion, sense of, 117
Motorcyclists, 212–217
acceleration and braking, 212
adverse weather conditions and, 215
carrying passengers, 215–216
crashes of, 217
lane position of, 212–213
riding in groups, 216
road conditions and, 215
turning, 214–215
using IPDE Process to protect, 213–216
Motor oil, recycling, 358
Mountains
driving in, 311–313
weather in, 312
Muffler, 351
Multilane roads, 87
changing to single lane road, 87
driving on, in rural areas, 299–301
entering, 301
passing on, 303–304

n
National Highway Safety Act, 5
**National Traffic and Motor Vehicle
Safety Act,** 5
Natural gas, 358
Natural laws and car control, 163–178
controlling force of impact, 175–178
gravity and energy of motion, 164–165
inflation and traction, 167
stopping distance, 173–174

tires and traction, 166–169
vehicle balance, 170–171
New vehicle, buying, 348–349
Night
dangers of driving at, 373
loss of forward vision at, 255
meeting vehicles at, 309
visibility at, 294
Night blindness, 115
Night vision, 115
No-fault insurance, 267
Non-controlled access, 321
No-parking zones, 35
No passing
at intersections, 305
on uphill roads, 304
No zone, 219
Nystagmus, 139

o
Objects
outside vehicle, 156–157
on road, 260
Odometer, 47
Off-road and obstruction ahead, 258
Off-road recovery, 257–259
Oil pressure warning light or gauge, 46
On-board diagnostics systems, 366
One-way streets, driving on, 286–288
Open zones, 83, 86
Operating costs, 9
**Operating while intoxicated or impaired
(OWI),** 138
Orderly visual search pattern, 83–84
Organ donor program, 13
Outside mirrors, 44–45, 64
Overdriving headlights, 230–231
Overhead engine, 254
Overinflation, 167
Overreaction, 106
Oversteering, 68, 239
Overtaking, 285
Over-the-counter medicines, 135
Ownership, cost of, 346

p
Parallel parking, 72–73
Parking, 71–74
angle, 71–74
handicapped, 35, 122
on hills, 74
parallel, 72–73
perpendicular, 71–72
restrictions on, 35

Parking brake, 42, 51, 243, 352
Parking lights, 97
Parkways, 321–322
Passenger-compartment fire, 256
Passengers
carrying, by motorcycles, 215–216
emotions and, 109
other, as distraction, 155
Passing, 285
being passed and, 219–220, 305–306, 333
of bicycle, 210
executing, 303
motorcyclists, 213
on multilane roads, 303–304
prohibition of, 304–306
on rural roads, 302–304
stopped school bus, 221
Passive railroad crossings, 197
Passive restraint device, 175
Path-of-travel restrictions, 196
Pedestrians, 206–208
crosswalks for, 34
injuries to, 31
responsibilities of, 208
Pedestrian signals, 30
Pedestrian signs, 24
Peer education, 144
Peer influence, 141
Peer pressure, 141–144
Peer refusal skills, 142–143
Penetration-resistant windshields, 178
Perception distance, 173
Perception time, 173
Peripheral vision, 113, 131
Permanent disabilities, 121–122
Perpendicular parking, 71–73
**Personal preparation in
long-distance travel,** 373
Personal reference point, 71
Physical limitations, 119–122
Physical senses, driving and,
112–118
Physical skills in driving task, 6
Pitch, 171
Planning your travel, 365–378
Point of no return, 185–186
Police
being stopped by, 139
calling for, 265
Policy, 267
Potholes
in road, 260
tire damage and, 260

Power-steering failure, 255
Power systems, maintaining, 350–351
Power wheels, loss of traction to, 239
Pre-departure equipment check, 377
Predicting in IPDE Process, 81, 88–91, 277, 329
Premiums, 267
　reduced, 269
Pre-owned vehicle, buying, 348–349
Prescription medicine, 135
Preventive maintenance, 350–355
　maintaining control systems, 351–355
　maintaining power systems, 350–351
Print resources, 370–371
Prohibition of passing, 304–306
Projectiles as distraction, 155
Propane, 358
Protected left turn, 193
Protective devices, 178
Protective gear for motorcyclists, 216
Public buses, 220
Public events as distractions, 158
Pull into driveway on left side, 70
Pull-out areas, 312

Radiator, checking fluid level in, 313
Railroad crossings, 34, 197–198
　active, 197
　crash data on, 310
　in rural driving, 309
　stalling on tracks, 253–254
　warning signs for, 24, 309
Rain, 208
　driving in, 232
　reduced traction in, 234–235
Ramp, entrance, 325–328
Ramp meter, 327
Ranges, searching, 83
Reaction distance, 174
Reaction time, 174
Rear defogger, 228
Rear-end collisions, 264
Rearview mirrors, 44–45, 50, 64
Rear wheels, loss of traction to, 239–240
Reasoning, effects of alcohol on, 129
Recreational vehicles, 375–376
Recycling centers, 358
Red, turns on, 194
Red arrows, 29
Red light, 27, 193
Red markers, 36
Reduced premiums, 269

Reduced traction, 234–241
　in ice, 236–237
　in snow, 236
Reduced visibility, 228–233
Reference point, 71
Reflective markers, 36
Reflex action, 130
Regulatory signs, 20–23
Remote-control key, 277
Reports, filing, after collision, 266
Residential areas, 207
Restraint device, 175
Restrictions
　line-of-sight, 196
　on parking, 35
　path-of-travel, 196
Reversible lanes, 35, 330–331
Riding the brake, 282–284
Right, backing, 65
Right angle parking, 71–73
Right of way, 189–190
Right side, backing into driveway on, 69
Right turn
　in entering multilane highway, 301
　by motorcyclists, 214
　on red, 28
　trucks making, 219
Risks
　in driving, 4
　effects of emotions on taking, 110
　managing, with IPDE Process, 79–100
　understanding factors of, 80
Road rage, 107
Roads, 4–5, 339
　conditions of, 169, 215
　desert, 314
　divided, 300
　driving on one-way, 286–288
　driving on two-way, 286
　features and conditions, 87
　markings for, 32–36
　　reflective, 36
　　rumble strips, 36
　　speed bumps, 36
　　stop lines and crosswalks, 34
　　white lane, 33
　　yellow lane, 32
　multilane, with center lines, 300
　no passing on uphill, 304
　object on, 260
　potholes in, 260
　rural, 294
　shape of, 172

　sharing, 205–222
　　with trucks, 218–220
　surface of, 88
　unexpected situations on crowded, 288
　users of, 4
Roadside hazards, 88
　in rural driving, 295
Roadway-contributed factors, 80
Rocking vehicle in snow, 236
Roll, 171
Roundabouts, 199–200
Routes, 374
Route signs, 25
Rubbernecking, 157
Rumble strips, 36
Runaway vehicle ramps, 312
Rural driving
　basic skills in, 296–301
　characteristics of, 294–295
　curves in, 297–298
　driving in, 293–314
　following distance in, 299
　following traffic in, 299
　hills in, 298
　intersections in, 299
　roadside hazards in, 295
　slow-moving vehicles in, 307
　traffic controls in, 295
Rural roads, 294
　passing on, 302–304

Safe driving, 338
Safe following distance, 244
Safe speed, determining, in rural driving, 294
Safety
　backing and, 65
　mirror usage and, 64–65
Safety belts, 5, 44, 175–176, 177
　light for, 47
Safety chain, 377
Safety features, 347–348
Safety stop, 186
Sandstorms, 314
Satellite systems, 360
Scanning, 85
School buses, 221
School crossings, 34
School-zone signs, 24
Scooters, 212
Searching, at intersections, 184–188, 213
Seat, analyzing, 50
Seat adjustment lever, 46

Security systems, 358–360
Seeing, 112–113
Selective seeing, 85–88
Semi-automatic transmission, 58
Sensors for security, 359
Sensory distractions, managing, 117
Shared left-turn lanes, 34, 35
Sharp curve, driving around, 261
Shift indicator positions, 43–44
Shift lever, 42, 51
Shoulders, 295
Side air bags, 177
Side-impact collision, 265
Side-impact panels, 178
Signals, 295
  controlled intersections with, 192–193
  DON'T WALK, 30
  flashing, 29
  pedestrian, 30
  traffic, 27, 281–283
  turning left at, 193–194
Signs, 295
  advisory speed, 298
  controlled intersections with, 192
  guide, 25
  international, 26–27
  pedestrian, 24
  regulatory, 20–23
  stop, 20–22
  warning, 24, 295, 297–298, 309
Single-lane roads, changing, from multilane road to, 87
Single lines, 32
Skidding, 238–240
Sleep, loss of, 218
Sleet, 208
Slippery roads, use lower gear on, 244
Slow-moving vehicles, 307, 309
Smell, 117
Smoking, 121
Snow, 208
  driving in, 232–233
  keep moving in, 244
  in mountain driving, 312
  reduced traction in, 236
Snowplows, 222
Social skills in driving task, 6
Space, managing, in city traffic, 281–285
Space cushion, 93
Specialized vehicles, 222
Special traffic lanes, 285

Speed, 172
  adjusting, 283
  controlled braking in reducing, 240–241
  controlling in maximizing fuel efficiency, 357
  deciding to change, 92–93
  determining, in rural driving, 294
  in rural areas, 296
Speed bumps, 36
Speed limits, 22, 331–332
  advisory, 298
  signs indicating, 22–23
Speedometer, 47
Speed smear, 116
Spur, 339
Stability of vehicle, 170–171
Stale green light, 192
Stalled engine, 253
Stalling on railroad tracks, 253–254
Standard reference points, 71
State highways, 320, 322
Static electricity, 354–355
Steering
  away from conflict, 97
  hand-over-hand, 52–53
  hand-to-hand, 53
  total failure of, 255
  of vehicle, 171
Steering system, 351
Steering wheel, 42
  hand position on, 50
  use of targets and, 52–53
Stimulant, 136
Stop
  deciding to, 186–187
  normal smooth, 55
Stop lines, 34
Stopping, after collision, 265
Stopping distance, 173–174
STOP sign, 20–22
Streets. *See* Roads
Student programs, 144
Students Against Destructive Decisions (SADD), 144
Sun glare, 229
Sun visor, 46
Suspension system, 353
Swerving, emergency, 258–259
Switchbacks, 311
Synergistic effect, 136

t

Tachometer, 47
Tailgating, 279, 332
Taillights, 97

Target, 52
Target area, 83
Temperature, 353
  tire pressure and, 167
Temperature light or gauge, 46, 254
Temporary disabilities, 119–121
Temporary illness or injury, 119–120
Theft prevention, 359
Three-point turnabout, 70
3-second following distance, 264, 278–279
T intersections, 184
Tire chains, 372
Tire monitor, 277
Tire pressure monitoring system (TPMS), 347
Tires, 352–353
  blowout of, 250–251
  changing, 251
  failure of, 250–251
    in desert driving, 313
  ice in tracks of, 237
  potholes and damage of, 260
  tread and traction of, 166–169, 354
Toll plazas, 339–340
Tornadoes, 242
Total brake failure, 252
Total steering failure, 255
Total stopping distance, 173–174
Towing techniques, 377
Traction, 166, 353
  ensuring good, 168–169
  loss of, 238–240
  reduced, 234–241
    on wet road, 234–235
  using, 168
Tractor trailer, 218
Traffic
  following, 278–279
    in rural areas, 299
  joining, 191
  meeting, 279–280
  meeting oncoming, in rural driving, 308–309
Traffic circles, 199
  signs for, 199
Traffic complexity, 276
Traffic control officer's signals, 30
Traffic controls, 88
  in rural driving, 295
Traffic density, 276
Traffic flow, 94–95
Traffic lights, 27–28
  computerized, 28
Traffic reports, 243

Traffic signals, 27
approaching, 281–283
Traffic signs, 20–26
control officer's signals, 30
guide, 25
international, 26–27
lights, 27–28
pedestrian signals, 30
regulatory signs, 20–23
shapes and colors, 20
warning, 23–24
Trailer hitch, 377
Trailers for recreational vehicles,
376–378
Transmission
manual, 57–58
semi-automatic, 58
Travel
local, 368–369
long distance, 370–373
planning your, 365–378
Tread wear, 353
Trucks
following large, 219
meeting large, 220
sharing road with, 218–220
Trumpet interchange, 324
Tunnel vision, 113
Turnabout, 68
three-point, 70
Turning, 68, 70
in front of bicycle, 210–211
at intersections, 300–301
on red, 194
Turning lanes, 35
Turnpikes, 321–322
Turn-signal indicators, 48
Turn-signal lever, 45
Turn-signal lights, 97
Two-way streets, driving on, 286
Two wheels off the road, 257–258

u

Ultraviolet radiation, 366
Uncontrolled intersections, 195–196
Underage drinking and driving, 139
Underinflation, 167
Understeer situation, 239
U.S. highways, 320, 322
Unprotected left turn, 193
Uphill roads, no passing on, 304
Used vehicle
buying, 348–349
inspection checklist, 349

U-turn, 196
midblock, 69

v

Vapor lock, 313
Variable electronic message signs, 157
**Variable ride-height suspension
(VRHS),** 348
Vehicle balance, 170–171
Vehicle check, 371–372
Vehicle-contributed factors, 80
Vehicle controls, 42
Vehicle equipment or controls, 153–154
Vehicle gauges, 46
Vehicle insurance, 267–269
Vehicles
basic operation of, 41–58
buying, 346–349
condition of, 168
cost of ownership of, 346
in deep water, 235, 252, 261–262
disabled, 338
distractions inside of, 152–155
distractions outside of, 156–158
effects of altitude on, 313
effects of heat on, 313
environment and, 366–367
exiting, 55–56
exiting parked, 211
fire of, 256
fuel-efficient, 356
getting into, 49–50
headlights meeting other, 230
malfunctions of, 250–256
navigation system for, 154, 370
position of, 98
preparation of, in long distance travel,
371–372
putting in motion, 54
recreational, 375–376
recycling, 358
routine maintenance for, 367
safety features of, 347–348
stopping behind, 187
turning, 68–70
type of, in determining insurance rates, 269
Vehicle speed and vision, 116
Velocitation, 338
Visibility
reduced, 207–208, 228–233
weather and, 231–233
Vision
aspects of, 84
effects of alcohol on, 130–131

factors that affect, 114–116
limitation on, in recreational vehicles, 375
Visual acuity, 112, 130
Visual distractions, 151
Visual lead, 297
Visual search pattern in rural areas, 297
Voltage meter, 46

w

Warning signs, 23–24
for curves, 297–298
graphics or pictures on, 295
for railroad crossings, 24, 309
Water, driving through, 235, 252, 261–262
Weather
adverse conditions, 211, 215
in mountains, 312
visibility and, 231–233
Weight check, 372–373
Wet roads
motorcyclists on, 214
reduced traction on, 234–235
Wheel lock-up, 55
White curbs, 35
White lane markings, 33
White markers, 36
Wind, 242
Windows
dirty, 228–229
icing up of, 237
Windshield wipers and washers, 45
Winter driving
equipment for, 372
tips for smooth, 243–244

y

Yaw, 171
Yellow arrows, 29
Yellow lane markings, 32
Yellow light, 27, 192–193
Yellow markers, 36
Yielding the right of way, 189–190
Yield sign, 22

z

Zero tolerance law, 137
Zone, 82
Zone checks, 185
Zone Control System, 7, 81, 82, 184
in highway driving, 329–330
in rural areas, 296
techniques for reduced visibility, 228

acknowledgments

Photographs Photo locators denoted as follows: Top (T), Center (C), Bottom (B), Left (L), Right (R), Background (Bkgd)

Cover (T,C) Kimball Stock; (B) Shutterstock; (CC) Shutterstock.

2 Corbis
5 (TCL) Alan Carey/The Image Works, Inc., (BCR) Jonathan Naurok/PhotoEdit, Inc., (TR) Rasica/Shutterstock
8 (CR) Tony Freeman/PhotoEdit, Inc.
18 Alan Schein/Corbis
22 (B) ©Image Source/Getty Images
24 (BR) Karina Zelentsova/Shutterstock
25 (BL) Getty Images
27 (BCR) ©Ryan McVay/Getty Images, (BCL, BC) Getty Images
40 Corbis
43 (BL) 123RF
49 (BR) Central Stock/Fotosearch
52 (TR) Bredemann Ford
53 (BR) American Driver and Traffic Safety Education Association Highway Safety Services, LLC
62 Dex Image/Corbis
78 Patrick Bennett/Corbis
87 (TR) ©Masterfile Royalty-Free
88 (TL) Jupiter Images
90 (TL) PhotoAlto/Fotosearch
91 (TR) Tony Freeman/PhotoEdit, Inc.
95 (TR) AGE Fotostock
103 (CL) iStockphoto
104 Alamy
108 (BL) Jupiter Images
114 (CL, BL) Prentice Hall
115 (BR) Jupiter Images
117 (BR) fotosearch/©Image Source
119 (BR) Cindy Charles/PhotoEdit, Inc.
121 (BR) Spencer Grant/PhotoEdit, Inc.
125 (TL) fStop/Fotosearch
126 Doug Menuez/Getty Images
133 (TR) ©Masterfile Royalty-Free
139 (TR) PhotoDisc, Inc./Fotosearch
140 (TL) Doug Menuez/Getty Images

141 (BR) Steve Skjold/PhotoEdit, Inc.
143 (BR) PhotoDisc, Inc./Fotosearch
144 (TL) Jupiter Images
151 (TR) ©Masterfile Royalty-Free
152 (BR) Jupiter Images
153 (TR) ©Masterfile Royalty-Free
154 (BC) Juniors Bildarchiv/Fotosearch/AGE Fotostock, (TL) Justin Lerner/Big Stock Photo
156 (BL) Tom Salyer/Alamy Stock Photo
157 (TR) David Zalubowski/©AP Images, (BR) David Zalubowski/Corbis
160 (CR) Big Cheese Photo/Fotosearch, (BR) Bill Ross/©AP Images
161 (CL) Andrew Manley/iStockphoto, (CR) Getty Images
162 Rick Gayle/Corbis
177 (BR, BC) ©Masterfile Royalty-Free, (BL) Getty Images
182 Jay Zimmerman/Corbis
199 (BR) ©Masterfile Royalty-Free, (BL) Alan Schein/Corbis
204 Rommel/Masterfile Corporation
206 (BL) Getty Images
207 fotogisele/Fotolia
210 (BL) AAA Foundation for Traffic Safety
212 (BL) Heiko Potthoff/iStockphoto
216 (T) AGE Fotostock
218 (BR) ©Masterfile Royalty-Free
221 (TR) Corbis
222 (TL) Carlos Osorio/©AP Images
226 Gloria Chomica/Masterfile Corporation
228 (B) ©Masterfile Royalty-Free
231 (BR) Comstock/Jupiter Images, (TR) Don Smith/Alamy Stock Photo
232 (B) Mulvehill/The Image Works, Inc.
233 (C) PhotoDisc, Inc./Fotosearch
234 (B) Robert Ginn/PhotoEdit, Inc.
236 (BL) Ed Andrieski/©AP Images
238 (TL) Fotosearch/Image100, (BL) Glow Images Inc./Fotosearch
244 (TL) Getty Images
247 (CL) PhotoDisc, Inc./Fotosearch
248 Ambrozinio/123RF
251 (TL) Jupiter Images

253 (TL) Stockbyte/Fotosearch
254 (T) Getty Images
261 (CR) Comstock/Jupiter Images, (CL) Jupiter Images
274 Atlantide Phototravel/Corbis
279 (BR) ©Masterfile Royalty-Free
282 (TL) AAA Foundation for Traffic Safety
286 (BL) Prentice Hall
288 (TL) Prentice Hall
290 (CR) AAA Foundation for Traffic Safety, (BR) Alex Segre/Alamy Images
291 (TR) AAA Foundation for Traffic Safety
292 Corbis
298 (TL) Getty Images
300 (TL) Getty Images
309 (TR) Getty Images
312 (BL) Jennifer Wright/Alamy Stock Photo, (TL) Spectrum EroStock/Robertstock
314 (TL) Tony Freeman/PhotoEdit, Inc.
318 Ron Neilbrugge/Alamy Images
323 (T, B) Alex MacLean/Landslides
324 (TL, CL) Alex MacLean/Landslides
326 (CL) Getty Images
327 (BR) Jupiter Images
328 (TL) Getty Images
330 (CL) Getty Images
331 (TL) PhotoDisc, Inc./Fotosearch
332 (T) Getty Images
339 (T) Getty Images
340 (C) Alan Schein/Corbis
343 (BL) Alex MacLean/Landslides, (TL) Jupiter Images
344 David Hammond/Corbis
347 (TR, TL) AGE Fotostock, (TC) Jupiter Images
348 (TL) Katsumi Kasahara/©AP Images
350 (BL) ©Masterfile Royalty-Free
355 (CR) Ross Anderson/©AP Images
356 (B) Getty Images
362 (CR) David R. Frazier/Alamy Images
364 ©Masterfile Royalty-Free
370 (BL) Corbis
372 (BL) ©Masterfile Royalty-Free
373 (TR) Corbis
380 (B) Bill Ross/Corbis.